6-13-5c
9/18 dk

Balanced Instruction:
Strategies and Skills in Whole Language

Balanced Instruction:
Strategies and Skills in Whole Language

Edited by

Ellen McIntyre, University of Louisville
and

Michael Pressley, University at Albany, State University of New York

Christopher-Gordon Publishers, Inc.
Norwood, MA

Credits

⇣ ——— ⇤

Every effort has been made to contact copyright holders for permission to reproduce borrowed material where necessary. We apologize for any oversights and would be happy to rectify them in future printings.

Figure 3.1 and Appendix of KEEP Literacy Benchmarks used with permission.

Figures 5.1 and 5.2, from Morrow, L. M. [1993]. *Literacy development in the early years: Helping children read and write.* Boston: Allyn & Bacon. Used with permission.

Christopher-Gordon Publishers, Inc.
480 Washington Street
Norwood, MA 02062

Printed in the United States of America

10 9 8 7 6 5 4 3 2 1   00 99 98 97 96

ISBN: 0-926842-56-0

Table of Contents

∞ ———— ∞

Preface xi

Acknowledgments xiii

Foreword, *P. David Pearson* xv

Chapter 1 Strategies and Skills in Whole Language:
An Introduction to Balanced Teaching 1

Ellen McIntyre, University of Louisville

Whole Language 3
Confusions and Uncertainty 8
Explicit Strategy and Skill Instruction 11
What's Different about this Book 13
Organization of this Book 14
References 15

Section I: Teaching Skills in Whole Language Classrooms 21

Chapter 2 Explicit Instruction Within a Whole Language Framework: Teaching Struggling Readers and Writers 23

Curt Dudley-Marling, York University, Toronto, Canada

A Socio-Psycholinguistic Perspective: Literacy as Social Practice 24
Reading and Writing Instruction in a Whole Language Classroom 26
Conclusion 35
References 36

Chapter 3 Explicit Instruction in the Context of the Readers'
and Writers' Workshops 39

Jacquelin H. Carroll, Cultural Learning Center at K'ala Waia'nae,
Roberta A. Wilson, Project Coordinator, PATTER, and
Kathryn H. Au, University of Hawaii

Readers' Workshop: Christine Tanioka's Fourth Grade Classroom 42
Writers' Workshop: Nora Okamoto's Fifth Grade Classroom 49
Conclusion 56
References 58
Appendix: KEEP Literacy Benchmarks 60

Chapter 4 Keeping It Whole in Whole Language: A First Grade
Teacher's Phonics Instruction in an Urban Whole
Language Classroom 65

Penny A. Freppon, University of Cincinnati
Linda Headings, public school teacher

Background 65
The Setting and the Children 66
Classroom Contexts and Meaningful Instruction 67
Learning to Teach Phonics 68
The Teaching/Assessing Process 69
Keeping Phonics Learning Whole and Reducing the Risks for Learners . 70
Organizing Instruction 72
Concluding Remarks 77
References 79

Chapter 5 Creating Rich Literacy Environments to Develop
Reading and Writing Skills in Early Childhood
Classrooms 83

Lesley Mandel Morrow, Rutgers University and
Muriel K. Rand, Jersey State College

Overview of the Chapter 85
Research and Perspectives about Literacy Rich Environments 85
Preparing Literacy-Rich Physical Environments that
Motivate Reading and Writing 87
Preparing the Social Environment to Develop Literacy Skills 96
Conclusion 99
References 102

Section II **Children's Development in Light of Instruction** 105

Chapter 6 Process Teaching with Direct Instruction and
Feedback in a University-based Clinic 107

Victoria Purcell-Gates, Director, Harvard Literacy Lab

The Harvard Literacy Lab 109
Lauren 111
David 117
Sam 121
Whole–to Part–to Whole: A Theoretical Frame for Process Learning 124
References 126

Chapter 7 Learning to Write in a Primary Special
Education Class 129

Laura Klenk, University at Buffalo, State University of New York
Annemarie S. Palincsar, University of Michigan

References 151

Section III Balancing Strategy Instruction
Within Whole Language 153

Chapter 8 Teaching Writing Strategies Within the Context
of A Whole Language Class 155

Steve Graham and Karen R. Harris, University of Maryland

Benefits 156
A Concern 158
Case Study One 160
Case Study Two 166
Conclusion 171
References 173

Chapter 9 Balanced Comprehension Instruction:
Transactional Strategies Instruction 177

Rachel Brown, University at Buffalo, State University of New York
Pamela Beard El-Dinary, Georgetown University
Michael Pressley, University at Albany, State University of New York

Strategies Teaching in Balanced Comprehension Instruction 177
A Description of Transactional Strategies Instruction 178
Conclusion 190
References 190

Chapter 10 Teaching Skills Through Learning Conversations
in Whole Language Classrooms 193

Laura Roehler and Mark Hallenbeck, Michigan State University
Meredith McLellan and Nancy Svoboda, Spartan Village School, Michigan

Using Learning Conversations 194
A Description of Their Whole Language Instruction 196
A Variety of Strategies 197
Learning Conversation One 198
Learning Conversation Two 201
Learning Conversation Three 203
Learning Conversation Four 204
Learning Conversation Five 206
Learning Conversation Six 208
Discussion 209

Conclusion 211
References 211

Chapter 11 Explicit Instruction for Early Learners:
Enhancing Reading Comprehension Using
a Multiple Strategy Repertoire 213

Linda Wold, Consolidated School District 118, Palos Heights, Illinois

The Adapted Word Chain Strategy 214
Adapted Word Chain Components 215
Motivation 215
Explicit Direct Instruction 216
Verbal Scaffolding 218
Using Think-Alouds 218
Reading the Story 219
Strategy Transfer 220
The Teacher's Response: Critical to Sense-Making 223
Discussion 223
References 225

Section IV Patterns of Teachers' Actions:
Balancing Instructional Perspective 229

Chapter 12 Explicit Teaching and Learning of Strategies
and Skills in Whole Language Classrooms 231

Ellen McIntyre, Diane Kyle, Ric A. Hovda, and Jean Anne Clyde,
University of Louisville

The Context 232
Characteristics of These Whole Language Classrooms 233
Explicit Teaching in a Whole Language Context 233
Teacher Explanations 234
Teacher Demonstrations 236
Children's Work as Demonstrations 238
Metacognitive Learning 239
Development of Metacognition: It Takes Time! 242
When and With Whom to Be Explicit 244
Conclusion 247
References 248

Chapter 13 The Nature of Outstanding Primary-Grades
Literacy Instruction 251

Michael Pressley and Ruth Wharton-McDonald,
University at Albany, State University of New York
Joan Rankin, University of Nebraska-Lincoln
Jennifer Mistretta and Linda Yokoi,
University at Albany, State University of New York
Shari Ettenberger, Mohanasen Public Schools, New York

Ms. Ettenberger Talks About Her Teaching 255
Surveys of Teaching Practices 262
Qualitative Study of Outstanding First Grade Literacy Instruction 264
Conclusion 266
References 267

Chapter 14 Concluding Reflections 277

Michael Pressley, University at Albany, State University of New York

A New Set of Hypotheses About Teaching
Need for Research 278
A Range of Potential Impacts 279
Potential Individual Differences With Respect to Instructional Needs 280
What Goes on When the Student Is Not With the Teacher? 281
Student Self-Regulation 282
Student Motivation 282
Active Learning 284
Diversity in Implementation of Balanced Teaching 284
Balanced Teaching as a General Model of Instruction 285
The Promise of Balanced Instruction 286
References 286

Epilogue 287
Ellen McIntyre, University of Louisville

Biographical Sketches 289
Index 301

Preface

—

Elementary literacy instruction is often characterized by extremes. A generation ago, the extremes that were debated were whole word versus phonics. Today, the extremes are whole language versus explicit strategy and skills instruction (for example, explicit instruction in decoding, comprehension, and composing skills). In contrast, this book advocates for neither one pole of an extreme nor another. Rather, it is a book that describes how strategy and skill instruction can be integrated in whole language instruction for potentially effective instruction. This is a book about balanced elementary-level literacy instruction, balanced in the sense that skills are taught in the context of instruction that is driven by reading and writing of authentic texts.

The contributors to this book recognize that strategies and skills must be developed and believe they are best learned and practiced during meaningful reading and writing experiences. The authors featured here have little confidence that decontextualized skills instruction will automatically transfer to natural reading and writing, a key assumption of traditional skills theorists. On the other hand, they also know that for many children the development of essential skills is not a natural by-product of immersion in reading and writing. The contributors believe that what works in elementary reading instruction is an interweaving of explicit strategy and skill instruction with rich reading and writing experiences. What they offer is their version of how explicit strategy and skill instruction fits within whole language philosophy.

The contributors to this volume did not hide their intellectual roots and strong assumptions about what is essential in instruction. The authors come from a variety of subfields within literacy—fields which some may think are at theoretical odds with each other. Some identify more strongly with whole language and others with explicit instruction. Some have backgrounds in psychology, while others are influenced more by anthropology. Some are known for strategy instruction with special needs children. A few are from early childhood programs and several are classroom teachers, including one Chapter One teacher. One purpose of this book is to get people who hold various perspectives to talk with one another, since they all want the same thing for children: the most effective instructional environment that meets the needs of all learners.

According to many of the teachers represented in this book, integrating strategy and skill instruction in whole language experiences is very, very hard to do. We believe that one way to begin doing it, however, is to study excellent examples of it, and assembling such examples and information about them is our primary motivation in editing this book. The teacher who decides to balance explicit instruction with authentic literacy experiences will undoubtedly feel like he or she is groping at first. That's all right. To be candid about it, all of us who are concerned with this kind of balanced literacy instruction are groping . . . including us as we tried to come to terms with the contents of these chapters. We invite you to consider these issues as you read the book.

—Ellen McIntyre
Michael Pressley

Acknowledgments

৪১ ──── ৫৪

Ellen McIntyre would like to express her deepest appreciation to the following people for their generous support in helping to make this book possible. First, I want to thank the many teachers who allowed me to visit their classrooms and ask them questions about their teaching. In particular, I wish to thank Marianne Davis from Cincinnati and JoAnn Archie, Helen Barnes, Tina Cron, Joy Spears, and Donna Stottman from Louisville.

A study which, in part, resulted in this book was funded by the International Reading Association Office of Education Research and Improvement at the United States Department of Education, and the University of Louisville. These grants provided me with the help necessary for analyzing mounds of data. I wish to thank the following graduate students for their help in analyzing these data and pushing my thinking: Opal Davis Dawson, Wendy Hames, and Denise Peterson.

I would also like to thank the chapter authors for their wonderful enlightening contributions to this book. They were completed in a timely way and made my job as editor easy. In addition, JoBeth Allen, Bob Calfee, Bill Harp, and Betty Schockley gave incredibly helpful, insightful, in-depth, and detailed reviews of an earlier version of this book. Penny Freppon, Diane Kyle, and Lesely Morrow discussed with me at length what this kind of instruction could mean for children; Lisa Delpit's work has inspired my thinking for this book; and P. David Pearson's keen understanding of the field and honest and sensible response to the sometimes ridiculous arguments we have has provided me with a model on which to base my own work.

I would like to thank Sue Canavan, publisher at Christopher-Gordon, for her energy and interest and help in this project. From the moment we met we acted as a team in pulling this book together. She has supported my ideas throughout the project.

Finally, I wish to thank my biggest supporter and fan, my husband, Bill Morison. His interest in my work and the ideas behind it provided a new "outsider's" lens through which to view teaching and learning.

Acknowledgments

❧ ———— ❧

Most of what Mike Pressley knows about balancing elementary language arts he learned while observing and working with teachers at Benchmark School in Media, Pennsylvania, and in public schools in Maryland and around Albany, New York. He is grateful to the many teachers who have permitted him to study their teaching. In recent years, he has talked with many other teachers on the topic, from California to New Hampshire, and they have increased his perspective further. During the past four years, he has been supported by the National Reading Research Center, funded by the United States Department of Education, Office of Educational Research and Improvement, and by various small grants from the University of Maryland at College Park and the University of New York. Then, there were the many conversations with Marilyn Adams, Valerie Anderson, Marsha Rolt, Barbara Conteh, Blauch Carus, Andre Carus, and others conncected with *Collections for Young Scholars,* as they hashed out a program determined to be balanced! Much of Pressley's writing in recent years originated in journals to himself after meeting with the *Collections for Young Scholars* colleagues, doing all possible to assemble arguments that would convince them about how to obtain the best skills instruction and whole language. That group especially sharpened each other's thinking by so challenging every supposition.

Foreword

❧ —— ☙

This is an important book, and it could not have come along at a better time. Teachers become confused when they read the professional literature and find the field split down the middle, taking sides on matters of what sorts of texts to read, what sorts of instruction to provide, and what sorts of procedures to use to assess student growth and accomplishment. Teachers like many of the new curricular ideas generated during the last decade, but they are not sure that they want to displace old ideas as they embrace new ones. This book provides teachers with the knowledge they will need to develop a lens which will allow them to resolve the conflicts they see in the profession's scholarly writing.

These are troubled times in both the schools and the academy. Hardly a week goes by without the release of another book or article complaining about the lack of skills (sometimes basic skills and sometimes higher order skills) of our high school graduates or the failure of our education schools to turn out teachers who can teach those skills. These attacks on our schools and our teachers should not surprise us. The systematic discreditation of public education and the teacher education system that feeds it is an essential premise in an increasingly popular argument to privatize education. In such an environment, with so many external forces seeking to overturn, or at least discredit, the good work done by teachers in our schools over the past few decades, our internal debates and squabbles within the literacy education field only play into the hands of these critics. They permit critics to put forward a convincing common-sense argument that goes something like, "Well, if those educators can't agree among themselves about how to teach reading, why should we let them decide on the curriculum for our kids?" If we want to preserve our current system of public education, if we want to build upon the knowledge about the teaching and learning of literacy that we have acquired in the past twenty years to create even richer learning opportunities for our children, we must find a common ground on which to stand while facing our critics and addressing their concerns.

This book is all about finding that common ground. The authors and editors build upon two important research and development efforts of the last twenty years to find that common ground. First and foremost, the book builds upon the whole language movement, which is, as its intellectual champions suggest (Edelsky, Altwerger, Flores, 1991; Goodman 1989), more of a philosophical disposition toward learning, knowing, and doing than it is a pedagogical approach to teaching. To say that this book and the ideas represented within it are based upon the whole language movement is to acknowledge its grounding in a substantial body of scholarship that undergirds the movement.

The first ground is constructivism. In the minds of the editors and authors, meaning is not regarded as a commodity that resides in texts to be reproduced by readers and reported to teachers. Meanings are complex negotiations between authors and readers through the medium of text within an environment that can dramatically influence the meaning construction process.

The second ground is the social nature of learning, language, and literacy. The premise is that all of these processes, even when we engage in them by ourselves, have a distinctively social character. Even in solitary situations, the writer hovers over our shoulder while we read, the reader is always there to guide our hand when we write, and the teacher in us is ever present when we make new discoveries. In schools and in everyday life, the social character of these processes is even more transparent: So much of what we learn, we learn with the assistance of others. So many of the textual interpretations we develop are negotiated during classroom discussions or informal conversations with friends. At least in everyday life, we write with a real audience in mind.

The third ground, which is intimately related to the second, is authenticity of text, task, and context. The basic premise here is that there is no need to create texts, tasks, and contexts that serve narrow instructional purposes. To the contrary, we need to frame instructional purposes around the texts, tasks, or contexts of everyday language and literacy. We need to let form follow function, to let teaching follow learning.

The fourth ground is integration, both among the language and between the language arts and other subject matter. To nurture integration among the language arts is to recognize that learning in one of the language arts supports learning in another. For example, the dispositions learned during critical reading activities help writers become better editors of their own work, and the knowledge of form that writers learn when they study genre and rhetorical structures is an invaluable aid in sorting out the ideas and relationships in the texts we encounter. To support integration between the language arts and other disciplines is to do neither more nor less than to situate reading and writing and oral language within real curricular learning contexts.

Second, this book builds upon a rich body of research, most of it less than twenty years old, that validates the efficacy of explicit instruction for the processes and strategies (some might call them skills) used by skilled readers and writers. This body of work (see Pearson, 1990; Pearson & Fielding, 1991; Pressley et al., 1989; Roehler & Duffy, 1991 for reviews) suggests that teachers who take the time to model strategies, explain their significance, and guide students in their acquisition can dramatically ameliorate students' understanding of text, both texts encountered in the instruction as well as new texts never before seen. Explicit instruction bears a family resemblance, albeit a weak one, to one of its intellectual predecessors, direct instruction, because of a common emphasis on clarity and systematicness on the presentation of skills and strategies. But the resemblance stops there. Within the tradition of explicit instruction, there are several characteristics that distinguish it from direct instruction, at least as direct instruction has been explicated by its advocates (Rosenshine, 1986). Explicit instruction is less likely to employ skill decomposition (breaking a complex skill down into manageable pieces), which is a staple of direct instruction, as a strategy for dealing with the complexity of important reading strategies. Instead, it is more likely to employ "scaffolding" as a tool for coping with complexity. In other words, teachers who work within this tradition are not likely to break down a skill into component parts, preferring instead to intervene in an instructional environment by providing clues, hints, questions, reformulations, and reflections that support students as they cope with a complex strategy or process. Second, explicit instruction is more likely than direct instruction to rely on authentic texts rather than special instructional texts in both initial instruction and later application. Specifically crafted texts are to be avoided lest we rectify a special world of texts and tasks. We can easily delude ourselves and our students into accepting the importance of skills that, in reality, apply only to texts that people would never read outside of the instructional worlds we have invented. We are less likely to fall into this counterproductive reification trap if we ground our curriculum in real texts and tasks, the kind everyday folks use in everyday reading and writing.

Like most marriages in real life, this one has its conflicts and un-resolved issues. The most glaring conflict turns on the question of when and why a skill, strategy, or concept would be taught. While many of the chapter authors who come to this wedding from the whole language side of the aisle are quite willing to endorse explicit instruction for any number of letter-sound correspondences or comprehension strategies, they resist any movement toward a systematic approach to skill teaching, an approach in which a scope and sequence would determine, in advance, the point in the curriculum at which a particular correspondence or strategy would be taught. Instead, they (see, for example, Dudley-Marling, this volume, or Freppon & Headings, this volume) argue for a need-driven approach to instruction: Let the teacher offer instruction to that student or group of students who demonstrate a need for it at exactly the moment when they need it. Others, from the skills side of the aisle, while not objecting to a need-driven approach, see it as unnecessarily difficult and subject to opportunities for overlooking important processes.

Conflicts notwithstanding, this is an important book. Situated firmly on these twin foundations of whole language and explicit instruction, the frameworks, concepts, and processes discussed in the chapters of this book hold great promise for the field of literacy education. They can answer questions for teachers who have been confused by the rhetoric of the debate between skills and whole language. They can provide a rationale for teachers who do not see a theoretical inconsistency between authenticity of task and explicit teaching. Most of all, because these ideas are based upon theoretically rich and empirically valid ideas, they can provide a consensus that will help restore public faith in our competence and convictions.

—P. David Pearson

Chapter 1

Strategies and Skills in Whole Language: An Introduction to Balanced Teaching

ଚ୍ଚ —— ଷ

Ellen McIntyre
University of Louisville

A fifth grade class is preparing for a trip to Washington, DC, and the students are making a relief map of the mall area. The teacher, Helen, is working with a small group of students as they build a model of the Lincoln Memorial. A few other students have made a model of the Vietnam Memorial after reading several books about the Wall. The class also just finished reading *Park's Quest,* a novel about a boy whose father died in Vietnam. Children have been writing in response to the book and other texts they have read about the Vietnam War. Like the character Park in the book, the students have written letters to people (fictional and real) involved in the war. They have prepared reports on the war and reactions to it. They also have written stories, poems, and personal reflections in response to this literature.

One child, Alesha, approaches Helen with a text she had been working on, also related to the theme. "Um, I'm not sure how to do this . . ." she begins. "I want to *report* my story, like a news reporter, but I'm not sure what words to use." Helen first asks Alesha why she chose to write a report. Alesha says, "Well, I'm not very good at stories, with details and all that. But, I think I can write a good report—with all the facts." Helen smiles and tells Alesha, "You know, news reports *do* have a lot of details. But I'll show you how to write them. A lot of you seem to be interested in report writing. I'll plan some time to meet with you about news writing tomorrow." She then retrieves her assessment notebook from a shelf and writes a note to herself.

The following day Helen meets with seven children, all of whom have elected to write news reports. She begins by showing about five minutes of the local news program she had taped the evening before that begins with a story about how local storms destroyed many homes, businesses, and schools. She prompts the children by saying, "Listen to the language she (the newscaster) uses and how she uses it . . . . You might even close your eyes so that you just hear words rather than see pictures." After the video, she asks the students, "What did you notice?"

At first, the children discuss the storm. Then Helen asks again, "What did you notice about the news report?"

Marcia replies, "I notice they start off showing pictures, then they actually tell what happened."

"Right. With TV, the story often begins with details—the interesting 'stuff.' Then they do a summary." Helen writes Marcia's observations on a chart paper labeled, 'News Report Writing.' She records a few other students' responses, and then adds her own, explaining, "Like Marcia said, her report is different from a newspaper report . . . . She started off with interesting details, and she let the camera grab your attention, too. She didn't begin with who, what, when, where like they often do in newspapers . . . ." (They had studied news writing and one child blurted out that newspapers don't always do that either!) Helen writes 'catchy, interesting beginning' on the chart. She tells the students that, on TV, the pictures can tell a lot, so if they choose to write TV reports they may want to consider accompanying their stories with pictures or a video. She explains that they must be careful that their report makes sense with or without pictures. After a discussion of the list of characteristics of news reports, Helen encourages the children to begin writing.

The vignette above illustrates how one teacher uses explicit instruction to teach writing strategies and skills in her whole language classroom. First, consider how the classroom community and Helen's instructional actions highlight good whole language teaching:

- Thematic instruction based on a common interest (trip to Washington)
- Authentic, functional experiences (reading literature about the trip)
- Hands-on, interdisciplinary activities related to the theme (building a model of the museum/monument area)
- Extensive reading of good literature
- Extensive writing of varied genre in response to good literature
- Respect for children's intentions (Alesha's decision to write a report)
- Assessment as an integral part of instruction (Helen keeps her anecdotal records handy)
- Small group instruction based on children's needs (report writing)

In addition to these instructional actions commonly found in whole language classrooms, Helen also explicitly teaches strategies and skills when necessary. Consider how she approached instruction, why she taught the skills she did, with whom she taught them (not all children), and when she taught them (when children needed them to accomplish their authentic tasks).

- She taught features of report writing (by showing and explaining the differences between "leads" of newspaper and TV reports).
- She taught effective wording which began with a demonstration of news report writing from TV.
- She taught students *how* to go about learning to write (by listening carefully to others).
- She provided a list of characteristics of report writing on chart paper to which students can refer.
- She taught only the children who needed this lesson.
- She taught these strategies and skills directly and explicitly.

Finally, in this short episode, Helen encourages the students to apply what they have just learned in the mini-lesson on news writing to their immediate report writing projects. In this lesson Helen not only exemplifies several principles of whole language teaching, she also makes sure that the students acquire the strategies of good writers and the specific skills of effective writing. This lesson is not unlike the literacy instruction portrayed in this book in which elementary teachers teach strategies and skills in their whole language classrooms.

Whole Language

A remarkable transformation is taking place in classrooms throughout the country. The teaching of reading, writing, and other language arts is moving from transmission or skills-based instructional orientations to more holistic perspectives. As in Helen's classroom, instruction in these classrooms emphasizes the functions and communicative nature of language. Teachers are increasingly interested in having their students read and write for real purposes, rather than answer questions and drill on skills (Goodman, Brooks, Meredith, & Goodman, 1987). Children in these classrooms are guided toward constructing meaning through reading self-selected texts and composing texts of many genres (Cambourne, 1988; Edelsky, Altwerger, & Flores, 1991; Goodman et al., 1987; Kamii, Manning, & Manning, 1991). When choices are honored and tasks are purposeful and open-ended, students are highly motivated and self-directed (Turner, 1995), thus fostering future reading and writing. Teachers who teach from this philosophy often call themselves whole language teachers.

The background of whole language is richly complex and comes from a variety of fields, including psychology, anthropology, linguistics, and education, to name a few. The movement has its roots in constructivism (Brooks & Brooks, 1993; Kamii, Manning, & Manning, 1991; Goodman, 1990; Reid, Kurkjian, & Carruthers, 1994), which views learning as the active *construction* of knowledge. Children's knowledge acquisition is built on current cognitive structures (or schemes) that enable them to interpret new information. Constructivism has its roots in developmental theory and is based on many of Piaget's notions of accommodation and assimilation in learning. Dewey's (1938) advocacy of direct experience for learning has also had an impact on constructivist theory. Dewey recommended that children solve real, authentic problems. In whole language classrooms, teachers guide students to construct knowledge through direct experience as they engage in authentic tasks (Edelsky, 1990; Goodman, 1986).

A key feature of constructivism is that learning occurs through interactions with the environment and others. One person often serves as a guide who provides the necessary support to the learner until the learner can achieve a task independently. This notion of "scaffolding" and the social aspect of learning theory is based largely on Russian psychologist Vygotsky's theory of learning (1956) and has been guiding the work of educators in recent decades. Children acquire knowledge not by internalizing it directly from the outside but by constructing it from the inside, in interaction with the environment (Bandura, 1977; Vygotsky, 1978).

Whole language has also been significantly influenced by linguists who emphasize the social nature of learning, but who also focus on learning through language use (Barnes, 1991; Halliday, 1984; Wells, 1986). Children learn language in naturally occurring contexts for authentic reasons in gradual stages that approximate adult language (Barnes, 1991; Cambourne, 1988; Halliday, 1984; Wells, 1986). Often it is through talk or writing that children come to new understandings (Barnes, 1991; Langer & Applebee, 1987; Marzano, 1991; Murnane, 1990). Whole language classroom practice involves less teacher-directed talk and activity, less use of textbooks as teaching tools, and more opportunities for cooperative learning than in more traditional classrooms.

The vision of the learner

One very telling hallmark of whole language philosophy is teachers' visions of the children themselves (Edelsky, Altwerger, & Flores, 1991; Watson, 1994). While teachers from all paradigms have respect for children, it is a written part of whole language philosophy. Whole language educators recognize that children come to school with vast knowledge, and they build on that knowledge. If children's knowledge is different from that of their teachers', these differences are viewed as opportunities, not as "deficits." Students' integrity as learners is honored (Reid, Kurkjian, & Carruthers, 1994; Strickland, 1994), and much of the curriculum is based on students' needs and interests.

Whole language teachers also have respect for children's language (Goodman, 1986). They do not deny children their "home" language, whether it be a cultural or regional dialect or foreign language. They also do not deny or view as deficient children's cultural understandings, behaviors, or "ways of taking" (Heath, 1983) from the classroom instruction. Again, the goal in whole language teaching is to understand children, respect them, like them, and use knowledge about them to make classroom decisions.

Whole language teachers also view children's curiosity and questioning as healthy signs of learning and not as classroom disruptions. They see children's mistakes as a natural part of learning— as approximations toward conventional reading and writing (Cambourne, 1988) and signs of and opportunities for growth (Goodman, 1986). Whole language instruction has the child at the center of the curriculum, and all decisions are made with the learner in mind (Edelsky, 1990; Goodman, 1986).

The vision of language and language learning

In whole language classrooms the focus of language learning is first and foremost on the construction of meaning (Harp, 1991; Goodman et al., 1987; Kamii, Manning, & Manning, 1991; Watson, 1994). Children learn language because they need to communicate; it develops in response to personal-social needs (Edelsky, 1990). People learn to talk by talking, read by reading, think by thinking (Harp, 1994). Language learning occurs informally and in meaningful contexts, is an active process, and happens in general, observable stages. Goodman (1986) captures the nature of learning in whole language classrooms:

Language learning "is easy when . . . it's real and natural, whole, sensible, interesting, relevant, belongs to the learner, is part of a real event, has social utility, has purpose for the learner, the learner chooses to use it, it's accessible to the learner, and the learner has power to use it" (p. 8).

It is not necessary to learn *about* language as one learns and uses language; however, learning about language also develops best and most usefully in the contexts of real literacy events (Edelsky, Altwerger, & Flores, 1991; Goodman, et al., 1987).

From a whole language view, comprehension of text is regarded as a constructive, transactive process. Rosenblatt (1978) has helped us understand that meaning lies in the readers of a text, not within the text. Thus, comprehension occurs as readers bring knowledge about the world and language to the text in order to gain personal under-standings. Studies of readers' processes have shown us that the successful reader's focus is always on making sense of text. Attention is on meaning, and anything else, such as letters, words, or grammar, only get full attention when the reader has trouble getting to the mean-ing (Goodman, 1986; Harp, 1991). Successful readers and writers are confident, display high degrees of control over the processes, use reading and writing for communication, and continue to engage in reading and writing. Proficient readers are strategic readers as well. They use prediction, inference, sampling, confirmation, and self-cor-rection strategies in order to construct meaning. In reading, comprehension is the only goal.

In writing, expression is the goal (Cambourne, 1988; Graves, 1983; Calkins, 1986). Good writers also have a sense of audience and pur-pose (Britton, Burgess, Martin, McCloud, & Rosen, 1975; Raphael, Englert, & Kirshner, 1989; Tierney & Shanahan, 1991), and they con-sider how to organize their texts and present their ideas in the best ways (Britton, et al., 1975; Mullis & Mellon, 1980; Graves, 1983). Good writing is clear, fluent, and delightful to read. One goal of whole language teaching is to help students write well. Classrooms that op-erate from this perspective are characterized by students who actively construct meaning in both reading and writing in order to become effective, skilled readers and writers.

Principles that guide teaching

The set of beliefs about how children learn and what is involved in effective language use described above have led to several principles for whole language teaching. The following actions are advocated by whole language theorists and practitioners. First, the classroom climate is characterized by a *positive view of the learners.* Teachers value and encourage risk-taking, and they create opportunities for success. Mutual trust exists among the students and the teachers in such a way that all can take risks.

The instructional focus is first and foremost on the creation of meaning (Goodman, 1986). To do this, whole language teachers *keep language whole.* That is, teachers do not teach language skills in isolation. Only after children understand reading and writing as meaning-creating processes are they exposed to the subskills (Harp, 1991). To maintain a focus on meaning, the work in these classrooms is *authentic* (Edelsky, 1990). Children write to get things done; read to find things out; listen to enjoy or learn something; or act in a play to better understand or appreciate something, or to express themselves. Children do things for a *purpose* in whole language classrooms (Edelsky, Altwerger, & Flores, 1991; Deegan, 1995).

Whole language teachers empower children to make *choices.* They encourage and allow students to express their opinions, needs, and desires. Students help choose tasks that make up the curriculum. Yet instruction is not all "funsy-wunsy" (Cambourne, 1988). The work students choose may be difficult, but they are expected to value the struggle (Cambourne, 1988). With choice comes responsibility, and children are taught and expected to choose work that helps them become independent learners. Independence is the ultimate goal of education (Pearson, 1989).

Literacy manifests itself in *sustained reading and writing* (Cambourne, 1988). Some whole language theorists have written that children learn to read by reading and learn to write by writing. While literacy learning is much more than that, all agree that in whole language classrooms, children "read, read, read and write, write, and write" (Harp, 1991, p. 3).

Whole language theorists and practitioners view the teacher as a *facilitator.* Teachers guide, support, monitor, and encourage children as they engage in authentic language tasks. Teaching in whole language classrooms has been described as "leading from behind" (Newman, 1985). The teacher motivates the learners, but also arranges the environment by providing appropriate materials, time, and opportunities for authentic experiences. Teachers monitor development and constantly assess children in light of what they know about how children learn. They provide individuals with needed experiences for further growth.

Harste (1994) has eloquently outlined some of the most salient effects the whole language movement has had on education. Among the many changes it has made in elementary schools across the nation, the movement has:

- helped educators see meaning as the core of language,
- helped educators have a new respect for children,
- helped teachers inspire writers rather than train spellers,
- helped teachers see themselves as researchers (pp. 145–146).

Happily, whole language is a fact of life in literacy curriculum and in research and is likely to remain a force for years to come (Pearson, 1989).

Confusions and Uncertainty

While the tasks and activities that often make up whole language teaching are enticing, one cannot assume instruction is effective simply because it is based on a list of classroom activities or even belief systems. Dyson (1984) warned us more than a decade ago to guard against defining good teaching as carrying out a set of instructional activities. Instead, effective instruction is a matter of making decisions about what is truly best for children. It involves deciding what to teach to whom, when, and how. These decisions and ambiguities about effective instruction have created much confusion and frustration for teachers attempting whole language (Dudley-Marling & Dippo, 1991; Gersten & Dimino, 1993; McIntyre, 1995a, 1995b). Many are still unclear about the role of "strategies" and "skills" in whole language even though decades of research have shown that good readers not only comprehend but can articulate their comprehension strategies (Baker & Brown, 1984; Roehler & Duffy, 1991; Paris, Lixon, & Wixon, 1986; Paris, Wasik, & Turner, 1991; Pearson & Fielding, 1991), and particular subskills of reading (such as phonics and word recognition) are prerequisites to reading acquisition (Adams, 1990; Clay, 1979; Ehri, 1991; Spear-Swerling & Sternberg, 1994; Stanovich, 1991).

The skepticism, confusion, and concern are valid. While the description of whole language (in its theoretical sense) carries great weight, the fact is that, in many classrooms, whole language is not being implemented as described above. In many places, children may not be getting instruction on strategies and skills for effective, independent reading and writing. Some beginning readers may not be taught to sound out words for fear that phonics will get in the way of meaning-making. Other children may be left to figure out on their own or with peers how to write more effectively or comprehend complex texts. In some places, teachers believe that instruction in skills is inappropriate in whole language classrooms:

> We've met lots of teachers who felt that the explicit teaching of read-ing and writing skills ran counter to the basic tenets of whole language teaching. A teacher in Toronto, for example, told us that she didn't teach spelling or punctuation because "I'm holistic" and "Whole lan-guage teachers don't teach skills." (Dudley-Marling & Dippo, 1991, p. 548)

Many emerging and novice whole language teachers are some-what confused about the role of spelling and phonics in the whole language philosophy (Powell & Hornsby, 1995; Templeton, 1991). Examples of comments follow:

> "I have been teaching phonics lessons in secret because I thought you weren't supposed to do that as a whole language teacher."
>
> "So, *are* we supposed to teach skills? Which ones?"
>
> "Who *cares* if kids can spell?" (McIntyre, 1994)

These views are so prevalent that the issue of skills instruction in whole language classrooms was a recent topic on National Public Radio's Morning Edition news program. In that story on reading in-struction in California, the reporter explained that many teachers in California said it was "politically incorrect" to admit to teaching phon-ics (NPR, September 14, 1995).

Educators express concern about strategy teaching as well. In their many observations of whole language classrooms, McKenna, Stahl, & Reinking found little integration of strategy instruction in authentic reading and writing tasks. Other educators worry that teach-ers are ignoring components of effective cognitive apprenticeship models of instruction (Brown, Collins, & Duguid, 1989) such as er-ror correction, feedback, and sequencing of events. The whole language movement needs to communicate more clearly how this kind of instruction fits into meaning-centered practice.

Despite early writings about explicit skills instruction (Cambourne, 1988) and strategy instruction (Goodman et al., 1987) and some ex-cellent efforts to clarify the place of strategies and skills in whole language (Newman & Church, 1990), many "myths" and misconceptions about whole language prevail. Through focusing on the negative aspects of traditional, skills-based programs and the primary purposes of whole language, advocates may have inadvertently sent implicit, contradictory messages about the role of strategies and skills in whole language. Dudley-Marling & Dippo (1991) explain, "We think they may get this impression from those of us who talk or write about whole language theory or practice, including people who are accepted as whole language 'authorities'" (p. 549). Those who write about whole language often use ambiguous language that says little about what teachers actually do (Dudley-Marling & Dippo, 1991). Thus, in these ways, the anti-skills message may have been communicated to teachers. (See Dudley-Marling, this volume, for further discussion of this issue.)

The role of the teacher

The role of the teacher is another concern of many educators who advocate whole language, but who may be skeptical about its implementation. If teachers are to "facilitate," they may think it inappropriate to demonstrate, explain, or instruct in any direct ways (Pearson, 1989). Indeed, that message has been communicated. Two years ago a new teacher was observed during what she labeled a "whole language lesson." She was asking the children to draw interpretations of a story she had just read them. She told them to "think about the setting of the story as I read." A child asked, "What is setting?" The teacher gulped, gave a furtive glance toward the observer and went on without answering the child. Later, when asked why she did not answer the student's question about setting, the teacher admitted, "I didn't know what I was supposed to do. In whole language you are supposed to let kids discover everything" (McIntyre, 1994). Other teachers have said:

> "I thought whole language was when you read a book and then did an activity with it," and

> "I keep watching and hoping my kids will learn how to use capitals and punctuation" (McIntyre, 1994).

Other research (Kulieke & Jones, 1993) has shown some children floundering in settings with little teacher direction. Still others (Stahl, Suttles, & Pagnucco, 1993) have found students in whole language classrooms reading much less challenging material than in traditional classrooms. One study (McIntyre, 1994) found some teachers who did not group for instruction because "whole language means whole class" (McIntyre, 1994). Clearly, the whole language movement has left teachers confused and uncertain about what and how to teach particular skills and strategies (McKenna, Stahl, & Reinking, 1994; Walmsley & Adams, 1993). The role of the teacher in whole language classrooms has not been communicated to many, and this has mani-fested itself in "bad examples" (Field & Jardine, 1994) of whole language.

Despite the confusion and uncertainty, whole language advocates maintain that whole language is not synonymous with benign neglect (Dudley-Marling & Dippo, 1991; Templeton, 1991). Whole language teachers can guide children's learning though modeling and coaching, and skills do not have to be ignored. There have been studies of the teaching of skills and strategies in whole language classrooms (McIntyre & Freppon, 1994; McIntyre, 1995b) and of direct and ex-plicit instruction within the same orientation (Fallon & Allen, 1994; Turner, 1995). And yet, in various ways, contradictory messages have still been communicated to the practitioners so invested in the whole language philosophy and practice. The messages they receive often ignore the extensive body of research on the essential skills necessary for beginning reading (See Adams, 1990, for example) and the effec-tiveness of explicit instruction on strategies.

Explicit Strategy and Skill Instruction

As stated, many studies have shown that good readers are not only able to comprehend but can articulate their comprehension strategies (Baker & Brown, 1984; Roehler & Duffy, 1991; Paris, Wasik, & Turner, 1991; Pearson & Fielding, 1991). Further, many studies show that subskills of reading such as phonemic awareness and automatic-ity in word recognition are skills necessarily developed on the way to becoming a conventional reader (Adams, 1990; Clay, 1979; Ehri, 1991; Spear-Swerling & Sternberg, 1994). Much research has shown that when children are explicitly taught these strategies and skills, they become better readers (Pearson & Dole, 1987; Palincsar & Brown, 1984; Pearson, 1985; Pressley et al., 1989).

Extensive research also shows that when teachers carefully ex-plain to students what is being learned, why it is being learned, when it will be used, and how it will be used, students learn more (Roehler,

Duffy, & Meloth, 1986; Palincsar, 1986; Roehler & Duffy, 1986; Rosenshine, 1986). Explicit instruction is not merely telling facts, but involves explanation (telling children the *whys, whats,* and *hows* of reading and writing) and modeling (including modeling thinking) (Roehler & Duffy, 1986). Further, when teachers regularly practice the use of "think-alouds" (Cambourne, 1988; Duffy, Roehler, & Herrmann, 1988), or modeling of cognitive processes (Tharpe & Gallimore, 1993), students learn more as well. Explanation and modeling can be ways of "scaffolding" (Bruner, 1960) or supporting students in accomplishing what they may not be able to do independently. Clearly, some children need explicit instruction on strategies and skills that others learn more easily. Delpit (1991) explains:

> The direct instruction of certain kinds of strategies would also help children acquire the culture of power because it would give them access to the major medium of power, written language . . . . It is often necessary to be explicit both with what you're trying to communicate and why that information is important (p. 542).

It is critical that the research on explicit strategy and skill instruction not be undervalued by teacher educators, school curriculum leaders, and teachers as we move toward more holistic instruction. As a field we can come to a better understanding of how these explicit instructional actions can be productively used in ways that honor children's backgrounds, interests, and abilities. We do not need to teach "isolated, meaningless, drilled 'subskills' . . . , but useful and usable knowledge which contributes to a student's ability to communicate effectively in standard, generally acceptable literary forms' (Delpit, 1988, p. 384) *"within the context of critical and creative thinking. . . ."* (Delpit, 1986).

Inclusion of strategy and skill instruction in whole language teaching may necessarily involve extensive, systematic explicit instruction, particularly for children for whom the language of school is not part of their culture (Delpit, 1986, 1988, 1991; Heath, 1983; Purcell-Gates, 1995). Does this mean a return to the meaningless drill of isolated skills and chanted direct instruction of the past? No. Nor does it mean an eclectic approach to teaching, but rather instruction on strategies and skills taught within authentic tasks so that instruction does not undermine/conflict with the principles of whole language instruction.

What's Different about this Book

This book represents a blending or synthesis of knowledge from a variety of perspectives about effective elementary literacy instruction. Authors with extensive research and teaching experience in the areas of whole language, strategy instruction, special education, emergent literacy, metacognition, and diverse cultures have contributed. Because this book represents a blending of perspectives, it quite understandably contains slightly different theoretical views. Across these chapters there are subtle differences in the authors' advocacy of explicit strategy and skill instruction. In addition, the degree to which authors believe teachers should honor the intentions of the learners as opposed to planning instruction they think is necessary also differs slightly. These differences are highlighted because they bring strength to the book. Teaching and learning are among the most complex human behaviors, and these differences in perspective and teaching strategies are natural. Readers are invited to take a critical stance as they delve into the classrooms of the teachers portrayed in this book.

In spite of some theoretical differences, the authors in this book share many assumptions in common about learning and effective literacy instruction. First, all of the authors believe that children come to school with knowledge upon which teachers can build. They respect children—their backgrounds, language, interests, and abilities. The authors believe children learn best what they want to learn and will engage in literacy more readily if tasks are functional. They believe children should engage more in the entire processes of reading and writing than in the practice of subskills of literacy. They believe children learn from each other in social, collaborative classrooms. They also, importantly, agree that the explicit instruction of strategies and skills can and should occur for some children, at some times, and in particular ways. This kind of instruction can occur spontaneously, of course, based on children's intentions, but it also may need to occur in planned, systematic ways. For many children, in fact, this kind of instruction *must* occur in order for them to become successful readers and writers.

The instruction the authors espouse is also similar. The teachers represented in this book use an assessment-to-instruction model of teaching. They first and foremost find out about the learners they teach, through both informal and formal means. Information from observations, interviews, collaboration with other teachers, read-alouds, written products, and tests all contribute to *what* teachers teach, *how* they instruct, with *whom*, and *when*. This model of whole language teaching is the most salient characteristic of the teachers represented in this book. When knowledge of the skills children have and those they need is apparent, teachers can then, and only then, make appropriate instructional decisions.

The strategies used to support children in their development are also similar across the teachers represented in this book. All the teachers use frequent demonstrations or modeling of reading and writing for functional, authentic purposes, and they model the specific strategies they want children to use for sense-making. They also demonstrate thinking processes to clarify how one might tackle reading and writing. All teachers use explicit and direct explanation of these processes. The practice of scaffolding to help children construct understandings is ever present throughout the book and is illustrated in whole class, small group, and one-on-one teaching situations. Finally, and perhaps most important, each teacher's primary goal is to help children become metacognitively aware of their own knowledge and skill in literacy in order to enable children to become decision-makers.

Organization of this Book

This book is organized to show how teachers in a variety of instructional settings balance instruction on skills and strategies within meaningful literacy experiences. The first section, "Teaching Skills in Whole Language Classrooms," includes several portraits of elementary classrooms showing how this kind of teaching is done. The second section of the book, "Children's Development in Light of Instruction," focuses on the development of learners. It highlights the relationship of assessment to instruction and how the knowledge of children can guide expert scaffolding. This section is followed by "Balancing Strategy Instruction Within Whole Language," which includes chapters detailing procedures of specific comprehension and composing strategies. The final section, "Patterns of Teacher Actions: Balancing Instructional Perspectives," includes chapters that describe the patterns of many teachers' instructional actions concerning explicit instruction on strategies and skills in their whole language classrooms. This section concludes with a reflective chapter about the instruction reviewed in this book.

Most edited books have some redundancy as well as gaps caused by material that is not covered. This book represents less of a problem with gaps and more with redundancy. Yet, I think this can be useful to readers and therefore I opted to edit little of the authors' literature reviews and the instructional strategies described across chapters. In fact, I was pleased to find that all the authors describe many of the same practices. This reinforcement can be useful to teachers who may appreciate varied examples of how particular strategies and skills can be taught. For example, while all the authors emphasize the need for frequent demonstrations of literacy skills, these demonstrations are shown in a variety of ways throughout the chapters. Readers can identify with particular teachers and children and classroom settings and visualize themselves teaching in this way.

As you read this book, I invite you to examine your own philosophical beliefs about learning and teaching. Please also analyze and criticize as you look at the instruction portrayed in this book in light of your own beliefs and practice. I hope that the chapters shape your thinking and help you internalize your own beliefs about the role of explicit strategy and skill instruction within meaningful, purposeful instruction.

References

Adams, M. J. (1990). *Beginning to read: Thinking and learning about print.* Cambridge, MA: MIT Press.

Baker, L., & Brown, A. L. (1984). Metacognitive skills and reading. In P. D. Pearson, R. Barr, M. L. Kamil, & P. Mosenthal (Eds.), *Handbook of reading research* (Volume 1, pp. 353-394). White Plains, NY: Longman.

Bandura, A. (1977). *Social learning theory.* Englewood Cliffs, NJ: Prentice-Hall, Inc.

Barnes, D. (1991). *From curriculum to communication.* Portsmouth, NH: Heinemann.

Britton, J., Burgess, T., Martin, N., McCloud, A., & Rosen, H. (1975). *The development of writing abilities 11-18.* London: Macmillan.

Brooks, J. G., & Brooks, M. G. (1993). *In search of understanding: The case for constructivist classrooms.* Alexandria, VA: Association for Supervision and Curriculum Development.

Brown, J., Collins, A., & Dugind, P. (1989). Situated cognition and the culture of learning. *Educational Leadership, 18,* 32–42.

Bruner, J. S. (1960). *The process of education.* Cambridge, MA: Harvard University Press.

Calkins, L. (1986). *The art of teaching writing.* Portsmouth, NH: Heinemann.

Cambourne, B. (1988). *The whole story: Natural learning and the acquisition of literacy in the classroom.* Scholastic, Inc.: New Zealand.

Clay, M. M. (1979). *The early detection of reading difficulties.* Portsmouth, NH: Heinemann.

Deegan, D. H. (1995). The necessity of debate: A comment on commentaries. *The Reading Teacher, 48,* 688–695.

Delpit, L. D. (1986). Skills and other dilemmas of a progressive black educator. *Harvard Educational Review, 56,* 379–385.

Delpit, L. D. (1988). The silenced dialogue: Power and pedagogy in teaching other people's children. *Harvard Educational Review, 58,* 280–287.

Delpit, L. D. (1991). [Interview with William H. Teale, editor of *Language Arts*]. *Language Arts, 68,* 541–547.

Dewey, J. (1938). *Experience and education.* New York: Macmillan.

Dudley-Marling, C., & Dippo, D. (1991). The language of whole language. *Language Arts, 68,* 548–554.

Duffy, G. D., & Roehler, L. (1987). Improving classroom reading instruction through the use of responsive elaboration. *Reading Teacher, 40,* 514–521.

Duffy, G. D., Roehler, L., & Herrmann, B. (1988). Modeling mental processes helps poor readers become strategic readers. *Reading Teacher, 41,* 762–767.

Dyson, A. H. (1984). Staying free to dance with the children: The dangers of sanctifying activities in the language arts curriculum. *English Education,* 134–145.

Edelsky, C. (1990). Whose agenda is it anyway? *Educational Researcher,* 19.

Edelsky, C., Altwerger, B., & Flores, B. (1991). *Whole language: What's the difference?* Portsmouth, NH: Heinemann.

Ehri, L. (1991). Development of the ability to read words. In R. Barr, M. L. Kamil, P. Mosenthal, & P. D. Pearson (Eds.), *Handbook of reading research II* (pp. 383–417). New York: Longman.

Fallon, I., & Allen, J. (1994). Where the deer and the cantaloupe play. *The Reading Teacher, 47,* 546–551.

Field, J. C., & Jardine, D. W. (1994). "Bad examples" as interpretive opportunities: On the need for whole language to own its own shadow. *Language Arts, 71,* 258–263.

Gersten, R., & Dimino, J. (1993). Visions and revisions: A special education perspective on the whole language controversy. *Remedial and Special Education, 14,* 5–13.

Goodman, K. S. (1986). *What's whole in whole language.* Portsmouth, NH: Heinemann.

Goodman, K. S. (1990). Whole language research: Foundations and development. *Elementary School Journal, 90,* 208–221.

Goodman, K. S., Brooks, E., Meredith, R., & Goodman, Y. M. (1987). *Language and thinking in school: A whole language curriculum* (3rd edition). New York: Richard C. Owen Publishers, Inc.

Graves, D. H. (1983). *Writing: Teachers and children at work.* Portsmouth, NH: Heinemann.

Halliday, M. (1984). Three aspects of children's language development: Learning language, learning through language, and learning about language. In Y. Goodman, M. Haussler, & D. Strickland (Eds.), *Oral and written language development research: Implications for instruction.* Urbana, IL: National Council of Teachers of English.

Harp, B. (1991). The whole language movement. In B. Harp (Ed.), *Assessment and evaluation in whole language programs.* Norwood, MA: Christopher-Gordon.

Harste, J. (1994). New questions, different inquiries. In C. Brown (Moderator), *Whole language: The debate.* Bloomington, IN: ERIC Clearing house on reading, English, and communication.

Heath, S.B. (1983). *Ways with words: Language, life, and work in communities and classrooms.* Cambridge: Cambridge University Press.

Kamii, C., Manning, M., & Manning, G. (1991). *Early literacy: A constructivist foundation for whole language.* Washington, DC: National Education Association.

Kulieke, M. J., & Jones, B. F. (1993). Cognitive instructional techniques in relation to whole language approaches. *Remedial and Special Education, 14,* 26–29.

Langer, J. A., & Applebee, A. N. (1987). *How writing shapes thinking: A study of teaching and learning.* Urbana, IL: National Council of Teachers of English.

Marzano, R. J. (1991). Language, the language arts, and thinking. In J. Flood, J. M. Jensen, D. Lapp, & J. R. Squire (Eds.), *Handbook of research on teaching the English language arts.* New York: Macmillan Publishing Company.

McIntyre, E. (1995b). Teaching and learning writing skills in a low-SES, urban primary classroom. *Journal of Reading Behavior, 27*, 213–242.

McIntyre, E. (1995a). The struggle for developmentally appropriate literacy instruction. *Journal of Research in Childhood Education, 9* (2).

McIntyre, E., & Freppon, P. A. (1994). A comparison of children's development of alphabetic knowledge in a skills-based and a whole language classroom. *Research in the Teaching of English, 28*, 391–417.

McIntyre, E. (1994). *Teaching skills in whole language classrooms.* Unpublished raw data.

McKenna, M. C., Stahl, S. A., & Reinking, D. (1994). A critical commentary on research, politics, and whole language. *Journal of Reading Behavior, 26*, 211–233.

McKenna, M. C., Stahl, S. A., & Reinking, D. (1994). On research, politics, and whole language. *Journal of Reading Behavior, 26*, 211–233.

Mullis, V. S., & Mellon, J. C. (1980). *Guidelines for describing three aspects of writing: Syntax, cohesion, and mechanics.* Denver, CO: Educational Commission of the States (ERIC Document Reproduction Service No. ED 205 572).

Murnane, Y. (1990). Writing as a thinking tool: How writing can foster metacognition. In B. Anderson (Ed.), *Teacher education for literacy around the world* (pp. 61–64). St. Cloud, MN: Organization of Teacher Educators for Reading.

National Public Radio (Morning Edition) (September 14, 1995).

Newman, J. M. (1985). *Whole language: Theory in use.* Portsmouth, NH: Heinemann.

Newman, J., & Church, S. (1990). Myths of whole language. *The Reading Teacher, 44.*

Palincsar, A. M. (1986). The role of dialogue in providing scaffolded instruction. *Educational Psychologist, 2*, 73–98.

Palincsar, A. M., & Brown, A. L. (1984). Reciprocal teaching of comprehension-fostering and comprehension-monitoring activities. *Cognition and Instruction, 1*, 117–175.

Palincsar, A. M., & Klenk, L. (1993). Broader visions encompanying literacy, learners, and context. *Remedial and Special Education, 14*, 19–25.

Paris, S. G., Lipson, M. Y., & Wixon, K. K. (1983). Becoming a strategic reader. *Contemporary Educational Psychology, 8*, 293–316.

Paris, S. G., Wasik, B. A., & Turner, J. C. (1991). The development of strategic readers. In R. Barr, M. L. Kamil, P. Mosenthal, & P. D. Pearson (Eds.), *Handbook of reading research, II* (pp. 609–640). New York: Longman.

Pearson, P. D. (1985). Changing the face of reading comprehension instruction. *The Reading Teacher, 38,* 724–738.

Pearson , P. D. (1989). Reading the whole language movement. *Elementary School Journal, 90,* 231–243.

Pearson, P. D., & Fielding, L. (1991). Comprehension instruction. In R. Barr, M. L. Kamil, P. Mosenthal, & P. D. Pearson (Eds.), *Handbook of reading research, II* (pp. 815–860). New York: Longman.

Pearson, P. D., & Dole, J. A. (1987). Explicit comprehension instruction: A review of research and a new conceptualization of instruction. *Elementary School Journal, 88,* 151–163.

Powell, D., & Hornsby, D. (1995). *Learning phonics and spelling in a whole language program.* New York: Scholastic Professional Books.

Pressley, M., Symons, S., Snyder, B. L., & Cariglia-Bull, T. (1989). Strategy instruction research comes of age. *Learning Disability Quarterly, 12,* 16–31.

Purcell-Gates, V. (1995). *Other people's words: The cycle of low literacy.* Cambridge, MA: Harvard University Press.

Raphael, T. E., Englert, C. E., & Kirshner, B. W. (1989). Students' metacognitive knowledge about writing. *Research in the Teaching of English, 25,* 291–313.

Reid, D. K., Kurkjian, C., & Carruthers, S. S. (1994). Special education teachers interpret constructivist teaching. *Remedial and Special Education, 15,* 267–280.

Roehler, L., & Duffy, G. D. (1986). Why are some teachers better explainers than others? *Journal of Education for Teaching, 12,* 273–284.

Roehler, L. R., & Duffy, G. D. (1991). Teachers' instructional actions. In R. Barr, M. L. Kamil, P. B. Mosenthal, & P. D. Pearson (Eds.), *Handbook of reading research (Volume II)* (pp. 861–884). New York: Longman.

Roehler, L. R., Duffy, G. D., & Meloth, M. (1986). What to be direct about in direct instruction. In T. Raphael and R. Reynolds (Eds.), *Contexts of School-based Literacy* (pp. 79–97). New York: Random House.

Rosenblatt, L. (1978). *The reader, the text, the poem.* Carbondale, IL: Southern Illinois University Press.

Rosenshine, B. (1986). Synthesis of research on explicit teaching. *Educational Leadership, 43,* 60–69.

Spear-Swerling, L., & Sternburg, R. J. (1994). The road not taken: An integrative theoretical model of reading disability. *Journal of Learning Disabilities, 27,* 91–103.

Stahl, S. A., Suttles, C. W., & Pagnucco, J. R. (1993). *The effects of traditional and process literacy instruction on first graders' reading and writing achievement and orientation toward reading.* Paper presented at the meeting of the American Educational Research Association, San Francisco.

Stanovich, K. E. (1991). Word recognition: Changing perspectives. In R. Barr, K. L. Kamil, P. Mosenthal, P. D. Pearson (Eds.), *Handbook of reading research, II* (pp. 418–452). New York: Longman.

Strickland, D. S. (1994). Educating African American learners at risk: Finding a better way. *Language Arts, 71,* 328–345.

Templeton, S. (1991). New trends in an historical perspective: The "what" and "why" of skills instruction in literacy. *Language Arts, 68,* 590–595.

Tharpe, R. & Gallimore, R. (1993). *Rousing minds to life.* New York: Cambridge University Press.

Tierney, R. J., & Shanahan, T. (1991). Research on the reading-writing relationship: Interactions, transactions, and outcomes. In R. Barr, M. L. Kamil, P. Mosenthal, & P. D. Pearson (Eds.), *Handbook of reading research, II* (pp.246–280). New York: Longman.

Turner, J. C. (1995). The influence of classroom contexts on young children's motivation for literacy. *Reading Research Quarterly, 30,* 410–441.

Vygotsky, L. (1978). *Mind in society: The development of higher psychological processes.* Cambridge, MA: Harvard University Press.

Walmsley, S. A., & Adams, E. L. (1993). Realities of "whole language." *Language Arts, 70,* 272–281.

Watson, D. (1994). Whole language: Why bother? *The Reading Teacher, 47,* 600–607.

Wells, G. (1986). *The meaning makers: Children learning language and using language to learn.* Portsmouth, NH: Heinemann.

Section I

Teaching Skills in Whole Language Classrooms

*"Immersing students in a print-rich environment is a neces-
sary, but not a sufficient, condition for literacy development.
Many students, especially struggling readers, require* frequent,
intense, *and* explicit *support and direction from their teachers"* (Dudley-Marling, Chapter 2).

This book begins with a group of chapters that describe how skill
instruction fits in whole language classrooms. Chapter 2 by Curt
Dudley-Marling shows how he taught a varied group of third graders
in his whole language classroom. Specifically, he tries to meet the
needs of the struggling readers and writers through immersing them
in print, demonstrating and explaining his own uses of and strategies
for reading and writing, and guiding them toward appropriate (not
too easy, not too hard) selection of material. He also describes how
he uses the strategies of assisted and repeating readings for children
who need much scaffolding as well as strategies for phonics and spelling. His goal as a third grade teacher was to help children make sense
of texts by responding to the needs and intentions of the individual
students. Some of the skills he taught in order to achieve this goal
included phonics and word recognition. His observations of learners
gave him a clear understanding of what readers do and how they
develop, which led to careful planning of what skills to teach the children in his class.

Chapter 3 by Jacquelin Carroll, Roberta Wilson, and Kathryn Au is a richly detailed description of readers' and writers' workshops in fourth and fifth grade classrooms. The authors show how the teachers incorporate skill instruction in classrooms in which students self-select reading materials and writing topics. How the teachers organize and manage time is also described. The instruction is based on careful assessment with an eye on learning "benchmarks," their statewide objectives for students. The instruction is both spontaneous and planned and is focused, ultimately, on student autonomy. The skills described range from responding to literature to figuring out unknown words, and they are taught through explanation, mediation (which may involve questioning and scaffolding), and demonstration in authentic contexts.

Chapter 4 by Penny Freppon and Linda Headings is a case study of a teacher's thinking and decision-making about why and how she teaches phonics in her first grade, whole language classroom. In this chapter, you will hear the teacher's (Linda Headings) actual words as she describes her instruction. Phonics in this first grade classroom is taught through authentic experiences such as reading books for enjoyment, writing letters, and even lining up for lunch. Linda's skill teaching is both spontaneous and planned and she describes how she makes time for whole class, small group, and one-on-one teaching every day. She uses authentic assessment strategies to further her understanding of her students in order to make the most appropriate instructional decisions.

The concluding chapter in this section, by Lesley Morrow and Muriel Rand, is a portrait of an early childhood whole language classroom. In it, they describe how the physical environment can be shaped to enhance the learning of early literacy skills. They emphasize that all materials in a room can be available for specific learning purposes (rather than for decoration). The descriptions of the centers are detailed and the authors provide highly specific guidelines for enabling children to learn literacy skills in self-directed environments. The teacher portrayed in this chapter models and explains to children how materials are to be used in this social, collaborative setting. The classroom setting described, the rules for enabling children to work independently and with peers, and the instructional strategies of the teachers are appropriate for all elementary teachers, not just early childhood specialists.

Chapter 2

Explicit Instruction Within a Whole Language Framework: Teaching Struggling Readers and Writers

ᵒᵒ ———— ᵒᵇ

Curt Dudley-Marling
York University, Toronto, Canada

The impression that whole language theory and practice precludes the direct, explicit teaching of reading skills and strategies is widespread (Cazden,1992; Shapiro, 1992; Spiegel, 1992) despite efforts by whole language proponents to be clear about the possibility of explicit instruction within a whole language framework (Dudley-Marling & Dippo, 1991; Dudley-Marling, 1995; Fountas & Hannigan, 1989; Freppon & Dahl, 1991; Newman & Church, 1990; Slaughter, 1988; Trachtenburg, 1990). Edelsky, Altwerger, and Flores (1991) make it clear that "whole language teachers *do* teach children how to spell words they are using, *do* teach appropriate punctuation for letters children are writing, *do* teach strategies for sounding out particular combinations of letters under particular circumstances" (p. 30). Good whole language teachers do teach skills, especially in the case of students for whom learning to read is a struggle. They differ from many teachers, however, in *how*, *when*, and *why* they teach skills, as well as in the meaning they attach to "skills."

In this chapter I draw on my experience as a third grade teacher to illustrate the nature of explicit instruction in a whole language program. To appreciate the character of explicit instruction within a whole language framework it is necessary to understand the theoretical position that underpins whole language. Therefore, I begin with a brief overview of the socio-psycholinguistic model of reading that informs whole language theory and practice.

A Socio-Psycholinguistic Perspective: Literacy as Social Practice

From a socio-psycholinguistic perspective, reading is a transactive, sociolinguistic process in which readers use a variety of cueing systems and sense-making strategies to construct meaning from print (Rosenblatt, 1978; Weaver, 1994). Reading is transactive in the sense that both readers and writers contribute something to the act of making meaning. Reading is a sociolinguistic process in that it is always used and understood in a sociocultural context that shapes the meaning of any text (Halliday, 1978).

The meaning of written language derives not so much from the content of words as from the social and cultural context within which it is used, including the "interplay of what went before and what will come later" (Bloome & Egan-Robertson, 1993, p. 309). From this perspective, words have meanings independent of the intentions of writers (Gee, 1990).

Every reading event involves the simultaneous orchestration of graphophonic, syntactic, semantic, and pragmatic cues within a sociocultural context (Goodman, 1994a, 1994b; Harste & Burke, 1978). These cueing systems interact with each other to facilitate the production or reception of other language cues. Edelsky (1984) observed that language systems "not only operate in context; they also are interdependent, each one having consequences for the other. In any instance of . . . language use, a choice in one system has ramifications for what choices or interpretations are possible in another" (p. 9).

The degree to which readers use various processing cues depends on such factors as the readers' purpose and background knowledge, the text, and the sociocultural context. Religious rituals, for example, may require people to *read* texts in languages they do not understand, relying on phonetic cues almost to the exclusion of semantic and syntactic cues. In this example, people read without comprehension, but not without meaning.

Viewing reading as social practice indicates that people do not learn to read *once and for all*. James Gee (1990) observes that the verb "read" can never be used intransitively. Instead, people learn to read texts in ways appropriate to the social and cultural setting. As social and cultural practices, reading and writing "involve specific ways of interacting with people, specific ways of using language . . . , specific sets of values for various kinds of behaviors, and specific sets of interpretations for understanding and guiding behavior" (Bloome, Harris, & Ludlum, 1991, p. 22). When people listen to a Gospel or read bits from the newspaper at the breakfast table, for example, they are involved in different ways of talking, interacting, thinking, valuing, and believing. Similarly, school reading lessons require students to display behaviors appropriate to a school setting—to act, think, and talk like a student (Bloome et al., 1991).

The assumption that students learn to read once and for all by mastering a set of autonomous skills underlies traditional approaches to school literacy. From this perspective, explicit instruction involves teaching a finite scope and sequence of discrete skills presumed to underlie *all* reading practices. However, from the point of view of literacy as social practice, various reading practices involve the use of different processes and strategies. The skills involved in an authoritative reading of a passage from a basal reader, for example, are not the same as a "critical" reading of a political campaign poster (see Fairclough, 1989). It is uncertain, therefore, whether the literacy skills and processes of one social context—the context of traditional school reading instruction, for example—are the same as the skills and processes of literacy in other social settings (Allington, 1994; Gee, 1990; Myers, 1992; Nespor, 1991). Myers (1992) concludes that "defining literacy skill as a collection of socially constructed practices . . . suggests that the traditional skill-based school instruction cannot transfer to literacy use in other contexts. The skills of exercises are not the same as the skills of literacy in other social contexts" (p. 302).

People do not learn the cues, processes, and strategies involved in reading particular texts in particular ways unless they have had experience in settings where texts of type X are read in way Y (Gee, 1990, p. 43). People have to be socialized in a *practice* to learn to read particular texts in specific ways (Gee, 1990, p. 43). Therefore, the goal of whole language teachers is to get students to use reading for a variety of purposes in a range of social and cultural settings. Believing that different reading practices entail different sorts of skills, whole language teachers do not endeavor to teach students *a* set of reading skills. Instead, whole language teachers use invitations, demonstrations, and explanations (Allington, 1994; Smith, 1981) to support students' intentions as they learn to use various cues, processes, and strategies as readers. In other words, whole language teachers offer explicit support to students who are attempting to fulfill specific language functions (for example, read a fictional story or read a letter from a friend) as they actively encourage students to expand the range of purposes for which they read, but they do not normally teach "skills" apart from the intentions of students. The rest of this chapter is an attempt to illustrate the nature of reading instruction in one whole language classroom.

Reading and Writing Instruction in a Whole Language Classroom

I took a leave from the university during the 1991-92 academic year to teach third grade. I collected a variety of data to help me "make sense" of teaching third grade, including 1500 pages of field notes (documentation and reflections on my experience), 70 hours of audio-tapes, copies of students' written work, photographs, and "environmental" print (for example, chart stories, sign-up sheets, written directions). I use these data to illustrate how I supported my students' reading development through the use of invitations, demonstrations, and explanations.

Immersing students in print

> When the class was reading the chart story, *Charles*[1] exclaimed, "Shyrose, it's your birthday?" I asked him how he knew and he told me he read it (pointing to the chart). (Field notes, October 10, 1991)

The fundamental assumption that guided my reading program was this: *people learn to read by reading.* I undertook to create a class-room environment that both invited students to read and modeled reading. I wrote a chart story every day that I hoped would invite less able readers to engage in reading. Charles's (a student with learning disabilities) comment about Shyrose's birthday indicates that the chart stories did invite reading. A few days later Charles glanced at the chart story and asked me, "You ran 30 miles last night?" (I had writ-ten "Last night I ran 3 miles . . .") On another occasion I overheard Nader, a student who was just learning English, carefully sound out "Ma-a-ay-poool L-leeefs" as he read the chart story.

I tried to take advantage of every opportunity to invite reading and demonstrate its uses. A discussion prompted by a picture of a gravestone in *The Haunting of Grade Three* (Maccarone, 1984) led me to bring in and display a collection of grave rubbings I had at home. These captured the interest of many of my students, especially the more able readers. I played my guitar and sang with my class as often as possible and, largely for the benefit of struggling readers, I

---

[1] All names used in this chapter are pseudonyms.

copied song lyrics onto chart paper. Song lyrics were a powerful invitation for many students. A few days after I introduced the song "The Cat Came Back," for example, I observed Jennifer, Catherine, and Barbara alternately reading and singing the lyrics, which were displayed on the blackboard.

My field notes indicate that the posting of written directions, announcements, samples of students' written work, comics and articles from the newspaper, posters, sign-up sheets, chart stories, and song lyrics frequently engaged my students in reading, but the most obvious way I invited my students to read was through the presence of books, including books that were considerate of the reading level and interests of my less able readers. My students also brought their own reading materials to school. A group of boys that included Charles spent weeks reading and discussing comic books they had brought from home. A group that included Nicholas, another struggling reader, read and discussed fan magazines they brought to school. Students sometimes discovered unexpected reading materials. Jennifer, Catherine, and Barbara, for example, often read lyrics from my song books, sometimes chorally. When they discovered the Beatles' "Sexy Sadie," which they thought was a "dirty song," it became a *must read* for everyone in our class.

The most enjoyable—and perhaps the most powerful—way I demonstrated the power of reading and invited my students to read was by reading to them. Reading to students can affect their reading vocabulary, reading comprehension, reading interests, and the quality of their oral language (Huck, 1979; McCormick, 1977). I read to my class three or four times each day and I took advantage of opportunities to read more often. If we had just a few minutes to fill, for example, I'd often read poems to my class.

From the perspective of whole language theory and practice, immersing students in a print-rich environment is a necessary, but not a sufficient, condition for literacy development. Many students, especially struggling readers, require *frequent, intense,* and *explicit* support and direction from their teachers. As Allington (1994) puts it, "All children need instruction, but some children need incredible amounts of close, personal instruction, usually clear and repeated demonstrations of how readers and writers go about reading and writing" (p. 23).

Explicit support and direction: Explanations and demonstrations

In this section I illustrate how explicit instruction might work in a whole language classroom by describing the explicit support and direction I offered my students. For purposes of this discussion I will focus on just three instructional goals: (1) helping students learn to select appropriate books; (2) improving students' reading fluency; and, (3) increasing the range of cueing systems and strategies students used to make sense of texts. It is important to point out that the instructional goals I developed for my students were based on routine and careful observations and analyses (for example, miscue analysis) of my students as they read a variety of texts in a range of social settings, including their response to my instructional support (for a comprehensive survey of assessment practices within a whole language framework see Rhodes & Shanklin, 1993).

Selecting appropriate reading material

> Today once again Charles just looked at the pictures in a book that was much too difficult for him . . . Roya also indicated that she had picked out a book that was too hard for her. (Field notes, September 9, 1991)

From a holistic perspective, readers use various cueing systems and strategies to construct meaning from texts. Texts with content and language beyond students' experience force them to rely almost exclusively on graphophonic cues. Since reading "involves the simultaneous orchestration of graphophonic, syntactic, and semantic cues" texts that oblige students to overrely on a single cueing system teach students little about what readers (normally) do in the process of reading. Therefore, the appropriate selection of texts is an important factor in students' reading development. And, since the process by which readers use various cues and strategies is a function of such factors as purpose, setting, and text, it is important that students be challenged to read a range of texts.

Many of my struggling readers had difficulty selecting books they could read independently. To help them learn to select appropriate books I dedicated a bookshelf to "not-too-difficult" books. I encouraged Charles, Lila, Martin, and other struggling readers to choose books from this shelf. I often spent several minutes at the beginning of each reading period helping students locate books that matched their interests and ability. Sometimes I interested students in books by reading to them individually and then suggesting that they "re-read" the books themselves. This worked particularly well with Charles.

Still, some students continued to select books I thought too difficult. I guessed that they chose "too difficult" books to protect their self-image, but I learned that struggling with difficult texts could be worthwhile *if students received sufficient support from their teacher or their peers.* Lila, for example, managed to cope with texts like *Amelia Bedelia's Family Album* (Parish, 1991), which she could not read independently, with the support of her friend Roya. Nader spent six weeks struggling with *Skinnybones* (Park, 1982), a book I'd read in class. With my help and the support of several classmates he was able to manage and, by the time he was finished, he was a much better reader.

I used a number of deliberate strategies to expand the range of students' reading and to encourage students to read more challenging texts. First of all, I read a variety of texts to my students, including folk-tales, mysteries, expository texts, and poetry. I also featured various genres in our book display. In December, for example, I supplemented my own collection with books from the public library to create a display of poetry books. I also influenced my students' reading selections by encouraging participation in literature-sharing groups, recommending particular books to individuals, and locating texts within particular genres that matched students' interests. I was able to interest Barbara in poetry by recommending a collection of poems about friends. When I brought several of the Hardy Boy books I'd read as a boy to class, I was able to interest Troy in mysteries. Supplementing the book collection in our classroom with books from the public library also enabled me to support my students' emerging interest in "scary" books.

Improving reading fluency

Several of my third graders were dysfluent readers who read word by word, in a stumbling, choppy manner. The primary strategies I used to improve students' reading fluency were assisted reading and repeated reading.

Assisted reading. Usually I began by sitting next to students and reading the book to them, sometimes pointing to each word as I read. Then the student and I would read the book together, but I would lower my voice when the student's reading was strong and raise it when the student needed support. For example:

> Read *The Big Enormous Turnip* (Shannon, 1988) with Nader. At some points I paused and he finished the lines (the more predictable/repetitive ones). At other points he read along with me . . . After I left him he re-read the story on his own (Field notes, September 26, 1991).

Assisted reading also encouraged students like Lila and Charles to use contextual information to make sense of words in text.

> Did assisted reading with Lila again using *Finders Keepers* (Will & Nicholas, 1989). Today I continued to read with her, even providing support for the parts I knew she could read. I was trying to use assisted reading to encourage her to read more quickly. She still tends to plod along, making it difficult for her to take advantage of contextual clues in the process of reading (May 20, 1992).

Later in the year I began reading texts chorally with Charles, Martin, and Lila to make more efficient use of my time. This didn't always work out, however. Martin, for example, often got frustrated with Lila, who read too slowly for him. Other variations of assisted reading I used included asking students to read along with audio-taped stories and paired reading. Early in the year I required my students to read with their partners on Fridays. I paired struggling readers with students who were able to provide helpful, unobtrusive support for their partners. Typically these were students who had younger brothers and sisters. We also did some whole class mini-lessons on how to support reading partners. When paired reading was no longer required, many students—including Charles, Martin, Lila, Nader, and Fatima—continued to read with partners. (For further details on procedures for assisted reading, see the chapter by Purcell-Gates in this volume.)

Repeated reading. I also tried to increase struggling students' reading fluency (and sight vocabularies) by encouraging the repeated reading of texts. When I did assisted reading with Charles, Lila, and Martin, for example, we often read the same text over several days until they could read it independently. The improvement in these students' reading fluency was consistent with the findings of other researchers who have reported significant gains in reading fluency in programs that combine assisted reading and repeated reading (Carbo, 1978; Hollingsworth, 1970; Samuels, 1979).

The opportunity to encourage students to repeatedly read texts often arose naturally. When my students asked to read books to the class I put up a sign-up sheet, but insisted that students practice their books before reading them to the class. A school-wide reading program that partnered my students with a first-grade class encouraged students to practice the books they were going to read with their younger "reading buddies." Lila, Martin, and Charles, perhaps anxious to avoid embarrassment, worked especially hard to practice their books.

Increasing the range of cueing systems and strategies students use to make sense of texts

Good readers use a range of cueing systems (that is, graphophonics, syntax, and semantics) and strategies (for example, predicting, re-reading, skipping unknown words as a means of taking advantage of contextual cues, skimming) to construct meaning from texts. Poor readers tend to overrely on a single cueing system and use fewer strategies as they read (Goodman, Watson, & Burke, 1987). Consider the following transcript that was made of Charles reading from *Clifford the Big Red Dog* (Bridwell, 1985).

Text	*Charles*
This is my dog . . .	This is my dog . . .
We play games.	We play great (pause) whatever.
I throw a stick, and he	I with, (pause) catch, (pause) I co-inss-i a stick, and he
brings it back to me.	be-its, bong, brah, big it to me brung it to me (sighs) whatever.
We play hide-and-seek.	He, he plays, We play hiding and go, hiding and seek.
I'm a good hide-and-seek . . .	I'm a, I'm, I am coming, or something, she, (long pause) he and sick, seek . . .

Charles tended to overrely on graphophonic cues to make sense of words in text. When he came to an unknown word he repeatedly sounded it out, often without much success. His oral reading miscues usually looked or sounded like the expected response, but were often semantically and/or syntactically inappropriate. Since he didn't have effective strategies for monitoring his comprehension or repairing his reading when sense-making broke down, Charles often accepted miscues that resulted in significant meaning changes. Lila and Martin exhibited similar profiles.

I used a variety of strategies to draw my students' attention to the range of cueing systems and sense-making strategies readers use in the process of reading and to teach students how to use these cues and strategies as they read. Since many of my struggling readers read word by word without much concern for "making sense" (for a discussion of this perspective see Goodman, Watson, & Burke, in press;

Goodman et al., 1987; Smith, 1994; Weaver, 1994), I often drew students' attention to miscues that resulted in meaningless text in an effort to get them to monitor their own reading comprehension. For example:

> During reading I listened to Lila and Charles read *Where the Wild Things Are* (Sendak, 1963) . . . When one of them read, ". . . roared their terrible eyes . . ." I went back and asked, "Do they ROAR their terrible eyes?" and they corrected their miscue (Field notes, April 6, 1992).

Similarly, when Benizar read:

> ". . . who were not especially [omitted] fradly [for friendly]," I asked her if this made sense. She agreed that it didn't and she corrected her miscue. A moment later she read, "Kack [for kick] off your blankets" and again I asked her if this made sense. She agreed it didn't and she was able to correct her miscue. (January 20, 1992)

I used a number of strategies to help students make sense of words in text. I encouraged students who overrelied on phonetic cues, for example, to skip unknown words they encountered when reading and come back to them after they'd read a bit more text. In this way, students learned to combine semantic and syntactic cues with phonetic cues to make sense, just as proficient readers do (Goodman et al., 1987). Sometimes I'd demonstrate this strategy when I read orally to the class and at least once I led a whole class discussion that was based on the question, "What do you do when you come to a word you don't know?" More often I'd offer individual support. In the following example I focused Nicholas's attention on the use of semantic and syntactic cues as well as the importance of "making sense" as he read from *Ralph S. Mouse* (Cleary, 1982).

Nicholas: *"When Ralph had . . . When Ralph had" (long pause)*

Curt: *"Why don't you skip that word [wiped] and come back."*

Nicholas: *"Off all the mud."*

Curt: *"Let's come back to this word now [pointing to 'wiped']. When Ralph had 'somethinged' off all the mud. What do you think that word might be?"*

Nicholas: *"When Ralph had off all the mud."*

Curt: *"That doesn't quite make sense. What he 'do' off all the mud?"*

Nicholas: *"I don't know."*

Curt:	*"What would you 'do' off all the mud?"*
Nicholas:	*"Wet it?"*
Curt:	*"Wetted off all the mud? Does that make sense? You walk into the house, you've got mud all over your shoes, what would you do?"*
Nicholas:	*"Like scrape it on the grass?"*
Curt:	*"Scrape it off. OK. What other ways might you deal with it?"*
Nicholas:	*"Um, leave your shoes outside."*
Curt:	*"Look at this word here [pointing to wipe]. What do you think that word might be, same as scrape?"*
Nicholas:	*"Like, maybe wash it off?"*
Curt:	*"OK, go ahead."* (May 12, 1992)

When some students were having difficulty dealing with proper names—for which neither contextual nor phonetic cues may be helpful—I augmented individual instruction with a whole class exercise.

> I wrote "I saw Mr. Solzhenitsyn in the park" on the board and asked the class if anyone could read this sentence. When no one was able to pronounce "Solzhenitsyn" I asked what they could do when they came to a name they couldn't pronounce. Barbara said, "You could make up a name." I offered that this is what I would do and we then brainstormed some possible names we could use as placeholders for "Mr. Solzhenitsyn." (Field notes, September 9, 1991)

I also used cloze tasks to encourage some students to expand the range of cues they used to make sense of texts. In early April, for example, I prepared a cloze task for Martin, Charles, and Lila based on the book, *I Know an Old Lady* (Chambliss, 1987), which they were reading with my assistance. Cloze tasks didn't work equally well for all students, however. Martin usually tried to locate the book on which the cloze was based and copy the missing words from the text. Copying from the book did encourage reading, but missed the point of the exercise. This was easily solved by briefly removing the books from circulation. But for Charles cloze was always a problem. Despite my instructions ("Put in any word that makes sense"), he tried to faithfully reproduce the text as it was in the book. I eventually overcame this difficulty by making up my own cloze passages, but Charles still needed some convincing that he could put any word in the blank.

> Charles was confused at first, saying that he didn't know this (he meant he didn't know the story from which the cloze came). I assured him that I had made up the story and he commented, "I can put anything in?" I told him he could as long as it made sense. (Field notes, March 24, 1992)

I also used explicit strategies to help students make better use of graphophonic cues. Sometimes I merely focused students' attention on graphophonic cues, as in the following example:

> When Charles came to the sentence, ". . . under the hen was quite an egg," he asked for help with "under" and I suggested he go on. When he came back he still had difficulty so I covered up "der" in under leaving "un" for him to sound out . . . (Field notes, January 6, 1992).

On other occasions I attempted to teach students about the regularities of English orthography.

> Nader read, "I was made [mad] about it." When he finished the page I went back to this miscue and asked him if it made sense. He agreed that it didn't and quickly corrected his miscue. Then we talked about the effect of the silent "e," making a list of words in which the short vowel had been made long by adding an "e" (e.g., mad/made, hat/hate, fat/fate . . .) (April 28, 1992)

I believe that my students learned the most about "sound-symbol relationships," however, through daily, whole class and individual spelling lessons (see Weaver, 1994). These lessons offered students some insight into the regularities of English orthography, which could support their use of graphophonic cues as they read various texts. The following spelling mini-lesson was typical of the individual support I provided.

> When Roya asked me how to spell "cartoon" I asked her how to spell "car." She said "c-a-r." Then I asked her how to spell "toon." She said, "ton," so I asked her how to spell "oo" and she said, "e." Then I asked her how to spell "moo" and she said, "moo." Then she knew how to spell "cartoon." (Field notes, April 6, 1992)

I supplemented these individual lessons with daily, three- to five-minute mini-lessons on some feature of English orthography. Typically, I asked the class to think of all the words they could that contained a particular feature (for example, words ending in "ing" or words sounding like "park") which I listed on chart paper. One of several lessons on "ing," for example, stimulated discussion of the effect of consonant doubling on vowels (for example, runing/running) and deleting the "silent e" after adding "ing."

Conclusion

My experience as a third grade teacher, my observations in whole language classrooms, and my reading of the literature on whole language theory and practice indicate that whole language teachers can—and usually do—engage in explicit instruction within a whole language framework. Explicit instruction in whole language classrooms differs, however, from traditional "skill" instruction in terms of how, when, and why reading skills are taught as well as the meaning attached to "skills."

First of all, whole language teachers do not teach a scope and sequence of discrete skills by following "an externally devised, school district-mandated curriculum sequence" (Edelsky et al., 1991, p. 30). From a socio-psycholinguistic perspective, readers use a variety of cueing systems and strategies to construct meaning from texts, but the strategies readers use and the relationship among cueing systems are not the same across reading practices. It may be that literacy as "a scope and sequence of discrete skills" is a reading practice, but it is uncertain that the skills of school literacy bear more than a faint resemblance to out-of-school literacies.

Whole language instruction is based on the assumption that reading and writing are infinitely complex processes, complicated by a range of psychological, social, cultural, and linguistic factors. Whole language teachers do not assume that they do or can know all that readers do in the process of reading. Therefore, whole language teachers offer the support students need to realize their intentions as readers by helping them discover and use various cueing systems and strategies in the process of reading. They may, for example, draw students' attention to certain regularities of English orthography, comprehension strategies, or the need to make sense *in support of what students are trying to do.* In this sense, whole language instruction is not systematic, because it responds to the needs and intentions of individual students and not a prescribed set of skills. Instruction within a whole language program is carefully considered, however, based as it is on careful planning, the painstaking observation of learners, and a clear theoretically-based understanding about what readers do in the process of reading.

Whole language teachers view learning to read as more of an apprenticeship than an accumulation of skills. Taking on the role of mentors—and not technicians—whole language teachers offer guidance and advice to developing readers. They point out what they've discovered about their own processes as readers as well as what they understand other readers do. They suggest strategies for dealing with words in text. They point out what they do when sense-making breaks down. In sum, whole language teachers do whatever is needed to help students make sense of texts, but always within the framework of the socio-psycholinguistic reading theory upon which whole language practice is based.

References

Allington, R. L. (1994). The schools we have. The schools we need. *Reading Teacher, 48*, 14–29.

Bloome, D. & Egan-Robertson, A. (1993). The social construction of intertextuality in classroom reading and writing lessons. *Reading Research Quarterly, 28*, 305–332.

Bloome, D., Harris, L. H., & Ludlum, D. E. (1991). Reading and writing as sociocultural activities: Politics and pedagogy in the classroom. *Topics in Language Disorders, 11*, 14–27.

Bridwell, N. (1985). *Clifford the big red dog*. New York: Scholastic.

Carbo, M. (1978). Teaching reading with talking books. *Reading Teacher, 32*, 267–73.

Cazden, C.B. (1992). *Whole language plus*. Portsmouth, NH: Heinemann.

Chambliss, M. (1987). *I know an old lady*. New York: Bantam Books.

Cleary, B. (1982). *Ralph S. Mouse*. New York: Morrow.

Dudley-Marling, C. (1995). Whole language: It's a matter of principles. *Reading and Writing Quarterly, 11*, 109–117.

Dudley-Marling, C. & Dippo, D. (1991). The language of whole language. *Language Arts, 68*, 548–554.

Dudley-Marling, C. & Dippo, D. (in press). What learning disability does: Sustaining the discourse of schooling. *Journal of Learning Disabilities*.

Edelsky, C., Altwerger, B., & Flores, B. (1991). *Whole language: What's the difference?* Portsmouth, NH: Heinemann.

Edelsky, C. (1984). The content of language arts software: A criticism. *Computers, Reading, and Language Arts, 1*, 8–11.

Fountas, I. C. & Hannigan, I. L. (1989). Making sense of whole language: The pursuit of informed teaching. *Childhood Education, 65*, 133–137.

Freppon, P. A. & Dahl, K. L. (1991). Learning about phonics in a whole language classroom. *Language Arts, 68,* 190–197.

Gee, J. P. (1990). *Social linguistics and literacies.* Philadelphia: Falmer.

Goodman, K. (1994a). *Phonics phacts.* Portsmouth, NH: Heinemann.

Goodman, K. (1994b). Reading, writing, and written texts: A transactional sociopsycholinguistic view. In R.B. Ruddell & H. Singer (Eds.), *Theoretical models and processes of reading* (pp. 1093–1130). Newark, DE: International Reading Association.

Goodman, Y., Watson, D. J., & Burke, C. L. (in press). *Reading strategies: Focus on comprehension* (Second edition). Katonah, NY: R. C. Owen.

Goodman, Y. M., Watson, D. J., & Burke, C. L. (1987). *Reading miscue inventory: Alternative procedures.* New York: Richard C. Owen.

Halliday, M. A. K. (1978). *Language as social semiotic.* Baltimore: University Park Press.

Harste, J. & Burke, C. (1978). Toward a socio-psycholinguistic model of reading comprehension. *Viewpoints in Teaching and Learning, 54,* 9-34.

Hollingsworth, P. M. (1970). An experiment with the impress method of teaching reading, *The Reading Teacher, 24,* 112–14.

Huck, C. (1979). Literature for all reasons. *Language Arts, 56,* 354–55.

Maccarone, G. (1984). *The haunting of grade three.* New York: Scholastic.

McCormick, S. (1977). You should read aloud to your children. *Language Arts, 54,* 139–43.

Myers, J. (1992). The social contexts of school and personal literacy. *Reading Research Quarterly, 27,* 297–333.

Nespor, J. (1991). The construction of school knowledge: A case study. In C. Mitchell & K. Weiler (Eds.), *Rewriting literacy* (pp. 169-188). Toronto: OISE Press.

Newman, J. M. & Church, S. M. (1990). Myths of whole language. *The Reading Teacher, 44,* 20–26.

Park, B. (1982). *Skinnybones.* New York: Bullseye Books.

Parish, P. (1991). *Amelia Bedelias family album.* New York: Greenwillow Books.

Rhodes, L. K. & Shanklin, N. (1993). *Windows into literacy: Assessing learners K–8.* Portsmouth, NH: Heinemann.

Rosenblatt, L. M. (1978). *The reader, the text, the poem.* Carbondale, IL: Southern Illinois Press.

Samuels, S. J. (1979). The method of repeated readings. *The Reading Teacher, 32,* 403–408.

Sendak, M. (1963). *Where the wild things are.* New York: Harper & Row.

Shannon, J. (1988). *The big enormous turnip: A Russian folktale.* Lakewood, CO: Link.

Shapiro, H. R. (1992). Debatable issues underlying whole-language philosophy: A speech-language pathologist's perspective. *Language, Speech, and Hearing Services in the Schools, 23,* 308–311.

Slaughter, H. (1988). Indirect and direct teaching in a whole language program. *The Reading Teacher, 42,* 30–34.

Smith, F. (1981). Demonstrations, engagement, and sensitivity: The choice between people and programs. *Language Arts, 58,* 634–42.

Smith, F. (1994). *Understanding reading: A psycholinguistic analysis of learning to read.* Hillsdale, NJ: Erlbaum.

Spiegel, D. L. 1992. Blending whole language and systematic direct instruction. *The Reading Teacher, 46,* 38–44.

Trachtenburg, P. (1990). Using children's literature to enhance phonics instruction. *The Reading Teacher, 43,* 648–652.

Weaver, C. (1994). *Reading process and practice: From sociopsycholinguistics to whole language.* Portsmouth, NH: Heinemann.

Will & Nicholas (1989). *Finders keepers.* San Diego, CA: Voyager Books.

Chapter 3

Explicit Instruction in the Context of the Readers' and Writers' Workshops

ℬ ———— ℭ

Jacquelin H. Carroll, Cultural Learning Center at Ka'ala Waia'nae,
Roberta A. Wilson, Project Coordinator, PATTER, **and**
Kathryn H. Au, University of Hawaii

The students in Nora Okamoto's fifth grade classroom were observed one morning in writers' workshop. Malia, writing at her desk, was heard to say, "I don't like my ending. I think I should add another paragraph to make it better." Jacob finished his draft and moved to the self-editing desk. He picked up a sheet of questions and began a self-conference before going to find a friend for a peer conference. Erin put her paper in the teacher editing box and told the observer, "I should go get an idea for my next piece." At the book rack, she skimmed through a few books and selected some. Sitting down, she began to add to her topic list. Kristin walked past and commented, "I need to get ideas for some more pieces." Kristin got her folder and sat next to Erin; the two had a conversation that gave each new ideas for topics.

Examples of students working thoughtfully on literacy activities without teacher intervention were commonplace in this classroom, because students learned skills that they could, and did, use independently. In this chapter we describe the experiences of Nora Okamoto and Christine Tanioka, teachers who incorporated skill instruction into authentic reading and writing contexts that fostered student autonomy. These teachers participated in a research project using a whole literacy curriculum in classrooms with Native Hawaiian students. In the process of achieving dramatic improvements in students' literacy, Nora, Chris, and their fellow teachers had to wrestle with issues of skill instruction. (For details about the research project and results, refer to Asam, et al., 1993, 1994.)

Chris and Nora used the whole literacy curriculum developed at the Kamehameha Elementary Education Program (KEEP) in Hawaii. The curriculum incorporated six aspects of literacy: ownership, the writing process, reading comprehension, language and vocabulary knowledge, word reading strategies, and voluntary reading. (For more information on the curriculum, refer to Asam, Au, Blake, Carroll, Jacobson, & Scheu, 1993.) Instruction in the curriculum was organized into a readers' workshop and a writers' workshop. The term *workshop* was used to establish a contrast with conventionally organized instruction, in which students often work individually to complete skill worksheets. In a readers' or writers' workshop, students are engaged in the full processes of reading and writing, not in the practice of skills in isolation. At any given moment, some students in readers' workshop may be reading silently, some may be engaged in discussion, and some may be writing responses to what they have read. In writers' workshop, some students may be drafting, some may be conferring with a partner, and others may be illustrating their published pieces. Examples of instruction are shown from the readers' workshop in Chris's classroom and the writers' workshop in Nora's classroom.

Changes in the way instruction is conceptualized are reflected in recent developments in educational psychology (Hiebert & Raphael, in press). In the past, when behaviorist and cognitive science perspectives dominated educational thinking, instruction was seen as the transmission of knowledge from teacher to student, with teachers as active senders and students as passive receivers of information. Current views proposed by constructivists and social constructivists suggest that knowledge is an exchange of ideas, a transaction between teacher and student, with both sides taking active roles in the learning process (Au & Carroll, in press; Moll, 1990).

Teachers such as Nora and Chris have turned to holistic approaches, especially the whole language philosophy, in response to these new views of instruction. At the core of whole language is the belief that classroom learning should involve students in the full processes of reading, writing, speaking, and listening, engaging students in meaningful activities like those that occur in the world outside the classroom. Instruction is seen as moving from the whole or the full process, to the part or the specific skills (Weaver, 1990). Skills are not taught in isolation, apart from their use in a context students can understand.

In a whole language setting, Chris, Nora, and other KEEP teachers provided students with explicit instruction aimed at the benchmarks in the KEEP curriculum. The benchmarks defined the outcomes for a hypothetical average student at the end of each grade level. They were established using sources that included the language arts guide prepared by the Hawaii State Department of Education, the reading objectives of the National Assessment of Educational Progress, research articles, a standardized test series, and scope and sequence charts of published reading and English programs. (See Appendix for the KEEP benchmarks for the six aspects of literacy.) More detailed descriptions were available for some benchmarks to clarify the expectations at different grade levels.

The benchmarks were stated more broadly than typical behavioral objectives. For example, the reading comprehension benchmark *comprehends and writes about characters, problem/goal, events, solution/outcome* incorporated specific skills such as sequence, but it did not imply that skills should be taught or tested separately or addressed apart from the reading of literature. To take another example, the writing process benchmark *corrects mechanics* subsumed such skills as capitalization and punctuation.

Student achievement was evaluated at mid-year and year-end through a portfolio assessment system. Students, teachers, and aides gathered evidence (usually two to three examples) that a student has met a particular benchmark. Evidence might take the form of writing samples, responses to literature, audiotapes of a student reading aloud, running records, anecdotal notes, or a student's self-reflections. Evidence was kept in portfolios, which were accessible to students. Students reviewed their portfolios, usually quarterly, and evaluated their growth and accomplishments.

To help students meet the benchmarks, Nora, Chris, and other KEEP teachers used a variety of instructional actions. One was *explanation*, "explicit teacher statements about what is being learned (declarative or propositional knowledge), why and when it will be used (conditional or situational knowledge), and how it is used (procedural knowledge)" (Roehler & Duffy, 1991, p. 867). Teachers used explanations, for example, to describe different types of story leads students could use in their writing, or to tell students about strategies they might use to determine the meanings of unfamiliar words that they encountered in their reading.

Another instructional action was *mediation*, "respond[ing] to students' interpretations [and] modifying instructional information in subsequent interactions to increase the likelihood that students will construct intended understandings" (Roehler & Duffy, 1991, p. 870). For example, teachers mediated students' understanding through questioning and scaffolding when confusions arose during literature discussions over the meaning of story events, or during writing conferences when students struggled to organize ideas on paper.

Still another instructional action was *demonstration*, described by Graves (1994) as the teacher's use of a personal example, such as her own journal entry or a book she is reading for herself, to show students how she performed a task that the students could do in the same way. Demonstration appears to be a particular form of what Roehler and Duffy termed modeling.

At the foundation of readers' and writers' workshop are two whole language trends: literature-based instruction and the process approach to writing. These will be described as they relate to the readers' workshop in Chris's classroom and the writers' workshop in Nora's classroom. Explicit instructional actions are highlighted in the examples of classroom instruction which follow.

Readers' Workshop: Christine Tanioka's Fourth Grade Classroom

Christine Tanioka, a 22-year veteran at Pahoa Elementary School in Pahoa, Hawaii, has worked with KEEP researchers for the last 14 years. Chris took a leading role in developing KEEP's upper grade curriculum, serving as one of the first teachers to try such activities as having students read novels and write in response to literature.

She and other KEEP teachers were influenced by reader response theory as a conceptual basis for the move to literature-based instruction. Rosenblatt (1978), a leading theorist, suggests that literature should evoke a personal response from the reader and that there is not just one way of reading literature. Rather, literature is read from one of two predominant stances, with the reader constantly shifting back and forth between the two. The first stance is aesthetic, or reading to enjoy the experience. The second stance is efferent, or reading to carry away information from the text. Rosenblatt's view implies that students should read works that evoke a strong response, and that they should have the opportunity to read both for enjoyment and to comprehend and interpret the text. Classroom reading activities consistent with reader response theory involve discussion and examination of ideas by students and teachers, not the search for a single right answer to a story's meaning. Observations in Chris's classroom showed students struggling to understand, interpret, and make personal connections to the events in the books they were reading.

Chris's thinking about her teaching changed considerably over the years. At first she used a basal, teacher's guide, and worksheets because they were common in elementary classrooms. "That's just what we did," she reflected. "But I felt the basals were uninteresting. The teacher was like a technician. And there were too many boundaries. I wanted to go outside those boundaries. I wanted to get children hooked on good literature." In discussing her goals for instruction, Chris explained that she wanted students to acquire strategies to become better readers, strategies that included both basic reading skills and more advanced thinking skills. She also wanted students to discover the joy of reading. Her ultimate goal was that students initiate learning for themselves, that is, that they know how to learn and choose to learn.

Chris set up her classroom to support and sustain the sense of belonging to a community of readers, of which she was an active and eager participant. The readers' workshop began with daily sustained silent reading, student book sharing, teacher read-alouds, and book recommendations by students and teacher. Next came mini-lessons, brief (5–10 minute) lessons used to present information about procedures, author's craft, or basic skills (Calkins, 1986). At least three times per week, students met for small group instruction. Later in the school year students participated in literature circles, which were book discussions where topics and the flow of conversation were managed by the students themselves (Short & Pierce, 1990; Peterson & Eeds, 1990). When students were not meeting with peers or the teacher, they read silently, read with a partner, wrote in their response journals about the books they were reading, or chose other follow-up activities from a menu. In addition, the class met monthly to read with their first grade book buddies. Several students voluntarily joined book clubs, meeting over lunch to discuss novels they had all chosen to read. Most students borrowed books from the class library to read at home and participated in reading incentive programs offered by local businesses.

Instruction grew out of Chris's goal to teach students the skills and strategies good readers employ to understand and appreciate text. Chris used the KEEP benchmarks to define specific objectives that would enable her to reach that goal. For example, in order to help students meet the benchmark *participates in small group reading discussions*, Chris knew she needed to teach students how to ask intelligent questions, make connections between story events and their own lives, and elaborate, clarify, and summarize their ideas.

Mini-lessons and small groups served as settings where Chris could plan to provide instruction focused on particular benchmarks. She knew ahead of time what she would be teaching on these occasions. Literature circles and book sharing gave Chris further opportunities for instruction. In these settings, however, she could not plan her lessons in advance, but kept the benchmarks in mind and waited for teachable moments to occur. Within all these settings, as described below, Chris used explanations, demonstrations, and mediation techniques to teach strategies and skills.

Mini-lessons

Chris used whole class mini-lessons to communicate information the class would need right away or in the near future. She determined these needs based on her own instructional goals, observations of students' reading behaviors, and analyses of students' work products. During mini-lessons, she frequently employed explanation as the most direct way to convey information in a short period of time. This was often followed by questioning to assess students' learning and, if necessary, mediate students' understanding. Chris then looked for opportunities to have students apply the skills and strategies she taught.

For example, one mini-lesson focused on different ways of responding to text. In this lesson, Chris wanted to show the class examples of how they could enlarge their repertoire of written responses and think about ideas in a story from additional perspectives. She felt this was needed because the students' responses, and often their story discussions, focused on surface features of the story or feelings that were not elaborated. Through this lesson, Chris wanted to help students work toward two reading comprehension benchmarks: *writes personal responses to literature* and *applies/connects theme to own life and experiences*.

Chris opened the mini-lesson by putting up an overhead from an article she had read in a research journal. "O.K.," she said, "this is an article some researchers wrote. They looked at the writings of fifth and sixth graders to see what the students said when they responded to books they were reading. The researchers noticed that students pictured things in their minds." Chris read an example of a student's response to *Summer of the Swans* (Byars, 1970). "You can tell she really put herself into the story—she visualized," Chris explained. "I liked it because it's not a hurried response; she took time to show us what she was picturing as she read." Chris then pointed to another section marked on the overhead. "In this one, the student puts herself in the character's place." She read the example and commented on it, then described and explained two other types of responses students had used. Finally, she reviewed. "O.K., what was the first type of response we talked about?"

"Visualize," a student said.

"Good. Next?"

"Put yourself in the characters' shoes."

"O.K.! Then?"

"Write poetry."

"Yes, you can respond in another form," Chris elaborated. "And finally?"

"Connections to your personal life."

Chris then asked the students to use one or two of these types of responses when they wrote in their reading response logs that morning. Reacting to *On My Honor* (Bauer, 1986), Kawika wrote: "I could feel my stomach muscles rise in fright. How could Tony drown so quick? Why didn't he yell or something?" Jarena, reading *A Taste of Blackberries* (Smith, 1973), wrote: "When I read the part when it said that Jamie, for my best friend, sure did aggravate me sometimes, that reminds me when me and T.J. were little and we used to play . . . dogs and cats. My brother [T.J.] would never quit barking like a dog . . . until we went to sleep. It was so irritating! Now that we are older I would also try not to have a fit over it." (The character in the story used the phrase, "don't have a fit over it.")

In another mini-lesson, Chris used the chart she created entitled "Steps That Help You Figure Out Unknown Words" to explain and describe different sources of information available to readers who encounter unfamiliar words. She wanted to help students work toward the language and vocabulary benchmark *uses multiple vocabulary strategies*. Steps on the chart included using the context of the sentences around the unknown word, noting prefixes and suffixes, looking for familiar words within the unknown word, dividing the word into syllables, and using references such as the dictionary or atlas. Chris followed up on this lesson in other settings.

Small group instruction

Small groups of students met with their teacher to talk about the novels and informational books they were reading. Mediation often occurred during these small group instruction sessions as Chris used techniques such as questioning, scaffolding, and the gradual release of responsibility (Pearson, 1985) to help students build their understanding of a story.

As students who were reading *Stone Fox* (Gardiner, 1980) met in a group, Chris led a discussion of important story events, characters, and personal reactions to the story. She had already given students open-ended questions or statements (for example, "What important events happened in this chapter?" "One thought I had while reading this chapter . . .") to help them prepare ideas for discussion. Students began by sharing their thoughts on interesting events in the chapter.

"Mr. Snyder nearly shot Searchlight!" Malani said.

Michael added, "Clifford Snyder came to collect taxes."

"He was afraid of the dog," Daniel speculated.

"Good observation," Chris told him. "How did you know that, Daniel?"

"It said his hand was shaking," Daniel responded. Chris asked the group to look back to the chapter to confirm that piece of information, a technique she was teaching them to use in discussion to support their reasoning.

Then Chris asked the students about some of the more difficult words in the chapter: "What did you think *ricochet* meant, Dane?"

"Out of control," Dane responded.

Chris nodded. "That's pretty close." Indicating the steps for figuring out unknown words chart described earlier, she asked, "What did you use to help you?"

Dane glanced at the chart and replied, "Context clues."

"What context clues help?" Chris asked the group. Several students looked through the chapter to find the specific context for that word.

Shanna thought she had found something important and read it aloud: "Cut through the air." Chris agreed. The students discussed other items on the chart and whether or not they would help in determining the meaning of this word.

Literature circles

Book discussions led by students, referred to as literature circles, were an outgrowth of children's experiences with small group reading instruction. During small group instruction, students learned how to talk about books by responding to questions their teacher posed and by bringing up questions of their own. During literature circles, students were given increasing responsibility to manage their own discussions, with the teacher as an equal participant or an outside observer. Chris frequently used demonstration as a teaching strategy to show students how she wanted them to carry out their discussions. She also used mediation to provide scaffolding as students worked toward independent discussions.

For example, when a small group met to discuss the first few chapters of *On My Honor,* Chris joined them. She had already explained that she would be listening to the discussion, but that she was not there to provide answers. She took the opportunity to note individual progress on the reading comprehension benchmark *participates in small group reading discussions*.

The students began by talking about the events of the chapter. When Keith mentioned that Tony, one of the characters, had jumped into the river, other students offered their opinions on this behavior. "I think it was dumb," Jessie stated. Several students agreed but did not expand on this idea any further.

"Why?" Chris asked.

"Tony can't swim!" they responded.

"How do you know that?" Chris asked, beginning to search the pages of her book. Others followed their teacher's example.

Sabrina located a passage and explained, "It says right here, 'He never noticed before what a poor swimmer Tony was.'"

Keith nodded, miming Tony's poor swimming stroke as he added, "He didn't even know how to breathe right." Dustin and Keith began talking about whether Tony was acting brave or just showing off. Chris asked the others what they thought and if they had noticed other information that might help them make sense of Tony's behavior. Keith and Kawika both gave examples of Tony's recklessness. Finally, some of the students talked about what they thought would happen next. "How many of you do that?" Chris asked the group. "As you read, do you predict? I was doing that, too." (For further examples of these kinds of "learning conversations," see the chapter by Roeller and Hallenback in this volume.)

Chris also demonstrated the kinds of written responses she wanted students to produce by sharing her own responses with them. During another literature circle meeting for *On My Honor,* Chris joined the group and shared an entry from her response journal. Her purpose was to show students the depth and quality of her thinking about the behavior of one of the story characters. She intended that the students see from her example how they might think about and respond to events in the story in more sophisticated ways. She prefaced her reading by saying, "I want to show you some things I was writing from chapters 5 and 6. I was so upset with one of the boys, I decided to write it down. I wrote a letter to one of the characters." After she shared her entry, which questioned the wisdom of the character's actions and expressed her indignation, the students talked about their own feelings and whether or not they would have done what the story character did. When the discussion ended, Chris told the group,

"Please feel free to write in your reading response logs about anything that bothers you or grabs you. Put your thoughts on paper. Don't wait for me to tell you."

Sharing

During the informal sharing done after teacher read-alouds and sustained silent reading, Chris opened the way for "teachable moments," those points in a discussion that seemed to lend themselves to further instruction. At these times, she used explanation, modeling, and mediation techniques in whatever way seemed most effective.

For example, after sustained silent reading, Chris asked the class if anyone wanted to tell something about the book they were reading. She noted students' participation for two ownership of reading benchmarks: *enjoys reading* and *talks about books with others.* Then she shared some passages from the book she was reading, *Journey to Jo'burg: A South African Story* (Naidoo, 1985). "Why did you mark that part?" a student asked, noticing her post-it. Chris explained how she marked parts of books she felt were important, interesting, or even confusing. These were parts she might reread herself, or share and discuss with someone. "I thought this part was important, and I wanted to share it with you. You can do the same thing with your books."

Chris also demonstrated her own love of books and enjoyment of reading. One day she brought in a large bag of books and told the class she wanted to share some books she had on her nightstand and was currently reading. One by one she pulled out her books and told the class what they were about and why they were important to her. Some were "how to" books on flower arranging and swimming, one was a popular novel recommended to her by a colleague, and several were children's books. These she said she loved most of all. "I used to hide my books so no one would know I read children's books. But not anymore!"

Writers' Workshop: Nora Okamoto's Fifth Grade Classroom

Nora Okamoto, also of Pahoa Elementary School, has been teaching for more than 20 years. Before she began work with the KEEP whole literacy curriculum three years ago, she had become discouraged about her work in the classroom and thought about quitting. She told a colleague:

> I don't think I can keep teaching much longer. I'm not making any difference with the students I need to reach. I can look at my class at the beginning of the year and tell you who will be at the top, middle, and bottom at the end of the year. I think I'll go and grow flowers!

Nora was frustrated with the traditional teaching of writing through skills in isolation. She found that, although students could do the exercises in the textbook, they did not apply the skills when they wrote. Nora wanted to try a holistic approach, and when the opportunity came to work with KEEP, she changed her writing instruction to implement a writers' workshop.

The writers' workshop grew out of the process approach to writing as described by Graves (1983, 1994), Calkins (1986, 1994), and others. This approach involves students in planning, drafting, revising, editing, and publishing their own pieces. Hansen (1987) points out that writers require time, choice, and response. A substantial block of time must be set aside for writing, every day if possible. Choice plays an important part, because good writing develops from inside, not from an external assignment. Students write best when they write about topics important to them. Response comes in the form of reactions from an audience—not just the teacher, but peers, parents, and others. Writers gauge the response to their pieces during conferences, when they read their work aloud in the author's chair, and when their published books are placed in the classroom library. As Hansen notes, the teacher can tell when the response system is working because students want to write. Observations in Nora's class showed students eagerly working independently and with peer and teacher support to develop and complete pieces on self-selected topics.

Nora's efforts to develop a successful writers' workshop led her to reflect on her teaching practices. In the past she had been guided by a textbook and teacher's guide. Now she had to rely on her own judgment of which benchmarks to teach when. After her first year of teaching toward the benchmarks, Nora decided to target certain benchmarks during each quarter of the school year. Knowing that she and the students would only have to worry about a few benchmarks at a time made the task easier. For example, Nora decided to concentrate on the benchmarks for planning and drafting in the first quarter. She had students revise, edit, and publish during this time but considered these activities to be of less importance. Once she developed this focus, she found she could integrate writing with instruction in science and social studies. At the end of each quarter, Nora evaluated and adjusted her plan for teaching the benchmarks. For example, sometimes she found she needed to spend more time on a particular benchmark.

Nora wanted evidence on which she could base her judgments about students' instructional needs as related to the benchmarks. For this purpose she wrote anecdotal notes and took the status of the class (Atwell, 1987) on a regular basis. She also analyzed samples of students' writing.

For example, during teacher-student conferences Nora kept a Teacher's Conference Record sheet for each student (see Figure 3-1 for examples) to note skills the student used correctly in the piece being discussed. She also taught one or two needed skills revealed by the writing piece. When she saw that several students lacked the same skill, she often addressed it in a mini-lesson. During one such mini-lesson on using paragraphs correctly, a writing process benchmark, Nora and the students created a list of qualities of a good paragraph, including interesting language, sentence variety, expression, description, and the use of transition words.

On a typical day, the writers' workshop began with the students seated on the carpet in the middle of the room as Nora conducted a mini-lesson. Following the mini-lesson, Nora asked each student, "What benchmark will you be working on today?" She recorded their answers on the status of the class form. Then students left to work

TEACHER'S CONFERENCE RECORD FOR _Gene_

TITLE OF PIECE & DATE	SKILLS USED CORRECTLY	SKILLS TAUGHT
9/15 Hi Flyer	Prewrite - Discover Map	Paragraphing
9/25 Almost Got Into a Fight	selects own topic Journal writing into personal narrative	confer w/ buddy confer w/ self
10/26 Fire Escape	Diagram - prewrite	Revise Titles
11/30 Hunting	Revised -added information -deleted	Paragraphing Revise for interesting words

TEACHER'S CONFERENCE RECORD FOR _Lani_

TITLE OF PIECE & DATE	SKILLS USED CORRECTLY	SKILLS TAUGHT
9/15 Horses of Oregon Personal narrative- abandoned after 2 weeks to work on another topic (difficulty recalling specifics)	Graphic organizer- sensory mapping Good attempt at description	-checking w/ others for recall of information
9/25 Soccer Game	Editing for punctuation and capitalization	-Titles - from what is written -Paragraphing
11/10 Glaciers (content-presentation)	-Information gathering -visual display w/ presentation was well planned	-using multiple sources -List resources -Label and date all parts -save everything

Figure 3-1. Sample of Teacher's Conference Record for two students in Nora Okamoto's class.

individually at their desks or went to the conference table to discuss their writing with their peers. Sometimes Nora called a small group to the carpet for a conference. Afterward, she referred to the status of the class to determine which students to check on. She moved around the room doing spot conferences, brief individual conversations to see what students were writing about and to provide skill instruction as needed (Atwell, 1987). About 10 minutes before the end of the period, Nora gathered the students for a Community Circle, an occasion for students to share accomplishments, learn from and help one another, and express appreciation to those who helped them (Gibbs, 1994).

Nora provided students with explicit instruction focused on the benchmarks in whole class, small group, and individual settings. Skills and strategies she determined were important for the entire class were taught in whole class mini-lessons. She conducted small group conferences when several students needed help in the same area. Like Chris, Nora set up structures so that she could learn of students' individual needs and capitalize on teachable moments. Spot conferences and Community Circle were two such structures. Within all these settings, Nora used explanation, demonstration, and mediation techniques.

Mini-lessons

Nora often used her own writing in whole class mini-lessons to demonstrate parts of the writing process for her students. For example, one day she worked on the benchmark *reconsiders and reorganizes writing* by showing students how she reshaped a piece of writing, changing it into another genre. Nora began by telling the students about a journal entry she had written about her father. She spoke about how hard it was to share her writing because the subject was a personal and emotional one. She talked about the feelings she had when her father experienced difficulties following the death of her mother. Nora explained how helpless she felt, not knowing what to do or say. She decided to write a piece about her father to express how much he meant to her. Then, reconsidering her writing, she saw how she could turn it into a poem, a less personal way to express her strong feelings. She showed the students how she circled thoughts and words from her journal entry and then began drafting. When Nora read the poem, the class was mesmerized. From this experience, Nora learned how powerful a teacher's demonstration could be. Both she and the students saw how the teacher who wrote and shared her writing became part of the classroom community of learners.

In another whole class mini-lesson, Nora used explanation. The students were working on research reports, and Nora wanted them to ask higher level questions about their topics. She explained that there were different kinds of questions, those that narrow and those that expand upon the topic. She had students suggest questions they could ask when conducting research on the lives of famous Americans.

"We have quite an extensive list of questions," Nora said. "Our next step—which questions will help you focus or zoom in on something. Mrs. Wilson had a graphic organizer she shared with me. It was titled fat and skinny questions. Any ideas on what that might mean?"

A student responded, "Fat questions expand your ideas. Skinny just gives one fact."

"Yeah," added another student, "like how old are you? Eleven."

"That's right," said Nora. "If you have used QAR [question-answer relationships; Raphael, 1986] you know about categories like that. So fat helps you expand, and skinny helps you focus or zoom in. Can we label questions like that?"

Nora had the students categorize the list of questions, using either an F or S. Afterward she told the class, "You did a good job. Now we know about questions that help us expand and questions that help us focus. You can use this in your research." Nora ended by releasing responsibility for using the strategy to the students, sharing her expectation that students would employ it in their research.

Conferences

Individual and small group conferences were regular features of Nora's writers' workshop. Because Nora used conferences to respond to immediate needs, she often had little time for advance planning. However, she felt a growing success as she built up a repertoire of successful techniques that she, other students, and professional writers used to deal with common problems in writing: organization, getting effective help from peer conferences, writing engaging leads, using interesting language to create a picture for the reader.

In a spot conference with Kaniela, Nora used scaffolding and coaching, forms of mediating. Kaniela had trouble organizing his writing logically, one of the writing process benchmarks. As he stared at his plan, a web on the baseball player Jackie Robinson, Nora asked him, "How are you going to start? What do you have here that will help you?"

Kaniela thought for a minute and replied, "When he was born."

"Can I highlight that?" Nora asked. He nodded and she highlighted that fact on his web. "What else do you have about his early life?" Kaniela pointed to another section, which Nora highlighted with the same pen. "I'm going to leave this pen with you," she said. "If you find anything else about his early life, you can highlight it. Another focus?"

Kaniela looked over his web and answered, "Why he became famous."

Nora responded, "O.K., I'll give you another color highlighter for that part, and then you need to decide on a third topic." Nora moved on to help another student. Through her words and by leaving the highlighter pens with Kaniela, she made it clear that he was to take responsibility for continuing to organize his piece along the lines she had shown him.

Ongoing assessment was an integral part of Nora's classroom. She conducted a benchmark conference with students whenever they finished a piece of writing. The purpose of this conference was to evaluate the student's progress and set future goals in an effort to reach the benchmark *sets goals and evaluates own achievement of writing*. Nora pointed out what the student had accomplished and together they decided on goals to be met in the student's next piece.

For example, Nora met with Andy for a benchmark conference on his fiction adventure story. They began by talking about what he had done well. He had written a complex plan for the story which was reflected in the detail of his piece. They agreed he had met the benchmark *participates in prewriting activities*. Then Andy and Nora talked about his future goals to improve his next piece of writing. Andy told Nora he wanted to use more interesting words in his next piece; he wasn't completely satisfied with the descriptions in his current piece. Nora asked if he had recently read any books with interesting or descriptive words. When he said he had, she suggested that he look at how the author used language to help the reader visualize a scene. She also told him writers varied their sentences to make their writing more interesting, and they discussed several examples to be sure Andy understood what Nora meant.

In a small group conference, Nora used scaffolding and questioning strategies to work with several students who were having trouble with a similar issue. These students tended to use vague language in their descriptions. Nora began by reminding them that the reader does not always have the same picture in his or her head that the writer does. The writer's responsibility is to create that picture as clearly as possible. "Here's a sentence," Nora said, writing a sentence on the board. "'I ordered a snack and a drink.' Suppose I tell you I'm at McDonald's. What do you see me ordering?" The students suggested french fries, a hamburger, and various other ideas. "How could I make it clearer?" Nora asked them.

"Write what you really ordered," Tiana declared.

"O.K. I'm going to say, 'I ordered a Happy Meal and a diet Coke.' Do we have the same picture now?" The students agreed. After working through a few more practice sentences, Nora told the group to look at their own pieces to find sentences that could be made more specific.

Community Circle

During the Community Circle, Nora looked for ways to capitalize on instruction given earlier or identify new instructional needs. For example, after the small group conference on using more explicit words, Nora began the Community Circle by asking, "How many of you found examples of unclear nouns and tried to make them clearer and more interesting?" Several students raised their hands.

Ikaika volunteered, "I changed part of my story. Want to hear it?" He read the first paragraph of his Halloween story, now filled with clear, precise nouns. Nora asked the class, "How many of you remember Ikaika's previous draft? What do you think now?"

"Better."

"I can picture the vampire now. He said the blood was dripping from its fangs."

"Good job," Nora told Ikaika. "You made it possible for your readers to see what you see."

Nora sometimes used Community Circle to check on students' ability to evaluate their learning of writing, one of the ownership of writing benchmarks. During one Community Circle, Allyson said she was having trouble writing a good lead. She asked the group for help with the lead for her piece about Indian tribes. "What can we do to help you?" Nora asked her. "Do you want to read us your lead?" Allyson agreed and decided to read just the first sentence. In order to focus the class' feedback and help Allyson identify her problem, Nora asked specifically, "What shall we listen for?"

"Just to see if the opening makes sense," Allyson replied. She read the first sentence aloud.

Kamuela commented, "The first sentence includes too much. You could say, 'Today we will be telling, showing, and teaching you about Indian tribes.'"

Bill offered, "You could say, 'Today we are going to teach you about different Indian cultures.'"

Nora asked, "Did you get the help you needed?" Allyson said yes, and the group went on to the next volunteer.

Nora's students showed their love of writing one day in April when she told them to wrap up their writing and get ready for Community Circle. "No, Mrs. Okamoto, we're not finished!" Kristin cried.

"Yeah!" several others agreed. "Can we pay you to let us write instead of going to lunch?" Erin asked.

Nora laughed. "O.K., class. I'll give you 10 more minutes and we'll go to lunch late."

Conclusion

Opportunities for choice in the KEEP writers' and readers' workshops enabled students to read, write, and share ideas about reading and writing according to their personal interests. At the same time, the KEEP benchmarks held students accountable for grade level standards. Knowing the expectations and given the responsibility, students in Nora's and Chris's classes were productively engaged in literacy activities that would help them meet these standards.

Achievement results in these classrooms were strong. Students who met all the benchmarks for their grade level were counted at grade level; those who met all the benchmarks for their own and the grade level above theirs were counted above grade level. All others were counted below grade level. From the most recent results of a study on program implementation and student achievement involving Chris, Nora, and 27 other high-implementing KEEP teachers, approximately two-thirds of the students in these classrooms were rated at or above grade level, and one-third were rated below. Baseline data prior to strong program implementation showed the reverse results: only one-third of the students at grade level, two-thirds below. (For more information, see Asam et al., 1994.)

In looking at the classroom conditions that foster successes such as these, we find several notable features. One is the authentic context of instruction, such as the readers' and writers' workshop. In classrooms like Nora's and Chris's, we see the power of self-selected writing topics and student-led literature discussions in motivating students to learn and practice literacy. Activities that are highly motivating may be especially important in maintaining older students' commitment to schoolwork (Edelsky, Draper, & Smith, 1983).

In these authentic contexts, the teacher's role as a learner is critical. Teachers like Chris and Nora, who see themselves as active participants in the learning process, communicate the value and usefulness of the skills and strategies they teach. When Nora read her journal entries to the class and talked about releasing painful feelings through her writing, she demonstrated that she used writing for meaningful purposes. When Chris shared the books she was reading with her class and explained why she read, she demonstrated a place for recreational reading in the life of an adult. The skills students are taught in classrooms like these take on greater significance; students see that skills are not used only for school, they are used for life.

The teacher's role as a facilitator is equally important. Teachers like Chris and Nora who follow a whole language philosophy know the importance of an exchange of ideas, a transaction between students and teacher. They consider students' contributions to be equal to their own. When students interpreted a story's theme differently from the teacher's viewpoint, Chris helped them to develop their own ideas as well as to consider hers. When a student decided to abandon a writing piece that the teacher felt had promise, Nora honored that decision and created a mechanism for the student to return to the piece later should he or she choose to do so.

The teachers' challenge was not only to provide planned instruction, but to capitalize on teachable moments. As the classroom observations suggest, explicit instruction on the skills and strategies embedded in the benchmarks became a dynamic process in which demonstration, explanation, and mediation all played a part. The purpose of explicit instruction was to enable students to be more effective readers, writers, and participants in the classroom community. The ultimate goal was to build students' ownership of literacy, as Kawika's end-of-year reflections express:

> On the first day of school, I did not like to read. I hated [to] read paperback novels. Novels was not my style. I only read one paperback novel. And it was called *Tough to Tackle*. It was good but I got tired of reading, so I stopped reading it. But in the second quarter I started to read like crazy. I read the books *Tough to Tackle, Dew Drop Dead, Holiday Inn, Quarterback Walk-On, A Taste of Blackberries,* and *On My Honor.* I started to read because I thought I would become a much better reader. And it came true.

References

Asam, C., Au, K., Blake, K., Carroll, J., Jacobson, H., Kunitake, M., & Scheu, J. (1993). *The demonstration classroom project: Report of year 1.* Kamehameha Elementary Education Program, Honolulu.

Asam, C., Au, K., Blake, K., Carroll, J., Jacobson, H., Kunitake, M., Oshiro, G. & Scheu, J. (1994). *The demonstration classroom project: Report of year 2.* Kamehameha Elementary Education Program, Honolulu.

Asam, C., Au, K., Blake, K., Carroll, J., Jacobson, H., & Scheu, J. (1993). *Literacy curriculum guide.* Honolulu: Kamehameha Schools/Bernice Pauahi Bishop Estate.

Atwell, N. (1987). *In the middle: Writing, reading, and learning with adolescents.* Portsmouth, NH: Boynton/Cook.

Au, K. H., & Carroll, J. C. (in press). Current research on classroom instruction: Goals, teachers' actions, and assessment. In D. L. Speece & B. K. Keogh (Eds.), *Research on classroom ecologies: Implications for inclusion of children with learning disabilities.* Hillsdale, NJ: Lawrence Erlbaum.

Bauer, M. D. (1986). *On my honor.* New York: Dell.

Byars, B. (1970). *Summer of the swans.* New York: Puffin.

Calkins, L. M. (1986). *The art of teaching writing.* Portsmouth, NH: Heinemann.

Calkins, L. M. (1994). *The art of teaching writing (new edition).* Portsmouth, NH: Heinemann.

Edelsky, C., Draper, K., & Smith, K. (1983). Hookin' em at the start of school in a whole language classroom. *Anthropology & Education Quarterly, 14* (4), 257–281.

Gardiner, J. R. (1980). *Stone Fox.* Scranton, PA: Harper & Row.

Gibbs, J. (1994). *Tribes: A new way of learning together.* Center Source Publications.

Graves, D. H. (1983). *Writing: Teachers and children at work.* Portsmouth, NH: Heinemann.

Graves, D. H. (1994). *A fresh look at writing.* Portsmouth, NH: Heinemann.

Hansen, J. (1987). *When writers read.* Portsmouth, NH: Heinemann.

Hiebert, E. H., & Raphael, T. E. (in press). Perspectives from educational psychology in literacy and literacy learning and their extensions to school practice. In R. Calfee (Ed.), *Handbook of Educational Psychology.*

Moll, L. C. (1990). Introduction. In L. C. Moll (Ed.), *Vygotsky and education: Instructional implications and applications of sociohistorical psychology.* Cambridge: Cambridge University Press, pp. 1–27.

Naidoo, B. (1985). *Journey to Jo'burg: A South African Story.* Scranton, PA: Harper & Row.

Pearson, P. D. (1985). Changing the face of reading comprehension instruction. *Reading Teacher, 38* (8), 724–738.

Peterson, R., & Eeds, M. (1990). Grand conversations: Literature groups in action. Jefferson City, MO: Scholastic.

Raphael, T. E. (1986). Teaching question-answer relationships, revisited. *Reading Teacher, 39* (6), 516–522.

Roehler, L. R., & Duffy, G. G. (1991). Teachers' instructional actions. In R. Barr, M. L. Kamil, P. Mosenthal, & P. D. Pearson (Eds.), *Handbook of reading research, Vol. II.* New York: Longman, pp. 861–883.

Rosenblatt, L. (1978). *The reader, the text, the poem: The transactional theory of the literary work.* Carbondale, IL: Southern Illinois University Press.

Short, K. G., & Pierce, K. M. (1990). *Talking about books.* Portsmouth, NH: Heinemann.

Smith, D. B. (1973). *A taste of blackberries.* Scranton, PA: Crowell.

Weaver, C. (1990). *Understanding whole language: From principles to practice.* Portsmouth, NH: Heinemann.

Appendix
KEEP Literacy Benchmarks

Language and Vocabulary Knowledge Benchmarks

Grade Level	K	1	2	3	4	5	6
Shows facility with language through quality responses during small group discussions	*	*	*	*	*	*	*
Notes and discusses new or interesting language in small groups			*	*	*	*	*
Uses clear, meaningful language to express ideas in written responses or summaries				*	*	*	*
Uses multiple vocabulary strategies				*	*	*	*
Responds in a variey of ways during small group discussions					*	*	*
Learns new or meaningful vocabulary from voluntary reading					*	*	*

Word Reading and Spelling Strategies Benchmarks

Grade Level	K	1	2	3	4	5	6
Attends to print during independent book reading	*						
Knows letter names and sounds	*						
Uses meaning cues		*	*	*			
Uses structure cues		*	*	*			
Uses visual cues		*	*	*			
Integrates cues		*	*	*			
Reads at grade level with 90% accuracy		*	*	*			
Self-corrects		*	*	*			

Reading/Listening Comprehension Benchmarks

Grade Level	K	1	2	3	4	5	6
INSTRUCTIONAL READING LEVEL							
Reads and comprehends text at grade level		*	*	*	*	*	*
Hears or reads literature that represents a variey of cultural perspectives	*	*	*	*	*	*	*
SMALL GROUP DISCUSSIONS							
Participates in small group reading discussions: teacher-led student-led	*	*	*	*	* *	* *	* *
Shares written responses to literature in small groups teacher-led student-led	*	*	*	*	* *	* *	* *
WRITTEN RESPONSE: Aesthetic							
Writes personal responses to literature: listening reading	*	 *	 *	 *	 *	 *	 *
Comprehends and writes about theme/author's message			*	*	*	*	*
Applies/connects theme to own life/experiences			*	*	*	*	*
Makes connections among different works of literature				*	*	*	*
Applies/connects content text information to own life/expereinces					*	*	*
WRITTEN RESPONSE: Efferent							
Comprehends and writes about characters and events (listening)	*						
Comprehends and writes about characters, problem/goal, events, solution/outcome		*	*				
Reads nonfiction and shows understanding of content			*	*	*	*	*
Writes summary that includes story elements				*	*	*	*
Reads different genres of fiction and shows understanding of genre characteristics					*	*	*
Understands elements of author's craft						*	*

Writing Process Benchmarks

Grade Level	K	1	2	3	4	5	6
HOLISTIC QUALITY OF WRITING							
Quality of writing average for grade level	*	*	*	*	*	*	*
PLANNING							
Selects own topics for writing	*	*	*	*	*	*	*
Particpates in prewriting activities		*	*	*	*	*	*
WRITING/DRAFTING							
Writes from own experience	*	*	*	*	*	*	*
Uses consonant sounds in inventive spelling to relate words to topics	*						
Relates sentences to topics		*	*	*	*	*	*
Organizes writing logically		*	*	*	*	*	*
Writes in a variety of formats				*	*	*	*
Writes in a variety of genres					*	*	*
REVISING							
Participates in writing conferences		*	*	*	*	*	*
Uses revising procedures		*	*	*	*	*	*
Uses interesting language (also may occur during drafting)		*	*	*	*	*	*
Varies sentences (also may occur during drafting)			*	*	*	*	*
Uses elements of author's craft to make writing interesting				*	*	*	*
Reconsiders and reorganizes writing						*	*
EDITING							
Corrects spelling	*	*	*	*	*	*	*
Corrects mechanics		*	*	*	*	*	*
Corrects grammar			*	*	*	*	*
Uses/corrects paragraphing				*	*	*	*
PUBLISHING							
Publishes one book	*						
Publishes two pieces with quality appropriate to grade level		*	*	*			
Publishes in two different forms		*	*	*	*	*	*
Shares published works with three different audiences		*	*	*	*	*	*
Publishes three pieces with quality appropriate to grade level					*	*	*

Ownership and Voluntary Reading Benchmarks

Grade Level	K	1	2	3	4	5	6
OWNERSHIP OF WRITING							
Enjoys writing	*	*	*	*	*	*	*
Shows confidence and pride in own writing	*	*	*	*	*	*	*
Shares own writing with others	*	*	*	*	*	*	*
Shows interest in others' writing	*	*	*	*	*	*	*
Writes in class for own purposes		*	*	*	*	*	*
Writes outside of class for own purposes			*	*	*	*	*
Makes connections between reading and writing				*	*	*	*
Sets goals and evaluates own achievement of writing					*	*	*
Gains insights through writing						*	*
OWNERSHIP OF READING/ VOLUNTARY READING							
Enjoys reading	*	*	*	*	*	*	*
Shows confidence and pride as a reader	*	*	*	*	*	*	*
Talks about books with others	*	*	*	*	*	*	*
Reads in class for own purposes		*	*	*	*	*	*
Reads outside of class for own purposes		*	*	*	*	*	*
Is developing reading preferences		*	*	*	*	*	*
Recommends books to others				*	*	*	*
Obtains books outside of class					*	*	*
Sets goals and evaluates own achievement of reading					*	*	*

Research Strategies Benchmarks

Grade Level	K	1	2	3	4	5	6
Obtains facts and ideas from a variety of informational texts			*	*	*	*	*
Uses a variety of reference materials				*	*	*	*
Uses graphic organizers				*	*	*	*
Uses a variety of library resources					*	*	*
Takes notes					*	*	*
Writes research report synthesizing information from multiple sources					*	*	*
Publishes research report or equivalent product					*	*	*
Uses a variety of outside resources						*	*

Chapter 4

Keeping It Whole in Whole Language: A First Grade Teacher's Phonics Instruction in an Urban Whole Language Classroom

 ℰ ⸻ ℭ℥

Penny A. Freppon, University of Cincinnati
Linda Headings, public school teacher

> I think phonics is a tool, a component of the reading process that should not be skipped or glossed over. I intentionally teach my students phonics, but I do so in a context that separates me from traditionalists. I consciously consider how the graphophonic system can be incorporated in meaningful ways in my classroom. (Linda Headings, first grade teacher)

Primary grade literacy instruction in whole language and skills-based (traditional) settings is fundamentally different. Yet, educators in both settings are very concerned about skill instruction. Teachers with a whole language philosophy and especially teachers interested in changing to a more holistic approach often have questions about the teaching of phonics. Their questions are important because the early grades are critical to school success and a lack of success in the primary grades often leads to failure in the upper grades (An Imperiled Generation, 1988). In this chapter we explore how one whole language teacher thinks about and implements first grade phonics instruction. One of the better ways to learn more about phonics teaching is through teachers' descriptions of their own instruction.

Background

In the past decade research on educational practice has increasingly focused on teachers' knowledge construction and the relationship of their understandings and classroom actions (Connelly & Clandinin,

1985; Schon, 1983). Understanding how teachers think about their practice holds great potential for improvement in education. Teacher thinking does not evolve in linear ways (Yinger, 1986). Instead, their classroom thinking and action come about through a recursive process. Teachers are constantly transacting with matters related to content, skills, political issues, human relationships, their beliefs about how children learn, and their knowledge of what children need to know to succeed in school. Teacher thinking and action will be in a state of change, possibly from external pressures such as curriculum mandates or from the individual teacher's need to grow professionally.

One significant impact of whole language philosophy is that teachers are more empowered (Rich, 1985). Whole language teaching requires a researcher/practitioner stance. Theory, texts, and experiences of others greatly inform the work of whole language teachers. However, the teachers believe that they are in the best position to make curricular and instructional decisions. Whole language classrooms are rich social learning environments in which extensive interactions with literature and an emphasis on process, empowerment, and decison making are hallmarks for both teachers and children (Rich, 1985; Smith, 1981). Rather than working to help children fit their learning to the curriculum and instruction, teachers with a whole language perspective create and manage curriculum and instruction according to the children's own needs and interests (DeFord, 1984).

In the following sections, we describe instructional contexts in one teacher's classroom. We also highlight her thinking in order to gain insights into the complexities of teaching a particular skill within a constructivist paradigm.

The Setting and the Children

The school in which Linda teaches is a large red Victorian brick building built over 100 years ago. Surrounded on all four sides by a large blacktop playground and high chain-linked fence, it is a familiar landmark in an urban, midwestern area. The majority of children in Linda's classroom are low-income, a population experiencing high rates of failure in public schools (Strickland, 1994). Many children come to school with a rich oral language background but without similar written language experiences. While a majority of these children need a great deal of instructional support in addition to the print-rich environment in Linda's classroom, some are more experienced and more readily take from the environment on their own. Thus, with respect to diversity, the children in this whole language first grade are no different from children in skills-based or traditional classrooms. They have a range of strengths and needs and they must learn to read independently within nine months. When asked what it means to be a whole language teacher, Linda's thoughts show this reality and the connections between place, people, and her own perspectives.

> I remember when I taught three different groups, had three different sets of workbooks, and three sets of board work and homework. I was not happy and neither were the children. When I told my kids we had to do one more workbook page, we *all* groaned. Today, being a whole language teacher means I'm able to reach all my children on their developmental level. I'm thinking of a little guy who was really struggling at the beginning of the year. He is still behind, but by March he had five published books. You know, that is really incredible. And he gets everybody's attention when he reads them. He is able to be like the other kids. That's what it is all about. I have such a wide range, but the way I teach now every child can succeed and that's what is important to me. They can all be writers and readers and all reach the success level even if they are not the same.

Classroom Contexts and Meaningful Instruction

Every school day the boys and girls in Linda's classroom engage in functional reading and writing. One essential instructional focus is to help children value and use oral and written language to communicate (Headings & Freppon, 1994). Displays of children's writing and art adorn the walls and flutter overhead on a clothes line strung from corner to corner. Interactive charts set at first graders' eye level require students' attention to get everyday needs met. For example, first thing in the morning the children use the charts to mark their attendance, choose from the lunch menu, and check to see what their classroom job is for the day. Children also use written language to leave messages for peers and the teacher, check in homework, check out books, and review the day's schedule.

Whole language teachers know the importance of the physical environment, and they shape their classrooms to invite children to read and write (Morrow & Rand chapter in this volume). Linda's room is filled with print, including interactive and manipulative books, big books, little books, trade books, child-made and teacher-made books, signs that tell about authors and stories, and interactive charts and songs that integrate math and other subjects with language arts. There is a classroom library area. Good literature abounds and the classroom includes places to rest and read comfortably, to listen to books on tape, and to engage in dramatic play by acting out a story with various manipulatives. Children's desks are grouped together in the center area, and the teacher's desk sits on the side, toward the back of the room.

The morning language arts block provides varied reading and writing opportunities. There is journal writing, a writers' workshop, and many opportunities to self-select reading materials and writing topics. Reading aloud and in-depth literature discussions among the children and the teacher also occur daily. Children work together and on their own and the teacher helps children in a variety of ways.

Children can learn about phonics meaningfully through teacher-guided reading/writing events and through their own use of letter/sound knowledge in student-generated reading/writing events (Freppon & Dahl, 1991; McIntyre & Freppon, 1994; Mills, O'Keefe, & Stephens, 1990). In this classroom, phonics instruction is kept whole as the teacher draws children's attention to this one part of written language. Because the children in this classroom frequently choose literacy events, and because they have time to use emerging alphabetic knowledge within a supportive context, learning is authentic to them. Reading and writing interactions are relevant because they occur to get everyday, ordinary things done. Written language events are empowering because both the teacher and the children are expert decision makers putting their knowledge to use.

Learning to Teach Phonics

Teacher knowledge is complex and multifaceted. Linda's knowledge of teaching is guided by a constructivist view of learning (Brooks & Brooks, 1993; Poplin, 1988). She knows that children themselves, within the context of their current understandings, create new meanings. Linda also uses her knowledge about cognitive development and the role of affect to shape instruction. Children's acquisition of positive attitudes and motivated behaviors is as important as their cognitive growth, and success in one area contributes to success in the other (Freppon, 1992; Turner, 1995).

In contrast to decontextualized, traditional phonics instruction, Linda's constructivist-based teaching of phonics is situated in real reading and writing contexts. She demonstrates and talks about how letters and speech sounds operate in written language while teaching students how to enjoy reading a book. This helps demystify phonics, which is abstract and difficult for some children to comprehend. Linda shows children how they, too, can work and gain control over this cueing system. They are expected to attend to, manipulate, and *use* alphabetic symbols to construct the texts they write and to help make sense of texts they read. Getting to this point was not easy, nor did it occur overnight. Linda gained expertise as a result of a conscious and sustained effort. As her discussion reveals, learning to teach within the whole language perspective was inseparable from learning how to assess or evaluate in new ways.

> When I began my transition to whole language teaching I took a great deal of time to monitor everything my students were doing. For instance, I frequently counted how many times a child used alphabetic sounds and standard spellings in her/his journal, and I learned their developmental patterns, such as using beginning consonants first. I took running records and combined this with basal end-of-unit tests even though we were not using basals. I see now how this helped me. Those years of intense record keeping and evaluation framed the observations and records I keep today. This knowledge contributes to my teaching decisions about whole groups, small reading groups, and individual learning goals for the children.

The Teaching/Assessing Process

Like other teachers, Linda must address district pupil performance objectives. In doing so, she engages in complex thinking and action that helps her meet all the objectives (Freppon, 1992). "Kid watching" (Goodman, Goodman, & Hood 1989) dominates the process through which Linda makes instructional decisions. Initially the focus is on finding out what the children know (Clay, 1979) by close observation and structured assessment. Throughout the year her teaching is informed by the children's responses. Tracking children's evolving understandings is essential, as she shows in the following comments:

> Observations are perpetual, but I really push myself to watch closely the first three months of school. All behaviors matter. I watch what they do with print, how they interact with one another about print, and whether they procrastinate or avoid interactions with written language. If a child continually cannot find her/his nametag on the attendance chart, that's a red flag! It usually means I have an early conference with parents and

volunteers to arrange working one-on-one with that child and to provide many meaningful experiences with print.

Using observations and assessments taken from Marie Clay's Reading Recovery program (1979) usually takes the month of September to complete. Children write a sentence that has been dictated orally to them, and their invented spelling is then scored according to Clay's procedures. Two of Clay's other evaluation techniques have been adapted. For example, children also write as many words as they believe they can spell conventionally in small groups and they participate in an alphabet assessment in which the scoring procedures have been adjusted. A reading attitude questionnaire is also given, and for those children able to read somewhat conventionally, Running Records are taken. Linda compiles all this information, watches for change, and works closely with children based on their strengths and needs. Anecdotal notes, written artifacts, and other materials are added to these initial assessments during the school year. Linda discusses some of her experiences below.

> Over the years I have reduced my record keeping because I feel less pressure from my administration and peers. But I still *watch*, write notes to myself, and keep checklists. For instance, in their writing I can see children using initial consonants, then ending consonants, later blends and vowels and experimentation with silent e and endings such as *ing*. I see children utilizing the skills I've taught in whole group such as word endings, and I watch them progress towards conventional reading and writing as those skills increased. These understandings help me make teaching decisions for the class and individual learning goals for children.

Keeping Phonics Learning Whole and Reducing the Risks for Learners

Teaching reading strategies and using the graphophonic cueing system begins on the first day of school when children are asked to put their name tags on the attendance chart. This shows that print carries meaning and that each child is important. Later that day, and for many days to come, lining up for lunch and recess also involves using the graphophonic cueing system with names. Linda holds up name cards that children read to line up. Hints are given if the children need support. For example, Linda may say the beginning letter sound or ask the child what the beginning letter and sound is. In these simple, functional activities there is opportunity to practice and to learn from others.

The following discussion shows one way Linda lets the children know that paying attention to and working on print is expected and beneficial.

> I focus on using children's names a lot, especially in the beginning months, because of the significance of names in their lives. Names carry power in giving us identity, and I can gather information by doing this, too. I can see who is unsure and who is not, who is trying to figure out not only her or his own name but also the names of others. Over the next month I use names to do language play, poetry, games and songs, and to engage with environmental print. That name immersion will be pulled back out and used when children have questions about invented spelling. "It starts like Bobby," I'll say, "Go find his name tag and see what letter his name starts with." I can use this with children who are poor risk takers or developmentally lagging. It also gives them the avenue to monitor their own learning. I teach and guide, and the child acts on his own and completes the process by finding Bobby's name and writing the letter B.

Whole class activities and transition time between activities fosters language play and opportunities to teach letter/sound relations. Children sing songs which include the "trick" of replacing the beginning letter in their name and pronouncing it instead with a blend or other letter sound. For example, in the name Mike, the *M* is replaced with *CH* and pronounced "Chike." This produces not only fun but great interest in the power of language as each child's name is so altered. Games that require reading of last names in order to get one's turn also help children attend to decoding. Singing, playing games, finding out what's for lunch, what one's job is and so on in this classroom also contribute to building community and trust. Children learn to *try* and to help each other. These experiences have a built-in connectedness that enables children to use graphophonic information to make sense of things they care about.

The lunch board is used by children throughout the school year to find out what's for lunch and to mark their choices. It looks a lot like the lunch board shown in Figure 4-1.

Each morning children gather around the lunch board and interact with and watch their peers as decisions and understandings are made public. Early in the school year the board has pictures *and* print; later on the pictures are removed to help children focus on and use print more. Much of the environmental print (job chart, homework and book check-in, etc.) that works to organize daily classroom life operates in this way. Activity with these organizers and other reading and writing events allows students to engage with written language

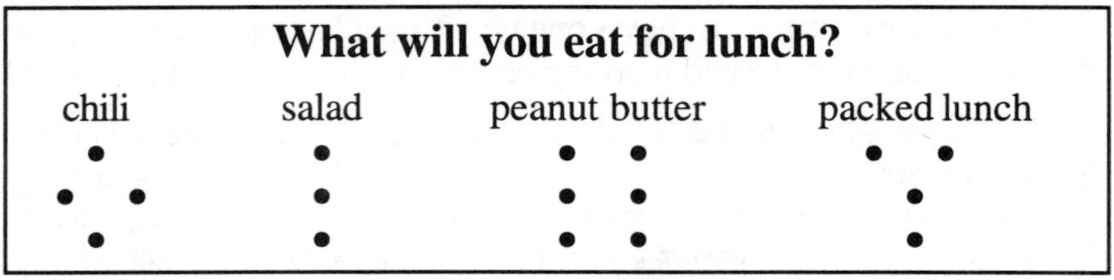

```
┌─────────────────────────────────────────────────────────┐
│            What will you eat for lunch?                    │
│                                                            │
│   chili       salad      peanut butter     packed lunch    │
│    •            •            •   •              •   •       │
│  •    •         •            •   •                •        │
│    •            •            •   •              •          │
└─────────────────────────────────────────────────────────┘
```

Figure 4-1.

and take chances in learning with very little risk of failure in the traditional sense. These supported, functional, and highly social experiences also help children build on what is known. This increases not only their learning opportunities but also that of their teacher, as Linda's discussion reveals.

> I can watch children each day when they try to figure out the main course for lunch. Standing close by as children circulate and get organized for the day allows me to give mini-lessons in a nonthreatening and unobtrusive way. If a picture word card of a taco is hanging on the lunch chart and I hear a child say "Burritos," I first listen for a self-correction. If I hear nothing, I intervene by asking the child to recheck. I ask, "What do you hear at the beginning of Burritos?" /B/. Let's look at the word card and see if that makes sense. This lunch board routine is used every day along with homework check-in, attendance board, lunch board, and job chart, etc. All kids must use them to get along. I try to take advantage of each potential learning opportunity in the classroom. I also find through teaching one child, others will follow my clues and help their peers when hesitation or doubt arises.

Classroom routines such as these help keep learning about phonics meaningful and children's risk of failure or embarrassment reduced. Children are explicitly told about how letters and speech sounds work in words. They are helped in ways that make sense to them and they get to practice authentically. Linda's teaching differs markedly from traditional teaching. Yet clearly, as shown in this and other discussions of whole language (Dudley-Marling & Dippo, 1991; Dudley-Marling, this volume; Edelsky, Altwerger, & Flores, 1991; Newman & Church, 1990), skill teaching is present.

Organizing Instruction

Linda conceptualizes her instruction in phonics as funnel shaped. Much of her teaching is spontaneous, based on children's evident needs and unforeseen learning opportunities. Her interactions are also, at times, thoroughly planned, based on knowledge of what children need to know about letter/sound relations. At the mouth of the funnel, instruction focuses on a wide audience such as the whole class. Learners' attention is guided toward letters and speech sound relations, and they "take from" these literacy events as they can, based on individual current knowledge and peer interactions. Farther down the funnel, instruction aims at a smaller audience where more specific support is provided. This occurs after careful planning for children who seem to need more phonics instruction. Again, the social group itself provides a supportive context. Finally, at the most discrete point, one-on-one teaching occurs during journal writing time, writing workshop, and in individual reading events. Here the social group is the teacher and a child (often with another child or two observing). In this teaching context individual learners are provided "concentrated" guidance in their use of letters to create texts and in their use of the graphophonic cueing system to read.

Whole group

Linda begins each week by introducing a new big book which is first read to the children and discussed at some length. In addition to the storyline, the illustrations and information about the author are discussed and enjoyed. Children read along with the teacher and may also illustrate and/or write as they create their own version of the big book. Using the big book to enjoy as literature and as a vehicle for teaching specific skills, Linda selects a focus such as letter/sound blends. Lessons are planned and carried out with both the strengths and needs of the children in mind and what Linda believes they need to know.

While whole group lessons are well planned, teaching also happens spontaneously. A child might respond with an insight such as "See the J, that's like Jake! And the S in swim, it's like Simon." Linda's comments below show that in addition to teaching children to attend to and learn about letter/sound relations, she also incorporates other skills, such as learning about the function of certain kinds of punctuation.

> My lessons are explicit and geared to the big book or chart chosen. For example, I cover the letter blends in words as Holdway (1979) suggests with post-it notes, and I read the text, asking the children to discuss with each other what they think the missing letters are when we come to these words. I may also use the cloze technique to help children learn

to depend on syntax and meaning and to work on predicting. Another time I may ask them to read just the parts in quotations while I read as narrator. I make sure some aspects of my instruction are easier and some are challenging, to reach students who are in different places. For instance, if I was working on a strategy of using middle consonants with the whole group, the majority of my focus would be there, but would also do something on vowels for those with more experience and some focus would be on beginning consonants for those who need it. It shouldn't all be too easy, because they need challenge, or too hard, because review and reinforcement are important. It's like a funnel. Whole group lessons and all the environmental print interactions are at the base with small reading groups, journals, and writer's workshop providing more focused instruction. I might work on middle consonants in whole group, using big books and charts of songs and poems I've made. Then I watch and encourage that application in other contexts such as journal writing.

The whole group activities described above assist in instructional organization. However, there is much more to it than that. This instructional context reveals deeply-held teacher beliefs about human learning. Because students' cognitive proficiencies, individual dispositions, and backgrounds with written language differ, Linda knows that students do not "take from" instruction in exactly the same ways. Some children are more tolerant of the stress accompanying challenging learning than others, and some have more knowledge on which to build. Whole group activities, such as having children discuss their ideas about letters and speech sounds with their neighbors, create a "social safety net" that encourages experimentation and risk taking. Learning becomes game-like and fun while teaching retains an explicit focus on letters and speech sounds. These instructional events also make the teacher's expectations clear: everyone works on learning these features of written language. The support of the group and Linda's positive view of errors as part of the developmental process of learning produces flexible situations in which individual students find levels of both comfort and tension. Thus, learning opportunities expand greatly.

Small group

Phonics and other strategy teaching such as predicting is carried out in reading groups of three to five children. Early in Linda's change to whole language groups these groups were organized heterogeneously. However, as shown in her discussion below, it became evident that her first grade students needed 20 to 30 minutes a day of instruction with peers who had similar reading needs.

> I love whole group, but when I hear "experts" say that you don't lose kids' attention in whole group, I say baloney! I lose less because of the ways I teach, but I still have kids who sit on the outskirts or avoid attending to print. So, I use small group and individual opportunities to teach specific strategies. Small groups help me target children who need specific help. Depending on my purpose, the groups are sometimes stable and sometimes not. Reading groups tend to be stable and homogeneous, particularly the first half of the school year. To me, this is an example of the way I visualize instruction being broadly, and also narrowly, focused. Grouping in my room is heterogeneous in most activities (whole group, free choice, most work times) and homogeneous in reading groups. The only published professional I've read who shares this view about first graders is Reggie Routman (1988). I remember feeling so relieved when I read that she thought homogeneous small groups are advantages because of beginning readers' wide range of understandings. Sometimes I think we forget that there is comfort, acceptance and encouragement among those who have things in common. Children need focused instruction according to their needs, which is why I use small group and one-on-one teaching.

In a small reading group, with children seated on the floor around her, Linda introduces the book by showing the title, author, and pictures and by discussing the storyline. She helps children make connections to their lives and to other books they have read whenever possible. Personal enjoyment of specific stories or story parts and characters are ever present. Linda models reading strategies and points to individual words as she reads the text. Students are then given the choice of reading the same book with a buddy or on their own. They are sometimes asked to discover the answer to a question about the story as they read. As children read their individual little books, their teacher watches and assists, shows how to use letter/sound relations and other strategies, such as skipping an unknown word and going back to it after reading the sentence. Linda also watches to see if a strategy is over used and she often reads along with those who need it most. She speaks words of encouragement and also asks, "What do you think?" and "How do you know?" These questions help children see which cueing system they are using, or might use, and keeps a focus on meaning making. As children finish their books, each one "checks in" with Linda. She asks them to share what they think and provides support to the child who is unsure or who responds in a fragmented way. Linda constantly rechecks on word recognition, use of phonics, and students' fluency.

One-on-one teaching

Journal time and writers' workshop provide rich opportunities for children and teacher to focus on phonics. Journals are used early in the school year and a full-fledged writers' workshop is gradually introduced as children learn more about writing. Linda's thoughts on her teaching in these contexts help show their importance.

> Journals are one of my favorite teaching tools. I see wonders, miracles, and plain hard work in journals when I track writing over the whole school year. I love it when a child realizes I can read her/his writing! Dialogue journals are a place where I *can get to it* (the teaching of skills and strategies), even if there is only a three-minute mini-lesson with each child. When I ask children to work on phonics in their journal, it is based on years of observing them develop through invented spelling and emergent writing. Their writing helps me understand their development. It helps me know when and what to focus on. I use individual teaching in journals in two ways. First, I ask the child to read my message. Here I can observe decoding strategies and make suggestions. I can really teach. Second, after the child has written a message and checks in with me to read it, I see successes emerge out of the confusions or errors that are often discovered. I usually make several points and discuss them with the child. Each child is asked to self-correct something before turning in the journal. Journal goals are made each quarter and shared with the child and parents.
>
> In writer's workshop, writing serves similar and different purposes. I still use both as a vehicles to teach phonics in the context of the child's own written message, but I also concentrate on story sense and other writing skills in workshop conferencing. Children choose pieces for publication and the graphophonic strategy, along with other strategies, are built on with the goal of becoming independent, well-published writers. We work on this for as long as it takes.

Early in the school year children use drawing heavily in their writing. As they gain writing skills and confidence, children gradually release this support and use drawing to elaborate and complement their texts. Journal writing responses between teacher and child are shared in whole group events and used to further build community and trust. The published books generated through the writer's workshop become part of the classroom library. These publications are shared with parents, other teachers and children, and administrators. As children acquire conventional reading proficiency, published works become a major force of encouragement and support in the learning of phonics.

Conclusion

Educators with a whole language perspective are influenced by a variety of forces. However, a common concern for *all* first grade teachers is grounded in the reality that if these young children do not learn to read by the end of first grade the consequences are nearly always very negative. Typically, nonconventional readers are tested and assigned to special classes or retained in first grade. We bring this chapter to a close with that in mind and with more discussion on the teaching of skills. In concluding we also draw on Field and Jardine's (1994) thoughtful discussion of whole language "owning its own shadow."

Many of those interested in whole language have consistently stressed that this philosophy does not necessarily exclude, or even advocate the exclusion of, explicit teaching (Church, 1994; Dudley-Marling, this volume; Headings & Freppon, 1994; McIntyre, 1995; Slaughter, 1988). However, because of the contextually-bound complexities of teaching and learning, these researchers and teachers also refuse to slot the teaching of skills into a simple "yes, you do—no, you don't" response.

Linda's explicit letter/sound teaching is deliberately structured to support and value the preconventional responses of young children. This brings us to another important point. While what is taught in any classroom is important, *how* it is taught is vital. Linda's phonics instruction strongly encourages experimentation and practice. The whole-part-whole nature of her instruction (see Purcell-Gates, this volume) and the "social safety net" of a whole language environment create multiple levels of support. Children don't receive traditional admonishments, bad marks, or the withholding of privileges such as recess as a result of their preconventional, emergent responses. However, they do receive clear messages on the importance of *working* on learning phonics. Linda believes, as do others, that providing good instruction means that school literacy expectations must be kept in mind (Delpit, 1988; Gee, 1990).

Throughout our discussion, elements of whole language (Goodman, 1986), holistic constructivism (Brooks & Brooks, 1993; Poplin, 1988), and explicit teaching (Roehler, Duffy & Meloth, 1986) are evident. Some of the elements most directly applicable to Linda's teaching and children's learning and examples from her classroom are noted below.

Children learn about language within the context of current understandings.

Example: In a transition activity, the children participate in using different beginning letter sounds to pronounce their names. The teacher works to provide this and other "open ended" learning opportunities.

Literacy learning is greatly influenced by young children's development.

Example: The teacher encourages working on vowel sounds or middle consonants only after a child can readily use beginning and ending letters and sounds. Children use their own language and emerging skills to create texts.

Trust and respect for each child is essential.

Example: Children self-select the majority of their reading and writing interactions and work with phonics according to their intentions. The teacher views the children as active learners and supports their efforts.

Learning is supported by whole-part-whole procedures involving problem solving.

Example: In a big book activity, the teacher moves back and forth focusing on the whole text, words and letters, and whole text again. Children "figure out" letter/sound relations within the context of a familiar story.

Explicit teaching is situated in highly familiar, functional contexts.

Example: The teacher uses the lunch board menu to help the child focus on the graphophonic cues. Interest in selecting lunch and the social group help support children's experimentations.

Explicit and implicit teaching necessitates risk taking.

Example: Children are part of a community of learners who regularly experiment with phonics. The teacher views her instruction as her *practice*. Instruction that "doesn't work" paves the way to understanding children's learning and improving instruction.

Children's errors and miscues are valued and invaluable.

Example: The teacher tracks children's growth and uses their emerging understandings to guide instruction. Children's emergent use of the graphophonic cueing system is essential to their and their teacher's learning.

Learning is supported when feelings are honored and passion is invited.

Example: As children become owners of their learning, their investment and excitement grows. The teacher knows that how children feel about learning phonics is important. She delights in and has respect for children's preferences, emergent responses, and intentions.

Our discussion of the teaching of phonics skills in whole language helps share something Field and Jardine (1994) believe is important. These authors call upon those interested in the many positive aspects of whole language to "take on" some difficult issues, as Mills, O'Keefe & Stephens did in their 1990 book on phonics instruction in a whole language first grade. Such discussions are a way of strengthening research and teaching. In this chapter we have made an effort to converse on this "touchy subject" a little more.

Teaching decisions about phonics instruction and the many other issues faced daily in classroom arise ". . . out of the midst of a rich nest of relations that have been established in the classroom, relations that involve responsibilities to the world and to children" (Field & Jardine 1994, p. 261). Our interpretation of whole language and constructivist instruction puts the teacher in the active role of decision maker, informed analyst, and expert language user. Such teachers have much to offer children and are responsible for providing instruction that helps ensure their success as much as possible.

References

An Imperiled Generation (1988). *A Carnegie Foundation Special Report.* Princeton, NJ: The Carnegie Foundation for the Advancement of Teaching.

Brooks, J. G., & Brooks, M. G. (1993). *In search of understanding: The case for constructivist classrooms.* Alexandria, VA: Association for Supervision and Curriculum Development.

Church, S. M. (1994). Is whole language really a warm fuzzy. *Reading Teacher, 47,* 362–369.

Clay, M. M. (1979). *The early detection of reading difficulties.* Portsmouth, NH: Heinemann.

Cochran-Smith, M. & Lytle, S. (1993). *Inside outside: Teacher research and knowledge.* New York: Teachers College Press.

Connelly, F. M., & Clandinin, D. J. (1985). Personal practical knowledge and the modes of knowing: Relevance for teaching and learning. In E. Eisner (Ed.), *Learning and teaching the ways of knowing.* Eighty Fourth Yearbook of the National Society for the Study of Education, part 2. Chicago: University of Chicago Press.

DeFord, D. E. (1984). Classroom contexts for literacy learning.In T. Raphael (Ed.), *The contexts of school-based literacy.* New York: Random House.

Delpit, L. (1988). The silenced dialogue. *Power and pedagogy in teaching other people's children.* Harvard Educational Review, 58, 280–287.

Dudley-Marling, C. & Dippo, D. (1991). The language of whole language. *Language Arts, 68,* 548–554.

Edelsky, C., Altweyer, B., & Flores, B. (1991). *Whole language: What's the difference?* Portsmouth, NH: Heinemann.

Field, J. C., & Jardine, D. W. (1994). "Bad examples" as interpretive opportunities: On the need for whole language to own its own shadow. *Language Arts, 71,* 258–263.

Freppon, P. A. (1991). An investigation of children's concepts of the purpose and nature of reading in different instructional settings. *The Journal of Reading Behavior: A Journal of Literacy, 23,* 139–163.

Freppon, P. A., & Dahl, K. (1991). Learning about phonics in a whole language classroom. *Language Arts, 69,* 192–200.

Freppon, P. A. (1992). Difficulties in evaluation in a traditional U.S. school. In C. Bouffler (Ed.), *Literacy evaluation: Issues and practicalities* (21–27). Newtown, Australia: Primary English Teaching Association.

Gee, J. P. (1990). *Social linguistics and literacies.* Philadelphia: Falmer.

Goodman, D. (1986). *What's whole in whole language.* Portsmouth, NH: Heinemann.

Goodman, K. S., Goodman, Y. M., & Hood, W. J. (1989). *The whole language evaluation book.* Portsmouth, NH: Heinemann.

Goswami, D., & Stillman, P. R. (1987). *Reclaiming the classroom: Teacher researcher as an agency for change.* Portsmouth, NH: Heinemann.

Headings, L., & Freppon, P. A. (1994). Taking the risk out of writing: Designing and implementing a program for low-SES children in a whole language first grade. *The Ohio Reading Teacher, 28,* 6–14.

Holdway, D. (1979) *The foundations of literacy.* Sydney: Ashton Scholastic.

McIntyre, E. (1995). The struggle for developmentally appropriate literacy instruction. *Journal of Research in Childhood Education.*

McIntyre, E. (1990). Young children's reading strategies as they read self-selected texts in school. *Early Childhood Research Quarterly, 5,* 265–277.

McIntyre, E., & Freppon, P. A., (1994). A comparison of children's development of alphabetic knowledge in a skills-based and a whole language classroom. *Research in the Teaching of English, 28,* 391–417.

Mills, H., O'Keefe, T., & Stephens, D. (1990). *Looking closely— Exploring the role of phonics in one whole language classroom.* Portsmouth, NH: Heinemann.

Newman, J. M. & Church; S. M. (1990). Myths of whole language. *Reading Teacher, 44,* 20–26.

Poplin, M. S. (1988). Holistic/constructivists principles of the teaching/ learning process: Implications for the field of learning disabilities. *Journal of Learning Disabilities, 21,* 401–416.

Purcell-Gates, V. (1988). Lexical and syntactic knowledge of written narrative held by well-read-to kindergartners and second graders. *Research in the Teaching of English, 22,* 128–160.

Rich, S. J. (1985). Restoring the power to teachers: The impact of "Whole Language." *Language Arts, 62,* 717–724.

Roehler, L. R., Duffy, G. D., & Meloth, M. (1986). What to be direct about in direct instruction. In T. Raphael & R. Reynolds (Eds.), *Contexts of School-based literacy.* (pp. 79–97). New York: Random House.

Routman, R. (1988). *Transitions.* Portsmouth, NH: Heinemann.

Schon, D. (1983). *The reflective practitioner: How professionals think in action.* New York: Basic Books.

Smith, F. (1981). Demonstrations, engagement, and sensitivity: The choice between people and programs. *Language Arts, 58,* 634–642.

Strickland, D. S. (1994). Educating African-American learners at risk: Finding a better way. *Language Arts, 71,* 328–345.

Turner, J. (1995). The influence of classroom context on young children's motivation for literacy. *Reading Research Quarterly, 30,* 410–441.

Yinger, R. J. (1986). Examining thought in action: A theoretical and methodological critique of research on interactive teaching. *Teaching and Teacher Education, 2,* 263–282.

Chapter 5

Creating Rich Literacy Environments to Develop Reading and Writing Skills in Early Childhood Classrooms

Lesley Mandel Morrow, Rutgers University and
Muriel K. Rand, Jersey City State College

With each thematic unit, Mrs. Millson helps her children design the dramatic play center to reflect the topic being studied. When learning about animals, the students in Mrs. Millson's combination kindergarten-first grade decided to create a veterinarian's office. The class had the opportunity to visit a veterinarian to help with their planning. They began redesigning the dramatic play center by creating a waiting room with chairs and a table filled with magazines and books. Mrs. Millson suggested hanging posters and pamphlets about good health practices for pets, which she had obtained from the veterinarian. The children made a poster that listed the doctors' hours, and added signs that said, "No Smoking" and "Check In With The Nurse When You Arrive." The nurse's table contained forms for patients to fill out, a telephone, telephone books, appointment cards, and a calendar. The veterinarian's office also contained patient folders, prescription pads, white coats, masks, gloves, cotton swabs, a toy doctors' kit, and stuffed animals. Blank paper, a stapler, pencils, markers, colored pencils, and crayons were placed in the area as well. The classroom computer was taken from the math center and relocated in the dramatic play area for keeping patient records and other files. The center design was a collaborative effort by the teacher and children. After preparing the environment with the children, Mrs. Millson focused on skill development by discussing and modeling the use of various materials. She suggested to them, "While you're waiting for your turn to see the doctor, you can read to your pet in the waiting area and the nurse can ask you to fill out forms. The receptionist might like to talk to patients on the phone about problems their pets are having, schedule appointments, and write out appointment cards. You can write bills for visits, accept payments, and give receipts. The doctor can fill out prescription forms and write up patient reports." Later, Mrs. Millson joined the children in the dramatic play area, pretending first to be the nurse, then the doctor, so that she could model the types of literacy behavior she wanted the children to try.

A week later, the children were fully engaged in this center. Jonnell sat in the waiting room reading the story "Caps for Sale" to her pet monkey. Damien joined him with his pet rabbit and listened. He asked if he could have a turn reading. Before they were finished, the nurse called Jonnell to come and answer some questions about her monkey's problems. When Jonnell finished filling out forms, she watched the two pets for Damien while he spoke with the nurse. Katie was acting as the doctor, and was examining a pet cat that was brought in by Emily. Katie wrote the animal's name and the owner's name in a file folder, and then picked up the prescription pad. She told Emily, "You see this? Now this says that you make sure that this teddy bear takes 100 pills every hour, until he feels better. Keep him in bed with covers, and be sure to give him lots of juice." Then she wrote down "100 PLS EVRY OWR" on the pad.

This anecdote from a study by Morrow (1990) describes a classroom environment that promotes the development of literacy skills by motivating the desire to read and write. The teacher, along with the children, prepared the physical environment. The teacher described and modeled the use of materials in the literacy-enriched play area. After this initial guidance, Mrs. Millson helped students in need of direction. As the children became more involved, she allowed the play to take place on its own and took the role of participator. The social collaborative setting provided for purposeful communication. The dramatic play theme allowed for the integration of play, literacy, and the content area theme. During their play, children pursued real-life behavior in caring for pets which involved meaningful and functional literacy activities. The teacher in this classroom was aware that the classroom environment helps develop critical literacy skills by motivating the children to communicate in varied ways.

Overview of the Chapter

The purpose of this chapter is to describe the physical and social aspects of the classroom environment that support literacy skill development. The chapter begins with a brief discussion of research and perspectives related to young children's literacy learning and the environment. Next we present practical information about creating physical environments that help literacy learning in young children. The role of the social environment, including guidelines for managing social collaborative activities, follows. Finally, observations of children engaged in reading and writing illustrate the skill development that occurs during social collaborative activities in a rich literacy environment.

Research and Perspectives about Literacy-Rich Environments

The whole language perspective emphasizes the important relationship between the classroom environment and children's early literacy development. From this perspective, literacy develops from authentic, meaningful, and functional experiences that use children's literature as their main source for actively involving children. These experiences take place within rich literacy environments created specifically to encourage children to practice skills they are learning. Instruction integrates literacy learning throughout the school day within different content areas while emphasizing social collaboration and self-regulated learning. Children as well as teachers become responsible for deciding instructional strategies, organizations, activities, and materials (Bergeron, 1990; Goodman, 1989; Graves, 1975).

Results from research show that the home environments of children who read early have similar features. These children had been read to since a very young age, had their questions regarding reading and writing answered, had parents who were avid readers, and came from homes in which reading was a frequent source of pleasure and relaxation. These literacy-rich environments provided access to reading and writing materials and encouragement to explore (Anbar, 1986; Clark, 1976; Morrow, 1983). The social aspects of the home environment, as well as the physical environment, were important in children's emergent literacy development. Teale's (1982) view of a supportive environment for early literacy development is one in which children's involvement in reading and writing activities is mediated by more literate others. According to his view, this social interaction teaches children the societal functions and conventions of reading and writing; they also link reading with enjoyment and satisfaction and thus increase their desire to engage in literacy activities.

Historically, theorists and philosophers who studied early childhood development emphasized the importance of the physical environment in learning and literacy development. Pestalozzi (Rusk & Scotland, 1970) and Froebel (1974) described the preparation of manipulative materials that would foster literacy development in real-life environments in which young children's learning could flourish. Montessori (1965) advocated a carefully prepared classroom environment intended to promote independent learning and recommended that each kind of material in the environment have its specific learning objective.

Based on these perspectives, a classroom designed to promote optimum literacy development will offer an abundant supply of materials for reading, writing, and oral language. While the majority of these materials are concentrated in a literacy center, literacy materials are also provided in content-area learning centers. Materials and settings throughout the classroom emulate real-life experiences and make literacy meaningful to children. They are based on information children already possess, and are functional so that children can see a need and purpose for using literacy. Careful attention to a classroom's physical design contributes to the success of such an instructional program.

General effects of classroom environments

Preparing a classroom's physical environment is often overlooked in planning instruction. Teachers tend to concentrate on pedagogical and interpersonal factors, but do not consider the physical context in which teaching and learning occur. They may direct their energies toward varying teaching strategies while the classroom setting remains relatively unchanged. When program and environment are not coordinated, "setting deprivation" often results, a situation in which the physical environment fails to support the activities of students (Spivak, 1973).

Instead of viewing the learning environment as background or scenery for teaching and learning, teachers can acknowledge the physical setting as an active influence on their own activities and attitudes and also that of the children (Loughlin & Martin, 1987; Morrow, 1990;

Rivlin & Weinstein, 1984; Sutfin, 1980). Research has shown many ways in which the physical design of the classroom affects the children's behavior. Rooms partitioned into smaller spaces have facilitated such behavior as peer and verbal interaction, fantasy, associative, and co-operative play more than rooms with large open spaces (Field, 1980). Children in carefully arranged rooms have shown more creative productivity and greater use of language-related activities than children in randomly arranged rooms (Moore, 1986; Nash, 1981). Literacy-enriched dramatic play areas based on themes have stimulated literacy activities and the enhancement of literacy skills (Morrow, 1990; Morrow & Rand, 1991a, 1991b; Neuman & Roskos, 1990, 1992). Dramatic play with story props has improved story production and comprehension, including recall of details and ability to sequence and interpret (Mandler & Johnson, 1977; Saltz & Johnson, 1974). Enhancing the physical setting also increases children's use of literacy centers. With increased use of the centers, children's literacy achievement improves as well (Morrow, 1992).

Preparing Literacy-Rich Physical Environments that Motivate Reading and Writing

By purposefully arranging the space and materials, teachers can use physical environments as an active, positive and pervasive influence on instruction. The following section gives suggestions for creating a literacy-rich physical environment to motivate reading and writing based on the research and ideas discussed so far.

Arranging the classroom

Although there is no single way to effectively arrange a classroom, we suggest one plan here as a guide (see Figure 5-1). Teachers are encouraged to adapt these suggestions to suit their needs and personal preferences and those of their children.

An ideal, literacy-rich classroom contains centers dedicated to particular activities or content areas, such as social studies, science, math, art, music, dramatic play, block play, and literacy. Centers contain general materials pertinent to the content area and materials specific to topics currently under study. Resources are primarily devoted to the content area but are designed to develop literacy skills as well. The materials are manipulative and activity oriented, and are designed so children can use them independently or in small groups.

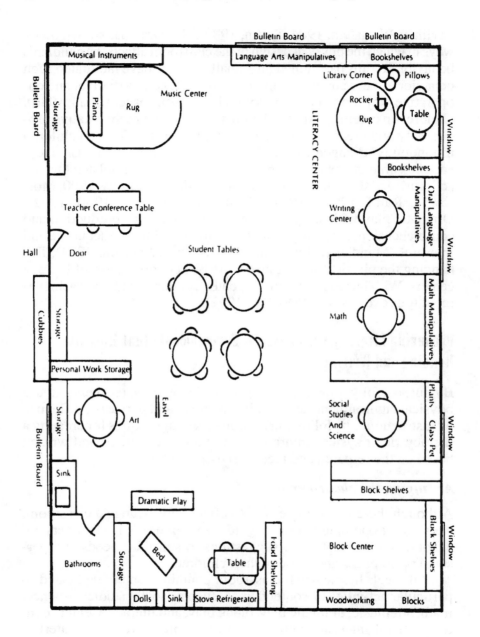

Figure 5-1. Early Childhood Classroom Floor Plan. (From Morrow, L. M. [1993]. *Literacy development in the early years: Helping children read and write.* Boston: Allyn & Bacon. Used with permission.)

Furniture that houses a center's materials separates them and serves as partitions. A center's materials are stored on tables, on shelves, or in boxes. Areas are accessible and labeled, and contain bulletin boards. Each piece of equipment in a center has its own designated spot so that teachers can direct children to specific items, and children can find and return them easily. Early in a school year, most centers hold only a small amount of items, with new materials added gradually as the year progresses.

Before new items are placed in centers, the teacher introduces them to the children (Montessori, 1965). This is often done in a whole class lesson. For example, if he or she were placing a felt board with story characters into the literacy center she would introduce the materials to the children by telling a story using the felt board. She would explain how the story is read or told while the figures are placed on the board. Children would be encouraged to work with the material, one reading or telling the story and the other manipulating the figures. In addition she would show the children the exact spot where the felt board is stored in the literacy center and where she felt the pieces are to be housed as well. She would encourage the children to read and tell stories for felt characters already in the literacy center, and to create figures for stories that do not have them. The retelling of stories with felt characters engages children in demonstrating comprehension of a story. The children must know the details, sequence, and be able to interpret characters' feelings in their presentation to others and organize all the parts of the story into a coherent whole.

When children are working in the centers, the teacher is a guide, a facilitator, as she/he works with individuals or small groups as they engage in activities. In the collaborative setting of a center, when children work together they collaborate and tutor each other, thus enhancing each other's skills development.

The room design supports whole group, small group, and individual instruction. (See chapter by Freppon and Headings, this volume, for details on instruction in these contexts.) Different types of lessons are appropriate for these different settings, and all of them serve an important purpose. The room environment supports the structure of the lesson. The teacher can hold large group instruction when the children are sitting at their desks or tables, or sitting on the floor. The literacy center and the music center are large enough for the entire class to meet together. The teacher should choose these lessons when he or she is able to meet the needs of a wide range of learners. For example, the teacher might conduct a brainstorming session before writing, or sing a song related to the theme. Storybook readings are highly appropriate for large group instruction since many different perspectives can be discussed.

A Teacher Conference Table provides space for small group and individualized instruction, necessary especially for skill development and interaction guided by an adult. The conference table is placed in a quiet area of the room to facilitate the instruction that occurs around it, but it is situated so the teacher can see the rest of the room where children are working independently. Explicit instruction on skills and strategies usually takes place in small groups or one-on-one. The teacher may bring together a small group of children who have the same skill needs to give extra help. The teacher may choose to group children who have similar interests. She may form "friendship groups" from time to time in order to give special attention and monitoring during skill or strategy teaching. The teacher may work with a child one-on-one when she feels she needs to work closely with a particular child or if the child works better alone. In this intimate setting, teachers can determine the skills needs of children and give direct instruction as needed. Work may be prescribed for children to practice skills learned when they go to center time.

The various centers also offer settings for independent and self-directed learning. Students practice what they learn and tutor others in the setting independent of the teacher.

On the classroom floor plan, the centers have been positioned so that areas where quiet work is typical (literacy, math, social studies, and science centers) are away from the noisy, more active centers (Dramatic Play, Blocks, Art).

Functional environmental print

Literacy-rich classrooms are filled with visually prominent functional print, such as labels on classroom items and areas. Signs communicate functional information and directions, such as *Quiet Please,* and *Please Put Materials Away After Using Them.* Charts labeled *Helpers, Daily Routines, Attendance,* and *Calendar* simplify classroom management (Morrow, 1993; Schickedanz, 1993). A notice board in a prominent place in the room is used to communicate with the children in writing. Experience charts display new words generated from themes, recipes used in the classroom, and science experiments conducted. This environmental print is actively used with the children or else it may soon go unnoticed. Children are encouraged to read it, copy it, and use words from the labels in their writing. When children use environmental print, they are developing a sight word vocabulary, they begin to recognize the visual elements of print for letter identification, and they use beginning sounds to read words. As they copy environmental print, they are developing motor skills for writing, making sound/symbol relations, and expanding their writing sight vocabulary.

The literacy center

A main feature of the literacy-rich environment in a classroom is the literacy center (see Figure 5-2). This center includes space and materials for writing, reading, oral language, and listening. The center is positioned in an area of the classroom in such a way that it is visually attractive and physically accessible. The effort of creating an inviting atmosphere for a classroom literacy center is rewarded by the increase in children's participation in the activities offered. This center is essential in making it possible for children to enjoy immediate access to literature. Researchers have found that children in classrooms with literacy centers read and write more often than do children whose classrooms don't have such materials (Morrow & Weinstein, 1986). Children should be involved in planning, designing, and managing the literacy center. They can help develop rules for its use, select a name for it, and keep it neat.

Although the literacy center is visible and inviting, partitions provide some privacy and physical definition. Five or six children can work in the center at one time. All children can take materials from the center to use in other parts of the room. Because much of the activity in the literacy center takes place on the floor, it is furnished with a throw rug and pillows or bean bag chairs. A rocking chair allows comfortable reading, and a private "cozy" spot for reading can be made from an oversized carton that has been painted or covered with contact paper. Stuffed animals also belong in the literacy center, especially if they are related to available books. A stuffed teddy bear, for instance, is placed next to a copy of *Bedtime for Frances* (Hoban, 1960) and other books in the Frances series, which tell about a family of bears. Children enjoy reading to stuffed animals, writing stories about them, or simply holding them as they look at books.

Books are stored in open-faced book shelving that is used for displaying titles about themes being studied. Regular bookshelves are also necessary to house five to eight books per child at three to four

Figure 5-2.   The literacy center. (From Morrow, L. M. [1993]. *Literacy development in the early years: Helping children read and write.* Boston: Allyn & Bacon. Used with permission.)

grade levels. The grade levels of books included reflects the classroom in which they have been placed. Books are color coded by categories, and represent different genres of children's literature, such as picture storybooks, poetry, informational books, magazines, biographies, fairy tales, novels, realistic literature, cookbooks, joke books, craft books, and so on. Interest in the books is kept high by rotating them on and off the shelves regularly.

To encourage home reading, children systematically check books out of the classroom literacy center to take home and read. Logs are provided to record books read and tasks completed during periods of independent reading and writing.

Other ways to encourage children to use the literacy center include posters displayed to point out the joys and importance of reading and writing and a bulletin board that provides a place for children to display their work. Literacy manipulatives such as feltboards with story characters from pieces of children's literature increase children's involvement in the center. These manipulatives, which include puppets, taped stories with headsets, chalktalks, roll stories, and prop stories, have been found to motivate children to engage in storytelling, storybook reading, and writing (Morrow & Weinstein, 1986).

The Author's Spot. The writing portion of the literacy center is often referred to as the Author's Spot. This section includes a table and chairs, and many writing materials such as colored markers, crayons, pencils (both regular and colored), paper, chalk, and a chalkboard. While various sizes and types of paper are available, most are unlined white paper or newsprint ranging in size from 8½" by 11" to 24" by 36". Index cards are available for children to record "Very Own Words," and the children's word collections are stored there. Writing folders, one for each child, are used to collect writing samples over the course of the school year. If available, a typewriter or computer adds to the center's usefulness.

Materials for making books are essential, including paper, hole punch, stapler, and construction paper for covers. Blank books prepared by the teacher, especially ones keyed to special occasions, invite children to fill in written messages and stories. Children's literature in the classroom collection becomes a catalyst for writing activities and ideas.

A bulletin board for children to display their own selected pieces of writing is required, but equally valuable are Message or Notice Boards used to exchange messages among members of the class and the teacher. Teachers find the Message Board helpful in sending messages to individual children as well as in posting important information for the class. Mailboxes, stationery, envelopes, and stamps for youngsters' incoming and outgoing mail may be placed in the writing center if a pen pal program is underway.

Integrating literacy materials into the content areas

Programs that motivate early literacy development require literacy-rich environments that support an integrated approach to literacy learning. Reading, writing, and oral language materials and activities are easily incorporated into subject area teaching, enabling these areas also to provide a source of literacy learning. Literacy becomes purposeful and takes on additional importance when integrated with other content areas (Dewey, 1966).

The literacy center just outlined incorporates materials that stimulate writing, reading, listening, and oral language. Materials are selected in the other content area centers throughout the classroom to create this same effect. Besides materials devoted to specific content areas, literacy materials are included as well. For example, centers contain things to read, materials with which to write, things to listen to, and activities to talk about. These materials create interest, new vocabulary and ideas, and a reason for participating in literacy activities. With each new theme studied, additional books, posters, artifacts, music, art projects, dramatic play materials, and scientific objects are added to create new interest.

When visiting another early childhood classroom also involved in the study of animals, we find that the teacher, Mr. Gravois, has extended the theme to all learning centers. To encourage literacy skill development, Mr. Gravois added the following materials and activities for students to participate in at the thematic centers.

Art center. Printed directions for making play dough were written on a chart for the art center. After following these directions, children created real or imaginary animals for a pretend zoo they designed in the block area. The children named their animals and wrote their names on index cards when they were placed in the zoo. This center encouraged skill development such as using knowledge about print when reading the recipe. Children practiced sound symbol relationships through writing the animal names on index cards. Children improved their skills at their own level in a functional context.

Music center. Children sang animal songs and the teacher wrote the words to new songs on chart paper that was displayed in the music center. The teacher encouraged the children to read or copy the charts. In this center, skills in vocabulary development were enhanced, and for the children who needed it, the relationship between oral language and written language was strengthened.

Science center. Mr. Gravois borrowed a setting hen whose eggs were ready to hatch. The class discussed the care of the hen. They started an experience chart when the hen arrived and added to it daily, recording the hen's behavior and the hatching of the eggs. They listed new vocabulary words on a wall chart and placed books about hens in the science area. Children kept journals of events concerning the hen. There were index cards in the center for children to record new "Very Own Words," relating to the hen. This center was rich in motivating experiences to develop early writing, vocabulary, and sight words.

Social studies center. Pictures of animals from different countries were placed in the social studies area along with a map highlighting where they come from. Children could match the animals to the appropriate place on the map. They also made their own books about animals around the world. During center time, Mr. Gravois helped some children identify beginning sounds by writing the animal names in their own books. He worked with other children who were conventional writers to focus more on mechanical skills of writing such as capitalization and punctuation.

Math center. Counting books that feature animals, such as *Count!* (Fleming, 1992) or *One, Two, Three to the Zoo* (Carle, 1968), were placed in the math center along with math manipulatives such as Unifix cubes. The children developed both math and literacy skills by matching the appropriate amount of manipulatives to the number names and number symbols in the books.

Dramatic play center. This area became a Pet Store. There were empty boxes of pet food, and other products for animals, all marked with prices. A Pet Supply Checklist was available for customers to decide what things they needed and how much they would cost. There were sales-slips for writing orders, receipts for purchases made, and a calculator to help figure totals. Animal magazines and pamphlets that discussed pet care were present in the store and pet posters labeled with animals' names hanging on the walls. Other materials included a sign that said OPEN one side and CLOSED on the other, with store hours posted as well. Stuffed animals were used as the pets for sale. They were placed in boxes that served as cages, labeled with their names. There were appointment cards for grooming pets and a checklist for owners to record activities necessary for maintaining a healthy pet. The environmental print and writing materials in this center provided the children a chance to practice literacy skills in a meaningful way.

Block play center. The block area became a zoo, housing animal figures, stuffed animals, and play dough animals created by the children in the art center. Children used the blocks to create cages and made labels for each animal and section of the zoo, such as "Petting Zoo," "Bird House," "Pony Rides," "Don't Feed the Animals," and "Don't Touch Us, We Bite." There were admission tickets and play money to purchase tickets and souvenirs. In many classrooms, literacy materials are not found in the block corner, but the simple addition of markers, paper, and index cards resulted in children's participation in writing activities.

Literacy center. Books and magazines about animals were highlighted on the open-faced bookshelves. The Author's Spot had animal-shaped blank books for writing animal stories. Many of the other center activities spread over into the literacy center as it became a central resource for information and materials.

Preparing the Social Environment to Develop Literacy Skills

In the whole language philosophy, social collaboration and interaction with adults and peers is an important factor for literacy learning. When children work in small groups in which social interactions are cooperative, their skill development and productivity increase (Johnson & Johnson, 1987; Slavin, 1983). Yager, Johnson, and Johnson (1985) posit two important elements in the dynamics of cooperative learning: (a) oral interaction among students, and (b) heterogeneity among group members. According to their findings, cooperative learning succeeds because it allows children to explain material to each other, to listen to each others' explanations, and to arrive at joint understandings of what they have shared.

The cooperative learning setting enables "more capable peers" to offer support to others. Cazden (1986) suggests that peer interaction allows students to attempt a range of roles they would be denied by traditional student-teacher roles. Forman and Cazden (1985) point out that learning occurs among peers when one student is observing, guiding, and correcting as another performs a task. The students accomplish more together than either could accomplish alone. Working with partners allows for similar learning opportunities as tutoring. Children engaged in task-oriented dialogue with peers can reach higher levels of understanding than they do when teachers present information didactically (Dewey, 1916).

Under what circumstances do young children socially interact in the most productive way when participating in center activities? What is the nature of the literacy and social activity that occurs? Not much research has focused on environmental contexts that promote cooperative learning with young children. Practical experience suggests that the ultimate goal for center time is for students to learn to direct their own behavior, make decisions, work together, stay on task, and be accountable for completing tasks. After many years of working with informal, moderate, and formal cooperative group structures, we have found that initially children need more formal guidelines to begin activities. With more experience, children can participate with less formal structure.

Guidelines for social collaborative activities

In setting up a social collaborative reading/writing period, students need guidelines for participating, such as: (1) Decide with whom you will work; (2) Choose the center where you wish to work; (3) Do only one or two activities in a given period; (4) Handle materials carefully; (5) Speak in soft voices; (6) Put materials back in their place before taking more; (7) Try new activities you haven't done before; (8) Work with people you haven't worked with before; (9) Stay with a group to complete tasks; (10) Record completed tasks in your log; (11) Be ready to share completed tasks with the class. It is important for teachers to remember that these guidelines take considerable time to teach and must be a focus early in the year.

Organizing cooperative learning groups.   In addition to general guidelines, rules for cooperating may include:

(1) When Working in Groups: Select a leader to help the group get started; Be sure that everyone has a job; Share materials; Take turns talking; Listen to your friends when they talk; Stay with your group.

(2) Helpful Things to Say to Group Members: I like your work; You did a good job; Can I help you?

(3) Check Your Work and How Well You Cooperated: Did you say helpful things? Did you help each other? Did you share materials? Did you take turns? Did you all have jobs? How well did your jobs get done?

When first initiating collaborative activities, some teachers assign children to centers, decide which activity they will participate in, and select leaders to organize the activity. Other teachers have children decide what activities they will do before the period begins. After participating in assigned groups with assigned activities, children can eventually make these decisions themselves, that is, choose people with whom to work, pick leaders, and select tasks. To help children select activities, a list of things to do at center time is helpful and should be reviewed.

The role of the teacher during this time is to teach procedures for using the centers, model behavior, work with individuals and small groups, and act as a facilitator in the classroom. Holdaway's (1979) view of literacy development suggests that children must first observe literacy behavior that is modeled. Next they can carry it out in a collaborative effort encouraged and assisted by an adult, and eventually continue independently. In a positive social environment for literacy learning, teachers provide modeling and scaffolding to support skill development.

Skill development during social collaborative activities

Preparing the environment for social collaborative activities allows children to engage in practicing and refining a variety of literacy skills. For example, children may write their own stories, and then prepare felt characters or a roll-movie for presenting them. Children improve reading comprehension by retelling stories in various ways, such as tape recordings, puppet shows, or dramatic presentations. The manipulative literacy materials in the centers allow the children to read and write through many different modalities and satisfy the individual learning styles of the children.

Children also engage in specific social behaviors that help improve literacy skills. They collaborate on tasks in which children help each other with reading words, coming up with ideas, or spelling. Learning also occurs through social conflicts when students disagree about spelling a word, or what should happen next in a story they are writing. According to Piaget and Inhelder (1969), this conflict enables children to study the options and negotiate a compromise or problem solve until a joint decision can be reached (Morrow, Sharkey, & Firestone, 1993).

The following observations from Mr. Gravois's room illustrate how social collaborative activities promote skill development both in literacy and in content areas.

In the **literacy center**, Jim, Patrick, and Damien were looking at books about animals as they relaxed on soft pillows, all of them clutching stuffed animals under their arms. Ivory read to Tiffany in the box called the "private spot." Tyshell and Alba used a felt board to tell the story of the *Three Billy Goat's Gruff*. Tyshell manipulated the characters and Alba told the story.

A group of children listened to a taped story of *The Little Red Hen* on headsets, tracking the print in the book as they listened. Each time they came to certain parts of the story they would chant aloud, "Not I," said the dog, "Not I," said the cat, "Not I," said the goat, and so on.

In the **social studies center**, Joseph and Marcel were making a book of animals from other countries. They used the magazine, *Ranger Rick,* to gather information. They were able to read the words *tiger* and *elephant* as they helped each other write these words in their own books. Katya and Tamar were looking through old issues of *National Geographic* magazine for animal pictures. They cut each one out, glued it on an index card, and labeled the animal's name. When they had done a few, they brought them over to the block corner where other children had begun making a zoo.

In the **music center**, three good friends were working out a rap about animals to present to the class later in the day. They were figuring out what words they could use to rhyme, and taking turns writing down what they had composed so far. Their teacher was planning to photocopy the words to their rap for the whole class to learn.

In the **science center,** Yolanda and Jovanna were discussing how the new baby chicks looked and acted. They discussed the color of the chicks and Yolanda thought they looked yellow, while Jovanna said they were more white. They argued a bit over who was right, and then called on the teacher to see what she thought. Mr. Gravois got some yellow and white items to compare the colors. Everyone agreed that they were a light yellow, or a whitish yellow color. The girls wrote their observations down in the class science journal.

Throughout the rest of the room, reading and writing materials became a natural part of the children's activities. They were able to work independently, practice needed skills, pursue their own interests, and develop a love for learning rooted in literacy. This was all possible because of the planning Mr. Gravois did in creating a supportive physical and social environment. Teachers who would like to evaluate and improve the literacy environment in their own classrooms can use the checklist in Figure 5.3 as a starting place.

Conclusion

The rich literacy environment described here allows for adult guidance and social interaction with peers. The room design promotes functional literacy through real-life experiences that are meaningful and interesting to the child (much like those described in the Dudley-Marling and Freppon & Headings chapters in this volume). It provides for the integration of literacy and content areas to add enthusiasm, motivation, and meaning. Space for personal growth is planned through direct instruction in small group and individual learning settings. Children learn independently and with peers through manipulation, exploration, and play.

The room design helps children associate literacy with enjoyment. With its appealing physical design, interesting activities, and the guidance of a competent teacher, the school environment that has been described will help children develop literacy through pleasurable, positive, and successful experiences. This will ensure a lifelong desire to refine and use literacy skills. The teacher who is dedicated to the development of literacy throughout the curriculum is like an architect who designs a learning environment that supports specific instructional strategies. Preparing a classroom for optimum literacy development includes not only instructional strategies, but also environmental planning, through the design of space and the selection and placement of materials in all content areas (Morrow, 1993).

Figure 5-3. Checklist for Evaluating and Improving the Literacy Environment.

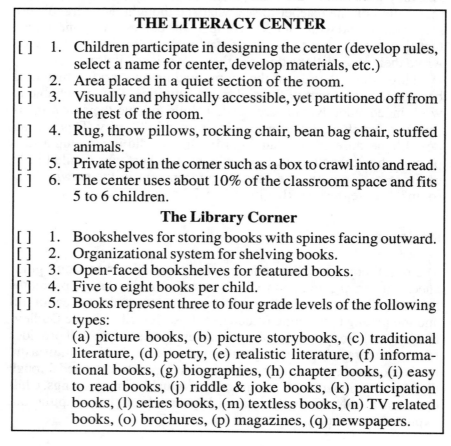

THE LITERACY CENTER

[ ] 1. Children participate in designing the center (develop rules, select a name for center, develop materials, etc.)
[ ] 2. Area placed in a quiet section of the room.
[ ] 3. Visually and physically accessible, yet partitioned off from the rest of the room.
[ ] 4. Rug, throw pillows, rocking chair, bean bag chair, stuffed animals.
[ ] 5. Private spot in the corner such as a box to crawl into and read.
[ ] 6. The center uses about 10% of the classroom space and fits 5 to 6 children.

The Library Corner

[ ] 1. Bookshelves for storing books with spines facing outward.
[ ] 2. Organizational system for shelving books.
[ ] 3. Open-faced bookshelves for featured books.
[ ] 4. Five to eight books per child.
[ ] 5. Books represent three to four grade levels of the following types:
(a) picture books, (b) picture storybooks, (c) traditional literature, (d) poetry, (e) realistic literature, (f) informational books, (g) biographies, (h) chapter books, (i) easy to read books, (j) riddle & joke books, (k) participation books, (l) series books, (m) textless books, (n) TV related books, (o) brochures, (p) magazines, (q) newspapers.

[ ]   6.   Twenty new books circulated every two weeks.
[ ]   7.   Check-out/check-in system for children to take books out daily.
[ ]   8.   Headsets and taped stories.
[ ]   9.   Felt board and story characters with related books.
[ ] 10.   Materials for constructing felt stories.
[ ] 11.   Other story manipulatives (roll-movie, puppets, etc., with related books).
[ ] 12.   System for recording books read (e.g., 3 x 5 cards hooked onto a bulletin board).

The Writing Center (The Author's Spot)

[ ]   1.   Tables and chairs.
[ ]   2.   Writing posters and bulletin board for children to display their writing themselves.
[ ]   3.   Writing utensils (pens, pencils, crayons, magic markers, colored pencils, etc.).
[ ]   4.   Writing materials (many varieties of paper in all sizes, booklets, pads).
[ ]   5.   Typewriter and/or computer.
[ ]   6.   Materials for writing stories and making them into books.
[ ]   7.   A message board for children to post messages for the teacher and students.
[ ]   8.   A place to store Very Own Words.
[ ]   9.   Folders for children to place samples of their writing.

Content Area Learning Centers

[ ]   1.   Environmental print, such as signs related to themes, directions, rules.
[ ]   2.   A calendar.
[ ]   3.   A current events board.
[ ]   4.   Appropriate books, magazines, & newspapers in all centers.
[ ]   5.   Writing utensils in all centers.
[ ]   6.   Varied types of paper in all centers.
[ ]   7.   A place for children to display their literacy work.

References

Anbar, A. (1986). Reading acquisition of preschool children without systematic instruction. *Early Childhood Research Quarterly, 1,* 69–84.

Bergeron, B. (1990). What does the term whole language mean? A definition from the literature. *Journal of Reading Behavior, 23,* 301–329.

Carle, E. (1968). *One, Two, Three to the zoo.* New York: Philomel.

Cazden, C. (1986). Classroom discourse. In M. C. Wittrock (Ed.), *The handbook of research in teaching, 3rd ed.* (pp. 432–463). NY: Macmillan.

Clark, M. M. (1976). *Young fluent readers.* Portsmouth, NH: Heinemann.

Dewey, J. (1966). *Democracy and education.* New York: Free Press. (Original work published in 1916)

Field, T. (1980). Preschool play: Effects of teacher/child ratios and organization of classroom space. *Child Study Journal, 10,* 191–205.

Fleming, D. (1992). *Count!* New York: Scholastic.

Forman, E., & Cazden, C. (1985). Exploring Vygotskian perspectives in education: The cognitive value of peer interaction. In J. Wertsch (Ed.), *Culture, communication, and cognition. Vygotskian perspectives.* Cambridge: Cambridge University Press.

Froebel, F. (1974). *The education of man.* Clifton, NJ: Augustus M. Kelly.

Goodman, K. S. (1989). Whole language research: Foundations of development. *Elementary School Journal, 90,* 207–220.

Graves, D. H. (1975). An examination of the writing process of seven-year-old children. *Research in the Teaching of English, 9,* 227–241.

Hoban, R. (1960). *Bedtime for Frances.* New York: Scholastic.

Holdaway, D. (1979). *The foundations of literacy.* Sydney: Ashton Scholastic.

Johnson, D. W., & Johnson, R. T. (1987). *Learning together and alone.* 2nd ed. Englewood Cliffs, NJ: Prentice-Hall.

Loughlin, C. E., & Martin, M. D. (1987). *Supporting literacy: Developing effective learning environments.* New York: Teachers College Press.

Mandler, J., & Johnson, N. (1977). Remembrance of things passed: Story structure and recall. *Cognitive Psychology, 9,* 111–151.

Montessori, M. (1965). *Spontaneous activity in education*. New York: Schocken Books.

Moore, G. (1986). Effects of the spatial definition of behavior settings on children's behavior: A quasi-experimental field study. *Journal of Environmental Psychology, 6 (3)*, 205–231.

Morrow, L. M. (1983). Home and school correlates of early interest in literature. *Journal of Educational Research, 76*, 221–230.

Morrow, L. M. (1990). Preparing the classroom environment to promote literacy during play. *Early Childhood Research Quarterly, 5*, 537–554.

Morrow, L. M. (1992). The impact of a literature-based program on literacy achievement, use of literature, and attitudes of children from minority backgrounds. *Reading Research Quarterly, 27*, 250–275.

Morrow, L. M. (1993). *Literacy development in the early years* (2nd ed.). Boston: Allyn and Bacon.

Morrow, L. M., & Rand, M. K. (1991a). Preparing the classroom environment to promote literacy during play. In J. Christie, (Ed.), *Play and early literacy development* (pp. 141–166). New York: SUNY Press.

Morrow, L. M., & Rand M. K. (1991b). Promoting literacy during play by designing early childhood classroom environments. *Reading Teacher, 44*, 396–402.

Morrow, L. M., Sharkey, E., & Firestone, W. A. (1993). Promoting independent reading and writing through self-directed literacy activities in a collaborative setting. *National Reading Research Center, Research Report No. 2* (pp. 1–26). Georgia & Maryland: University of Georgia and Maryland.

Morrow, L. M., & Weinstein, C. S. (1986). Encouraging voluntary reading: The impact of a literature program on children's use of library centers. *Reading Research Quarterly, 21*, 330–346.

Nash, B. (1981). The effects of classroom spatial organization on four- and five-year-old children's learning. *British Journal of Educational Psychology, 51*, 144–155.

Neuman, S., & Roskos, K. (1990). The influence of literacy-enriched play settings on preschoolers' engagement with written language. In J. Zutell and S. McCormick (Eds.), *Literacy theory and research: Analyses from multiple paradigms. Thirty-ninth yearbook of the National Reading Conference* (pp. 179–187). Chicago: NRC.

Neuman, S., & Roskos, K. (1992). Literacy objects as cultural tools: Effects on children's literacy behaviors in play. *Reading Research Quarterly, 27* (3), 202–225.

Piaget, J., & Inhelder, B. (1969). *The psychology of the child.* New York: Basic Books.

Rivlin, L., & Weinstein, C. (1984). Educational issues, school settings, and environmental psychology. *Journal of Environmental Psychology, 4,* 347–364.

Rusk, R., & Scotland, J. (1979). *Doctrines of the great educators.* New York: St. Martin's Press.

Saltz, E., & Johnson, J. (1974). Training for thematic-fantasy play in culturally disadvantaged children: Preliminary results. *Journal of Educational Psychology, 66 (4),* 623–630.

Schickedanz, J. A. (1993). Designing the early childhood classroom environment to facilitate literacy development. In B. Spodek & O. N. Saracho (Eds.), *Language and literacy in early childhood education: Yearbook in early childhood education, Vol. 4.* New York: Teachers College Press.

Slavin, R. E. (1983). Non-cognitive outcomes. In J. M. Levine & M. C. Wang (Eds.), *Teacher and student perceptions: Implications for learning* (pp. 341–366). Hillsdale, NJ: Erlbaum.

Spivak, M. (1973). Archetypal place. *Architectural Forum, 140,* 44–49.

Sutfin, H. (1980). *The effects on children's behavior of a change in the physical design of a kindergarten classroom.* Doctoral Dissertation, Boston University.

Teale, W. (1982). Toward a theory of how children learn to read and write naturally. *Language Arts, 59,* 555–570.

Yager, S., Johnson, D. W., & Johnson, R. T. (1985). Oral discussion, group to individual transfer, and achievement in cooperative learning groups. *Journal of Educational Psychology, 77,* 60–66.

Section II

Children's Development in Light of Instruction

"Never can teachers forget that, while it is useful to 'work' on pieces of the system in isolation at times, when these pieces are put back into the whole system and it is operating in process, those pieces will never look, or operate, the same as they did in the isolated work. Thus, the more the pieces can be worked on in process, *the more assured one is that the whole process will improve"* (Purcell-Gates, Chapter 6).

Teachers must understand how children develop in order to link instructional decisions to what children need. The two chapters in this section focus on children's development by highlighting children's growth in light of specific instructional strategies. In Chapter 6, Victoria Purcell-Gates describes three children with reading and writing problems and how they were tutored at Harvard University's Literacy Lab, which operates from a whole language philosophy. You will meet Lauren, a 10-year-old who could read aloud only at a primer level and who could not read silently with comprehension when she began attending the Literacy Lab. You will meet David, a fifth grader, who demonstrated a clear discrepancy between his literacy performance and his abilities. And Sam, a seven-year-old who came to the Lab with little print exposure. Interwoven with careful and extensive informal and formal assessment, the tutors instructed these children from a whole-to-part-to-whole model, using direct and explicit skill instruction when children seemed to need it and always moving back to authentic reading and writing experiences. This chapter describes how tutors worked with children on phonics, context clues, decoding, spelling, monitoring comprehension, and more. After much strategy instruction and constructive feedback, all three children made advances in their literacy learning. Through the detailed descriptions of the expert scaffolding that was conducted to help these learners, this chapter emphasizes that isolated instruction on skills must always be immediately followed with use of the skill during actual reading and writing.

Chapter 7, by Laura Klenk and Annemarie Palincsar, is a case study of one child's literacy development. Kevin is a six-year-old whose physician diagnosed him with ADHD and prescribed Ritalin. He is distractable, has a high activity level, processes information slowly, has difficulty remembering, and is impulsive. Literacy learning is difficult for him, and he often does not want to participate, even in the best instructional circumstances. His work often looks random and it does not occur in a linear fashion. Yet, through his written texts across one year and careful scaffolding by a researcher, we see his development and his success as a literacy learner. Readers can examine the milestones made by Kevin to understand early literacy development and the kind of scaffolding that enables children like Kevin to succeed. The chapter ends with suggestions that are offered to teachers of similar children.

Chapter 6

Process Teaching with Direct Instruction and Feedback in a University-based Clinic

℆ ——— ℈

Victoria Purcell-Gates
Director, Harvard Literacy Lab

Try to remember what it was like to learn to ride a bike. In addition, recall, or imagine, yourself teaching a child to ride a bike. This "bike riding" metaphor captures to a large degree the ways in which direct instruction is woven into the holistic literacy learning environment instantiated in the Harvard Literacy Lab at the Harvard Graduate School of Education. When learning to ride a bicycle, learners need to situate themselves in an authentic bike-riding environment. That is, one cannot begin to learn to ride a bicycle unless one (a) has a bike, (b) is willing to get on it, (c) has the intention to move forward in space, and (d) is located on a surface over which bikes can be, and usually are, ridden. Given the above prerequisites, most learners need to have an experienced bike rider with them to guide them through the learning process. It helps if this experienced rider is also perceptive and sensitive to ways in which learners can "go wrong" with different parts of the overall process of riding a bike so that the learner can be notified of the problem and receive suggestions for eradicating it.

The bike riding "teacher" usually begins by holding the bike steady while the learner gets on and begins to get a feel for the balancing feat required. However, as soon as possible, the teacher "pushes off" by propelling the bike forward, holding onto both the handlebars and the back of the seat upon which the learner is sitting. The degree of support needed at this point, as at all points in the learning process, derives from characteristics about the learner such as (a) experience, (b) preference for different types of support, (c) comfort level with various degrees of risk, and (d) speed of learning.

Right from the beginning, the teacher directly instructs the learner about processes he/she must engage in to "ride" as the bicycle is propelled forward: "put your feet on the pedals," "hold onto the handlebars," "move your hands so that your knuckles are on top of the bars," "keep the left foot on the pedal as it goes around," "push down with your knee as the pedal goes down," "No! Don't peddle backwards!" And so on. The teacher, in response to the actions of the learner, and interpreting those actions against her/his knowledge about how bike riding is done, provides clear, explicit instructions to the fledgling bicycler as said bicycler is *in the process of* actually trying to ride a bike.

The strong, two-handed support, or scaffold (described above), is gradually replaced by support that is diminished in response, again, to the learner's displayed ability to "stay on, up, and moving" (Vygotsky, 1978). Thus, the supporter's one-handed grip will often replace the two-handed one; the supporter may completely release the bicycle but so subtly that the rider is unaware of the change; the teacher may reduce the support to a mere presence, running along beside the new rider and shouting encouragement only to again grasp the back of the seat and the handlebars as the rider confronts an unexpected difficulty. As soon as the learner is capable of riding without support and appears to have the basic parts of the process under control, the teacher backs off, allowing experience over time with bike riding to complete the learning process.

While this metaphor can be deconstructed and/or extended in numerous directions, the important point for our purposes here is to reflect on the teaching behavior of providing clear, explicit directions, and corrections, to the learner as he/she is trying to accomplish, master, the process of interest. Reading and writing are both processes, and learning to read and write must be undertaken as one would any process: get on and try to do it. Teachers are most helpful to learners if they can provide the support called for at any given moment, perceive and respond to ways in which the learner is performing pieces of the process (while trying to accomplish the whole process), and provide feedback to the learner in ways intended to allow him/her to get on with it and gain mastery over the process, in this case reading and writing. It is this metaphor or teaching/learning that guides and describes the instruction at the Harvard Literacy Lab.

The Harvard Literacy Lab

The Literacy Lab is an integral part of the Language and Literacy program at the Harvard Graduate School of Education. Designed to provide practicum experience for graduate students enrolled in my course on diagnosis and instruction for remedial readers and writers, it accepts on a first-come, first-serve basis students in grades 1–12 who are experiencing difficulties learning to read and write in school. All of the students are self-referred by their parents, often at the recommendation of other parents and/or teachers. Graduate students work one-to-one with students for an hour twice a week. Their focus is to arrive at an in-depth understanding of the nature of the literacy difficulties experienced by their assigned students and to provide individually designed instruction for their students based upon this understanding.

Students who seek help in the literacy lab

The students who attend the Lab exhibit a variety of difficulties with reading and writing. Word recognition, decoding, comprehension, vocabulary, spelling, composition, study skills—each and all of these, alone and in varying combinations, represent areas of difficulty for the Lab students. Because of our proximity to a large number of medical centers and hospitals—each with their own clinics for children with special needs—about one third of the clientele each year at the Lab is made up of children, referred by the clinics, with diagnosed neurologically-based learning disabilities. The policy is to accept anyone whose name is placed on the waiting list, excluding no students for type of difficulty or reported prognosis of success/failure. Thus, at any one time, observers can see first and second graders who still have not focused on print and who exhibit early emergent literacy behaviors, ninth graders who cannot read beyond memorized Dr. Seuss books and who cannot write more than a few sentences with unconventional spelling and punctuation, seventh graders who like to read Judy Blume books but cannot comprehend their social studies texts, developmentally delayed ten-year-olds with neurologically-based motor and perceptual problems who have yet to read or write anything beyond letters and simple words in a workbook, and second-language learners, from both literate and nonliterate homes, who are trying to learn both the language of the United States and the language of books.

Diagnosis, assessment, and instruction in the Literacy Lab

The diagnosis and instruction in the Literacy Lab is holistic and re-flects a view of literacy acquisition that is grounded in psycholinguistic and sociolinguistic research and theory (Clay, 1991; Dyson, 1989; Goodman, Smith, Meredith, & Goodman, 1987; Harste, 1984; Purcell-Gates, 1988, 1995). In essence, this means that learners are encouraged to read and write authentic texts for authentic reasons. In the process of doing so, they are assisted by their teachers in gaining control over the various strategies needed to read and write. The theory underly-ing this program views the reading and writing processes as meaning-centered and involving synergistic transactions among the linguistic systems of syntax, semantics, graphophonics and pragmat-ics. It is only when these individual systems are working together to create meaning that the process can be said to be working efficiently, fluently, and effectively. Teachers in the Literacy Lab consider it their role to help the learners gain control of the entire process by engaging in reading and writing while attending to those systems which need work in order to make the whole move forward.

Reading and writing are taught/learned, not through a succession of isolated skill work, but, rather, in the context of the actual reading and writing of real texts. This means that the majority of the material available for instruction consists of literature, both fiction and nonfic-tion, reference materials, journals, stationery, and other materials for writing. Separate material for the teaching and learning of phonic skills is also available for teacher reference and selective use with students. Phonic skill is also taught incidentally during the reading and writing activities. The Lab teachers/tutors may pull out pieces of the process for focused work but always operate from the whole and back to the whole (the "whole" being whole texts read or written for authentic purposes). I often refer to this focusing on a piece of the process as "side-of-the-pool" activities, referring to the process of learning to swim: while it is sometimes necessary and beneficial to work on kicks or arm strokes in isolation at the side of the pool, one must apply those lessons right away to actual attempts to propel one-self through water with all of the systems working at once and synergistically in order to actually learn to swim.

Assessment and diagnosis in the Literacy Lab is both informal and formal. Standardized achievement tests are given to provide practice for the graduate students-in-training and to place the clinic students on a national norm. Assessment for instruction (diagnosis) is accom-

plished through informal measures such as informal reading invento-
ries, teacher-made informal assessments, and skilled teacher
observation during reading and writing events. These include assessments of the following: (a) attitudes, beliefs, and habits about and of
reading and writing; (b) comprehension of narrative and expository
text; (c) writing of narrative and expository texts; (d) knowledge of
graphophonemic relationships; (e) vocabulary and concept knowledge (in relation to required school reading); and (f) coordinated and
effective use of the linguistic cueing systems during reading. A recursive relationship exists between diagnosis and instruction in the Literacy
Lab. As students respond to instructional moves by their teachers,
careful note is taken of areas of difficulty, ease, frustration, or confusion. These observations form the basis of future instruction as well
as documentation of the nature of the difficulty. The assessment pro-
tocol for the Literacy Lab also includes extensive information from
parents, school records and teacher reports, observations of Lab students in their regular school contexts, and records of medical and
educational assessments performed outside of the schools or the Lab.

To illustrate the ways in which direct instruction is woven throughout the holistic literacy learning in the Lab, I have selected from our
files three Lab students who exhibited very different needs, received
focused direct instruction to meet those needs, and who have since
"graduated" with good prognosis for their futures. It is important to
keep in mind as you read these accounts that the definition of direct
instruction used in this chapter and in the Harvard Literacy Lab does
not mean mindless drill of isolated skills, but "clear, unambiguous
explanation of how one goes about reading and writing" (Purcell-
Gates, 1995). All of the teaching and learning was taking place within
the context of holistic literacy learning described above.

Lauren[1]

Lauren was almost 10 years old and in the fourth grade when she
began attending the Literacy Lab. She had a cheerful, willing-to-work
disposition, and previous teachers described her as highly social, happy,
cooperative, motivated and enthusiastic. She loved to dance and had
recently joined the city ballet corp for children.

---

[1]All of the names used in this report are pseudonyms.

Lauren exhibited severe reading and writing problems, however. On the Stanford Diagnostic Reading Test (1984), Reading Comprehension, she scored in the 7th percentile; according to the Analytical Reading Inventory (Woods & Moe, 1989), she was reading independently only at the primer level. Reports from school and close observations of her reading and writing in the Lab confirmed that she experienced severe word recognition/decoding and encoding problems. Her writing was labored, as was her oral reading. She could not read silently at all, explaining that when she did no one could help her when she had problems. She came with a family history of difficulty learning to read, a medical history indicative of oxygen deprivation at birth, and an inherited medical condition, Thalassemia Minor, a rare form of anemia which results in severe fatigue which affects attention.

Our observations confirmed the description provided by a nearby hospital educational clinic: While reading connected text, Lauren could recognize more words than she could in a word list. However, she tended to read word-by-word and did not apply contextual or syntactic cues to aid in her word recognition. Her attempts to decode words more often than not resulted in nonwords that she accepted without making attempts at self-correction so that she might attain meaning. When writing, she chose to write syntactically simple sentences, using "simple" words (for example, *I lvov my cat.*), struggling to encode them phonetically and spending an inordinate amount of time "figuring" them out. Several assessments done at the clinic suggested an overall weakness in visual memory and phonics analysis, probably due to inherited dyslexic-type difficulties, compounded by possible neurological damage at birth. At their suggestion, Lauren had been participating in structured, synthetic phonics instruction at school (Orton-Gillingham), which, according to her mother, she absolutely hated.

Focus on strengths to get going

In the Lab, we decided to work, initially, on her nonproductive pattern of reading word by word and ignoring contextual cues for word recognition. It was possible that her attempt to use only the graphophonic cueing system—her weakest—was a result of her instruction in school and was making a serious problem worse. To build fluency, and get her "going again" in the overall process of processing print to gain meaning, her teacher instituted the Repeated Reading technique (Allington, 1977; Lipson & Wixon, 1991; Samuels, 1979). For the Repeated Reading technique, a student reads and rereads a piece of challenging text until he/she reaches a predetermined level of fluency. The student's reading is timed and the teacher notes all reading errors and aided words. At the end of the reading, the number of errors and aided words are subtracted from the total number of words read and the results are graphed for the student so that the student can visually appreciate her progress. This technique increases fluency by facilitating automatic recognition of words encountered repeatedly and by the repeated presentation of those words in natural, connected text, which allows the reader to employ phrasing and intonation and improve over the readings.

Lauren chose the book *Millions of Cats* by Wanda G'ag (1928) for this activity. She showed a 78 percent increase in reading performance by the end of her third reread. At the end of the second session, Lauren showed a 61 percent reading performance increase from the fourth read to the sixth repeated reading and an 11 percent reading performance increase from the seventh read to the ninth reread on the third day. Overall, she showed a 120 percent reading rate and accuracy increase from the first to the third day.

During this first semester in the Lab, Lauren also worked to gain fluency in writing. Her relatively strong comprehension skills and experiences with stories read aloud led her on several occasions to decide to rewrite endings to stories and short books which she decided did not "make sense." During these writing activities, her teacher urged her to compose natural-sounding text, employing the invented spelling she was so good at. These texts were then rewritten with conventional spelling, with Lauren contributing to this editing process in heavily scaffolded sessions.

While space constraints prohibit a more thorough description of the many reading and writing activities Lauren participated in during this initial semester, they all were focused on encouraging her to read more on her independent reading level, working on building fluency and integrating the various strategies needed for effective reading. Her writing activities, including personal and third-person narrative, personal letters and journal writing, and an expository text on the city ballet, were all focused on increasing her fluency and complexity of written language. By the beginning of the second semester, we could document an increase in fluency and comfort in her reading and writing. This was confirmed by her classroom teacher and her mother.

Scaffolded instruction focusing on needs

In early February of this first year, Lauren appeared to go through a rapid reading growth spurt. From one session to the next, during a three-week period, she showed an increase in reading fluency and a decrease in decoding difficulties. She appeared to shift her emphasis from "word calling" to "reading for meaning." She showed an increase in using contextual clues and a decrease in reliance on phonetic decoding strategies.

Two different direct instruction techniques characterize the instruction she received this semester. For one of them, she was explicitly taught to skip an unknown word and use contextual clues to identify the word. When she began employing this strategy, she showed rapid reading improvement in the areas of fluency, fine detail recall and overall comprehension. The other technique involved scaffolded readings with both peers in the Lab and with her Lab teacher. She was paired with another child at times for peer reading. Her teacher deliberately chose a child who was reading at a slightly higher level. Lauren and her partner would alternate reading aloud from a tradebook; this activity suited both Lauren's highly social nature and need for peer interaction and her need to practice her emerging reading strategies with accessible text. With her teacher, Lauren voiced an interest in reading "adult-looking books." To accommodate this request, her teacher introduced her to Judy Blume's *Tales of a Fourth Grade Nothing* (1972). Her reading in this text was more halting than on the less challenging texts she had been using. However, with help, she appeared to be able to undertake the challenge. Over the next few months, she exhibited more self-corrections and frequently used the "skipping strategy" to identify unknown words. To further aid Lauren on this text, she and her teacher took turns reading paragraphs. At times, her teacher would encounter "unfamiliar words," or misread whole sentences which changed the meaning of the text, and would request Lauren's help in sorting out the difficulties. Lauren loved this turnabout in roles, and quickly proved adept at focusing her tutor on effective reading strategies.

Lauren ended this first year at the Lab with a notable increase in fluency and the possession of good strategies for employing all cues for the meaningful processing of text. She still had considerable difficulty with sound/symbol associations and retention of sight vocabulary for both reading and writing. Her Lab teacher noted in her final case report on Lauren that her writing was very slow and she often appeared to have difficulty "keeping up" with the pace of her thoughts as she wrote. Her performance on the alternate form of the SDRT (1984), Reading Comprehension showed little movement, with her score placing her again at the 7th percentile as compared to the national norm.

Now that we're going, strengthening the weak areas

When Lauren returned in the fall (to a "new" Lab teacher), her teachers and her mother were reporting that (a) she seemed much more relaxed and confident; and (b) her literacy problems were still evident in the areas of oral reading, decoding, and visual perceptual discrimination. In the Lab, her strength in comprehension and newly acquired strategies for integrating the cueing systems were graphically displayed in the results of the Analytical Reading Inventory (Woods & Moe, 1989) assessment. According to this assessment, although she could read words at an independent level *in isolation* only at the first grade level, she could accurately identify words and comprehend text *in narrative context* at an independent level up to the fifth grade level. Compared to her performance on this assessment, she had moved her independent reading level for narrative text reading from the primer to the fifth grade level. Her SDRT (1984), Reading Comprehension score showed no movement from the previous spring.

Based on the above, we decided the focus of instruction for her this year would be to attempt to strengthen her skill in her area of weakness: word recognition, decoding, and spelling. This would be done within the context of continued reading and writing of real texts for real reasons. In addition, we instituted an independent, silent reading schedule for Lauren, with her mother's cooperation. Lauren was to devote an increasing amount of time (we began with 10 minutes, gradually increasing this to 30) each evening reading by herself for enjoyment at her independent reading level. She was encouraged to "read out loud" to herself, if she needed to, to aid in her visual recognition of words, but this was to be an independent activity.

Each Lab session, Lauren and her teacher would select troublesome words from the texts she was reading and writing to focus upon. Many of these words were the "simple" sight words like *to, too,* and *two* or *through* and *though*; others were the multisyllabic words which were hard for her to visually process. Multimodal techniques were used to aid Lauren in mastering the words. Each word would be written on an index card, traced with colored felt pens or with her index finger as she named each letter, read the word, closed her eyes and attempted to visualize the word, letter by letter, tracing in air as she did so. These words would be added to word banks and to growing "word walls" (Cunningham, 1991) and reviewed each session.

To address the difficulty with multisyllabic words, Lauren's teacher introduced the strategy of "chunking" words to replace her tendency to sound out these words letter by letter. (Lauren revealed to her teacher that she tended to forget the beginnings of multisyllabic words while sounding out at the letter level because it takes so long to get to the end of the word!) Within the context of reading Roald Dahl's *Fantastic Mr. Fox* (1970), Lauren's teacher modeled the strategy of looking for bigger "parts" within a word and decoding at that level. Her teacher describes how Lauren then, when encountering the word *tremendous*, responded to her directive to cover all but the first part of the word, then the next, and so on. She covered all but *trem* and correctly pronounced it. She then did the same for *end* and *ous*. She then put the three parts together and read *tremendous*. The teacher reports that, from this time on, she continued to model this strategy, and Lauren began to use it spontaneously over the remainder of the term.

In the course of instruction during this year, Lauren and her teacher generated a list of specific strategies she could use when reading that would support her "weak" area of visual processing of print. This list was typed out and Lauren carried it with her:

IDEAS

1. Use finger or the back of a pen or pencil to point at the word you're saying.
2. Use an index card.
3. Chunk long words; cover parts.
4. Look at all of the letters; ends too!

Lauren's reading and writing improved dramatically over the course of this year. By the end of this second year in the Lab she was aware of her strengths and weaknesses, equipped with specific strategies to effectively read and write, and confident that she could continue to apply these strategies in the future as she continued to develop as a reader and a writer. Even her score on a standardized, timed[2] reading achievement

---

[2]Actually, given Lauren's dyslexia, which severely affected her speed of visual processing, timed tests were ruled inappropriate for her and their results considered invalid. Thus, soon after beginning at the Lab she was allowed to take all tests in an untimed mode. However, it is not possible to interpret raw scores achieved on an untimed basis on a normed standardized test so I do not report her results in the untimed conditions.

test showed impressive growth at the end of the year! She placed in the 24th percentile on the SDRT (1984), Reading Comprehension test, a movement of 17 percentile points since she began attending the Lab. She graduated from the Lab, and subsequent reports from her mother indicate that she is continuing to read and write successfully both in and out of school, with appropriate classroom support for her learning disability.

David

Unlike Lauren, David first appeared at the Literacy Lab angry, sullen, and discouraged. He was beginning the fifth grade at an open/progressive private school where the average performance of the students was well above "grade level." Previous testing at private clinics revealed a severe visual-motor difficulty which seriously affected his ability to "decode and encode" written language. An optometric evaluation reported "limited eye teaming, an inability to focus his eyes properly, and an inability to track print properly." This difficulty stood out against a background of assessed intelligence in the "very superior" range and an impressive store of background knowledge and accompanying oral vocabulary knowledge. Both of David's parents were research scientists employed at a prestigious private university.

Standardized, norm-referenced tests of reading comprehension given by the outside clinic and within the Literacy Lab placed David solidly in the average range. On the SDRT (1984), administered in the Lab, he scored in the 59th percentile. These scores were considered low, however, for someone of David's intelligence and knowledge store. The contributions of his visual-motor difficulties to his problems with reading and writing were apparent in his scores on the decoding and spelling subtests of the Wide Range Achievement Test which was administered by a private clinic the preceding year. These scores placed him in the 30th and 27th percentiles (national norms), respectively. David's teachers reported his unhappiness with literacy tasks, his unwillingness to read aloud or to write, and his difficulties with decoding and spelling words, during which he would mix up "pieces" of one word with others. They also reported that he had problems comprehending text and organizing his writing. His performance on the ARI (Woods & Moe, 1989) in the Lab placed his independent reading level at the third grade, his instructional at the fourth to fifth grades, and his frustration at the fifth to sixth grades. He performed at the eighth grade level for listening comprehension, confirming the impression that he was performing below his ability.

David's reading and writing in the Literacy Lab revealed the extent of his problems. In the beginning of the semester, he could not monitor his reading when decoding problems destroyed the meaning of the text. For example, when he read a sentence like *The boy was bored*, he would read it as *The boy was bread* and move along without realizing that this did not make sense. His tutor noted his consistent tendency to tire if a reading activity exceeded 15 minutes, after which his miscues increased dramatically. His written texts consisted of series of unconnected sentences with no beginning, middle, or end, and little organization. Spelling and punctuation problems were severe.

A few good strategies to gain momentum and build confidence

When we first met, David was understandably frustrated and depressed at his inability to read and write in accordance with his overall ability and as compared to his peers. Through perseverance and humor, his quite talented tutor broke down his resistance after four lab sessions and, from that point on, David engaged actively in the literacy activities in the Lab.

These activities focused on providing David with compensatory strategies for reading and writing and on reinvolving him in literacy activities by convincing him that all was not hopeless, that he could, by utilizing the strategies being taught, overcome, or override, his difficulties and become actively engaged in comprehending and producing written text to serve his purposes.

By utilizing a bookmark, placed under each sentence being read, David's visual tracking improved and his incidences of incorporating pieces of other words with those being read decreased. During his second semester in the Lab, David's tutor began employing the Neurological Impress Method (Heckelman, 1966, 1969), in conjunction with the visual tracking aid, which combined to improve David's ability to visually process the text. For this technique, the teacher sits slightly behind the student and reads along with him/her for not more than 10–15 minutes. Specific guidelines are recommended (Lipson & Wixson, 1991).

1. The teacher should maintain a reasonable, fluent pace of reading. The point is for the student to match the fluency of the teacher, not vice versa.
2. The teacher runs a finger smoothly along the print as it is being read.
3. The teacher does not launch a discussion of comprehension and does not use this experience to teach word recognition or word analysis strategies (p. 528).

For other oral reading events, David's tutor also limited the time to 10–15 minutes to avoid the strain on his visual system that resulted in an increase in miscues. For these oral reading activities, David chose books by Matt Christopher, Roald Dahl, and Brian Jacques over the course of the year as well as *The Velveteen Rabbit* (Williams, 1983). While he read, David's tutor would coach him in reading strategies, reminding him to "make sense"; to self-correct when he lost meaning; to think about what he was reading. Over the course of the year, he showed steady progress in monitoring the text for meaning.

David's comprehension of text read both silently and orally also improved through activities such as Reciprocal Questioning (ReQuest), Question-Answer Relationships (QARs), and Self-Monitoring Approach to Reading (SMART). ReQuest (Manzo, 1969) helps the reader learn to formulate questions and set purposes for reading. David and his tutor would both read silently from text (which was often assigned by his school). Once they had finished, they would take turns asking questions of the other about the text. They did this with varying units of text: a sentence, a paragraph, a "section," or a heading.

Working with his tutor, David, with the QARs (Raphael, 1982, 1986) activity, learned to recognize the relationships between comprehension questions and their answer sources (Pearson & Johnson, 1978): (a) information explicit in the text; (b) information which can be inferred from the text by putting together different parts of the text; and (c) information which can only be constructed by referring to personal knowledge. David found this strategy extremely useful for his school-assigned readings and projects.

Using the SMART (Vaughan & Estes, 1986) technique, David's tutor also taught him, as he read along in text, to keep track of his ongoing comprehension by either putting a check mark in the margin, indicating that he understood, or a question mark to flag confusion. David would then go back and explain in his own words the concepts, or ideas, that he understood. For those areas flagged with question marks, David's tutor, through modeling, coaching, and gradual release of support, taught him to reread, identify the problem (for example, whether it lay with a particular unknown word or in a relationship between words or ideas), and generate ways to deal with the problem(s), such as using a dictionary, rereading the text, or asking for help.

David also worked hard to become a writer. Every lab session included uninterrupted journal writing, where fluency was stressed. In addition, David worked with his tutor on a series of writing events. He produced an autobiographical essay as an outgrowth of the common Lab practice of composing written "introductory descriptive paragraphs" to accompany Polaroid photos taken at the beginning of each academic year and posted around the Lab for all to see, read, and learn about each other—students as well as tutors. As David worked on his essay, his tutor helped him to produce a semantic map (a way of organizing ideas on paper visually so that relationships and interconnections among them can be seen) to structure it, and provided ongoing instruction on organizing writing into sentence and paragraph forms. Other writing activities, all of them incorporating this type of coaching/instruction, included the rewriting of a classic fairy tale, and writing letters to NASA requesting information.

During his second semester in the Lab, David collaborated with another student, who was also in the fifth grade, on a research project that involved both reading and writing. Three sessions were used for this collaborative process, with both boys sharing ideas and supporting each other during the initial writing stage through the final editing. In addition, a computer was used to aid them in their collaboration and to help them edit the final text.

Throughout these writing activities, David's significant spelling problems were addressed via several approaches. David's tutor provided direct instruction for common patterns of spelling difficulty. These included words ending in the suffix -tion and silent -e, homonym pairs, contractions, and the pluralization of certain nouns (for example, glasses, taxes, wishes). All of these patterns of difficulty emerged in the process of the writing activities and involved words David wished to use in his written texts.

In addition to the direct instruction, David's tutor also prepared a Spelling Notebook for him to use for problem words. Throughout the year, David added to this notebook, organized alphabetically like a dictionary, and increasingly relied upon it during his writing activities. He also used it at school and at home for his schoolwork. Finally, David learned to use the spell-check in the word processing program he was using in the Lab, and his parents soon provided him with a computer and word processing program at home.

By the end of the year, David had improved both his reading and writing. His parents and teachers reported a real increase in his *willingness* to read and write as well as a noted improvement in his *ability* to do so. Improved spelling was noted by his teacher, his parents, and his tutor in the Lab. He was now writing organized, informative texts, and felt empowered, with the aid of his mapping strategies, to continue to do so. Post testing on an alternate form of the SDRT (1984), Reading Comprehension, placed him in the 7th stanine, 79th percentile, a growth of 20 percentiles as compared to his showing in the fall. We all felt that he was now reading and writing at levels much closer to his intellectual abilities. His visual difficulties continued unabated, however, as evidenced in his continuing to tire visually after about 15 minutes of print-focused work. We recommended that he return to the optometrist for renewed visual therapy because it had apparently helped in the past.

Sam

Sam's history differed radically from Lauren's and David's. We first heard about Sam when we received a referral form from his great-aunt, who wrote:

> When my grandnephew, Sam, came to live (with me) last December (2 days before Xmas break) he was placed in 1st grade because he was six on 09-09-92. However, Sam was in Kindergarten in (a southern city). Consequently, he didn't know all of the alphabet. He worked hard. But now he is placed in (a) learning disabled homeroom with 7 others and allowed to go to a 1st grade class for art and music only. Yesterday, I asked that he be placed with 2nd grade or 1st grade all day and be provided with a reading tutor like last year. Please help Sam.

According to his great-aunt, Sam was physically abused, neglected, and abandoned by his mother for months at a time, and she left him with relatives in several states. Both his mother and his father were substance abusers, and his father was currently in jail. The summer after he came to live with his great-aunt (and just prior to beginning at the Literacy Lab), he was hospitalized in a psychological evaluation center for 10 days. A psychiatric evaluation conducted three months earlier had diagnosed moderate to severe emotional and conduct disturbance with Post Traumatic Stress Disorder indicated as "very possible." By the time we saw him at the Lab, Sam was seven years old and involved in both group and individual therapy.

Before he came to live with his great-aunt, Sam had virtually no exposure to print or books. Personnel at his school reported that when he first enrolled, he did not know the names of the letters or how to hold a book. His aunt's home, however, was rich with literacy materials and activities. His home now included children's and adults' magazines, children's and adults' fiction and nonfiction books, newspapers, and work- and church-related literature. His great-aunt read and wrote for many and various purposes and reported reading daily to Sam from fairy tales, Dr. Seuss books, and books directed at older audiences, such as *Sounder* (Armstrong, 1969) and *Of Mice and Men* (Steinbeck, 1937)!

Sam had made a great deal of progress in his literacy development since he had moved in with his great-aunt. However, because of his emotional and cognitive state when he first appeared at his new school (and was placed ahead by one grade because of his age), school personnel had diagnosed him as learning and emotionally disabled and placed him in a special class where the extreme difficulties of the other children precluded further literacy progress. As his great-aunt worked to remedy this at his school, we set about to move him toward independence as a reader and a writer.

At the Literacy Lab, we evaluated Sam's knowledge of reading and writing through the battery of assessments in Clay's *The Early Detection of Reading Difficulties* (1979). This included the Concepts of Print Test, the Letter Identification Score Sheet, the "Ready to Read" Word Test, the Dictation Test, and the Writing Vocabulary Test. Our assessment also included careful observation by his tutor as she engaged him in reading and writing activities. In general, Sam looked like a beginning reader/writer on all of these assessments: he scored in the 4th stanine on the Concepts About Print Test (normed on 282 urban children, ages 6:0 to 7:0 in 1978), experiencing difficulties mainly with punctuation and within word alterations; he could identify all of the letters in the alphabet; he knew some simple sight words; and spelled either by memory or with advanced invented spelling strategies, utilizing letter names for sounds for only a few phonemes. His tutor diagnosed a strength in identifying beginning and ending consonant sounds in writing words and a weakness in representing vowel sounds.

Sam's dominant reading strategy was to identify words as wholes, using both semantic and syntactic cueing systems, and only rarely utilizing the graphophonic one. When he encountered a word not in his reading vocabulary, his first response was to substitute a word that seemed to fit both semantically and syntactically. Because he was reading simple, predictable books in the lab, he was able to draw on his memory for much of his reading. On the few occasions that he did employ graphophonic knowledge, he attended only to the first letter of the word. He rarely produced semantically inappropriate miscues, and the majority of his syntactic-impacting miscues were related to his dialect.

Careful consideration of the assessment and observational data led us to conclude after several weeks that Sam, at this point, understood almost all of the functional and language-specific concepts related to the reading process. The piece of the picture he was now ready to learn, and needed to learn, was the role of graphophonics in the processing of print. Thus, his tutor set out to help him do this.

Every session with Sam involved rereading familiar books, reading new, but predictable books, a focused lesson on vowel sounds, endings sounds, or sight words, and the application of these skills in the context of a writing activity that related to one or more of the books he had just read. Sam loved games, and his tutor presented most of the direct instruction of graphophonics in a game-like context. A typical lesson went like this: Sam's tutor would read to him from simple, predictable books. Following this, she would present him with sentence strips from the story and ask him to order them to match the sequence in the book (Ekwall & Shanker, 1985). He would then read them back and reorder them as needed. As he proceeded with this activity, his tutor would coach him with thoughts about logical order, references back to the story, cause and effect, and so on. Following this, Sam would read to his tutor from several books he had chosen from a pre-selected group. His tutor would make careful note of patterns of difficulties. This reading would generally be followed by a phonics or word analysis game. One game that Sam engaged in many times was "WordMaker," which his tutor had devised. Utilizing a tagboard sleeve/letter holder and pre-selected consonants and vowels printed on tagboard cards, Sam would compete with his tutor in making real words (Cunningham, 1991). The pre-selection of the letters allowed his tutor to focus on noted patterns of difficulties Sam had encountered in his reading and writing. Following the focused phonics work, Sam would usually engage in different writing activities, such as preparing directions for a fortune hunt that he would present to either another child in the Lab or to one of the supervisors.

While Sam's focus and reading and writing behaviors varied some-what across sessions due to physical and/or emotional fatigue (related to his therapy session for the most part), he quickly began to make dramatic progress. His tutor reported that a "diagnosis" was almost impossible to formulate because his abilities underwent such rapid change from session to session. "You can literally see him learning to read and write within one session."

By the close of the first semester, Sam had impressive advances in his reading and writing. He was capable of independent reading at an advanced first grade level. Both his reading and his writing revealed evidence of his increased knowledge of sound/symbol(s) relationships, both consonants *and* vowels. He had been removed from the special needs classroom and was functioning relatively well within a regular first grade room, with resource room sup-port. We expected to continue working with him, and we recommended continued exposure to written stories, with a focus on comprehension and vocabulary. We also recommended contin-ued focus on the graphophonic system and the modeling of a variety of reading strategies. However, several life circumstances led Sam's aunt to move from the city at this time, taking Sam with her. She was pleased with his progress, though, and vowed to continue providing Sam with literacy instruction that incorporated our many suggestions.

Whole-to-Part-to-Whole: A Theoretical Frame for Process Learning

The three case studies just described illustrate the ways in which di-rect skill instruction can be incorporated within a holistic literacy program for learners who are experiencing problems learning to read and/or write. The theory upon which this program rests embodies several learning principles: (a) Language is learned as it is used to fulfill meaningful, authentic functions and cannot be learned for its own sake, in isolation from function; (b) The components (sounds, syntax, semantics, pragmatics) of language are learned as they trans-act synergistically during authentic use, not separately to mastery; (c) Language develops through social interaction; and (d) Language de-velopment proceeds recursively in an expanding variety of contexts, not from simple to higher order sequentially (Bakhtin in Todorov, 1984; Goodman, et al., 1987; Harste, 1984; Rhodes & Dudley-Marling, 1988; Vygotsky, 1978).

Most helpful for teachers in such a program is the notion of the synergistic workings of the pieces of a process. Never can the teachers forget that, while it is useful to "work" on pieces of the system in isolation at times, when these pieces are put back into the whole system and it is operating in process, those pieces will never look, or operate, the same as they did in the isolated work. Thus, the more the pieces can be worked on *in process,* the more assured one is that the whole process will improve.

The assessment/diagnostic component of the Literacy Lab program allows us (a) to view the children against their age peers to the limited extent allowed by normed achievement tests and (b) to obtain a wide view of individual learners as they engage in the processes of reading and writing for different purposes across different contexts. The focus of these assessments is to discover the parts of the process that are and are not working well. This allows us to direct the learner toward abandoning his/her dysfunctional beliefs and strategies and to maintain and adopt those that will allow for further development.

The practice of providing direct and clear feedback to the learners regarding the ways in which they are employing both effective and ineffective strategies for reading and writing is key to this program. Again, the bike riding metaphor brings this home. In the clinic, as the learner reads and writes, the teacher provides such feedback as "that doesn't make sense," "you spell the number 2 as 't-w-o,' not 't-o-o,'" or "you need to put a comma after the 'Dear John' in a letter." The learner is not left to "discover" the rules at this point. Rather, the teacher is there as a coach and a facilitator, observing him/her, and providing relevant information and instruction at the time it is needed with proficiency as the goal.

Holistic clinic literacy instruction with direct, learner-centered, strategy teaching is engaging and effective. The learners read and write—often for the first time—real texts for their own purposes. They are supported as they do this by knowledgeable teachers who can tell them which dysfunctional strategies to abandon and provide them with effective strategies to enable them to get on with the process of reading and writing.

References

Allington, R. (1977). If they don't read much how they ever gonna get good? *Journal of Reading, 21,* 57–61.

Armstrong, W. H. (1969). *Sounder.* New York, NY: Harper & Row.

Blume, J. (1972). *Tales of a fourth grade nothing.* South Holland, IL: Yearling Books.

Clay, M. M. (1979). *The early detection of reading difficulties,* third edition. Aukland, New Zealand: Heinemann.

Clay, M. M. (1991). *Becoming literate: The construction of inner control.* Aukland, New Zealand: Heinemann.

Cunningham, P. M. (1991). *Phonics they use: Words for reading and writing.* New York, NY: HarperCollins.

Dahl, R. (1970). *Fantastic Mr. Fox.* New York, NY: Puffin Books.

Dyson, A. (1989). *Multiple worlds of child writers: Friends learning to write.* New York: Teachers College Press.

Ekwall, E. & Shanker, J. L. (1985). *Teaching reading in the elementary school.* Columbus, OH: Charles E. Merrill.

Ga'g, W. (1928). *Millions of Cats.* New York, NY: Coward-McCann.

Goodman, K., Smith, E. B., Meredith, R., & Goodman, Y. M. (1987). *Language and thinking in school.* New York, NY: Richard C. Owen.

Harste, J. (1984). Examining our assumptions: A transactional view of literacy and learning. *Research in the Teaching of English, 18,* 84–108.

Heckelman, R. G. (1966). Using the neurological impress remedial technique. *Academic Therapy Quarterly, 1,* 235–239.

Heckelman, R. G. (1969). Neurological impress method of remedial reading instruction. *Academic Therapy Quarterly, 4,* 277–282.

Lipson, M. Y., & Wixson, K. K. (1991). *Assessment and instruction of reading disability: An interactive approach.* New York, NY: HarperCollins.

Manzo, A. V. (1969). The request procedure. *Journal of Reading, 13,* 123–126.

Pearson, P. D., & Johnson, D. (1978). *Teaching reading comprehension.* New York, NY: Holt, Rinehart & Winston.

Purcell-Gates, V. (1988). Lexical and syntactic knowledge of written narrative held by well-read-to kindergartners and second graders. *Research in the Teaching of English, 22,* 128–160.

Purcell-Gates, V. (1995). *Other people's words: The cycle of low literacy.* Cambridge, MA: Harvard University Press.

Raphael, T. E. (1982). Question-answering strategies for children. *The Reading Teacher, 36,* 186–190.

Raphael, T. E. (1986). Teaching question-answer relationships, revisited. *The Reading Teacher, 39,* 516–522.

Rhodes, L. K. & Dudle-Marling, C. (1988). *Readers and writers with a difference.* Portsmouth, NH: Heinemann.

Samuels, S. J. (1979). The method of repeated reading. *The Reading Teacher, 32,* 403–408.

Stanford diagnostic reading test. (1984). San Antonio, TX: The Psychological Corporation.

Steinbeck, J. (1937). *Of mice and men.* Toronto: Bantam Books.

Todorov, T. (1984). *Michail Bakhtin: The dialogical principle.* Minneapolis, MN: The University of Minnesota Press.

Vaughan, J. L., & Estes, T. H. (1986). *Teaching reading in the elementary school.* Columbus, OH: Charles E. Merrill.

Vygotsky, L. S. (1978). *Mind in society.* Cambridge, MA: Harvard University Press.

Williams, M. (1983). *The velveteen rabbit.* Boston, MA: David R. Godine.

Woods, L. M. & Moe, A. J. (1989). *Analytical reading inventory, fourth edition.* Columbus, OH: Merrill.

Chapter 7

Learning to Write in a Primary Special Education Class

Laura Klenk
University at Buffalo, State University of New York
Annemarie S. Palincsar
University of Michigan

Imagine that you are brought to a field and told to run as fast as you can from one spot on the field to the next; sometimes when you arrive at the next spot you are told to keep running after you have reached your purported destination—only to be told to then return to the destination; at other times you are told to come to an immediate, jarring stop at the spot; and, yet again, at other times you are told to hurl yourself at the target spot. Imagine that you engage in these mysterious exercises day in and day out over a number of months. At first there is some satisfaction in achieving speed, or hurling yourself in less painful ways, but in time, your interest in these seemingly pointless activities begins to wane. You perform only to be compliant and you invest as little of yourself in these actions as is necessary.

Now imagine the same routine, except that punctuating these sessions are opportunities to "play ball." With the experience of playing even a few games behind you, the intermittent practice sessions take on a whole new sense of purpose; as you practice you can feel the heat of the pitcher as she chases your heels to first base and, mustering every bit of strength you have, you tear through the base. Staging a steal from second base, you leap—arms outstretched and propelling the rest of your body—to hug third base. With each experience, the mystery fades, replaced by a set of personal goals and expectations regarding your performance.

We use this scenario to illustrate the difference between learning out of context and learning through practical action. In this chapter, we want to take you on a journey with a young student named Kevin who, while he has been inundated with activities related to using print, has never had the opportunity to—metaphorically speaking—"play ball." The purpose of our journey with Kevin was to help him make connections between putting symbols on paper—an activity with which he was extremely familiar—and using writing to communicate. Our retelling of this journey is guided by multiple goals, which include describing (a) Laura's (the first author) attempts to recruit Kevin to this journey and sustain his engagement, (b) Kevin's cognitive and affective responses to these invitations, and (c) the tools and constructs that we used to understand and describe Kevin's progress on this journey and to guide instructional decision making.

Before we begin the story of Kevin and Laura's journey, we want to present a few principles that have guided our thinking about the instruction of writing with young learners who are experiencing school-related difficulties. The first principle we have adopted in our work with Kevin, and children like Kevin, is that writing must be understood and approached as a developmental process. From this perspective, we are reminded that writing is initially an act of play and not an act of remembering or representing. Typically, children at the ages of two and three, while they may grasp the outward manifestations of writing, even emulating forms of writing that they have seen adults engage in, are unable to relate to writing as a tool or as a means toward some end. As children make the transition to using writing for mnemonic purposes, they may adopt forms of writing (for example, scribbles, shapes, and lines) that look less like the conventional ways of writing with which they have been playing but which are meaningful to the child as ways of representing or recording ideas. Most children who are about to enter school, where they will be formally introduced to symbolic alphabetic writing, understand the instrumentality of print. While it may be a few years before the child uses conventional forms, the child is aware that he or she can use signs to communicate (Gundlach, 1982; Luria, 1929).

This awareness is a critical dimension of writing development and one that we find ourselves particularly concerned about when we consider the writing development of children who are experiencing developmental delays. Often, when children enter school, the emphasis is on manipulating written language as a code, rather than the purposeful uses of writing. The rationale for this practice is not hard to appreciate; the hope is that by the time the child has matured to the point of using writing in authentic ways, she or he will have mastered the tools of writing, and will have acquired a sense of the conventions and logic of writing. For youngsters with developmental delays, this process of mastering the code may be a protracted one; furthermore, the child may be pursuing this mastery without any appreciation for its usefulness in achieving personal goals. As we discuss Kevin's engagement in print activities, we will highlight these developmental issues and describe how we attempt to accommodate his current understandings and uses of print, while at the same time nudging him to more complete understandings and uses of print.

In addition to a developmental perspective, our work has been greatly influenced by a sociocultural perspective (Cole, 1993; Cook-Gumperz, 1986). This perspective reminds us that children don't become writers by simply observing this activity going on about them but rather by experimenting with writing, by becoming active participants in a community that uses writing for a broad array of purposes that promote making meaning and sharing meaning with others. This perspective has been especially useful in designing contexts in which children with developmental delays might become writers. As we describe Kevin's journey, we will describe our successes and challenges in establishing contexts where Kevin could experience writing in social and interactive ways, such as through the use of writing conferences and author's chair. Furthermore, we will depict the role of teacher as one of assisting performance (Tharpe & Gallimore, 1989), supporting Kevin's efforts and guiding him to more refined uses of writing.

Kevin is one of a number of special education students with whom we have conducted literacy research. Two primary goals provided the motivation for this research. First, we sought to describe, from an emergent literacy perspective, how young children identified as learning disabled learn to read and write. Second, and in collaboration with special education teachers, we sought to investigate effective literacy instruction for these children, based on the principles described above.[1] In the first portion of this chapter, we describe the specific context in

[1]The study reported in this paper was conducted as part of a program of research funded by a grant (#H023C90076) awarded by The Office of Special Education Programs to Annemarie Palincsar and Carole Sue Englert, co-principal investigators, Taffy Raphael, and James Gavelek.

which this research occurred, focusing on the nature of literacy activities in this context. We describe some of the procedural aspects of introducing new contexts for literacy learning in this setting. We then introduce Kevin, sharing the kinds of information traditionally collected on children identified as learning disabled, as well as assessment information that has been guided by a developmental perspective. The final portion of the chapter characterizes "the journey."

Context. This study took place in a self-contained special education class with seven children, six to eight years old, in grades one and two. Most of the children had been identified as learning disabled or developmentally delayed in preschool or kindergarten. Their difficulties in school ranged from mild to severe delays in social, cognitive, speech/language, and motor development. The children received reading instruction from the special education teacher individually or in pairs, based on their placement in the preprimer levels of a basal reading series. Whether judged by conventional or emergent literacy standards, these youngsters had fallen behind their age peers in literacy acquisition.

Introducing writing. We began the project by situating writing activities in a socially meaningful context: the newspaper. For two weeks, the special education teacher led class explorations and discussions of local newspapers. She and Laura explained to the children that they could learn from the paper even if they could not read the words, and we encouraged them to talk about what they saw in the newspapers. The children identified advertisements, sports reports, weather maps, the television guide, and other features of newspapers. As they shared with the class their discoveries, the children related newspaper features to their own lives—telling us about the television shows they liked to watch, or about shopping trips to stores, and so on. The class also took a field trip to the local newspaper office where they observed many facets of newspaper production, such as reporters working at their computers, the paper folding machine, and the news wire machine.

Following this introduction to the newspaper, Laura demonstrated for the children steps in story writing, including the generation of ideas for potential story topics, planning the composition, and thinking aloud as we made spelling decisions. To involve the children more actively in these demonstrations, she solicited their ideas for possible spellings ("birthday—what sound does birthday start with?"). Along with the teacher, she emphasized to the children that they could write stories even if they did not know how to spell all the words.

Following these demonstrations, each child was given a steno pad, or "News Book." The teacher explained that they would have time to write their own news every day. Weekly sharing sessions were instituted, during which time the children took turns coming to the "Author's Chair" at the front of the class to read the news they had written during that week. Our goal for the sharing time was to establish the foundation for a community of writers. Most often, the children were free to write about any topic of their choosing. At other times the teacher assigned topics based on themes from their content area classes such as the solar system, Black History, meal worms, dinosaurs, and book reports, among others. Twice during the school year, we published a class newspaper. The children practiced reading their stories to each other, and later shared the newspaper with students and teachers in other classes.

Scaffolding. In addition to conducting writing demonstrations for the whole class, Laura worked with the children individually to support, or scaffold, their attempts to write stories. According to sociohistorical theory (Vygotsky, 1978) scaffolding refers to assistance that is offered to a child in the context of a holistic, social activity. That is, the activity—in this case story writing—is approached as a complete task rather than being broken down into discrete parts, such as handwriting or spelling practice. The adult assists the child as necessary to complete the task. Laura's decisions in scaffolding were adjusted to meet the individual needs of the children. To illustrate these principles and the developmental progression we witnessed during the course of the school year, we present a case study of Kevin, one youngster in this class. We have chosen Kevin's case study for two reasons. First, his profile is a classic textbook case of a child with a specific learning disability, both in terms of his performance in school and on traditional psychoeducational assessments, displaying a severe discrepancy between his perceived average ability and the severe delays in his acquisition of academic skills (for cases of children with similar profiles, see Purcell-Gates, this volume). Second, the painfully slow progress made by Kevin in writing over the course of the school year affords a poignant but realistic case from which we will discuss the dilemmas encountered by teachers when making instructional decisions for children with significant learning problems, and will illustrate, in slow motion, milestones in his writing development. These illustrations are particularly relevant, we feel, given the current trend of inclusion models for serving children with learning problems, in which general education teachers are becoming increasingly responsible for the instruction of children such as Kevin.

We begin with a review of Kevin's history in school, based on the information contained in his special education records. Then we describe Kevin's participation in our year-long project, with a detailed analysis of his writing development. We note here that we did not read Kevin's special education files until the end of the school year, in order to avoid prejudgments based on information in the file.

Kevin. Kevin was seven years old and just beginning grade one in the special education class when we first met him. Kevin's history in school is typical for young children in special education. He had been diagnosed as exhibiting Attention Deficit Disorder with Hyperactivity (ADHD) when he was four years old and in preschool. Ritalin was prescribed to control the hyperactivity. Despite the medical treatment and two years of attendance in a special education preschool program, Kevin was not successful in kindergarten. He was retained for a second year, during which he was referred to his school district's Multidisciplinary Evaluation Team (MET) to determine whether or not he was eligible for special education services. The primary concerns were summed up by his kindergarten teacher as: distractibility, high activity level, slowness processing information, difficulty remembering letters and numbers, and impulsivity (which his teachers regarded as "unintentional").

Based on information in the kindergarten teacher's referral, a complete battery of psychoeducational and speech/language assessments was administered by members of the MET. Kevin's chronological age at the time of testing was six years three months. He obtained average or low-average scores on tests of cognitive ability (WISC-R), and general academic knowledge (Woodcock Johnson-R). However, his performance on all of the skills sections (letter identification, applied problems, and dictation) were deficient. He could write his name and recognize colors, but he knew only one letter and could only count to four. The psychologist concluded that "Dealing visually and auditorily with symbolic content is very difficult for Kevin." Results of a speech and language assessment were also mixed, but the examiner concluded that Kevin's speech and language skills were "appropriate to his cognitive ability," and thus he did not qualify for speech/language services. However, the MET concluded that Kevin was eligible for learning disability services due to the "severe discrepancy between [Kevin's] average ability and deficient achievement."

When we met Kevin, he was anything but hyperactive. His blank facial expression gave the impression of a child who was emotionally and cognitively disengaged. In psychological terms, he displayed a flat affect. Kevin was reluctant to speak in class. He rarely volunteered comments or answers, and, when called on, Kevin spoke in a whisper that was difficult to hear, even in face-to-face conversations. We audiotaped many of our sessions with the children in this class, but even when the microphone was placed within inches of Kevin's mouth, his voice was usually inaudible on the tape. Kevin seemed to lack self-confidence, shielding his journal and seatwork with one arm, effectively hiding his efforts from curious adults. During independent seatwork time, he frequently sought assistance from the teacher or a child seated near him for directions on completing each step of the daily assignments. Kevin was also reluctant to participate in sharing his weekly news from the "Author's Chair," often stating that he was "not done yet" with his stories. As the other children took turns sharing their news, Kevin would hastily add to what he had written earlier during the week. He was often the last child to read during these sessions, and he relied on the teacher to first read what we had dictated from his writing. He would repeat after the teacher in a hushed voice. Because of his passivity, we found it easy to overlook this verbally and physically subdued youngster in group activities.

Despite his lack of confidence regarding school work and his passivity during group instruction and independent work time, Kevin was not socially isolated. He enjoyed building Lego constructions with his classmates during free time, and his athletic skills surpassed most of his age-mates, making him a popular playmate on the school playground.

Literacy Profile. In mid-September, we administered several emergent reading and writing tasks to Kevin, in order to learn about his knowledge of print. On Clay's (1979) *Concepts of Print Test,* Kevin demonstrated appropriate book-handling behaviors (directionality for page turns and following print), but his knowledge of specific print features was nonexistent. He lacked basic literacy concepts such as speech-to-print match, and he was unable to identify punctuation marks, match upper- and lower-case letters, or isolate letters and words in a short line of text. When asked to "Write all the words you know," Kevin produced only one word—his name. Unlike many younger children, Kevin could not spell "mom," "dad," or his brother's name. He was not able to identify any sight words on a preprimer word list, nor was he able to make any letter-sound matches on a dictation test.

With regard to alphabet knowledge, Kevin identified only eight upper-case letters (A, K, W, B, O, E, V, T) when the letters were presented out of sequence. Kevin was completely reliant on singing the "A-B-C song" to complete this task. When he lost his place, he would go back to the beginning of the song and start over. Even so, most of the letters he recognized were in either his first or last name. When presented with the lower-case letters, Kevin simply followed the alphabet sequence without regard to the presentation of the letters. When he came to the "x, y, and z" phrase in the song, he pointed to a letter as he said "and," as if this word were another letter in the sequence. Interestingly, he did associate some upper-case letters with the names of his classmates. Ferreiro (1986) and others have observed that preschool children often claim a single letter to represent a person whose name begins with that letter. That Kevin could make these associations but still not identify all of these letters out of sequence demonstrates the inconsistency in his literacy development.

Two additional emergent literacy tasks, Sulzby's (1985, 1989) emergent storybook reading and story writing, were presented to Kevin. In the first case, we asked him to read *Curious George Rides a Bike* (H. A. Rey, 1952), a story that the special education teacher had read to the class. Kevin's independent reenactment of *Curious George* was based solely on the illustrations; he neither pointed to nor focused his eyes on the print. Most episodes of the story were briefly retold in words that were "similar to the original text" (Sulzby, 1985). His intonation, in Sulzby's terms, was distinctly oral ("telling the story" as opposed to "reading the story"), indicating that Kevin possessed little tacit knowledge of written language patterns. This reenactment is not atypical for preschoolers and children in kindergarten, but for a child of Kevin's age and school experience, it indicates an immature understanding of written language.

With regard to writing development, Kevin's first original story (see Figure 7-1) is a "prephonemic" composition (Temple, Nathan, Temple, & Burris, 1993); that is, Kevin did not yet display any under-standing of the connections between phonology (sounds) and orthography (spelling). He wrote instead with random strings of let-ters that contained many repetitions of the letter "B," along with elements of his name (E, V, i, n) and some numerals. The erasures indicate that Kevin was concerned about the appearance of his text. An interesting feature of this writing is Kevin's use of dash-like marks to separate some of the letters. In our first demonstration of "kid writing," we explained to the children that, if they were unsure of what letter to write, they could draw a line. This strategy is helpful to children who are spelling phonemically, as it allows them to move along when they get stuck on a spelling. It is possible that Kevin remembered the strategy, though it does not appear again in any other writings he produced, perhaps because it did not yet serve a functional purpose for him. Kevin's story confirmed what the other measures showed—he demonstrated a stable sense of directionality, beginning each line on the left side, and moving from the top to the bottom of the page. This writing shows as well that Kevin lacked a knowledge of specific print features, that he did not yet have a stable concept of word, and he was unable to match letters with sounds. Given that letter identification, speech-to-print match, and phonemic awareness are important prerequisites to conventional literacy (Bryant, 1990; Temple, et al., 1993; Walsh, Price, & Gillingham, 1988), the results of this assessment suggested that, despite four years of instruction in preschool and kindergarten, Kevin's development as a reader and writer was severely delayed.

Traditionally, literacy instruction for learning disabled children such as Kevin has focused on improving their perceptual and motor skills. Authentic reading and writing activities are often postponed until the children demonstrate a mastery of handwriting, phonic skills, decoding, and spelling. For example, Kevin's prior experiences with school literacy had been limited to copying short poems from the chalkboard and tracing or copying letters on worksheets. The intent of our writing project in Kevin's class was to provide meaningful literacy activities through which the children could acquire basic print concepts and skills as they simultaneously discovered the social and communica-

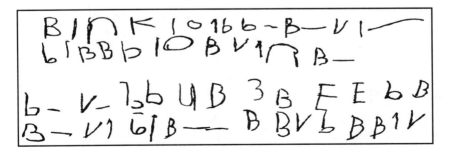

Figure 7-1.   September. Kevin's first original writing, random letters with elements of Kevin's name: "Dogs jumping on a hoop. This is a circus here. They have dogs here."

tive functions of literacy. We now turn to Kevin's participation in the project, to document his progress in writing and our attempts to support his efforts.

Response to writing activities. As "news writing" became part of the morning routine in Kevin's class, he began to experiment with printed forms, some days producing tall letters that filled the page, other days producing fat "bubble" (outlined) letters. He continued to rely on the letters in his name—along with "B," to fill the pages of his newsbook. A selection from late October, seen in Figure 7-2, shows several rows of repeated letters, along with the names of some of Kevin's classmates, copied from the nametags that were taped to the desks. Name lists were frequently written by all of the children in the class. Kevin varied the size and shape of the letters he printed, as in Figure 7-3, which he began with thick, filled-in letters, then completed with three-inch-tall letters. In addition to writing names of friends and producing strings of random letters, Kevin also practiced copying from the chalkboard. In Figure 7-4, from mid-November, we see that he has copied the date and month. We did not encourage or discourage copying; over time, a greater variety of letters began to show up in Kevin's daily newsbook entries.

Figure 7-2. Late October. Random letters and letter-like forms. Names of classmates copied from nametags: Jimmy, Mia, Brandon.

Figure 7-3. November. Kevin experiments with letter shapes and size.

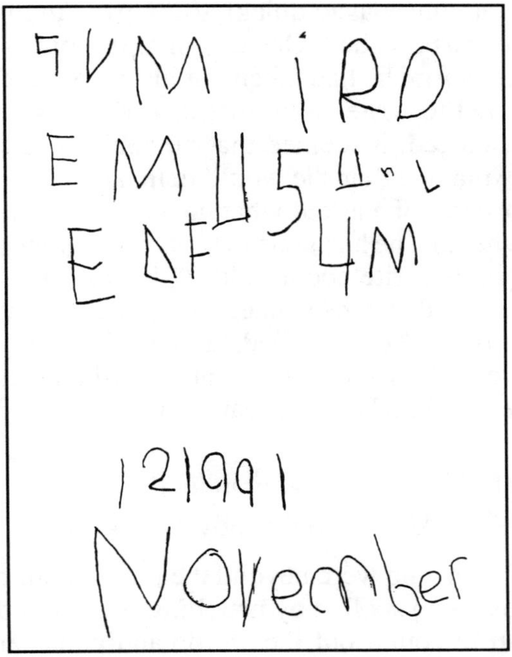

Figure 7-4. Mid-November. Random letter strings with name elements; date and temperature (45°) copied from the chalkboard.

Kevin remained reluctant to be observed as he wrote, making it difficult for us to offer assistance and suggestions as we did for his classmates. Although he enjoyed the applause and praise he received when he read stories from the Author's Chair, he continued to be the last to volunteer each week. In whole language terms, Kevin was not a confident risk taker. However, in his own quiet way, he was paying attention to his classmates' efforts. His topic choices often mirrored theirs, and he followed their lead on mechanical aspects as well. For example, when two other boys took out their rulers and began making line designs in their newsbooks, Kevin followed suit. When other children began copying slogans ("Say no to drugs," "Take a bite out of crime," "This is your brain on drugs"), Kevin "read" the same slogans from his writing. He also listened carefully as the other children shared their stories from the "Author's Chair." One day a classmate read a rather convoluted story about a man who had a heart attack, died, was taken to the hospital, and had needles stuck in his arms. Kevin queried, "If someone has a heart attack, how can they have needles in their arms?" This question sparked a group discussion, which ultimately led the young author to revise his story.

As we circulated around the classroom during writing time, we always stopped by Kevin's desk to ask about his news stories. A tactic Kevin used to avoid interactions was to quickly fill a page in his newsbook and then tell us he was finished. One day in mid-November, Laura approached Kevin before he had taken out his newsbook, and asked him what he wanted to write about that day. Kevin said that he was very tired, and, indeed, it seemed that he could barely keep his eyes open. Laura explained that she would help, and began to prompt him for possible topics. She asked what he had done over the weekend, and Kevin told her that he had gone to his grandmother's house. "Is that what you want to write about today?" Laura asked. Kevin acquiesced, and Laura asked how he wanted to begin the story. Resigned to having lost his privacy, Kevin replied, "I like going to my grandma's house." Laura pressed for more information. "She takes me to the movies," added Kevin. With Laura repeating his story word by word, Kevin wrote:

> R WTinDR (I like going to my grandma's house.)
>
> ET DRWE (She takes me to the movies).

When working with children who were beyond the prephonemic stage of spelling, that is, those who spelled by matching sounds and letters, we encouraged them to sound out the words and consider possible letter-sound matches. At this time, Kevin was not yet attending to or discriminating individual sounds. The fact that he used one letter per word in this story might have indicated that he was beginning to form a more stable concept of word. However, this was not an independent task, and the process of representing each word with a letter was wearisome. In fact, Kevin became even more diligent about evading us during writing time following this session. Not only was Kevin unwilling to take risks with spelling, he successfully avoided interactions that might have nudged him to a more sophisticated understanding of writing.

Despite his reluctance to work with us, Kevin continued to experiment on his own. He began to add drawings to his daily entries, revealing his interest in Ninja Turtles, sports, seasonal and holiday activities, and he continued to follow the lead of classmates, producing many pages of personal "I like ____" statements ("I like the American flag," "I like my teacher," "I like water when it rains"). Gradually, illustrations took prominence over the text, though Kevin always added a label to his pictures. Figure 7-5 shows

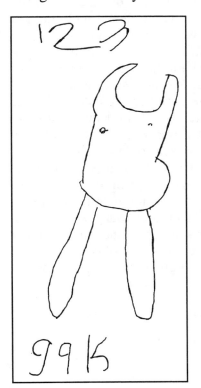

an entry from late January, with a rather primitive drawing of a cow labeled, "g a K," which Kevin read as "I like cows." Because Kevin did not vocalize as he wrote, it was not possible to know for certain whether he was trying to represent the /k/ sound in "cows," or whether the three letters each represented a word. The numbers at the top of the page indicate the date: 1/23 (January 23).

By February, Kevin had become accustomed to the routine established for news writing, and was becoming more tolerant of Laura's "intrusions" to observe and assist him. The class had been studying the life cycle of mealworms, and Kevin produced, on his own, a drawing of a

Figure 7-5.   Late January. "I like cows."

mealworm with the following label: "KPbpB," which he read to Laura as, "I like mealworms" (see Figure 7-6). Laura first responded to the content of the story, prompting Kevin for more information: "Why do you like mealworms?" Kevin answered, "They crawl." Laura asked Kevin to explain how mealworms crawl. "On their legs," responded Kevin. As Kevin added another line of print to his story, Laura turned her attention to the phonemic representation of the information, prompting him to listen for sounds as she repeated the words in the new line:

Z   K K   n   Z   L
They crawl on their legs.

Several significant features in this writing can be noted. First, Kevin is beginning to make approximate letter-sound matches. The /th/ sound in "they" and "their" is phonetically close to /z/. Both sounds are produced at the front of the mouth, with the tongue against the back of the teeth. Kevin appropriately used the "K" from his name to represent the initial consonant sound in "crawl," and he recognized the "L" in "legs." His omission of vowel sounds is typical for children in the early phonemic stage of writing. It is also interesting to note that Kevin used dots to separate some of the words in this sentence. That he marked word boundaries is another sign that the concept of word was becoming established in his mind. It is also significant to note that Kevin crossed out one letter in the sentence, indicating that he had begun to realize that he could make choices in deciding how to spell words. It must also be noted that Kevin was able to write at a higher level when the task of spelling was scaffolded for him.

Kevin was finally gaining some control over the process of spelling, but, as with most emergent writers, his progress was more recursive than linear. He continued to rely on random letter and number strings, or copying from environmental print for many of his stories. Spelling on his own remained an arduous task, and one that he did not usually attempt on his own; however, he remained more receptive to assistance. In late February, again with a great deal of assistance in sounding out words, Kevin wrote:

i 9LAGD NENTLNDO YTH Wi BRR   TREVOR

I played Nintendo   with my brother Trevor.

(See Figure 7-7.)

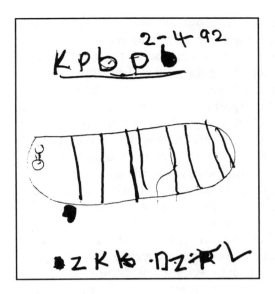

Figure 7-6.
February "I like mealworms.
They crawl on their legs."

Figure 7-7.
Late February.
Letter-name
spelling "I played
Nintendo with my
brother Trevor."

Kevin's spelling had advanced to the point where he was now able to write more than one sound per word. He represented long vowel sounds ("a" in played, "o" in Nintendo, and "i" in my). Temple, et al. (1993) describe this stage of writing as "letter-name spelling." His substitutions are typical, and quite appropriate. He used an "e" for the short "i" sound in Nintendo, and a "y" to represent the /w/ in "with." The "p" in played is printed backwards, and the "M" in my is upside-down, but Kevin added a period when asked what was needed at the end of the sentence.

This piece represents a leap of progress for Kevin, not only in terms of print knowledge, but in his level of attention and effort given to the task of writing. Rather than moving on to the next word as soon as he had written one letter, Kevin tolerated prompts to listen for additional sounds ("What else do you hear when you say Nintendo?"). His effort here is significant because, in addition to the developmental issues that made writing difficult for Kevin, his motivation was adversely affected by a certain aspect of the daily class routine. That is, the children were expected to complete their "seatwork" independently; as soon as their work was finished and received approval from the teacher, the children were dismissed to free play time. During the course of the school year, the children began to compete with each other to be the first one finished. Ample time was allotted for the children to finish their seatwork and to write in their newsbooks, but when they became concerned about finishing ahead of each other, their attention to writing was diminished. Kevin was no exception; thus, his progress in writing remained inconsistent. He wrote more, and with greater detail, when he had one-to-one assistance. For instance, several weeks after writing the Nintendo story, Kevin drew a race car and hastily added several lines of random letters and letter-like marks, which he read as, "I like fast cars because they get away from bad people." On other days, he fulfilled his obligation to write in the newsbook with loosely scrawled, primitive illustrations.

So far, Kevin's writing development parallels that of many children in kindergarten and first grade. From random letter strings, he began to represent words with one consonant, then gradually began to add long vowel sounds. What set Kevin apart from other children was the difficulty with which these gains in remembering letter shapes and making the letter-sound associations were achieved. The following transcript excerpts are taken from a session in mid-March. Laura began by prompting Kevin to identify and discuss a topic (he chose space travel). She then guided him through the writing process, holding his story in memory and scaffolding the process of letter-sound identification.

1. L: OK, what's the first thing you want to put in your story today?
2. K: I want to put up a flag on the moon.
3. L: All right, let's write that. How are you going to start that? I,

4. K: [Writes "I," then moves to another sound, possibly for "moon"]. M.

5. L: [Refocuses Kevin's attention on the next word] Want, say the word first. /w/ /w/.

6. K: Want, want, "Y"?

7. L: O.K.

8. K: How do you make "Y"?

9. L: How do you make "Y"? You show me how you make it.

10. K: [writes "R"]

11. L: I want . . . [retrieving the sentence]

12. K: A "I"?

13. L: You've already got the "I." Wanttt [oversounds on the final consonant].

14. K: Want,/t/, "T"?

15. L: I hear a "T."

16. K: [Writes T, moves on to the next word] To [or "two"]

17. L: /T/ to.

18. K: To? [or "two"]

19. L: To.

20. K: [Writes "2," moves on to the next word]. Put,

21. L: To what?

22. K: To put up.

23. L: OK, I want to put, /p/

24. K: "P"?

25. L: Very good. P, [calls Kevin's attention to the alphabet chart on the wall] like by the pear, right next to the O. I want to put . . . Do you hear anymore in "put"? [pause] You say it, put.

26. K: Pud, /ae/, /ae/,

27. L: /uh/

28. K: "E"?

29. L: OK.

30. K: [Moves on to the next word, "up," sounding out the final consonant]. Bah, B?

31. L: OK. I want to put up a

32. K: E? [Adds "E." He has run out of room on the line]
33. L: You can start over here. Flag, how do you write flag? /f/ /f/
34. K: V?
35. L: V, do you remember how to make a V? S, T, U, V [Laura traces the shape of "V" on Kevin's arm. Kevin writes "Y"]. That's a Y, this is a V. Flag, do you hear anymore in "flag"?
36. K: /puh/, P?
37. L: In flag do you hear a /p/? I don't. [rereads the sentence]. Put up a flag, flllagg.
38. K: V?
39. L: [Realizes that Kevin does not hear the /l/ in flag.] You've got the V, that's at the beginning. Do you hear anything at the end, flag /g/ /g/,
40. K: /g/ /g/, D?
41. L: OK. Let's read it so far. [K & L read together, word by word]. I want to put up a flag.
42. K: N? [Has probably already moved ahead to the next word, "in"].
43. L: Well, what are you going to say? I want to put up a flag . . .
44. K: I wantt, T?
45. L: No, we're right here now [slides finger under sentence as she reads], I want to put up a flag [pauses for Kevin to complete the sentence]
46. K: In, in
47. L: [trying to get Kevin to complete his thought before writing] In what?
48. K: Sbace. [oversounds on /p/]
49. L: O.K. In, [thinks K is trying to spell "in"]
50. K: Buh, B? [trying to sound out "sbace"]
51. L: Innn, what do you hear in inn, /n/?
52. K: Ind, B? [still trying to spell "sbace"]
53. L: Innn.
54. K: N.
55. L: OK. [Kevin writes "N"] Sssss [Laura begins to sound out "space"]
56. K: Space, C?
57. L: Yes, C. What else could it be?
58. K: S? [Kevin and his classmates have been taught that some sounds can be spelled by more than one letter]
59. L: Umhmm. [Kevin writes "S"] Space.

60. K: Bu, buh, B?
61. L: Umhmm. [Kevin writes "B"]. O.K. Would you read it again for me?
62. K: I,
63. L: want
64. K: want to put up a flag in space.

From this transcript, we see some progress in Kevin's writing. Most of his letter-sound matches are accurate or close approximations, including some vowel sounds (lines 28, 32); in addition, he used more than one letter to represent some of the words (want, put, flag, space). Kevin continued to struggle with recognition of some letter shapes (lines 9, 25, 35), and he did not recall the spelling of basic sight words from his reading instruction—he printed the numeral "2" for the word "to" (lines 16–20), and he could not remember the spelling of other sight words such as "a" and "in."

Discussion of assistance. A primary goal for the assistance Laura provided Kevin was to sustain a level of fluency in the writing. To this end, she assisted him in recognizing and representing the phonemes in the words he was trying to spell, and to help Kevin represent each word in the sentence by redirecting his efforts when his attention to the phonemic issues caused him to lose track of the sentence. Through-

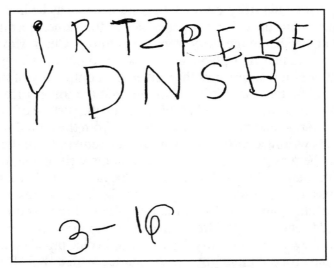

Figure 7-8.   Mid-March. "I want to put up a flag in space."
I Rt   2 P   EB E YD N SB

out the episode, Laura maintained the constructivist stance that Kevin could construct a complete story (albeit a brief one), providing assistance and information as required to move the story along. In several instances, Laura repeated the story to get Kevin to focus on the next word, or to vocalize the word before he began to write (lines 5, 41, 45, 47). Kevin was still accustomed to producing letter strings at random, and the process of making a decision about how to represent sounds was not yet automatic for him. Laura agreed with Kevin's choice of letters when his representations were phonetically close (lines 7, 15, 25, 29, 35). In some cases, when Kevin's choice was grossly inaccurate, or when Laura knew that there had been a class discussion relating to a particular letter-sound relationship, she redirected him to a more accurate choice (lines 37, 57, 58).

It must be noted that Laura could not always anticipate Kevin's "next move," thereby complicating the scaffolding process. In lines 16–20, for instance, Kevin's "to" actually meant "2." In lines 49–53, Kevin needed only two more words to complete the sentence: "in space." The word "space" seemed to be more salient for him than "in," and Kevin tried to sound out "space." Confused by his repetition of /b/ (for the /p/ in space), Laura tried to redirect Kevin to the word "in." As the transcript shows, several exchanges were required to coordinate their efforts.

When Kevin had completed the sentence and decided not to add anything else to his story, he read the sentence just as he had written it: "I want to put up a flag in space." Later the same morning, and again when he shared the story from the Author's Chair, Kevin read the story as he had first planned it: "I want to put up a flag on the moon." It does not surprise us that, given the complexity of the writing process, he lost the original thought. But the images Kevin had seen of American astronauts planting a flag on the surface of the moon returned after he had gained some distance from the actual writing.

Kevin's writing continued to vary for the remainder of the school year. That he was gaining independence in his writing and thinking about print was not always obvious to us. One day in late April, Kevin's teacher was modeling storywriting for the class. As she described her recent birthday party, she listed the gifts she had received from her family and friends. The children called out spelling suggestions to her, and when she wrote "c-a-n-d-y," a thin, timid voice piped up from the midst of the group: "I thought 'candy' started with a 'K.'" It was not until we listened to the audiotape of this session that we realized— with some astonishment—that the voice belonged to Kevin.

Progress. At the end of the school year Kevin was able to identify 42 letters, as compared to eight at the beginning of the year. He recognized most of the upper-case letters, but remained confused by several lower-case letters: j for f, one for l and i, r for h, p for q, and b for d. On the test of dictation, Kevin's score improved from 0 to 13 accurate letter-sound matches. Equally significant, he made 19 attempts as compared to only 4 on the pretest. On all of the other measures, Kevin showed little if any progress. With regard to the Concepts of Print test, Kevin was now able to demonstrate word by word matching, and he could isolate the first and last letter of a word. He still could not label punctuation marks, nor was he able to identify misspellings of common words. His score on the word writing test remained the same (only one conventional spelling), but this time he attempted to write 10 words—names of classmates and color words, several of which were missing only one letter. Previously he had made only three attempts. On the sight word test, Kevin attempted to read 14 of 20 words, compared to only one attempt made on the pretest. However, he recognized only one word, "can," which he may have memorized from his preprimer. Interestingly, Kevin spelled the words he could not read, again, confusing some letters for numbers (he read "look" as "One-O" and "little" as "One-I-T-T-One-E"). This confusion between reading and spelling is yet another sign of delay in Kevin's progress towards conventional literacy.

Discussion. We introduced Kevin as a textbook case of a child with a learning disability. His literacy-learning experiences paralleled the ball-playing analogy with which we opened this chapter. Every day, Kevin copied unfamiliar words from the chalkboard and completed handwriting worksheets, tracing and printing row after row of letters. These speed and accuracy drills were punctuated by opportunities for Kevin to "play ball"—to create original texts based on his own real-life experiences and aspirations, and to share these texts with his schoolmates, from whom he received applause and admiration. In the process, Kevin encountered the dilemmas faced by all beginning authors—choosing topics, matching letters and sounds, and recalling letter shapes. Kevin's story serves as a reminder that children do not acquire literacy concepts and skills simply through formal, direct instruction—recall that Kevin had four years of schooling before we met him. Rather, children—both those who learn easily and those who learn with difficulty—construct their own understandings of print, understandings that do not always match conventional forms or our preconceived notions of developmental stages. This enterprise of knowledge construction occurs in the context of activities that are personally meaningful, socially purposeful, and, for children like Kevin, that are accompanied by intense assistance within the individual child's "zone of proximal development." Kevin's "zone" was bounded by several factors, including:

- his limited memory for letter names and shapes;
- his (mis)articulation of some sounds and words;
- his limited but increasing awareness of the syllabic principle;
- his lack of phoneme awareness, including the ability to distinguish individual sounds and the ability to match these sounds with letters.

We visited Kevin one year later to see how he was faring. When given the opportunity to write anything he wanted, Kevin decided without hesitation to write a letter to one of his former classmates, a task he managed with independence and fluency, if not by conventional means. He insisted that Laura write the name of his friend in cursive, but the rest of the effort was his own:

D   J,   I x   u   s   e. Yd   u   K   b   to ds sy
Dear J____, I wish you was here. Would you come back to this school?

D   ue Reb   ths tin Y   ot pp et   a   t   a   a t
Do you remember the time we went to Putt-Putt and you got a lot of tickets.

Then I took you home. Kevin.
    I n   o   p   Kevin

Kevin continued to lag behind his age mates, but his confidence in himself as a writer was growing. His letter also demonstrates that he now understood the communicative power and social nature of writing, in this case, as a means of renewing a friendship.

Kevin's story serves as a powerful reminder that young children with special needs do benefit from authentic, personally meaningful opportunities to engage in reading and writing, but that these activities must be accompanied by supportive assistance as the children confront the complexities of print. While we often fumbled in our interactions with Kevin, we were able to scaffold story writing for him—and his classmates—in several ways. We offer these suggestions to other teachers who seek to engage children in authentic writing activities:

- Encourage children to plan their stories orally before they begin to write.
- When working individually with a child, begin with the expectation that he/she does have some knowledge of letter-sound relationships. Ask, "What do *you* hear?" and "What else do you hear?" when repeating words.
- Respect the child's current understanding of print—observe and document the lines demarcating his/her "zone of proximal development," and provide assistance within this zone. For example, when the child makes a logical approximation in matching letters and sounds, accept this decision and move on to the next sound or word.
- Provide opportunities for the children to share their stories with each other.
- At times, translate the child's writing into conventional print (as we did with the class newspapers) so that he/she has the opportunity to practice reading familiar, original text.
- Your emotional/moral support is essential to providing the child with an incentive to complete the task. Writing requires intense effort from children who are learning easily; for those with learning difficulties, the task is formidable. Stay composed and relaxed, and the child will sense your confidence in his/her ability.

We are committed to creating opportunities for children like Kevin to participate as full members of the literate community. We are hopeful that his story will encourage other teachers to persevere with children who seem to be making little or no progress in achieving conventional literacy.

References

Bryant, P. E. (1990). Phonological development and reading. In P. D. Pumfrey & C. D. Elliott, (Eds.), *Children's difficulties in reading, spelling and writing: Challenges and responses,* 63–82. London: The Falmer Press.

Clay, M. M. (1979). *The early detection of reading difficulties.* Auckland, New Zealand: Heinemann.

Cole, M. (1993). *Vygotsky and writing: Reflections from a distant discipline.* Paper presented at the Conference on College Composition and Communication. San Diego, April 2.

Cook-Gumperz, J. (1986). Introduction: The social construction of literacy. In J. Cook-Gumperz, (Ed.), *The social construction of literacy,* 1–15. NY: Cambridge University Press.

Gundlach, R. (1982). Children as writers: The beginnings of learning to write. In M. Nystrand, (Ed.), *What writers know,* 129–148. New York: Academic Press.

Luria, A. R. (1929). *The development of writing in the child.* Moscow: Academy of Communist Education.

Read, C. (1971). Preschool children's knowledge of English phonology. *Harvard Educational Review* 41:*1,* 1–34.

Rey, H. A. (1952). *Curious George rides a bike.* Boston: Houghton Mifflin.

Sulzby, E. (1985). Children's emergent reading of favorite storybooks: A developmental study. *Reading Research Quarterly.* 20, 458–481.

Sulzby, E. (1989). Forms of writing and rereading from writing: A preliminary report. In J. Mason (Ed.), *Reading and writing connections,* 31–63. Needham Heights, MA: Allyn & Bacon.

Temple, C., Nathan, R., Temple, F., & Burris, N. A. (1993). *The beginnings of writing.* Needham Heights, MA: Allyn & Bacon.

Tharpe, R., & Gallimore, R. (1989). *Rousing minds to life.* New York: Cambridge University Press.

Vygotsky, L. (1978). *Mind in society: The development of higher psychological processes.* Edited by M. Cole, V. John-Steiner, S. Scribner, & Souberman (Eds. and Trans.). Cambridge: Harvard University Press.

Walsh, D. J., Price, G. G., & Gillingham, M. G. (1988). The critical but transitory importance of letter naming. *Reading Research Quarterly, 23:1, 108–122.*

Section III

Balancing Strategy Instruction
Within Whole Language

ᵍ⌐ ──────────────── ⌐ᵍ

*"If whole language or process writing are to be successful
with students of varying abilities and backgrounds, then teachers need to be flexible and resourceful in applying them. It is
important to acknowledge that there are children in whole
language and process writing programs who struggle with
writing and reading. If we are to help these children be successful readers and writers, we must be open to building
bridges across different teaching philosophies"* (Graham &
Harris, Chapter 8).

This section highlights procedures for teaching specific reading and
writing strategies. Chapter 8 by Steve Graham and Karen Harris describes strategy instruction that occurs in the context of a writer's
workshop. Their chapter highlights two specific instructional strategies for writing: story elements for narrative writing and report writing
for expository texts. The authors describe a progression from more
teacher-directed instruction to more student-directed autonomy; however, they emphasize that the progression is not linear. Teachers may
need to go back and be direct and explicit with some children many
times in order for them to be successful. The authors describe how
the teacher uses charts, discussion, and mnemonic devices in further
efforts to make the strategies explicit for students. While the teacher
portrayed is a special education teacher collaborating in a fifth grade
classroom, the strategies described are appropriate for all elementary
children.

In Chapter 9, Rachel Brown, Pamela Beard El-Dinary, and Michael Pressley describe reading comprehension strategies designed to improve students' comprehension of text. They describe instruction in which students are taught to articulate a repertoire of strategies, including prediction, verification, visualization, summarization, and the generation of relevant background knowledge. The second grade teacher portrayed in this chapter uses explanation (of what to do during reading and *why*), demonstration (such as thinking aloud), and scaffolding (including responsive elaboration) to encourage students' acquisition and use of these strategies. These authors emphasize the recursive nature of explicit instruction and the need for teachers to respond to learners' needs for particular skill instruction.

In Chapter 10, Laura Roehler and Mark Hallenback illustrate how teachers can teach literacy skills through naturally occurring conversations about the topics the students are studying. These conversations focus on such strategies as activating background knowledge, summarizing, paraphrasing, and self-monitoring. The chapter includes the verbatim conversations of the teacher and students to allow readers a window into how skills are taught through discussion. While the strategies in her chapter take place with English as a Second Language students in a whole language context, *all* teachers of *all* children can benefit from thinking about their classroom conversations with children as an authentic place to teach skills and strategies.

In the final chapter in this section, Linda Wold describes a specific teacher-directed reading strategy designed to help children make connections among what they know, stories, titles, and illustrations in books for beginning readers. Linda is a Chapter One reading teacher who collaborates with the regular classroom teacher in deciding what instructional strategies the children need. She uses motivational talk, thinking aloud, and scaffolded instruction in a whole class setting to teach her strategy. Like all whole language instruction, the focus of this strategy teaching is on enabling the children to transfer the skill to their authentic reading contexts.

Chapter 8

Teaching Writing Strategies
Within the Context of A Whole Language Class

~ ───── ~

Steve Graham
Karen R. Harris
University of Maryland

In recent years, writing instruction based on constructivistic principles has become increasingly popular with teachers. By the late 1980s, for example, 40 percent of teachers reported using a process approach to teaching writing (Applebee, 1989). Process writing teachers provide children with extended opportunities for writing about self-selected topics and emphasize students' ownership of their writing projects. They assume that children have meaningful things to say and look for ways to help them learn how to say what they want to say. They act as a facilitator, creating an atmosphere (both nonthreatening and supportive) in which students can flourish and take risks while writing for real purposes and real audiences. They also use mini-lessons, peer collaboration, writing conferences, modeling, sharing, and classroom dialogue to deliver personalized and individually tailored assistance and instruction (Atwell, 1987; Graves, 1983).

Process writing instruction shares many of the same underlying principles as whole language teaching, and is often integrated into whole language instructional programs (Goodman, 1992; Vacca & Rasinski, 1992). Whole language teachers stress that learning to write and read is as natural as learning to speak and, therefore, is best learned through real use (rather than practice exercises) in meaningful and authentic contexts. They also emphasize that learning to write and read should focus on meaning and process, not form. Learning is further viewed as integrative, so that learning in any one area of language helps learning in other areas. In whole language classrooms, teachers strive to develop a community of learners who share and help each other, make personal choices about what they read and write, take ownership and responsibility for their learning, take risks in their reading and writing, and evaluate their efforts and progress.

Benefits

More time spent writing

The beliefs about learning and writing that underlie whole language and the process approach to writing benefit young writers in several important ways. One potential advantage is that students will spend more time writing. Both process writing and whole language teaching emphasize that learning to write well is dependent on frequent and meaningful writing.

In many traditional classrooms, little time is set aside in the school day for writing. Studies by Bridge and Hiebert (1985) and Christenson, Thurlow, Ysseldyke, and McVicar (1989), for example, found that both regular students and students receiving special services spent most of their writing time completing transcription activities (copying, handwriting exercises, filling in blanks, and so forth), seldom composed text of more than a sentence in length, and rarely wrote for a real audience. This approach to teaching writing reminds us of a recent Peanuts cartoon. Charlie Brown's little sister, Sally, is drawing lines on a piece of paper and informs him that she is practicing her underlining. She continues practicing, further informing him, "If I ever write something worth underlining, I'll be ready."

In contrast, Fisher and Hiebert (1990) found that students in whole language classes spent six times as much time writing as students in skills-oriented classes. Increasing children's writing time is an essential ingredient in current efforts to improve writing instruction. Young writers need plenty of opportunities to apply and develop their emerging writing skills in meaningful ways. It is hard to imagine, for instance, that students will develop effective strategies for planning and revising, sensitivity to the needs of their readers, or a strong knowledge base about how to write if the bulk of their instruction involves decontextualized spelling, handwriting, and grammar exercises.

Increased self-regulation

Another potential advantage of whole language and process writing is that many of the key components, such as choice, ownership, self-evaluation, peer collaboration, and a supportive environment, are aimed at creating conditions that foster self-regulation (Corno, 1992). We believe that helping young authors more fully develop this quality is an important goal in writing instruction (Graham & Harris, 1994a, 1994b; Harris & Graham, 1992a, 1992b). As others have noted (Hayes & Flower, 1986), skilled writing is not a passive activity. It is intentional and resourceful. Skilled writers establish goals for their writing, deftly manipulate the environment and the cognitive tools at their disposal in order to achieve these goals, and monitor their progress—adjusting and shifting resources and goals as necessary.

Developing writers, however, often employ a different, less sophisticated strategy when composing (Scardamalia & Bereiter, 1986). They retrieve from memory any information that is somewhat topic appropriate and then simply write it down, making little attempt to evaluate it or rework it in light of other rhetorical goals. This retrieve-and-write process typically functions like an automated and encapsulated program, operating largely without children's metacognitive control (McCutchen, 1988).

Many of the instructional procedures common to whole language and process writing confront this automated retrieve-and-write strategy head on, paving the way for children to incorporate additional self-regulatory procedures into their writing (McCutchen, 1988). In a cooperative writing situation, for instance, there are other collaborators who disrupt the automated retrieve-and-write process by suggesting ideas of their own and rejecting others. The tension of composing collaboratively forces students into other modes of writing, often requiring more reflection and resourcefulness, as they try to accommodate each others' ideas and writing styles.

Integrative learning

Whole language places considerable emphasis on the integrative nature of learning, stressing that writing and reading work together to support literacy development (Goodman, 1992). There are numerous examples of how learning in one area of language helps learning in writing, including acquiring rhetorical knowledge from reading (Bereiter & Scardamalia, 1984), learning the correct spelling of words from reading (Callaway, McDaniel, & Mason, 1972), or using knowledge of word meanings to spell a word (for example, use a related word to spell a reduced vowel: compete, competition).

A Concern

Despite the potential advantages of whole language and process writing, these teaching philosophies have generated considerable controversy among educators working with children who are likely to experience difficulty with literacy learning (cf. Pressley & Rankin, 1994; Spiegel, 1992). Both philosophies are primarily based on indirect rather than direct teaching methods. Consequently, there is some concern that the methods used by whole language and process teachers are not powerful enough for children with learning or writing problems. In whole language or process writing classrooms these students may not learn all the skills or strategies needed for effective reading and writing (cf. Harris & Graham, 1994; Mather, 1992).

This is not to say that whole language or process writing teachers ignore the skills and strategies underlying effective writing. In process writing, for instance, higher-order writing skills and strategies are emphasized as teachers create a predictable classroom routine where planning and revising are expected and encouraged, provide feedback and assistance in carrying out these processes during individual and group conferences, create learning communities where students assist each other in planning and revising their text, and deliver process-oriented instruction through mini-lessons (MacArthur, Schwartz, & Graham, 1991a).

The cognitive process and strategies underlying planning and revising, however, are not the primary focus of many teachers who use process writing. The development of these processes and strategies are often secondary to the focus on content and communication (DeGroff, 1992; Fitzgerald & Stamm, 1990). Perhaps more important, process teachers primarily strive to facilitate children's "natural" development of planning and revising over long periods of time and through questions and "gentle" response during conferences, sharing, and so forth. Explicit instruction in using specific planning and revising strategies is mostly limited to on-the-spot teaching and short mini-lessons (often no more than five to 10 minutes in length) delivered in response to needs that have spontaneously arisen as children write. While both of these instructional tools are useful, many students may require more extensive, structured, systematic, and explicit instruction in order to master the skills and strategies underlying complex processes such as planning and revising (Dudley-Marling, this volume; also see Freppon & Headings and McIntyre, et al., this volume, on teachers' perspectives on this issue). A considerable amount of research, for example, demonstrates that students with special needs often do not acquire a variety of cognitive and metacognitive strategies unless detailed and explicit instruction is provided (Brown & Campione, 1990).

The role of direct instruction (by certain definitions) is viewed as undesirable by some whole language and process experts. Goodman (1992), for example, indicates that direct instruction is incompatible with whole language because "it is not only narrow, but unscientific, and misconceived" (p. 197). We believe, however, that a balanced and integrative stance is desirable, especially for students who are likely to have difficulty with literary learning (Brown, El-Dinary, and Pressley, this volume; Harris & Graham, 1994; Pressley, et al., this volume). This does not mean that we should throw out the proverbial baby with the bath water, though. We enthusiastically endorse whole language and process writing principles. It is essential that learning is integrative; tasks are meaningful and authentic; students choose, evaluate, take risks, share, and collaborate; and teachers create supportive learning environments. We would expand the teacher's role, however, so that more extensive and explicit instruction is provided in the processes and strategies underlying effective writing.[1] In the current chapter, we provide two case studies of how planning processes for narrative and expository writing were explicitly taught within the context of a whole language and process writing class. Similar examples of teaching a revision strategy within a process writing context are available in a paper by MacArthur, Schwartz, and Graham (1991b).

---

[1]We would also argue that a more balanced approach needs to be applied to the teaching of handwriting and spelling in whole language and process approaches. Issues and recommendations concerning the teaching of these text production skills are addressed in Graham (1992), Graham and Harris (1994a), and Harris and Graham (1994).

Case Study One

The setting

The first case study examines how Barbara Danoff taught a strategy for planning and writing a story, as well as procedures for regulating use of the strategy and the writing process, in the context of a whole language classroom (see Danoff, Harris, & Graham [1993] for outcome data on the teaching of this strategy). Barbara is a special education teacher who works directly in the regular classroom. In some instances, Barbara supports regular class teachers by providing additional instructional assistance to students with special needs and any other students who may need help. For instance, during a lesson, she may work with an individual or small group of students, providing additional explanation, modeling, or guided practice. At other times, she takes the lead in crafting and delivering instruction in conjunction with the general education teacher.

While writing is emphasized throughout the day, students in Barbara's school also have a Writers' Workshop period. During this time, students consult with their peers when planning and revising their work, conference regularly with teachers about their work, share their completed and in-progress work with classmates, select pieces for publication, and reflect on their accomplishments and challenges in a journal. While students typically choose the topics for their papers, the genre is often specified by the teachers. This is in accordance with a county-wide curriculum that specifies the types of genres to be covered at each grade.

Barbara's decision to embed strategy instruction within the context of Writer's Workshop began with her observation that many of the stories in the portfolios of a class of fifth grade students commonly failed to include basic parts of a story. She further noted that all of the students could improve their story writing by including greater detail and elaboration, as well as more goals and actions. After several discussions with the collaborating fifth grade teacher, it was decided that Barbara would offer instruction in a story grammar strategy designed to enhance advanced planning and content generation. The teachers both felt that knowledge and use of the story grammar strategy would also benefit some of the students in terms of reading comprehension and would be of use to all of the students in middle school the following year, when they would face increased demands for specific writing products, such as book reports and biographies. (See also Brown, El-Dinary, and Pressley, this volume.)

Most of the students in this fifth grade class enjoyed writing. A few who found writing particularly challenging, though, were very anxious about it. Most, but not all, of these students had been identified as having learning disabilities. Barbara wanted to help the anxious students establish a stronger sense of motivation, enhanced self-efficacy, and more internal attributions (or an overall "I can do this if I try" attitude).

Barbara used procedures from the Self-Regulated Strategy Development model (Graham & Harris, 1993; Harris & Graham, 1992a) to teach the strategy. This model is designed to help students learn, maintain, and generalize academic strategies, as well as use a variety of self-regulation procedures for managing the target strategies and developing positive attitudes and beliefs. In terms of self-regulation, she decided to include (on an individual basis) self-instructions, proximal goal setting, self-monitoring (including self-assessment and self-recording), and self-reinforcement as part of the instructional program. The strategy and accompanying self-regulation procedures were introduced through an extended series of mini-lessons offered during the writing period. Once Barbara modeled how to use the strategy, students were encouraged to use it (during collaborative practice and independent performance) as they wrote stories during the writing period.

Instruction

Stage 1: Initial conference. Barbara began with a conference with the entire class, offering to teach a story writing strategy to those students interested in learning it. The class discussed what they knew about story writing, including the parts that are commonly found in a story (setting, characters' goals, actions to achieve goals, ending, and characters' reactions). They also talked about the goals for learning the strategy (to write better stories: ones that are more fun for you to write and more fun for others to read) and how including and expanding story parts can improve a story. Barbara further described the procedures for learning the strategy, emphasizing the students' roles as collaborators (including the possibility of serving as a peer tutor for other students who wished to learn the strategy in the future) and the importance of effort in strategy mastery. All of the students decided to participate in the mini-lessons on the story writing strategy.

Stage 2: Preskill development. During the first mini-lesson, the class resumed and expanded its previous discussion on the types of elements commonly included in the two major components of a story:

setting (main characters, locale, and time of the story) and episode (characters' goals or aims, actions to achieve goals, results of actions, and characters' reactions). This included identifying examples of these elements in the literature they were currently reading, highlighting the different ways authors used and developed story parts. To promote linkages to reading, the class further considered how "we can use our knowledge of story parts to help us get the author's meaning." The class then spent some time generating ideas for story parts, using differing story origins. Finally, students selected two or three previously written stories from their portfolios and determined which story elements were present in each story. At this point, Barbara met with students, individually or in small groups, to introduce and explain the purpose of self-assessment and graphing (to monitor the completeness of their stories and the effects of learning the strategy), demonstrate how to graph the number of story parts included in a story, and how they would continue to use the graph for self-recording. For those students who used all or nearly all of the parts in their stories, Barbara discussed with them how more detail, elaboration, and action could improve their parts.

Stage 3: Discussion of the composition strategy. In the second minilesson, Barbara introduced the story grammar strategy; each student had a chart listing the strategy steps and a mnemonic for remembering the questions for the parts of a story (step 3). The strategy and mnemonics were as follows:

The Strategy:

1. Think of a story you would like to share with others.
2. Let your mind be free.
3. Write down the story part reminder (mnemonic):
   W-W-W-   What = 2   How = 2
4. Make notes of your ideas for each part.
5. Write your story—use good parts; add, elaborate, or revise as you go; make sense.

The Mnemonic:

Who is the main character; who else is in the story?
When does the story take place?
Where does the story take place?
What does the main character do or want to do; what do other characters do?

<u>What</u> happens when the main character does or tries to do it?
   What happens with other characters?
<u>How</u> does the story end?
<u>How</u> does the main character feel; how do other characters feel?

Barbara asked the students what they thought the reason for each step might be. The class then discussed when and how to use the strategy; linkages to writing book reports, biographies, other compositions, and to reading were stressed at this time. Discussion also focused on the importance of student effort in learning the strategy, since a strategy cannot work if it hasn't been mastered (this was meant to serve both attributional and goal-setting functions). Barbara further illustrated the types of things she would say to herself to free up her mind and think of good ideas and parts while planning or writing. This included statements such as "Let my mind be free" and "Take my time; good ideas will come to me." After considering how these self-statements were helpful, students developed their own preferred creativity self-statements, recorded them on paper, and practiced using them.

Stage 4: Modeling. During the third mini-lesson, Barbara shared a story idea with her students that she had been thinking about, and modeled (while "thinking out loud") how to use the strategy to further develop the idea. The students participated during modeling by helping her as she planned and made notes for each story part, and as she wrote the first draft of her story (changes to her plans were made several times as she wrote). While planning and writing, Barbara used self-instructions that involved problem definition, planning, self-evaluation, self-reinforcement, and coping. When the story was finished, the class discussed the importance of what we say to ourselves as we work and write (students volunteered examples of personal positive, and sometimes negative, self-statements they used when writing) and identified the purpose of the different types of self-statements used by Barbara. Next, they developed (and recorded on a card) personal self-statements they planned to use while writing. Examples of students' personalized self-statements included: "How am I doing so far?" "I can do this if I try." "Slow down; take my time." Barbara then asked the students if they could suggest any changes they thought would make the strategy better. No changes were proposed at this point. While Barbara continued to ask students for suggested changes in later mini-lessons, no changes were made by this group (Barbara had taught the strategy for several years; changes had been made in the strategy and instructional procedures in earlier years).

Stage 5: Memorization of the strategy and mnemonic. Barbara asked her students to memorize the steps of the strategy, the mnemonic, and several self-statements they planned to use. Practice in memorizing this information was done either alone or with a partner, using methods selected by the students. These items were memorized easily by some students, while others needed more extended practice (some students continued to work on memorizing as they began using the strategy to write stories).

Stage 6: Collaborative practice. During this stage, students received assistance from the teacher (as needed) as they started to apply the story writing strategy and the accompanying self-regulation procedures during Writer's Workshop. Barbara (or the classroom teacher) collaboratively planned a story with each student who needed assistance, and made sure students were using the strategy steps and mnemonic appropriately. Use of self-statements was prompted as appropriate during writing and at other times as well; this continued throughout instruction and afterwards as needed.

As they worked with individual students, the two teachers modified their input and support to meet each child's needs (sometimes students provided assistance to each other). Assistance included helping students determine self-statements especially useful to them, prompting and providing guidance, as well as re-explanations and modeling. In some cases, assistance concentrated on planning for greater detail and elaboration, or incorporating more goals and actions on the part of story characters. Scaffolding, including students' use of charts and self-statement lists, was faded individually, and the two teachers started encouraging students to use their self-statements covertly (in their own head) if they weren't already doing so.

As students worked on their stories, the two teachers encouraged them to use goal-setting, self-monitoring (continuing use of the graphs), and self-reinforcement procedures in conjunction with the story writing strategy. The goal, which could be met by using the story writing strategy, was to include all of the story parts. Thus, when a student completed a story (or sooner if preferred), the student and one of the teachers identified the story parts independently, compared counts, filled in the student's graph, and then compared this number to the goal. Collaborative practice took less time than anticipated, with most of the students ready for independent performance after two or three collaborative experiences. Students who continued to need collaboration in the writing process received it from the teachers and peers as appropriate.

A conference was also held with the entire group to discuss and plan for strategy maintenance and generalization. The students decided that it would be helpful to have several review and booster sessions and discussed opportunities they might have for generalization (one student reported using the strategy in English class when they read stories, another reported using it to help write outlines).

Stage 7: Independent performance. At this point, students planned and wrote stories independently. Barbara and the regular classroom teacher provided positive and constructive feedback as needed. While some students still relied on their charts and lists of self-statements, they were encouraged to try working without them. By this time, many of the students wrote the mnemonic at the top of a piece of "planning" paper (using it as a reminder as they generated writing notes), and some students no longer wrote out ideas for all of the story parts in advance of writing. They told Barbara they had the parts in their heads and were ready to write (this was not viewed as a problem unless the student then left out story parts). The teachers encouraged students to continue using independently the goal setting and self-monitoring (graphing) procedures on at least two more stories during this stage. After that, students were told that using these procedures in the future was up to them.

The class held a group meeting to formally evaluate the strategy and the instructional procedures. The students indicated that the strategy was helpful and they were pleased with their use of it. The mnemonic was most frequently nominated as the most enjoyable aspect of instruction. One student replied, "The W-W-W, What = 2, How = 2 builds up your resources." The regular class teacher commented that she could see "light bulbs going off" as the students worked to master the strategy. As one student told her, "Now this story writing makes sense." Based on comments made during writing conferences, Barbara also believed that positive changes were occurring in students' attitudes toward writing and their self-efficacy, especially for those students who had been most anxious about writing to begin with.

Changes in students' writing performance are illustrated in the story presented below. This story was written after strategy instruction by a student whose preinstructional stories did not contain a plot or theme and typically just described an event, such as a frog jumping from one lily pad to another.

Dreams! Dreams! Dreams!

Once there was a penguin named Rubin. There was nothing special about Rubin. He was just a black and white penguin. Rubin lived in the San Diego Zoo. He loved the zoo. Then one day he saw a boy that came to visit the zoo wearing shorts with sailboats on them. Rubin loved the shorts. Rubin also wanted them. That night Rubin had a dream. It was about Rubin getting the shorts. Once he got the shorts he gotten a Walkman. Rubin dreamed that after he had got the walkman, he turned it on and started to dance. Rubin danced all night in his dream. When Rubin got up he was sad because he had only dreamed it.

This story contained all of the basic elements emphasized in the story grammar strategy. The main character was Rubin who once lived at the San Diego Zoo (setting: who, when, and where). He wanted the shorts he saw (the character's goal) and obtained them in a dream (actions to obtain the goal). The story ends when he wakes up without the shorts and his other acquisition, the Walkman (ending). Not surprisingly, Rubin is sad (reaction) because he really didn't obtain the coveted shorts or the Walkman.

Finally, during the group meeting, Barbara further initiated a discussion of the strategy's weaknesses and talked about other story structures. The teachers and students discussed different kinds of stories (for example, tall tales); the students indicated that they would like to learn about these in future mini-lessons. The class also revisited their plans for maintenance and generalization, and shared instances where these had occurred. One student, for instance, reported using the strategy to write a "tall tale" in another class, while another child used it when writing a story for the school newspaper. Other students indicated they used it during journal writing. These reports were confirmed by the students' teachers (one fourth grade teacher adopted the strategy for use during both reading and writing in her classroom); use of self-statements in other classes was noted as well.

Case Study Two

The setting

Our second case study again involves Barbara Danoff. This time, however, she helped students develop a report writing strategy in a general education class of 25 fifth grade students during Writers' Workshop.

The class included four students with learning disabilities and was team-taught by Barbara and a regular education teacher. Most of the students in this class had already learned the story grammar strategy as described in the first case study.

The report writing strategy was primarily taught by Barbara, with the regular class teacher providing help as needed. It should be noted that the general education teacher and other teachers in the school planned to teach the strategy in their other classes after observing and conferencing with Barbara about the process. Barbara also met with special education teachers from three other county schools who were helping students learn the report writing strategy (MacArthur, Schwartz, Graham, Molby, & Harris, 1994).

For the story writing strategy, instruction initially involved a series of mini-lessons during Writers' Workshop. Because the report writing strategy was more complicated and difficult to learn, the Workshop was temporarily suspended during the initial stages of instruction. Once students started using the strategy together (collaborative practice), though, the Workshop returned to its previous format. Barbara also incorporated a number of cooperative learning procedures into the instructional process. Students were already familiar with these procedures, as they were used throughout the school.

Before deciding to teach the report writing strategy, Barbara carefully considered what she knew about report writing, the students in this class, and the types of assignments they would be expected to complete now and in the near future. They currently wrote reports for their social studies class, and Barbara anticipated that the demand for this type of writing would increase considerably next year in middle school. Furthermore, Barbara and the regular fifth grade teachers' assessments indicated that the students were not particularly adept at report writing. Report writing involves generating and organizing information from multiple sources (background knowledge, information from other written sources, and so forth). While the students were able to brainstorm their own ideas with little difficulty, their skills in organizing collected information (through webs, outlines, or other organizational aids) varied considerably, and they were not adept at reading to locate expository information for writing. Barbara also thought that some of the students, including the four students with learning disabilities, would find it difficult to regulate and monitor a task of this complexity. For these students, and several others, she believed it would be important to include instructional components that would help them persist, compensate for difficulties in retrieving and remembering information, and help establish an "I can do this" attitude.

In describing Barbara's instruction in the second case study, we primarily describe the lessons provided to the class as a whole. Barbara found it necessary, however, to schedule additional time (in the classroom) to work with the students with learning disabilities and other students who were having difficulty learning the strategy. In addition, when students started to use the strategy (during collaborative practice and independent performance), Barbara focused most of her attention on students who needed greater support to learn the strategy; this included the four students with learning disabilities and a few other students. The general education teacher assisted the other students in the class during these times.

Instruction

Stage 1: Initial conference. Barbara held a conference with the class to discuss the goals of instruction. They examined how students had written an earlier report (either writing solely from prior knowledge or mostly copying verbatim facts from reading material). Barbara indicated that she thought the class would profit from learning a strategy for report writing; their reports would become more informative and better organized as well as more fun for others to read. She briefly described the strategy and indicated that the procedures used to learn the story writing strategy would again be used to learn this strategy. She also stressed the importance of effort in strategy mastery and students' roles as collaborators. All of the students indicated a willingness to learn the strategy.

Stage 2: Preskill development. In a lesson with the whole class, Barbara next focused on the characteristics of a good report. After generating ideas on how people work together cooperatively (for example, using nice words, staying on topic, looking at the speaker, and so on), cooperative groups were formed and students brainstormed and discussed what makes a good report (for example, "it makes sense") and why it is important to write good reports (for example, "Prepares you for high school." "To help organize ideas." "So others can understand your writing."). Each group was responsible for sharing their ideas with the class as a whole.

In the next lesson, students were assigned to small groups of three (a reader, a writer, and a manager) and given an example of a good report written by a former student. Their task was to identify what made it a good report. When the groups shared their ideas, Barbara organized them on the blackboard using a semantic web. She also asked students to share any weaknesses they identified in their assigned report. Next, students were asked to reexamine the ideas they had brainstormed in the previous lesson to see how their knowledge of "good reports" had changed. An uncompleted semantic web was then passed out and each group was asked to use it to organize the information in their assigned report. At this point, students were also asked to assess their progress (self-monitoring) by keeping a log in their journal on what they were learning.

By involving students in activities involving brainstorming and semantic webbing, Barbara not only made sure that they understood the purpose of report writing and the characteristics of a good report, she was further able to assess their facility in using these two strategies—both were critical components of the report writing strategy. This assessment allowed her to determine whether students needed additional work on these two strategies.

Stage 3: Discussion of the composition strategy. During the next lesson, Barbara described in detail the report writing strategy to small groups of students; each student received a small chart listing the strategy steps. The strategy included the following steps: (1) choose a topic; (2) brainstorm all you know and would like to know about the topic; (3) organize your ideas by main points and detail on a web; (4) read to find new information and verify the accuracy of already generated material (add, delete, and modify information on the web as necessary); (5) write your report using information from the web, but continue planning as you write; and (6) check to be sure you used everything you wanted to from the web.

Barbara asked students what they thought the reason for each step might be. They then discussed when and how to use the strategy, drawing linkages to social studies and other writing assignments.

Stage 4: Memorization of the strategy.[2] As a homework assignment, students were asked to memorize the strategy steps, using the following key words as reminders: topic, brainstorm, organize, read, write

---

[2]Barbara decides to do *Memorization of the Strategy* before *Modeling*.

and say more, check. The regular class teacher encouraged students to make up a silly sentence (mnemonic) to help them remember the steps. While most of the students memorized the steps easily, the students with learning disabilities and several other students required some additional practice rehearsing the steps of the strategy.

Stage 5: Modeling. In several subsequent lessons, Barbara modeled (while "thinking out loud") how to use the strategy to write a report. Using an overhead projector, she extensively involved the class in helping her plan, write, and revise the report. While composing, Barbara used a variety of self-statements, including problem definition ("What do I need to do?"), planning ("I need to figure out what I know about this topic."), self-evaluation ("Does this make sense?"), self-reinforcement ("I did a good job on that part."), and coping ("Keep trying: I will think of some other ideas."). Students also volunteered helpful self-statements. Once the report was completed, students were asked to volunteer personal self-statements they had previously used to help them regulate their behavior, particularly when learning the story writing strategy (for example, "Let my mind be free."). A discussion also ensued on the importance of what we say to ourselves, and the class identified the purpose of the self-statements used by Barbara during modeling. Students then developed and recorded their own self-statements for helping them regulate their use of the report writing strategy and the writing process. Statements developed and later used by students included: "I can do it." "Am I doing it right?" "I did a good job." "I need to reread my paper." Finally, Barbara asked the students how the strategy might be made more effective. The class agreed at this point to cross out brainstormed items as they were transferred to the semantic web.

Stage 6: Collaborative practice. Students now began to use the strategy to write their own reports, receiving assistance from Barbara and the regular classroom teacher as needed. During individual conferences, the two teachers encouraged students to use a writing checklist (introduced earlier in the year) to evaluate their written product and make decisions about needed revisions. Students also continued to reflect on what they were learning in their journals. Use of the checklist and the journal as well as the personalized self-statements were encouraged as needed. As students became more adept in using the strategy, reliance on the teacher and instructional materials (charts with strategy steps and personalized self-statements) was faded, and Barbara began encouraging students to use their self-statements silently to themselves.

Stage 7: Independent performance. While most of the students were ready for the final stage of instruction after only two or three collaborative experiences, it took the students with learning disabilities more time to learn to use the strategy. As a result, additional instructional time was provided for these students to practice using the strategy.

During both collaborative practice and independent performance, students shared their opinions on how to make the strategy better. This included (a) do brainstorming and webbing together; (b) don't brainstorm for unfamiliar topics; and (c) number on the web what will appear first in the report, second, third, and so forth. Some students personalized the report writing strategy by following one or more of these suggestions. The class also considered how to encourage continued use of the strategy. This included identifying opportunities for using the strategy in the near future, and recognizing problems that might occur and how to address them. In addition, the class set a goal to use the strategy in their social studies class, and agreed to participate in a review and booster session to help promote maintenance and generalization.

Conclusion

As we noted in the beginning of this paper, whole language and process writing represent a marked improvement over what has previously passed as writing instruction for many students. No one intervention, however, can address the complex nature of school success or failure (Harris & Pressley, 1991). If whole language or process writing is to be successful with students of varying abilities and backgrounds, then teachers need to be flexible and resourceful in applying them. It is important to acknowledge that there are children in whole language and process writing classrooms who struggle with writing and reading. If we are to help these children be successful readers and writers, we must be open to building bridges across different teaching philosophies.

Despite the heated rhetoric surrounding the whole language debate, many whole language teachers have already begun building bridges. For instance, Slaughter (1988) indicated that many of the teachers she interviewed used both indirect and direct methods of teaching. Similarly, Dahl and Freppon (1991) and McIntyre and Freppon (1994) observed that whole language teachers were very responsive to children's individual needs, providing direct instruction in phonics and other skills as needed. (One of the teachers from the above-mentioned studies, Linda Headings is co-author of Chapter 4 in this volume).

As the case studies presented in this chapter illustrate, students who participate in constructivistic teaching, such as whole language and process writing, can benefit from explicit and extended strategy instruction. This is not surprising, because strategy instruction complements and supports both of these teaching philosophies in several significant ways. For example, process writing teachers place considerable value on the importance of planning and revising when writing. Strategy instruction supports this emphasis by making the cognitive processes involved in planning and revising more visible and concrete, helping students develop new and more sophisticated tools for accomplishing their writing goals. In addition, students in process writing classrooms are encouraged to be active and responsible participants in their own learning. This includes making decisions about their own work, managing and directing the process of writing, and assessing the effects of their efforts. The type of strategy instruction illustrated in this chapter strengthens students' self-reliance by emphasizing and teaching strategies for goal setting, self-assessment, and self-instruction.

Finally, many of the tenets underlying whole language and strategy instruction are similar. Similarities include (a) students constructing knowledge in interaction with a more competent adult; (b) the teacher continually assessing students' competence in order to determine how to structure learning; (c) nonscripted dialogues between teachers and students about their work; (d) students providing assistance and feedback to each other; (e) acceptance of individual differences in students' rate of progress; (f) emphasis on learning through understanding; and (g) teachers encouraging students to apply what they know to new tasks, including the creative transformation of teacher-modeled skills or processes by students (Graham & Harris, 1994a). Thus, while there are differences between strategy instruction and whole language (mainly centering on explicitness in teaching), they are not incompatible, as both are firmly rooted in constructivistic views of learning (Harris & Pressley, 1991).

In closing, the case studies presented in this chapter provide one example of how bridges can be constructed between whole language and other teaching philosophies. We would like to encourage teachers to build additional bridges that more securely link the teaching of writing and reading processes with the principles of whole language.

References

Applebee, A. (1989, November). *National study of the teaching of literature in the secondary school.* Paper presented at the National Reading Conference, Austin, TX.

Atwell. N. (1987). *In the middle: Reading, writing, and learning from adolescents.* Portsmith, NH: Heinemann.

Bereiter, C., & Scardamalia, M. (1984). Learning about writing from reading. *Written Communication, 1,* 163–188.

Bridge, C., & Hiebert, E. (1985). A comparison of classroom writing practices, teachers' perceptions of their writing instruction, and textbook recommendations on writing practices. *Elementary School Journal, 86,* 155–172.

Brown, A., & Campione, J. (1990). Interactive learning environments and the teaching of science and mathematics. In M. Gardner, J. Green, F. Reif, A. Schoenfield, A. di Sessa, & E. Stage (Eds.), *Toward a scientific practice of science education* (pp. 112–139). Hillsdale, NJ: Erlbaum.

Callaway, B., McDaniel, H., & Mason, G. (1972). Five methods of teaching language arts: A comparison. *Elementary English, 49,* 1240–1245.

Christenson, S., Thurlow, M., Ysseldyke, J., & McVicar, R. (1989). Written language instruction for students with mild handicaps: Is there enough quantity to ensure quality. *Learning Disability Quarterly, 12,* 219–229.

Corno, L. (1992). Encouraging students to take responsibility for learning and performance. *Elementary School Journal, 93,* 69–83.

Dahl, K., & Freppon, P. (1991). Literacy learning in whole-language classrooms: An analysis of low socioeconomic urban children learning to read and write in kindergarten. In J. Zutell & S. McCormick (Eds.), *Learner factors/teacher factors: Issues in literacy research and instruction* (pp. 149–158). Chicago, IL: National Reading Conference.

Danoff, B., Harris, K. R., & Graham, S. (1993). Incorporating strategy instruction within the writing process in the regular classroom: Effects on normally achieving and learning disabled students' writing. *Journal of Reading Behavior, 25,* 295–322.

DeGroff, L. (1992). Process-writing teachers' responses to fourth-grade writers' first drafts. *Elementary School Journal, 93,* 131–144.

Fisher, C., & Hiebert, E. (1990). Characteristics of tasks in two approaches to literacy instruction. *Elementary School Journal, 91,* 3–18.

Fitzgerald, J., & Stamm, C. (1990). Effects of group conferences on first graders' revision in writing. *Written Communication, 7,* 96–135.

Goodman, K. (1992). I didn't found whole language. *The Reading Teacher, 46,* 188–199.

Graham, S. (1992). Issues in handwriting instruction. *Focus on Exceptional Children, 25,* 1–14.

Graham, S., & Harris, K. R. (1993). Self-regulated strategy development: Helping students with learning problems develop as writers. *Elementary School Journal, 94,* 169–181.

Graham, S., & Harris, K. R. (1994a). Implications of constructivism for teaching writing to students with special needs. *Journal of Special Education, 28,* 275–289.

Graham, S., & Harris, K. R. (1994b). The role of development of self-regulation in the writing process. In D. Schunk & B. Zimmerman (Eds.), *Self-regulation of learning and performance: Issues and educational applications* (pp. 203–228). New York: Lawrence Erlbaum.

Graves, D. (1983). *Writing: Teachers and children at work.* Exeter NH: Heinemann.

Harris, K. R., & Graham, S. (1992a). *Helping young writers master the craft: Strategy instruction and self-regulation in the writing process.* Cambridge, MA: Brookline.

Harris, K. R., & Graham, S. (1992b). Self-regulated strategy development: A part of the writing process. In M. Pressley, K. R. Harris, & J. Guthrie (Eds.), *Promoting academic competence and literacy in school* (pp. 277–309). San Diego: Academic Press.

Harris, K. R., & Graham, S. (1994). Constructivism: Principles, paradigms, and integration. *Journal of Special Education, 28,* 233–247.

Harris, K. R., & Pressley, M. (1991). The nature of cognitive strategy instruction: Interactive strategy construction. *Exceptional Children, 57,* 392–404.

Hayes, J., & Flower, L. (1986). Writing research and the writer. *American Psychologist, 41,* 1106–1113.

MacArthur, C., Schwartz, S., & Graham, S. (1991a). A model for writing instruction: Integrating word processing and strategy instruction into a process approach to writing. *Learning Disabilities Research and Practice, 6,* 230–236.

MacArthur, C., Schwartz, S., & Graham, S. (1991b). Effects of a reciprocal peer revision strategy in special education classrooms. *Learning Disabilities Research and Practice, 6,* 201–210.

MacArthur, C., Schwartz, S., Graham, S., Molloy, D., & Harris, K. (1994). *Case studies of classroom instruction in a semantic webbing strategy.* Unpublished raw data.

Mather, N. (1992). Whole language reading instruction for students with learning disabilities: Caught in the cross fire. *Learning Disabilities Research and Practice, 7,* 87–95.

McCutchen, D. (1988). "Functional automaticity" in children's writing. *Written Communication, 5,* 306–324.

McIntyre, E., & Freppon, P. (1994). A comparison of children's development of alphabetic knowledge in a skill-based and a whole language classroom. *Research in the Teaching of English, 28,* 391–417.

Pressley, M., & Rankin, J. (1994). More about whole language methods of reading instruction for students at risk for early reading failure. *Learning Disabilities Research and Practice, 9,* 157–168.

Scardamalia, M., & Bereiter, C. (1986). Written composition. In M. Wittrock (Ed.), *Handbook of research on teaching* (3rd Ed., pp. 778–803). New York: Macmillan.

Slaughter, H. (1988). Indirect and direct teaching in a whole language program. *The Reading Teacher, 42,* 30–34.

Spiegel, D. (1992). Blending whole language and systematic direct instruction. *The Reading Teacher, 46,* 38–44.

Vacca, R., & Rasinski, T. (1992). *Case studies in whole language.* Fort Worth TX: Harcourt, Brace, Jovanovich.

Chapter 9

Balanced Comprehension Instruction: Transactional Strategies Instruction

ℰꙄ ——— ℭℬ

Rachel Brown
University at Buffalo, State University of New York
Pamela Beard El-Dinary
Georgetown University
Michael Pressley
University at Albany, State University of New York

In recent years, we have studied how reading strategies can be taught well in environments in which the following conditions exist: (1) students are exposed daily to reading, writing, listening, and speaking activities in an integrated fashion; and (2) students' individual needs and interests are taken into account. In recent years, we have studied how reading strategies can be taught well in such environments. We refer to this type of balanced comprehension instruction as *transactional strategies instruction* (TSI; Pressley, et al., 1992) to distinguish it from other types of strategies instruction described in the literature.

Strategies Teaching in Balanced Comprehension Instruction

There is no question that coordinated use of comprehension strategies is a critical component of effective reading. Skilled readers use strategies flexibly when they attempt to navigate their way through difficult texts (Pressley & Afflerbach, 1995). When students are taught to use comprehension strategies, their comprehension improves (see, for example, Bereiter & Bird, 1985; Collins, 1991; Duffy et al., 1987; Palincsar & Brown, 1984). These instructional successes aimed at stimulating the constructively responsive use of comprehension strategies observed in excellent readers motivated some educators to adopt comprehension strategies instruction and adapt it to their settings (see also Pressley, Brown, El-Dinary & Afflerbach, in press).

In recent years, we have worked as part of a team to study the teaching and learning of reading strategies in school-based settings. Our work has been a collaborative effort with program developers and teachers. We have documented together how these educators developed and implemented the strategies interventions now deployed in their schools. In the following section we summarize key aspects of the balanced comprehension instruction we studied.

A Description of Transactional Strategies Instruction

Transactional strategies instruction has several important character-istics: (1) an emphasis on teaching a coordinated set of comprehension strategies; (2) an explicit model for instruction that focuses on read-ing as a process; and (3) an integrated approach to teaching cognitive, aesthetic, and affective responding in a social setting.

A coordinated set of powerful strategies

TSI students learn to use a small set of strategies as they read. The strategies are included to improve students' memory, monitoring, and comprehension of text. TSI teachers teach each strategy thoroughly. The comprehension strategies include the following: (1) anticipating upcoming events in text (that is, *predicting*), (2) checking the accu-racy of predictions using the text or the reader's prior knowledge or experiences (that is, *verifying*), (3) picturing text content (*visualiz-ing*), (4) stating main ideas or retelling important information (*summarizing*), (5) linking relevant background knowledge with the text (that is, *making connections*), and (6) checking one's understand-ing of the text (that is, *monitoring*).

Students also learn strategies for tackling unknown words and resolving problems they face while they read. These include several *fix-it strategies* such as: (1) skipping over the problem and continuing to read, (2) guessing by using picture or word clues, (3) rereading the confusing word or section, and (4) looking back in the text to help clarify a confusion.

Instruction in these strategies occurs over several years. Students are encouraged to use strategies they are learning when they partici-pate in small or whole group readings of text as well as during paired and independent reading activities. Students are taught to use strategies when reading both narrative and expository texts, and to apply them when reading in diverse content areas (for example, science and social studies texts, math word problems). Moreover, students are taught to make decisions about which strategy is most appropriate for a situation and to judge for themselves whether the strategy they used was effective.

Explicit instruction in transactional strategies instruction

TSI students are explicitly taught how to use the repertoire of strategies they are acquiring to facilitate their understanding, interpretation, and memory of text. The instruction is consistent with Duffy et al.'s (1986) direct explanation approach and Pearson and Gallagher's (1983) explicit instruction approach (see Figure 9-1).

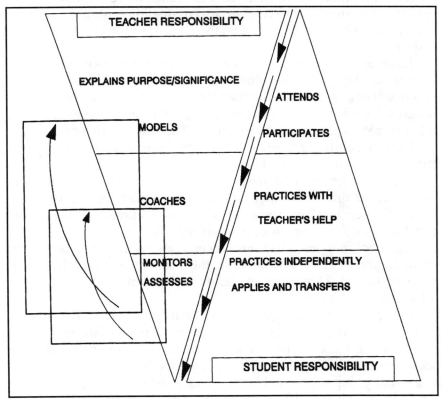

Figure 9-1.   Model for Explicit Instruction

Based on: Bergman, J. L. (1992) and Pearson, P. D. & Gallagher, M. C. (1983).

The top section of the figure represents early strategies instruction, when the teacher bears most of the responsibility for using strategies to comprehend text. The teacher provides a rationale for learning about strategies, defines and explains strategies at points where they are appropriate to the text, and models use of the strategies while he or she verbalizes thinking for students (that is, *thinking aloud*).

As instruction continues, teacher and student responsibilities become more equal, as represented by the middle section of the figure. During this phase of instruction, the teacher coaches students by providing reminders and hints about strategies they can use. Students practice the strategies, often thinking aloud so that the teacher and other group members can "see" the student's line of thought. When students think aloud, they share with each other their thoughts, feelings, connections to themselves and to other texts, descriptions of details, interpretations of motives and events, discussion of themes, and use of strategies. The teacher also frequently rephrases what the student said or did, elaborating on the student's thought processes or actions.

Eventually, the teacher turns over even more responsibility to the student, as depicted in the bottom third of Figure 9-1. As students practice using strategies, the teacher continues monitoring student progress, re-explaining strategies as necessary until students use the repertoire of strategies independently. The teacher also encourages students to identify and seek out new situations in which to apply the strategies they have learned.

Although the instruction described here generally proceeds from more teacher-directed to more student-independent, it is not entirely linear. Rather, teachers respond to students' immediate needs and capabilities during the processing of text. Therefore, they explain, model, coach, and release control recursively, as the arrow on the left of the figure suggests. For example, the teacher may re-explain strategies or model them more explicitly in light of students' specific difficulties with the text.

In the next section, we describe various phases of this model, including specific examples to illustrate key aspects of the instruction we observed. The examples included here were from a representative second grade reading lesson, taught by Mrs. Reston (a pseudonym) to a small group of low-achieving readers who read "Mushroom in the Rain" (Ginsburg, 1991). In the story, an ant seeks shelter from a storm by hiding under a small mushroom. Several animals, increasing in size, wander by in succession, asking to stay under the mushroom until the rain stops. Later, a rabbit races toward the mushroom, trying to elude a fox. The animals hide the rabbit under the mushroom. When the rain stops, the animals emerge, attempting to understand how they all fit under the mushroom.

Explicit explanations. In the initial phase of instruction, the teacher extensively *explained* the strategies (see Figure 9-1). The explanations were explicit, in that students are not just told the information they need to learn. They also are provided with a rationale for the value of that information. For example, the teacher frequently discussed with students why, when, and where to use the strategies to support their meaning-making efforts.

In the following excerpt, Mrs. Reston began her lesson by discussing with students the characteristics of good readers and by reviewing a number of strategies students can use while reading. During the review, students mentioned the strategy of making connections—that is, using prior knowledge to relate the story currently being read to other experiences or stories previously encountered. As the group discussed the purpose of using this strategy, Mrs. Reston asked:

T: When you're reading, do good readers think all the time?

S: Yes.

T: Do sometimes those thoughts just come into your brain as you're reading?

S: Yes.

T: That happens to me. That happens to all good readers. Thoughts hit your brain; you retrieve them. Remember we talked about the brain kind of being like a file cabinet, and you have a storage, you have file drawers for all the books you've read, and file folders with all the information inside? And when you read something, it . . . opens up that drawer, and out comes that information, and you say, "Oh yes, I remember." It's good to talk about that and share that with the group. What about talking so much . . . that you forget what's happening in the story that you're reading? Is that a good idea?

S: No. (Many students.)

T: So you just do a quick think-aloud connection, right? And then go right back to the text because you certainly don't want to forget what's going on in the print . . . and you're understanding right then . . .

In this segment, Mrs. Reston explicitly explained how storage of information in memory can be compared to a filing cabinet that students can draw upon when making associations. She also addressed one potential problem with making connections—and *why* it is a problem. That is, readers may go off on a tangent, talking about their experiences and forgetting their primary goal—to use their background knowledge to facilitate comprehension of the text they are reading.

Modeling. Also during the first phase of explicit instruction, the teacher *modeled* her own use of strategies to interpret text. She thought aloud for her students about her own text processing (see Bereiter & Bird, 1985, on instructional uses of thinking aloud and Duffy, Roehler, & Herrmann, 1988, on mental modeling). Prior to reading "Mushroom in the Rain," Mrs. Reston reminded students to use all their strategies. However, she stressed that in this lesson she would particularly attend to visualizing content. She read the title and first page and modeled her thinking processes.

T: One day, well, I, let's see, the title's the "Mushroom in the Rain." I know what mushrooms are because we've been studying plants, and we saw a filmstrip just the day before yesterday.

(She paused and then read the first page.)

T: Well, I know what a clearing is, it's where, in the woods, where they've taken down a lot of trees, or it's an open space where there aren't a lot of tall bushes and trees and things like that. Well, I guess for an ant, though, that could be pretty small. I'm visualizing a clearing as a . . . big place without trees. But I'll bet a clearing for a little tiny ant would just be a place where there are maybe bits of leaves to make shadows, but just maybe, . . . grass growing around. And so he's looking, he's looking for something to act sort of like a . . .

S: . . . cover.

S: . . . umbrella.

T: . . . like an umbrella, like an umbrella, to keep him, to keep him dry until the rain stops.

(She continued to read: "He sat there waiting for the rain to stop, but the rain came down and came down.")

T: You know, that's happened to me, what I'm picturing. I'm visualizing when I was stranded here at school, without my car, with my bag of school papers to grade, waiting under the overhang, that was almost like my umbrella, waiting for the rain to slow down a little bit, so that I could walk home to my house. Gosh, sometimes it seems like forever till the rain stops. Has that ever happened to you?

Mrs. Reston also modeled by talking about her personal experience with using a strategy, serving as a model of what an expert reader does while reading. For example, when students talked about visualizing, the teacher described her use of visualizing:

T: Do you know what I do when I'm reading? I try, as I'm reading a novel, to make a picture in my mind of the events that are taking place. If the story takes place in the setting of a woods, I try to visualize the woods in my brain, and I try to visualize what's happening, and it helps me remember when I want to summarize, when I want to look back, and try to think what's happened so far. I try to think with my brain, but also use my visualizing strategy to picture, oh yes, this is what happened first, yes, this is what happened second, and that helps me remember.

By talking about her own experiences with visualizing, Mrs. Reston provided a reference for what good readers do. She explicitly explained how she uses visualizing to support her recall of chronologically or sequentially ordered information. (see Chapter 12 by McIntyre et al. in this volume for more examples of teachers' thinking aloud about their reading and writing processes).

Scaffolding. Explaining and modeling strategies is the first step in instruction that encourages students to use strategies for themselves. The next step is to give students a chance to try out the strategies, while guiding their attempts. The teacher provides support or *scaffolds* the instruction, gradually ceding responsibility to students as they become more proficient (Wood, Bruner, & Ross, 1976). The middle section of Figure 9-1 represents how teacher and student responsibilities become more equal at this phase of instruction. The teacher's responsibility is to coach students by providing reminders and hints about strategies they can use. The students' responsibility is to practice the strategies, trying the kinds of thinking processes the teacher has modeled. The teacher also provides frequent feedback through *responsive elaboration* (Duffy & Roehler, 1987), in which the teacher rephrases what the student said or did, elaborating on the thought processes and strategies the student demonstrated.

Guidance is provided as students require it. Mrs. Reston coached, provided hints, and restated students' comments and questions to elaborate and clarify them. In its simplest form, support was provided as Mrs. Reston cued students to apply their knowledge of strategies when they encountered an unknown word:

S: I can't figure out what he did with his tail but all . . .

T: Okay, so what can you do, because you've got some strategies you can use.

S: Skip it and go on.

T: Why don't you try that?

If the selected strategy does not work, Mrs. Reston typically suggests that students apply a different strategy. If a student still has difficulty, the teacher guides the student through the process or models her use of a strategy while explicitly explaining her thinking.

In another example of scaffolding, Mrs. Reston channeled students' attention to thinking about when to use different strategies through use of an analogy and questioning:

T: How do you know which . . . [strategy] to pull out? . . . A carpenter doesn't pull out a hammer when he wants to screw in a screw . . . Now, as expert readers you have to make decisions about which strategy to use, which one will work. Do you want to make a prediction at the end of the story, necessarily? Do you want to use a fix-up strategy if you know all the words and you understand what the story's about? Do you want to visualize? If there's a picture right there and, gee, that's exactly what you're thinking is happening in the story, it looks just like what you're imagining? How do you know when to make a connection . . . [or] think aloud . . . How do you know?

Sometimes support to an individual reader is provided by the group. During the "Mushroom" lesson, a student had trouble reading. The teacher and students in the reading group concurred that rereading the last page was an appropriate strategy to use.

T: Would you like to choral read that? Okay, choral read that last paragraph.

S: I think we should choral read the whole thing. It doesn't make sense.

T: It doesn't?

S: No.

T: Would that be all right with the group? Let's choral read the page? Okay?

S: Doesn't really make sense because he skipped a few words.

The teacher seized this opportune moment to reinforce what good readers can do to resolve a problem:

T: "Well, ... why don't we reread it. I think that's a good ... idea. .... I do that. I go back and reread when I don't understand. That's what good readers do. Let's go back to the top of the page then ... "

The group reread the page together. The student who had trouble was supported in his attempt to construct meaning. Through her actions, Mrs. Reston reminded students that there is something they can do besides sitting and staring at unknown words or waiting for someone to call out an answer. The teacher also saved the student from a potentially ego-damaging event by showing that sometimes even good readers experience difficulty and that they can go back and reread. This takes the onus off the student and transforms the episode into a learning opportunity for all.

Instead of simply commenting about a student's accuracy (for example, "You're right." or "That's incorrect."), the teacher provided re-explanations to extend students' thinking. Often these re-explanations are nested in cycles of coaching and hinting. Such explicit elaborations are opportunities for clarification, review, and fine-tuning of strategic knowledge. For instance, in reviewing comprehension strategies, Mrs. Reston questioned students:

T: What other strategy do we use? You've mentioned problem solving, or fix-up strategies, predicting, summarizing. There are two more that we've learned this year.

S: Think-aloud.

T: And what's that?

S: When you, uh, predict what's gonna happen next.

T: You might use think-aloud to make a prediction. How else do we use think-alouds?

S: Uh, when sometimes after you summarize you sometimes think aloud.

T: And what might you say when you're thinking aloud? Can you think of an example? We talk out loud when we summarize and

we talk out loud when we predict, and we talk out loud, sometimes, when we're using those fix-up strategies, but when we think
aloud, there's something else we can do . . . and I'm gonna give
you a little hint. It's about making . . .

S: Connections.

In this example, the group reviewed the process of thinking aloud.
Mrs. Reston re-explained the ways in which thinking aloud can support interpretive processing. She also cued students to think of another
way thinking aloud could be used.

Self-regulated use of strategies. After much practice, the strategies
teacher decreases cues and feedback even more (see Figure 9-1). As
students begin to use strategies independently, the teacher re-explains
strategies only when necessary. Throughout this period, the students
are asked to *evaluate* the effectiveness of their strategies use. The
teacher also encourages students to use the strategies they have learned
in new contexts (for example, when reading during science instruction or when reading alone during silent reading).

One important component of teaching students the worth of using strategies independently is to have them reflect on their own
strategies use and observe how strategies enhance their reading performance. In this excerpt, Mrs. Reston ended the lesson by evaluating
students' use of strategies:

T: Well, what I'm so impressed with is the fact that you chose strategies to help you understand, and I heard some strategies you
used that I didn't help you [with]. In the beginning of second
grade, I had to say, "Okay, today we're all going to make predictions; today we're all going to summarize; today we're all going
to try to visualize."

S: I remember that.

T: Do you remember that? Do you remember when we practiced
and practiced and practiced? . . . I don't have to do that anymore
because now you're the bosses of your reading. You choose the
strategies that help you understand. And I am very proud of your
thinking. I hope you carry all these strategies in your strategy bag,
which is sort of imaginary, isn't it? . . . I hope you carry them to
third grade and to fourth grade, and to fifth grade, and the rest of
your life because they'll always help you. They help me. And if
they help me, and I'm a grown-up, they certainly are gonna help
you every step along the way. Give yourselves pats on the back

for doing such a super, super thinking job. You got more out of this story, I think, than I did when I read it! Good job!

The integrated, on-line instruction of cognitive, affective, and aesthetic responding in a social setting

In strategies instruction lessons, much occurs concurrently. Students are learning strategies. They are learning how to understand text literally and interpretively. They are learning how to respond aesthetically (for example, to the artistry of the literary piece) and affectively (that is, on an emotional level) to texts. They also are learning to make connections to other genres, authors, and books. This highly integrated form of instruction all occurs naturally, sparked by information in the text, as well as by other students' comments and instructional needs. All of this activity occurs amidst lively social interactions that are always part of reading group.

The social setting provides students with an opportunity to observe the on-line processing of other members in the group. What we mean by integrated on-line instruction is that cognitive, interpretive, and aesthetic responses all occurred *while* group members interacted with each other and the text. By reading and processing text in a group, on-line meaning-making is distributed among teachers and students. Over time, students who observe and practice on-line processing in reading groups learn to process and respond similarly on their own (Vygotsky, 1978).

Mrs. Reston, like other strategies instruction teachers, interwove into her lesson the elements of cognitive, affective, and aesthetic processing of text. After reading a segment, a student thought aloud. Thinking aloud consisted of retelling what happened, making or verifying a prediction, or stating an interpretation. Other students, on their own or in response to teacher prompting, reacted to or elaborated on the first student's ideas. In this way, collaborative, interpretive dialogues unfolded. The discussions of text focused on diverse content, cued in response to students' background knowledge, personal experiences, interests, and the text.

We can see how these various elements come together in the following excerpt. When Mrs. Reston finished visualizing (after reading the first page), a student spontaneously volunteered:

S: I have a prediction, . . . this is gonna be like, . . . "The Mitten" one, like . . . all these insects are gonna try to come in.

T: You think so?

S: Yeah.

The student made a connection based on picture clues that this story would be similar to another story the group read much earlier in the year. In that story, different animals of increasing size ventured into a mitten to escape the ravages of a winter storm. The teacher indicated that the group should try to verify the student's prediction as they read on. After reading the next page, another student agreed that this story is similar to "The Mitten." Students discussed the animals that entered the mitten, noting a discrepancy. A student clarified by stating that there are a couple of versions of "The Mitten." Students continued taking turns, reading aloud, responding, discussing. As the lesson proceeded, students revised their predictions and shared new insights. Throughout these discussions, Mrs. Reston rephrased comments and sought elaboration. However, she did not explicitly state her own interpretation of story events, as is evident in this excerpt:

T: Could you imagine what that would feel like if you were the rabbit?

S: Squished.

S: Like, ooaah . . .

S: I know what I'd feel.

S: I'd feel like a flattened pancake.

S: Because I have a ton of stuffed animals and sometimes I pretend I'm a rabbit at night and I'm squashed by all my stuffed animals because I have about 17 of them.

T: And you sleep with them all?

S: Yeah.

T: So you know what crowded is like.

S: My brother has about two of them in his room, or four, but I have a ton of them.

T: (Calls on another student who has a hand raised.)

S: Uh, when it says mushroom, it's like it's a room, it's like a house, and then a room.

T: Oh, is it acting like their house in a way? It is a shelter, isn't it? It is a shelter.

S: A "mush-**room**" (emphasis on room).

S: Like an igloo.

S: (A different student) With all these people in it, but it's kind of like a room, but lots of people in it, so, a room, but, people are mushed in there.

T: Are they kind of smooshed all together?

S: Yeah, **mush**-room (emphasis on "mush"-ed into room).

In the example, it was apparent how various types of responding were integrated into the lesson. Students used predictions based on their prior knowledge to advance ideas; other students supported or refuted their comments. Students inferred how the animals must have felt, projecting the animals' experiences onto themselves. They related elements of the book to their own very personal experiences. Moreover, they built on each others' observations, constructing meaning collaboratively.

Transactional strategies instruction in whole language classrooms

The term "transactional" captures three theoretical perspectives that are critical in describing transactional strategies instruction that occurs in excellent whole language settings. Text interpretations are encouraged through transactions between reader knowledge and text content, consistent with Louise Rosenblatt's (1978) reader response theory. Teachers believe that the meaning of a text does not reside in the text alone, simply awaiting extraction by the reader. Nor do they believe the meaning is only in the mind of the reader. Instead, meaning is seen as constructed, a result of transactions between the reader's background experiences and the information in the text. Consistent with this view, students are encouraged to bring their knowledge to bear on the text and to rely on strategies to help them as they construct meaning from text.

The transactions between a reader and a text do not occur in a vacuum. Rather, teachers and students act as a literary community, using strategies to construct and evaluate interpretations of text together. Meaning is determined through group discussion rather than by a reader reading alone. This definition of "transaction" has its roots in organizational psychology (for example, Hutchins, 1991; Wegner, 1987), where researchers have studied how group members develop understandings through transactions with others that they would not have developed on their own. In this sense, group members socially construct the meaning of a text (see, for instance, Resnick, Levine, & Teasley, 1991). The meaning that emerges during reading groups is the result of problem-solving involving all the minds in the group.

Balanced comprehension instruction that included TSI in whole language classrooms is transactional in another sense as well. Transactions occur among group members in the sense of the term as it is used in developmental psychology (for example, Bell, 1968; Bjorklund, 1989, pp. 228-231; Sameroff, 1975). That is, when teachers teach the use of strategies to support text interpretation, how one group member reacts is largely determined by what other participants in the group are doing and saying. Therefore, teachers do not decide in advance the questions they will ask students, the support they will give students, or the specific way a lesson will unfold. Instead, the lesson emerges in direct response to students' reactions and needs. In this sense, instructional activities during group reading are largely co-determined.

Conclusion

Transactional strategies instruction provides a socially supportive environment that fosters strategic and interpretive transactions with text and with other readers. Such an environment encourages students to make choices about how to process text, such as using strategies to support reflective responding. It is the totality of the package—the emphasis on strategic knowledge and use, the explicit instruction of how to use strategies to respond to text in multiple ways, and the on-line integrated instruction and construction of meaning that occurs in a socially supported context—that makes TSI a particularly rich form of instruction. Moreover, we believe that TSI can occur in excellent whole language settings.

References

Bell, R. Q. (1968). A reinterpretation of the direction of effects in studies of socialization. *Psychological Review, 78,* 81–95.

Bereiter, C., & Bird, M. (1985). Use of thinking aloud in identification and teaching of reading comprehension strategies. *Cognition and Instruction, 2,* 131–156.

Bergman, J. L. (1992). SAIL—A way to success and independence for low-achieving readers. *The Reading Teacher, 45* (8), 598–602.

Bjorklund, D. F. (1989). *Children's thinking: Developmental function and individual differences.* Monterey, CA: Brooks/Cole.

Collins, C. (1991). Reading instruction that increases thinking abilities. *Journal of Reading, 34,* 510–516.

Duffy, G. G., & Roehler, L. R. (1987). Improving reading instruction through the use of responsive elaboration. *The Reading Teacher, 40,* 514–520.

Duffy, G. G., Roehler, L. R., & Herrmann, B. A. (1988). Modeling mental processes helps poor readers become strategic readers. *The Reading Teacher, 41,* 762–767.

Duffy, G. G., Roehler, L. R., Meloth, M. S., Vavrus, L. G., Book, C., Putnam, J., & Wesselman, R. (1986). The relationship between explicit verbal explanations during reading skill instruction and student awareness and achievement: A study of reading teacher effects. *Reading Research Quarterly, 21*(3), 237–252.

Duffy, G. G., Roehler, L. R., Sivan, E., Rackliffe, G., Book, C., Meloth, M. S., Vavrus, L. G., Wesselman, R., Putnam, J., & Bassiri, D. (1987). Effects of explaining the reasoning associated with using reading strategies. *Reading Research Quarterly, 22,* 347–368.

Ginsburg, M. (1991). Mushroom in the rain. In D. Alvermann, C. A. Bridge, B. A. Schmidt, L. W. Searfoss, P. Winograd, & S.G. Paris (Eds.), *My best bear hug* (pp. 144–154). Lexington, MA: D. C. Heath.

Hutchins, E. (1991). The social organization of distributed cognition. In L. Resnick, J. M. Levine, & S. D. Teasley (Eds.), *Perspectives on socially shared cognition* (pp. 283–307). Washington, DC: American Psychological Association.

Palincsar, A. S., & Brown, A. L. (1984). Reciprocal teaching of comprehension-fostering and comprehension-monitoring activities. *Cognition and Instruction, 1,* 117–175.

Pearson, P. D., & Gallagher, M. C. (1983). The instruction of reading comprehension. *Contemporary Educational Psychology, 8,* 317–344.

Pressley, M., & Afflerbach, P. (1995). *Verbal protocols of reading: The nature of constructively responsive reading.* Hillsdale, NJ: Erlbaum.

Pressley, M., Brown, R., El-Dinary, P. B., & Afflerbach, P. (in press). The comprehension instruction that students need: Instruction fostering constructively responsive reading. *Learning Disabilities Research and Practice.*

Pressley, M., El-Dinary, P. B., Gaskins, I., Schuder, T., Bergman, J. L., Almasi, J., Brown, R. (1992). Beyond direct explanation: Transactional instruction of reading comprehension strategies. *Elementary School Journal, 92,* 513–555.

Resnick, L. (1991). Shared cognition: Thinking as social practice. In L. B. Resnick, J. M. Levine, & S. D. Teasley, (Eds.), *Perspectives on socially shared cognition* (pp. 1–20). Washington: American Psychological Association.

Rosenblatt, L. M. (1978). *The reader, the text, the poem: The transactional theory of literary work.* Carbondale: Southern Illinois University Press.

Sameroff, A. J. (1975). Early influences on development: Fact or fancy? *Merrill-Palmer Quarterly, 21,* 267–294.

Vygotsky, L. S. (1978). *Mind in society: The development of higher psychological processes.* M. Cole, V. John-Steiner, S. Scribner, & E. Souberman (Eds. and Trans.). Cambridge: Harvard University Press.

Wegner, D. M. (1987). Transactive memory: A contemporary analysis of the group mind. In B. Mullen & I. G. Goethals (Eds.), *Theories of group behavior* (pp. 185–208). New York: Springer-Verlag.

Wood, D., Bruner, J.S., & Ross, G. (1976). The role of tutoring in problem solving. *Journal of Child Psychology and Psychiatry, 17,* 89–100.

Chapter 10

Teaching Skills Through Learning Conversations in Whole Language Classrooms

ℬ ────── ℭ

Laura Roehler, Mark Hallenbeck
Michigan State University
Meredith McClellan, Nancy Svoboda
Spartan Village Elementary School

The sense of completeness and closure nurtured by whole language has generated widespread discussion within the educational community. In some quarters it summons the deep devotion typically reserved for works of art, motherhood, and apple pie. Whole language makes so much intuitive sense that its rightful place in the contemporary philosophy of literacy teaching and learning is seldom questioned; as such, the structures upon which effective whole language instruction are built frequently go unexamined. Yet, just as a fine painting is best appreciated by understanding the impact of individual brush strokes, the image of effective language is brought into clearer focus through analysis of its component patterns and strategies. Distinct features stand out for a moment; but they remain connected to a larger, growing, evolving image. The wholeness of language is not ruptured; rather, its components are simply better understood and valued as parts of a whole.

Effective literacy educators help students become strategic language users who not only understand the elements of language, but also appreciate its larger image. These students are aware of connections, patterns, and integrations within and across literacy events. They know when, how, and why to use specific words and word groups.

The patterns and sequences of their language allow seamless communication and clarification to occur. On the other hand, when misunderstandings and miscues occur, effective language users know how, why, and when to repair the damage. In so doing, students increase their language expertise (Duffy, Roehler, Sivan, et al., 1987).

Language users do not necessarily acquire this expertise "naturally." With the help of strategies, learners can move toward whole language outcomes. Learners can develop positive attitudes and dispositions about language and its uses. They can learn how to reason and think their way through challenges. They can learn about important information that is relevant and useful. Strategies support the development of expertise within the whole language philosophical approach. The whole language image is empty without strategy usage. Likewise, isolated strategies and application of strategies are useless without connections to a larger language image. For students to develop expertise in language, they need both the whole language image and its component literacy strategies. It is the interweaving of these two that creates optimum literacy conditions.

Using Learning Conversations

One set of teachers decided to create such optimum learning conditions for their students who were in English as Second Language (ESL) classes. All students were in first year classes that met for an hour at a time four or five times a week. The teachers wanted to help their students develop the dispositions of valuing, respecting and being responsible for self and others while using language. They also wanted to help students understand why language is important and how to use it orally and in written form. Finally, they wanted to help students generate and gain knowledge about important concepts as language was shared.

Because these teachers believe that knowledge is internalized through the use of language in social situations (Vygotsky, 1978; Wertsch, 1985), conversations were selected as a primary means to gain and generate knowledge. These conversations were designed so that all participants could learn. They created situations where students felt that their ideas mattered, where information could come from any participant, and where the task was to learn and share. All participants played two roles. Sometimes a participant was a learner and sometimes the participant was one who had important information to share with others. The classroom teachers moved out of the role of information-giver only and became learners and sharers, too. These conversations were called learning conversations because all participants had opportunities to learn.

Learning conversations are very similar to instructional conversations, which are "discussion-based lessons geared toward creating richly textured opportunities for students' conceptual and linguistic development" (Goldenberg, 1992, p. 317). During instructional conversations, teachers focus on concepts that are relevant for students and have educational value. Background information on a topic is activated, teachers build on the students' ideas and guide the students to new levels of understanding. Learning conversations incorporate the important features of instructional conversations and go one step further. The teachers not only teach, they also learn. They co-construct knowledge with the students. They join conversations where all ideas, comments, and questions matter. All participants value and respect their own ideas and the ideas of others. They also feel responsible for themselves and others (Roehler, McLellan and Svoboda, 1993). As a result, students increase their ability to analyze, their critical thinking ability, the quality of their reflections, and their abilities to interact and work together. Teachers learn to create learning opportunities in which they can participate as learners and sharers of information. These conversations are embedded within activities such as the generation of questions, brainstorming, the generation of comments that activated background knowledge and the creation of maps that connect information. These learning conversations then lead to written drafts that are shared in subsequent conversations. Conversations become the prime vehicle of learning.

After three years of using these strategies in their whole language classrooms, the teachers became curious about the successes of their learning opportunities. They discovered that their students had gained from one to five years on the Metropolitan Reading Test. Their students took leadership in small group and whole group discussions in the ESL classroom and back in their grade level classroom. Their writing was high quality, often winning awards in local authorship contests.

In order for the teachers to strengthen their inquiry, they asked three other educators to join the team. The new members had the responsibilities of analyzing lesson transcripts, observing lessons, interviewing the teachers and interacting with students in order to determine why the learning conversations were so successful. The guiding question was, "What constitutes successful learning conversations in our ESL classroom?" They wanted to know why students had such high gain levels in language expertise and why they were so eager to participate as members of a group.

A Description of Their Whole Language Instruction

The teaching and learning experience was designed to focus on learning conversations within the literacy cycle (Duffy & Roehler, 1993). Within this literacy cycle, conversations played a major role as expertise in reading and writing grew. Because knowledge is acquired in social situations and the students already talked to their families, friends, and acquaintances on an ongoing, comfortable basis, the pattern of learning during conversations was used. The literacy cycle was initiated with guided reading and writing whereby the teachers created opportunities to read, talk, and then write around selected topics. Reading and writing included formats such as books, journals, poems, magazines, and newspaper articles. Films were observed and discussed. These literacy events were stimulated by learning conversations and provided the basis for future learning conversations. These conversations led to the creation of rough drafts of stories, articles, poems, and books that occurred both individually or in groups. Specific, explicit, and adaptive instruction in reading and writing occurred within learning conversations as needed.

If students wanted to share their beginning ideas, seek additional ideas, or had difficulty in creating rough drafts, they joined a group at the sharing table where students and/or teachers met to discuss the emerging rough drafts. Some reading and writing and many learning conversations occurred at this time. Students returned to the sharing table and revised as often as needed. Eventually, students took their latest drafts to the editing table where the collaborative team and/or the students provided assessment of content, mechanics, and form. Once again, reading, writing, and conversations occurred. After written products were assessed, the final drafts were shared at the author's chair (Graves & Hansen, 1983) and the literacy cycle began again. Ongoing authentic reading, writing, and learning conversations occurred continuously throughout the literacy cycle.

Within this literacy cycle, the ESL students progressed through a variety of units. Background knowledge was activated by student-generated and teacher-generated questions and comments. This type of activity was followed by brainstorming, during which the students generated lists and cognitive maps about what they had learned. The lists and maps became the basis for writing and additional reading. Students' interest was maintained as they generated additional questions and comments as knowledge within the various units was developed. Learning was completed as written products were read in the author's chair and shared in other classrooms. The teaching and learning experiences occurred within the literacy cycle, reflecting a whole language image that incorporated strategy instruction.

These teachers, however, did not assume students would learn the content of text (particularly nonfiction) through reading self-selected materials or shared texts on topics of study. They did not assume students would construct their own knowledge without specific guidance from the teacher. Therefore, within these whole language classrooms, these teachers made a specific point to conduct learning conversations about topics the students were reading about. It was their intention to make learning explicit in their whole language classrooms. (See McIntyre et al., in this volume, for additional ways teachers make learning explicit in whole language classrooms.)

A Variety of Strategies

Because they believed students cannot be left to discover everything on their own, these teachers used direct, explicit instruction to guide learning through conversation. Four oral discourse strategies were used by the teachers. The strategies usually occurred in varying combinations as conversations progressed; rarely was one strategy used alone. All strategies were initially modeled during interactions in learning conversations by the teachers, with students subsequently using the strategies as they participated. The strategies used in their learning conversations included:

- *Making Connections*—when teachers activate students' background knowledge in relation to text or material to be learned, provide definitions, show relationships, preface remarks, and summarize what was said or read. This strategy helps students make connections to what they know, an essential component of whole language instruction (Goodman, 1992).

- *Respecting Ownership*—when teachers model language that signifies ownership of ideas on the part of students. This is done through asking for consensus, using personal plural pronouns, asking for clarification, asking permission of the students, allowing students' ideas to develop, and using language that signals an assumption that students are competent.
- *Making Thinking Visible*—which involves creating invitations for students to clarify their thinking, reinforcing what has been asked or said, clarifying what was said, or asking questions.
- *Monitoring the Flow of Conversation*—when teachers use language that moves the conversation forward, paraphrasing, and verifying student understanding.

The learning conversations presented here were part of a unit study on plants. Several oral language skills are included in each learning conversation. Not all of the skills in each conversation are noted.

Learning Conversation One

The first learning conversation occurred at the beginning of a lesson where science content was being reviewed. One of the teachers asked what had been learned. A student responded and the teacher prefaced her next statement by signaling what she was going to ask of the students. She then provided an opportunity for students to activate their background knowledge.

S: . . . We learned to read books and then we talked about what we read and we wrote about roots—that almost all the water that root takes has been taken by the roots, and they have hair and they have veins and they take water. Water goes up in the plant and the food goes down.

T: Okay. Well, I'm really interested in seeing if we can put together our knowledge about plants. Remember what a concept map looks like. Or what webbing is like. Do you remember talking about webbing or a concept map? It's sort of an organization about information. First you take the big idea and put it in the middle. What was the big idea so far in science? What was the main thing the chapter was about? The great big chapter.

S: About plants. About green plants.

Note that the teacher told the students what she was interested in as a preface to her subsequent statements. She then voiced a series of questions and comments to activate what the students knew about concept maps and plants.

In the next sequence within the first learning conversation, the teacher modeled the strategy of ownership by asking for consensus and using personal plural pronouns.

T: Green plants? Okay, would everyone agree that that was what we talked about? So if we were to put up on the board "green plants," then that would be the middle of our map—that would be the center of it. So we could put up "green plants," then, in the middle. Now Tina, you just talked to me about the roots, right?

S: Yeah. They have hair, and their hair is . . . every plant has to have millions of those hairs. And almost all the water that root has taken has been taken by the root hair.

T: So in your remembering and thinking about the chapter, do you think that roots are an important piece of information about green plants?

S: Umm, yeah.

In the next sequence within the first learning conversation, the teacher modeled a third strategy, how to make her thinking visible by offering an invitation to the students.

T: So we want to put that on the map, then, as an important piece of information. And now with roots, you've given us some information that's important about roots. Now out of what you've said, what do you think would be important about these roots—the hairs?

S: Yeah. Their hair and . . .

T: Okay. So we want to put that hair off of the roots. And now what did she say was the purpose of the hair? Why is hair on the roots so important to us? Do you remember, Saram?

S: She said that hair was important because it picks up the water.

T: Because that's the way the water gets in. So it's very important to have water in the plant. Now why is that?

S: So the plant won't dry or anything.

T: Yeah. Because we need what? The plant is how much water?

S: The water goes up to the leaves.

S: I think the root is important because it stores food.

T: Okay, so that would be another reason off of root. So that would go off of roots, wouldn't it? "Stores food."

T: Do you remember the name of the part of the root? What they called the root that stores food?

S: Tap root?

T: That was right—the tap root.

T: Okay, so off of the root, then, we want a line that says "tap root." And then under that, it's important because . . . What did Saram say?

S: That it takes the food . . . makes the food . . .

T: Stores the food. Okay.

In the next segment of the conversation, a student made connections by providing a definition of tap roots and the conversation continued.

S: You know . . . Can I say something about tap root? It says in here "A tap root is one of the thick main roots that store food for the plant."

T: So they store food for the plant. That's good. Now, in what you've read so far, and thinking about your notes or looking at your notes, is there anything else about roots that's important in terms of what you've read, or even what you've wondered about? You know, we can have questions, too. We can put our questions off to the side if a question occurs. Sima?

S: Umm . . . maybe roots hold the plant?

T: Okay. So roots hold the plant what? Up?

S: Yeah.

In the last segment of the first learning conversation, the teacher used another ownership strategy. She asked the participants to help her clarify the thinking of the group.

T: Okay, so the roots have a function of . . . how would we put that? Who can help me?

T: Can we use the word anchor? Do you know that word, anchor?

T: To hold it steady, hold it up, hold it in one place? Would that make sense?

In summary, the first learning conversation contained the oral language strategy of making connections where developing ownership and making thinking visible were used. The second strategy of making connections included prefacing, activating background knowledge, and providing definitions. The third strategy of developing ownership included finding consensus, using personal plural pronouns, and seeking clarification. The fourth strategy of making thinking visible included providing invitations. These teachers do not leave learning to chance, but make special efforts to work in several strategies in their lessons in a "natural" conversational way. (See Dudley-Marling, this volume, and McIntyre et al., this volume, for more examples of teaching through conversation.)

Learning Conversation Two

The second learning conversation occurred immediately after the first one. In this conversation, students and teachers talked about tap roots as they continued to co-construct the concept map about plants. The participants developed their notions about tap roots until a teacher monitored the flow of conversation when she highlighted the differences between the edible parts of carrots and corn.

S: And a carrot is a tap root that we can eat.

T: Oh. Well, that's interesting. So some tap roots are edible.

S: And we are talking about tap roots—remember what you say at the lunch table? Beets . . .

T: Well, then we ought to put that . . . Do you want to put that off of tap root?

S: Well, actually it doesn't have anything to do with green plants or not green plants. It wouldn't have anything to do on the board.

S: I know something that could go with green plants. Carrots.

T: Carrots or potatoes . . .

S: Carrots are not green plants.

S: I don't know—maybe it has something to do with it . . .

S: Does it?

S: You know, this chapter is not—. I think . . .

T: These are good questions . . .

T: Good questions—very good questions.

S: But how come if this is a chapter on green plants, how come they put all the things that are not green plants?

S: It might be because maybe it's important for us to know that we eat something like that.

T: Well, how did we know that we could eat the tap root? Where did that information come from: What does it say there? From your notes or from looking back—what does the book say about . . . ?

S: I think the tap roots you can sometimes eat because they're growing like under the ground. Some food like carrots that grow under the ground, but the leaves are up.

T: And they're green.

S: Yeah, but some has . . . underground they have roots, and up is the food area.

T: So corn, for instance, has roots under the ground and we eat the part that's above the ground. But, with a carrot, we eat what's under the ground.

The conversation continued until a teacher used the strategy of developing ownership. She asked permission of the students to add "edible" to the concept map.

T: And sometimes we use what's on top of the ground just as a plant— a pretty green plant.

S: Can I put something else on this side?

T: Okay, let's finish up with tap root, then we'll come back and add that in. What I'm wondering, is can we put up there that the tap root is edible? Is that something that . . .

S: . . . The green plant needs.

T: Yeah, the green plant needs it, but in addition to that, we can eat it.

T: Can I add that? "Edible?"

S: Yeah.

In summary, the teachers monitored the flow of conversation by highlighting the line of conversation and the strategy of developing ownership by asking permission. While guiding the conversations, this teacher shows respect for learners' contributions, a key component to holistic instruction (Watson, 1994).

Learning Conversation Three

This conversation opens with a teacher asking the students to help her remember what happened on the previous day.

T: Now we did have a discussion yesterday and I need my memory refreshed. We learned about the tap root of the carrot and the beet. We thought about other things that we can eat. And then we got to thinking about onions and potatoes and some of the other vegetables. And somewhere in the back of my mind I remember calling those kinds of plants tubers. We talked about it a while— is the tuber or those big bulb kinds of growths the same as a tap root or different?

The teacher used the strategy of developing ownership by asking students to help her refresh her memory. Another teacher then reinforced the question that was raised and asked the group if her wording of the correction was accurate.

T: Well, I think that's a good question to put up there. We'll see if we can't find the answer to it. So one question would be "Are tap roots and plants that have tubers the same?" Is that right? Would that be a way to put the question?

S: A tuber is a plant? I mean, a vegetable?

T: Yes. A tuber is a vegetable.

S: And they have tap roots?

T: Well, that's the question. A tuber would be a kind of vegetable, but what we don't . . .

S: I don't hear it.

T: Well, I don't hear it very often either, and I grew up on a farm. You'd think I would have known.

Later:

T: I'm not sure that says what I want it to say. Help me. "Are plants that have tap roots and tubers the same?" That's not really what I mean.

S: The tubers have tap roots!

S: Are tubers and tap roots the same?

T: Okay. That sounds right.

And still later:

T: And then we'll have to see if we can find some books that answer that question. Okay, Saram, you said you wanted to add something else to our map?

In the earlier part of the conversation, the teacher helped make thinking visible by reinforcing what had been asked. This strategy is similar to the metacognitive strategies shown in the chapter by McIntyre et al., in this volume. The learning conversation continued as a teacher asked for help. She assumed the students were competent participants. The teacher used the strategy of developing ownership by assuming that the students were competent. This learning conversation ended as a teacher moved the conversation forward by monitoring the flow of conversation.

Learning Conversation Four

The fourth learning conversation occurred later in the lesson as the participants focused on co-constructing information about the stem and continued to create the concept map. A student provided information about the stem and the conversation continued. A teacher used the strategy of developing ownership when she asked the students if anything else needed to be added, and again the conversation continued.

S: Yeah. The stem to transport the water. And the food goes down. . . .

T: Okay, so would stems be the same as the roots? Is that important? Would we draw a line off of green plants and put stems in there? Okay, let's do that. And then the purpose of the stem is to what?

S: Transport food and water.

T: O.K., transport food and water.

T: So I would put that off of stem.

T: Anyone want to add anything else about the stem? We'll get back to your roots in just a minute. Tina or Tiajun? Do you want to add something about stems? If you remember something, looking at your notes, we can go back and add it.

S: And there are some veins.

S: But that's not in the stem.

T: So veins would be off from stems, also. And what are the veins for?

S: Some of the veins carry water for the leaves. Some veins carry food . . .

T: We have "stems," and under that we have "transports food and water," and then we have "veins." Is it the veins in the stems that's transporting the food and water?

S: Yeah.

T: So we want to just erase that one line from stems and connect it to veins, right? Because that's the part of the stem that transports food and water.

S: Yeah. The stem to the vein and then vein to the stem.

T: So does that capture what you're saying? Good. Sina?

In the next segment a teacher made her thinking visible as she clarified the role of the stem in a plant.

S: Stem is a part of the plant between the roots and the leaves.

T: O.K., the stem is the part between the roots and the leaves. Now where would we put this on the map? Where would that piece of information go?

In the final segment of this learning conversation the participants completed their talk about stems and a teacher made connections by summarizing.

T: We have two major parts already in this map. We have the roots . . .

S: Maybe put it in the middle.

T: The stems connect the roots and the leaves. Is that what you said? So could we draw a line off of stems that says, "Connect roots and leaves?"

S: Maybe we could have that stuff, and this is leaves and this is roots.

T: What would be in the middle?

S: So it comes between stems and leaves.

T: So could we take that piece of information, draw a line of stems, and put "connects the roots and the leaves?" Does that make sense, Tiajun? Saram?

S: Yeah. I'm not sure.

T: Let's put it up there, and then we can take it off if we don't like it there. We know that the stem is the part in the plant that comes between the roots and the leaves. That's good because we know that with the roots, that holds the plant up. The stem is the part that connects the roots and the leaves. So that seems to be important information. Saram?

In summary, the teachers developed ownership by encouraging idea development by the students. They made their thinking visible by clarifying the role of the stem and they made connections by summarizing the information that had been co-constructed.

Learning Conversation Five

The fifth learning conversation occurred later in the lesson as the participants began to discuss how the plants make food. One student asked the question about how the plants get materials for food making. Other students made connections by showing relationships.

S: I think on the leaf because, see, sun come on the leaf, air come on the leaf, and then water come when __. Water going this way and going on the leaf the same as air.

S: That's the same thing.

S: I think because it messes up, the water goes up the leaf so sunlight goes there and the air goes there, so it gets all the things that it needs. It messes up and that makes its food. So the food goes down so food comes back here because it doesn't mix well itself. It goes down to the roots so the roots can grow longer.

T: So in some cases, then, the food would go underneath to like where the carrot is. That would become the food? But sometimes the food would go to make like corn—that's on top.

S: Yeah. It can go maybe on top, too.

The conversation continued as a teacher gave ownership of the question to Saram. After Saram responded, the teacher then monitored the flow of conversation by checking and verifying student understanding.

T: Let's see. The question, Saram, say your question again.

S: What part of the plant makes food?

T: Now we had two answers that said it was in the leaf, and that's what you said, too, Tina. Right? That it was in the leaves. Does everybody agree that we think the food is made in the leaves? We don't know for certain where it goes, but it's made there.

The participants continued the conversation until a teacher monitored the flow of conversation by paraphrasing what happens when water falls on leaves. In these examples, students use language to learn (Mayher, Lester, & Pradl, 1983) and co-construct meaning through conversations.

S: That's where plants store stuff.

T: That's right, because we have it right there, don't we? Sure. So you found it in your book and it was up there, too. That stores the food. Saram.

S: I think when the sun shines, it make food right here.

T: Then it goes back down in here and is stored, right?

S: Yeah. I think water goes from the roots to the stem, stem to the leaf. But when food come in on the leaf, the leaf to the stem, stem to the root.

T: So the other way around. Saram?

S: On this spot, right here, it says that. I think I agree with Sina.

S: When the sun come, they make food.

T: So the roots couldn't make food unless they were in the sun. But they're not in the sun. Where are they?

S: On the ground.

S: They can't get air either. It's the air that goes over here. Everything goes, the sun goes on the leaf, and the air goes on the leaf, and the water goes on the leaf. The water goes, that's the place that on the picture they showed. Sun goes here, air goes here, and the water goes here. So that's when it messes up and it goes down.

S: Where the sun is, . . . The air can be anywhere.

S: I think we should read this part.

S: I have a question. There is the food, it's made in the leave, then and the sun and the air is going to the leave, then why does the water go down the root and up the leave? Why don't the water just go the leave?

T: O.K. Does someone think they have an answer for that? Sina?

S: Sometimes there's water down here, down on the ground, and sometimes rain coming. It can't drop—I mean, all this from this rain some waters on the leaf, it can't fly out. It rain drop down. So there's a lot of water down there than going up.

T: So when it rains, the water would fall on the leaves. But because of gravity, it would just keep rolling right off and going down, wouldn't it? Into the ground, and the ground absorbs it. Then, what would the roots do?

S: Brings it up. I think I know why because when you give water to the plant, you don't really give it to the leaf, you give it to the soil.

S: Because of the roots that can take it up. I think the leaves are getting down, so it slips down. That's why we're putting all the water on the ground. So then the water can go in, under where the roots are so the roots can pick it up and the water goes up. Under the picture, under this picture, it shows how plants get materials for the food making. So these are the only materials that it makes food from. That's under here, so it's definitely that they make food in the leaves because everything goes on this place.

Learning Conversation Six

The last learning conversation included in this conversation occurred as the participants were discussing whether plants need water, how often plants need water, and the best places for plants to get water. A teacher summarized the conversation and the students contributed information about the length of the roots and how often plants should be watered. A student used the strategy of making thinking visible by asking a challenging question. A student responded and another student made her thinking visible by stating a conjecture, "If you don't believe that there's no water underground, you could prove it in many ways." The students responded to the conjecture, and another student concluded this learning conversation by using the strategy of making her thinking visible by elaborating on the question, ". . . how can it get the water?"

S: How do grass get water? We don't water grass. Do they get it from underground?

S: How would it grow if you don't water it?

S: If you don't believe that there's no water underground, you could prove it in many ways.

S: There's kind of soil that is in the beach. That soil there's none water in there.

S: That's sand.

S: But this soil, what you talking about, that's—there is water. I know that. But in the desert, if the water's really deep, when the plant is really small, how can it get the water? It doesn't have that big the roots. It doesn't have that big to grow that big and take the water.

S: Some roots just suck it up like a vacuum cleaner.

Discussion

In these classrooms, which operated from a whole language philosophy, the teachers did not assume students would learn science content through reading text, even if the text was of interest to the students. Instead, they used learning conversations as a vehicle for making the content of the topic they studied explicit for students.

The described strategies in these conversations seem to increase the learning opportunities. As strategies were modeled by the teachers within the conversation, they became an expected component that provided support and challenge for the students. The students had more opportunities to learn and were given help as they learned how to talk to each other and teachers.

When oral discourse strategies were compared to reading and writing strategies, many similarities were found. Pearson, Roehler, Dole, and Duffy (1992) identified major reading comprehension strategies shown by research to be effective. All seven of the comprehension strategies overlapped the oral discourse strategies. Their first comprehension strategy, searching for connections between what is known and what is encountered while reading text, is similar to the strategy of Making Connections, which includes providing definitions, showing relationships, activating background knowledge, and prefacing. Their second comprehension strategy, monitoring the adequacy of the models of text meaning that are being built, is similar to Monitoring the Flow of Conversation group, which includes strategies of paraphrasing, checking for and verifying understanding, and moving the conversation consciously forward. Their third comprehension strategy, determining what's important in the text, is similar to Making Thinking Visible by offering conjectures and Monitoring the Flow of Conversation through highlighting a line of conversation. Their fourth comprehension strategy, repairing faulty comprehension when sense-making breaks down, is similar to Making Thinking Visible through clarifying. Their fifth comprehension strategy, drawing inferences during and after reading, is similar to Making Thinking Visible through elaborating. Their sixth comprehension strategy, synthesizing information is similar to Making Connections through summarizing. Their last comprehension strategy, asking questions, is similar to issuing invitations and generating challenging questions and/or comments, also a strategy for Making Thinking Visible.

It is not surprising that many of the oral discourse strategies were similar to the strategies found in reading and writing. See Tierney and Shanahan (1991) for an excellent comparison of the research on reading and writing relationships. What was surprising was the use of a number of oral discourse strategies that signaled ownership by all for the contents of the learning conversations and greater equity among all participants, especially between students and teachers. The teachers modeled the use of all the strategies in this category. They asked permission of the students before using their ideas. They encouraged and allowed idea development. They assumed the students were competent and verified that competency as it appeared. They signaled specific student ownership appropriately. They admitted difficulty in making sense of discussed topics and ideas or remembering important pieces of information while seeking clarification when the participants seemed to need it. They also requested opportunities to refresh their own memories. The teachers used personal plural pronouns and sought consensus often. Again, students emulated these strategies as the learning conversations progressed.

The use of these oral discourse strategies as used by teachers and students appear to move the learning of students beyond the normal subject matter curriculum and more into the hidden curriculum or implicit curriculum often discussed in educational literature. Valued components of the hidden curriculum were made explicit through the use of oral discourse strategies and gradually became interwoven, usable elements for the students as the learning conversations progressed. The addition of oral discourse strategies did not seem to decrease subject matter learning, it seemed to increase subject matter learning, as noted by the scores on the Metropolitan Reading Test. The students' scores ranged from non-readers to primary grade readers at the beginning of the school year to scores that ranged from grade level to sixth and seventh grade levels at the end of the school year. The students' writing improved in quality and quantity and their leadership in group discussions increased. Talking in ways that reflects connections in the ideas being shared, that monitors the flow of conversation, that makes thinking visible and supports the development of ownership and equity makes learning explicit in these classrooms.

Conclusion

The study answered the question of what constitutes successful learning opportunities in an ESL classroom. The inquiry showed that certain oral discourse strategies seemed to play a role in developing expertise in the subject matter curriculum and in the hidden curriculum. Apparently, once again, what teachers say and do affects what students learn (Duffy, Roehler, Sivan, et al., 1987).

Of particular interest was the role of modeling of the teachers in the development of the oral discourse strategies. Students were able to see and hear the teachers using oral discourse strategies during the social exchanges within the learning conversations. They were not just told about these strategies, they were immersed in conversations where they were used. If we want certain dispositions, strategies, and ways of thinking to be second nature and habits for our children, we need to help them form these important patterns of thinking, feeling, and doing by living those patterns in ways that are clearly understandable. Modeling is one of the ways. Plato summed up this need centuries ago when he asked:

> For have you not perceived that imitations, whether of bodily gestures, tones of voice or modes of thought, if they be persevered in from an early age, are apt to grow into habits and second natures?

> —Plato

References

Duffy, G., & Roehler, L. (1993). *Improving reading instruction: A decision-making approach.* New York: McGraw-Hill.

Duffy, G., Roehler, L., Sivan, E., Rackliffe, G., Book, C., Meloth, M., Vavrus, L., Wesselman, R., Putnam, J., & Bassiri, D. (1987). Effects of explaining the reasoning associated with using reading strategies. *Reading Research Quarterly,* 22, 347–368.

Goldenberg, C. (1992). Instructional conversations: Promoting comprehension through discussion. *The Reading Teacher,* 46, 316–326.

Goodman, K. (1992). Whole language research: Foundations and development. In S. Samuels & A. Farstrup (Eds.), *What research has to say about reading instruction.* Newark, DE: International Reading Association.

Graves, D. H., & Hansen, J. (1983). The Author's Chair. *Language Arts, 60,* 176–183.

Pearson, P. D., Roehler, L., Dole, J., & Duffy, G. (1992). Developing expertise in reading comprehension. In S. Samuels & A. Farstrup (Eds.), *What research has to say about reading instruction,* 2nd Ed. Newark, Delaware: International Reading Association.

Roehler, L., McLellan, M., & Svoboda, N. (1993). *University professors and public school teachers: A case for mutuality in classroom-based collaboration.* Paper presented at the annual conference of the American Education Research Association, Atlanta.

Tierney, R. J., & Shanahan, T. (1991). Research on the reading-writing relationship: Interactions, transactions, and outcomes. In R. Barr, M. Kamil, P. Mosenthal, & P. D. Pearson (Eds.), *Handbook of reading research volume II* (pp. 246–280). New York: Longman Publishing Group.

Vygotsky, L. S. (1978). *Mind in society.* Cambridge, MA: Harvard University Press.

Watson, D. (1994). Whole language: Why bother? *Reading Teacher, 47,* 600–607.

Wertsch, J. V. (Ed.). (1985). *Vygotsky and the social formation of mind.* Cambridge, MA: Harvard University Press.

Chapter 11

Explicit Instruction for Early Learners: Enhancing Reading Comprehension Using a Multiple Strategy Repertoire

ℬ ———— ℭ

Linda Wold
Palos Consolidated School District 118, Palos Heights, Illinois

As in most whole language classrooms, the instruction described in this chapter is focused on children's construction of meaning. The first grade teacher in this classroom creates opportunities for children to read and enjoy books in a variety of contexts: whole class, small groups, triads, partners, and individually. Some of these contexts are planned and some of them occur naturally. The teacher engages the children in talk about books—always with a focus on meaning—in all of these contexts. Children naturally collaborate on reading and discussing these books with and without the teacher.

Within this classroom environment, the classroom teacher consistently searches for relevant strategies to make reading memorable. She is dynamic in the sense that she cultivates a disposition to engage with text (Beck & Dole, 1992), intended to promote in beginning readers a deep cognizance of how their reading-thinking processes affect reading comprehension. The teacher attempts to be sensitive to the ever-changing needs of novice readers, modifying reading instruction to accommodate diversity.

As a Chapter I reading resource teacher for grade one, I collaborate with this whole language teacher by providing in-class reading instruction for developing readers and occasional whole group strategy lessons. Strategy instruction fits into this classroom reading practice as a way for students to develop "strategic ingenuity" (Palincsar, 1986, p. 122), an approach to combining self-regulated learning and effort in different learning contexts, resulting in adaptive strategy use.

The classroom teacher saw the need for a strategy lesson intended to increase children's comprehension and suggested that I conduct a lesson with the entire class. Since the whole class was familiar with predicting, I decided to present an adaption of the Word Chain prediction strategy. The Word Chain[1] (Abromitis, 1992) is a brainstorming vocabulary activity, focused on making word associations with related words, similar to clustering (Rico, 1994). When the chain is linked with explicit, informative feedback that redirects learners back to the text and to their own sense-making while reading, it helps children become autonomous readers.

Adapting the Chain as a cognitive strategy to increase reading-thinking connections developed after my realization that students and even adults don't always notice links among titles, illustrations, and text. I realized that novice readers have very similar problems when they encounter words they don't know. My Chapter I students often rely only on the words in the title of a book without noticing the illustrations to predict story words and events. When readers don't know the title of a book, they need resources to develop alternative ways to make reading-thinking connections. Explicit scaffolded support, the kind of guided direction used in Adapted Word Chains, is one way to encourage students' sense-making.

This chapter delineates an Adapted Word Chain strategy procedure used in a first grade whole language classroom in a public school in Illinois. Specific, encouraging teacher feedback, illustrated throughout the chapter, underlies this procedure, intended to increase students' reading autonomy. This description is followed by a table which summarizes the steps of the procedure.

The Adapted Word Chain Strategy

Initially designed to tap students' prior knowledge and create meaningful associations for new words, the Word Chain activity promotes brainstorming word meanings and relationships. Several words, written from a previously read story and distributed to individuals or pairs of students, are linked by chains from left to right by relatedness or

---

[1]While Abromitis sees Word Chains as a single strategy, it is my understanding that the Adapted Word Chain is most effective as a multiple strategy repertoire which includes think alouds, prediction, and self-questioning.

patterning. Teacher-generated word lists or students' self-selected words are used to construct the linked chain. In this example, students used the word "reading" in Abromitis's brainstorming model to develop the Word Chain from a list of words, relating each word to the adjacent link: reading—books—letters—words—stories—titles—authors—poems—rhythm—songs.

Adapted Word Chain Components

The Adapted Word Chain[2] components, woven throughout the strategy sequence, include the following:

1. motivation, created by an encouraging context for prediction.
2. explicit direct instruction, guided by teachers' think-alouds.
3. verbal scaffolded direction, demonstrated by teachers' dynamic and supportive instruction.

I presented the strategy as a cognitive coach, infusing motivational prompts about good readers, providing encouraging support when necessary, and rehearsing what students already know about prediction. Before we began I encouraged students to develop a context for reading-thinking in which they could do the very things that good readers do, using prediction as a way to strengthen their developing knowledge systems (Pressley, Borkowski, & Schneider, 1987). Because prediction plays such a powerful role in learning, I explained to the students, using think-alouds (see Brown, El-Dinary, & Pressley, this volume; McIntyre, et al., this volume), how I choose books to read. Carefully describing my own ambivalence in book selections and sharing my prediction strategies as I read the titles and jackets of books, I revealed how I predict my selection of a captivating story. My thinking aloud was intended to explain that prediction is a strategy that good readers use.

Motivation

The following introduction established the willingness of students to explore new ways to learn about reading and prediction.

---

[2]The Adapted Word Chain, while cohesive (which makes it work), is constructed by explicit and overlapping strategy components embedded in think-alouds, predictions, and self-questioning.

T: We aren't just born smart. We have to learn how to get smarter every day. Today we're going to learn about a strategy that good readers use. It's a strategy that helps readers learn how to predict words and events in a story, and that helps students learn how to become better readers. It's called Word Chains. Do you remember what prediction means?

S: Um, make up what the story's about.

T: Yes, you make up or predict what the story might be about. So I'm going to ask you to do that today. Did you ever make paper chains at holiday time?

All: Yes!

T: Well, this activity is like making paper chains, only you make chains in your head with words. Pretty neat, isn't it?

All: Yeah.

T: It's something that good readers do and helps you to understand the story before you read it. When you predict from the title of the book and the pictures, sometimes you actually know what the words are. You connect those words to the story just like paper chains. Using Word Chains helps you to learn more about prediction. Let's try Word Chains together.

My encouraging motivational prompt about learning to get smarter every day was intended to help students understand, from this informative, encouraging feedback, that it takes effort and thinking to get smart. Additionally, I wanted them to recognize that they could develop reading competency by using a strategy that good readers use. Developing such self-efficacy beliefs (Bandura, 1986, 1993) is an important process for all learners, but especially for children who believe they are unable to accomplish certain tasks even though their peers feel capable of something quite similar.

I included a brief rehearsal of the meaning of "prediction" and what it means to use prediction in the Chain context. I tried to cultivate a sense of how prediction can be used to increase strategic reading-thinking power, enhancing Word Chain connections that bridge what learners know with what they don't know.

Explicit Direct Instruction

Using think-alouds as a way to enhance comprehension (Spiegel, 1992), I presented Margaret Mahy's book, *The Fight on the Hill*

(1988), a story about pigs and goats who fight over territory and whose confrontation yields such distress that the animals resolve their problems with humanely characterized compassion, I modeled chain predictions. I demonstrated how to connect our predicted words on the blackboard, just like paper chains. In our visual Chain diagram, we connected the known with the unknown, just like good readers do. Our strategy session continued as students predicted their own Chain words for our blueprint on the board. I used every opportunity to let students make their own paper chain connections with words and ideas they could picture happening in the story.

Students created their own Word Chains by predicting the relationship between the book's title, *The Fight on the Hill*, and the book's cover illustrations.

T: If you look at the picture on the cover of this book and the title, you can predict what words might be in the story. You try to make a connection between the *title* of the book and the *picture*. Can you think of a word that might be in this story?

S: Friend.

T: Friend, Why did you say "friend"?

S: Because "friend" is in the title.

T: Yes, it looks like "friend" in the title. I like the way you noticed the beginning letter. Let's look carefully and read it together. The title actually says, *The Fight on the Hill*. Now I'm going to write "friend" on our Word Chain and you decide after we talk about our predictions if you think we should include that word in our Chain. OK? That might be an important word on our Chain. If we look at the picture and the title, *The Fight on the Hill,* what other words can you predict? Remember you can use words in the title.

S: Animals.

T: Animals. I like the way you used the picture clues to figure out your prediction. Do you want to tell me what kind of animals or use the word "animals"?

S: Pig.

T: If you use the picture clues, would you say "pig"?

S: Pigs.

T: What is the difference between "pig" and "pigs"?

S: There's an "s" on the end of "pigs."

T: I like the way you noticed more than one pig! How did you figure that out? (Write on chain.)

S: I heard the sound of "s" at the end of the word.

T: I noticed you made the word match the picture of "pigs," that's what good readers do! Can you think of another word that we can add?

Verbal Scaffolding

The students added predictions to the Word Chain, carefully using the picture clues and the title to predict words that might be in the story. I encouraged students to predict connections like single word pretellings, based on their prior knowledge (Irwin & Baker, 1989) and intuitions. My verbal scaffolded direction was based on students' immediate needs and my overriding concerns to facilitate their self-management skills. Sometimes I stopped to explicitly instruct, noticing that someone used an "s" at the end of the word to describe more than one animal; to affectively support, commenting on something I liked that a student demonstrated; to redirect, asking students to refer to the print or illustrations to use reading-thinking frames; to think aloud, repeating my own questions about words that might be in the story. We also rehearsed the growing list of words chorally. This activity added word recognition opportunities for students who were insecure about reading and allowed them many risk-free chances to respond or listen within the group.

Using Think-Alouds

At one point a student predicted "the," which prompted our discussion about predicting picture words in our Chain. I used a think-aloud to verbalize my mental processes when choosing words for the chain.

T: The word "the" is an excellent prediction because that word is often in titles. I want you to stick with picture words, though, so you can imagine a story in your mind as we go along. This will help you understand the story. Picture words are words that we can imagine a picture of something happening. When I think of a picture word, like "pigs," I can imagine a picture of sloppy, muddy pigs in my mind. Should we include "the" or should we try to choose a picture word in the title?

S: (Same student) Fight.

T: Do you think that prediction makes sense and why?

All: Yes! It's in the story title.

T: I like the way you figured out a picture word for our Chain.

After a few minutes, our list contained the following words: pigs, goat, fight, basket, sky, sweating, friends. After I made up a story invention to make sense out of the Chain words similar to McGinley and Denner's (1987) story impressions, we practiced reading our list together. In step four of the Chain sequence, I described my story invention as my own think-aloud, telling what I thought would happen in *The Fight on the Hill.* Thinking through possible connections suggested a way for students to pre-tell stories.

T: Now, this is our Word Chain, and I'm going to make up a story invention using all the words. That's what good readers do, they pretend they know the story. So I'm going to predict a story from these words on our Chain and at the end of the story, we will have to decide if my story prediction is true. (The story invention is plotted below.)

The *pigs* and the *goats* had a *fight.* They both wanted the baseball in that *basket* and they wanted to throw the baseball high up into the *sky.* They were playing so hard, they were all *sweating*! Finally, at the end of the story, instead of fighting, they became *friends.*

Using "I wonder" think-alouds to instigate self-questioning, I made my own private thinking public before reading the text in shared book fashion:

- I'm wondering if the pigs and goats will really have a fight?
- I'm wondering if animals fight for a reason, and if they're really sweating?
- And I'm also wondering (looking at the inside title page differently illustrated) if the animals will become friends again?

Reading the Story

After this sequence, I actually read the story to the children. We simply enjoyed it together. Because we had created a number of predictions about the story together, the children seemed especially interested and closely attended. I also asked the students to listen carefully to the story and determine if my invention was true. Markman (1981) tells us of this critical point in prediction: Readers must be able to confirm or disconfirm a prediction to decide whether or not they understand, which plays a key role in the Adapted Word Chain. Because this self-evaluation process leads to the development of self-regulated behavior, it is an imperative step in the learning process. Students are being asked to be the evaluators, articulated by teachers' encouraging feedback. Readers need to be the ones to determine what they know about the predicted Chain words by thinking about whether or not the predicted story makes sense as well as how it differs from the actual story meaning. When students invent their own Chain stories, they will repeat this evaluative process independently to confirm and disconfirm their predictions.

In following Markman's confirmation sequence, first I asked the audience to confirm or disconfirm my story invention after I read the book aloud to the group. Then, I asked the students to do the same as they examined the Chain words on the blackboard. After each part of the story invention, the students gave feedback about the invented sentences:

- (Pointing to the word chain) The pigs and the goats had a fight over the baseball in the basket. Did that really happen? "No!"
- Did they want to throw that baseball high into the sky? "No!"
- And they were playing so hard, they were sweating? "Yes!"
- At the very end, did they become friends? "Yes!"

T: So my invented story was a little different than the real story. After you read the story with a Word Chain, you have to decide whether the predicted Chain words should be kept on the Chain or crossed off. Now, we have to decide if those words were really in the story. When you predict from the title of the book and story illustrations, you can see that you already know some of the story words. That's what good readers do!

Following the story prediction with the actual text, students continued confirming and disconfirming the selected words on the Chain. They unanimously included "pigs," "goats," and "basket." A discussion ensued as students conferred on the word "sky" since the word wasn't actually read in the story. Eventually "sky" was disconfirmed and crossed off our Word Chain, but added to our list of words we wanted to learn. Students were to justify their answers for keeping the word on the Chain.

Strategy Transfer

Following a choral rereading of the Word Chain words, I asked the children to think about getting smarter in first grade. Based on my ongoing studies with repeated Word Chain practices, I knew if readers connected this strategy with what good readers do, they would be more likely to practice it and eventually own it as part of their reading strategy repertoire.

After I explained ways that Word Chains can help us think about reading, I asked students to tell me if Word Chains might help them get smarter when they read other stories (step seven). A unanimous response told me that they thought so, but when I asked them how it would help they could only say, "When you read a book!" They couldn't verbalize exactly how prediction gives us an insider's view to the story vocabulary and events. I knew that young learners' ability to verbalize their thinking is somewhat limited, but direct application of this behavior can improve such understanding (Brown, 1987; Brown, Campione, & Day, 1981) and that it develops over time (McIntyre et al., in this volume).

Thus, immediately following the strategy instruction, I asked students to practice making their own Word Chains with *The Chick and the Duckling* (Ginsburg, 1972). I wanted to see if they could transfer the strategy sequences to another text and if the process seemed helpful. While holding up a big book of *The Chick and the Duckling,* we followed the exact Chain strategy that we had just completed. I read the title of the book and waited to see if students could apply and generalize what they had learned, with less explicit instruction from me (Wood, Bruner, & Ross, 1976). When I asked students about using the Adapted Word Chain with this new story, they began to predict spontaneously from the book's cover illustration. One of my Chapter I students said, "You can tell the duck went for a walk." Another child mentioned, "The butterflies were coming."

Next, we practiced the "how to" part of the reading-thinking strategy with assigned buddy readers. The students quickly paired up to attempt their own Word Chains. As the classroom teacher and I circulated throughout the room, we reminded students to put only one word in each circle of the chain and used such motivational prompts as, "I like the way you're using good picture words to tell us about the story."

During learning talk (Wells & Chang-Wells, 1992) or classroom conversation it became apparent that children quickly understood the paper Chain idea and enjoyed making their own Chain connections. Within a few minutes, *The Chick and the Duckling* was transformed into a graphic chain of new vocabularies and insights. The strategy sequence continued, using the same steps as *The Fight on the Hill,* followed by the story read-aloud and final phase of confirming and disconfirming the story invention and the new Word Chain. Observing these young six-year-olds as they clearly demonstrated their Word Chain knowledge base in a new context, I realized that they were at various zones of proximal development (Vygotsky, 1978), stretching to think and connect reading. While using the strategy and talking about it with classmates, students came to understand the utility of Word Chains (Pressley, Borkowski, & O'Sullivan, 1984). They had opportunities to learn when and where to use the Word Chain strategy, as well as how to adapt the procedure to new situations.

In the evaluation segment, children jointly discussed their contributions and suggestions about Word Chains, followed by explicit talk concerning what they were understanding in reading. Students made comments like, "We can read better," and "Sometimes I know the words." Many students came to know it well and appreciate its cognitive importance as a reading strategy. For example, a group of Chapter I students taught Word Chains to younger siblings in kindergarten using their take-home readings. Others have brought back Word Chain examples, developed from their at-home readings, to share with the class. Table 11-1 summarizes the procedures for this reading comprehension strategy.

Table 11-1.   Word Chain Procedures for Pre-reading Activities

Word chains are free-association prediction activities that help students discover connections between known words and new story vocabulary and events.

Strategy sequence:
1. Develop prediction understanding through think-alouds.
2. Think aloud and predict the relationship between the title of the book and the illustrations.
3. Verbalize possible words that may be found in the story and visually link them on the blackboard. First experiences should use five to six words and expand appropriately.
4. Model the story invention based on the words chosen.
5. Present a shared reading of the story. Confirm or disconfirm the story invention and Chain words that match the story.
6. Cross off all inappropriate words on the chain and ask for justification.
7. Decide how and where this strategy is useful.
8. Rehearse the strategy in pairs or triads, using a blank Chain diagram. Support student engagement by citing their examples.
9. Invite readers' contributions and suggestions.
10. Talk about what we've learned today.

The Teacher's Response: Critical to Sense-Making

Cognitive coaching sustains the framework of the Adapted Word Chain and represents a metacognitive approach to define the thinking interactions between teachers and students (Paris & Winograd, 1990). We used cognitive coaching nested in an affective support system (Dinkmeyer & McKay, 1976; McCombs & Whisler, 1989). That is, there was explicit instruction and modeling (Duffy, et al., 1987), plus verbal scaffolded practice (Wood et al., 1976), all presented in an encouraging, affectively positive context (Bandura, 1993) intended to motivate developing readers' autonomy.

Other ongoing, encouraging commentary supported students' developing reader autonomy. In my responses, "I liked the way you used the picture clues to make your prediction," and "I like the way you noticed the difference between one goat and more than one goat," I encouraged readers to rethink what they had done to make the prediction or notice the word differences. By rethinking the process of how students responded as good readers, I asked readers to connect such positive reading-thinking to repeated behaviors.

Finally, selective, informative feedback also encourages readers' autonomy. Examples of this kind of teacher response are listed in Table 11-2.

Instead of praising students' products as, "You did a good job thinking about that prediction," which they understand as a teacher's opinion of how well they have done, I consistently encourage students to evaluate the quality of their own performance. I intend to help students learn how to appraise their own work and build confidence in self-evaluation processes, leading to reader autonomy (Clay, 1979; Dinkmeyer & McKay, 1976; Routman, 1991; Walker, 1992).

Discussion

How can the classroom teacher make reading instruction explicit and understandable, especially for students who are unable to integrate what they know with what they are currently learning? I found that verbal think-alouds made reading more accessible to those students who had trouble integrating new information. They disclosed my private thinking as public knowledge and helped readers to scaffold in such a way that they could visualize my metacomprehension thinking as an alternative sense-making posture.

Table 11-2. Supportive Teacher Feedback for Developing Learners' Self-Control

- You're doing exactly what good readers do.
- I heard you thinking out loud to make story sense. That's a good reader strategy.
- What did you just do to help make the story predictions?
- It could be the word you just read. Does it look like the word?
- I liked the way you worked hard to make that match. What did you use as a clue?
- Good readers like to notice _____. I like the way you noticed _____ to figure out the pattern. (Name the strategy that was used.)
- I liked the way you made sense out of a difficult word. How did you do that?
- I noticed that you were _____ (name activity) when you came to the hard part. What did you do? Why did that help you? Or, why was that part hard for you?
- I noticed the way you used the picture clues to figure out the hard part. That's a good reader strategy.
- Sometimes I notice that you reread to make story sense. How does that help you?
- What are some of the good reader strategies that you are using?
- What strategy did you just use that helped you solve the problem?

When students heard me talk about holiday paper chains, they seemed to easily understand the Word Chain example. (These children were familiar with making holiday chains.) As I talked about choosing library books to read, my think-aloud showed how I predicted what I thought would be enjoyable reading. This mental modeling (Duffy, Roehler, & Herrmann, 1988) revealed metacognitive processing as a significant aspect of learning (Paris & Winograd, 1990; Pressley, Borkowski, & O'Sullivan, 1985; Vye, Delclos, Burns, & Bransford, 1988), steering the readers' focus toward strategic reading (Paris et al., 1983).

The intention of teaching Word Chains via think-alouds, predictions, and self-questioning is to shed light on the invisible, inner thinking that occurs during authentic reading. The easy connection to something most first graders seem to know, paper chains, brings this strategy directly into their own scheme of understanding. In the process of learning how to learn through direct, explicit instruction, and repeated strategy practice, students develop the habitual response of knowing when and how to use such a comprehension support. My readers had begun to attribute their successes and failures in reading to their efforts rather than to their innate abilities (Brophy, 1988; Weiner, 1974).

The effects of using the Adapted Word Chain strategy seem to be spilling into this whole language classroom's reading practices as the teacher supported her readers with reading-thinking ideas that nurture autonomous reading. Gradually our young community of readers is starting to make the magical paper chain connections (Paley, 1986) that deepen and enhance their repertoire of reading sense-making strategies.

References

Abromitis, B. (Ed.). (1992). *New directions in vocabulary.* Rolling Meadows, IL: Blue Ribbon Press.

Bandura, A. (1986). *Social foundations of thought and action.* Englewood Cliffs, NJ: Prentice-Hall.

Bandura, A. (1993). Perceived self-efficacy in cognitive development and functioning. *Educational Psychologist, 28*(2), 117–148.

Beck, I. L., & Dole, J. A. (1992). Reading and thinking with history and science text. In C. Collins, & J. N. Mangieri (Eds.), *Teaching thinking: An agenda for the twenty-first century* (pp. 3–21). Hillsdale, NJ: Erlbaum.

Brophy, J. (1988). Research linking teacher behavior to student achievement: Potential implications for instruction of Chapter I students. *Educational Psychologist, 23,* 235–286.

Brown, A. (1987). Metacognition, executive control, self-regulation, and other more mysterious mechanisms. In F. E. Weinert, & R. H. Kluwe, *Metacognition, motivation, and understanding* (pp. 65–116). Hillsdale, NJ: Erlbaum.

Brown, A. L., Campione, J. C., & Day, J. D. (1981). Learning to learn: On training students to learn from texts. *Educational Researcher, 10*(2), 14–21.

Clay, M. M. (1979). *The early detection of reading difficulties* (3rd ed.). Auckland, New Zealand: Heinemann.

Dinkmeyer, D., & McKay, G. D. (1976). *Systematic training for effective parenting.* Circle Pines, MN: AGS.

Duffy, G. G., Roehler, L. R., & Herrmann, B. A. (1988). Modeling mental processes helps poor readers become strategic readers. *The Reading Teacher, 41*(8), 362–367.

Duffy, G. G., Roehler, L., Sivan, E., Rackliffe, G., Book, C., Meloth, M., Vavrus, L., Wesselman, R., Putnam, J., & Bassiri, D. (1987). Explaining the reasoning associated with using strategies. *Reading Research Quarterly, 22*(3), 347–368.

Ginsburg, M. (1972). *The chick and the duckling* (V. Suteyev, Trans.). New York: Macmillan.

Graves, D. H. (1990). *Discover your own literacy.* Portsmouth, NH: Heinemann.

Irwin, J. W., & Baker, I. (1989). *Promoting active reading comprehension strategies: A resource book for teachers.* Englewood Cliffs, NJ: Prentice Hall.

Mahy, M. (1988). *The fight on the hill.* Auckland, New Zealand: Shortland Publishing Ltd.

Markman, E. M. (1981). Comprehension monitoring. In W. P. Dickson (Ed.), *Children's oral communication skills* (pp. 320–357). New York: Academic Press.

McCombs, B. L., & Whisler, J. S. (1989). The role of affective variables in autonomous learning. *Educational Psychologist, 24*(3), 277–306.

McGinley, W. J., & Denner, P. R. (1987). Story impressions: A prereading/writing activity. *The Journal of Reading, 31*(3), 248–253.

Paley, V. (1986). On listening to what children have to say. *Harvard Educational Review, 56*(2), 122–131.

Palinscar, A. (1986). Metacognitive strategy instruction. *Exceptional Children, 53*(2), 118–124.

Paris, S. G., Lipson, M. Y., & Wixson, K. K. (1983). Becoming a strategic reader. *Contemporary Educational Psychology, 8,* 293–316.

Paris, S. G., & Winograd, P. (1990). How metacognition can promote academic learning and instruction. In B. F. Jones, & L. Idol (Eds.), *Dimensions of thinking and cognitive instruction* (pp. 15–51). Hillsdale, NJ: Erlbaum.

Pressley, M., Borkowski, J. G., & O'Sullivan, J. T. (1984). Memory strategy instruction is made of this: Metamemory and durable strategy use. *Educational Psychologist, 19*(2), 94–107.

Pressley, M., Borkowski, J. G., & O'Sullivan, J. T. (1985). Children's metamemory and the teaching of memory strategies. In D.L. Forrest-Pressley, G. E. MacKinnon, & T. G. Waller (Eds.), *Metacognition, cognition, and human performance: Vol 1. Theoretical perspectives* (pp. 111–153). Orlando, FL: Academic Press.

Pressley, M., Borkowski, J.G., & Schneider, W. (1987). Cognitive strategies: Good strategy users coordinate metacognition and knowledge. In R. Vasta (Ed.), *Annals of child development* (Vol. 4, pp. 89–129). Greenwich, CT: JAI Press.

Rico, G. L. (1994). *Writing the natural way.* New York: G. P. Putnam's Sons.

Routman, R. (1991). *Invitations: Changing as teachers and learners, K-12.* Portsmouth, NH: Heinemann.

Spiegel, D. L. (1992). Blending whole language and systematic direct instruction. *The Reading Teacher, 46*(1), 38–44.

Vye, N. J., Delclos, V. R., Burns, M. S., & Bransford, J. D. (1988). Teaching thinking and problem-solving: Illustrations and issues. In R. J. Sternberg & E. E. Smith (Eds.), *The psychology of human thought* (pp. 337–365). New York: Cambridge University.

Vygotsky, L. (1978). *Mind and society: The development of higher order thinking processes.* Cambridge, MA: Harvard University Press.

Walker, B. (1992). *Supporting struggling readers.* Markham, Ontario: Pippin.

Weiner, B. (1974). *Achievement motivation and attribution theory.* Morristown, NJ: General Learning Press.

Wells, G., & Chang-Wells, G. L. (1992). *Constructing knowledge together: Classrooms as centers of inquiry and literacy.* Portsmouth, NH: Heinemann.

Wood, P., Bruner, J., & Ross, G. (1976). The role of tutoring in problem-solving. *Journal of Child Psychology and Psychiatry, 17,* 89–100.

Section IV

Patterns of Teachers' Actions: Balancing Instructional Perspective

  ∽ ——————————————————— ∾

"Especially important . . . the instruction reported by special education and regular education teachers for weaker students was balanced, involving both explicit instruction of decoding and other skills in the context of rich authentic reading and writing" (Pressley et al., Chapter 13.)

The chapters in this section result from studies of many outstanding whole language teachers who teach strategies and skills within authentic tasks and activities. The final chapter is a reflection about issues involved in explicit strategy and skill teaching in whole language contexts by Michael Pressley.

In Chapter 12, Ellen McIntyre, Diane Kyle, Ric Hovda, and Jean Anne Clyde report on the instructional patterns of 10 whole language teachers and how they taught reading and writing skills. The instructional strategies used include demonstration, explanation, and using children's work as demonstrations. These 10 teachers regularly encouraged children to explain their thinking and to report on what they knew through speaking, projects, and writing. The teachers used many prompts and questions that also encouraged student thinking. The teachers describe how many of these instructional actions led to students' metacognitive understanding, a constant goal. This chapter shows teachers' decision making and their struggles and concerns along the way. It also highlights how careful assessment can enable teachers to know what skills to teach which children, when, and why.

In Chapter 13 Michael Pressley, Joan Rankin, Ruth Wharton-McDonald, Jennifer Mistretta, Linda Yokoi, and Shari Ettenberger also describe patterns of outstanding primary grades literacy instruction. These teachers unambiguously balance whole language and direct and explicit skills instruction. A table summarizing outstanding primary-level teaching is accompanied by a description of a morning in a first grade teacher's classroom. The final chapter by Michael Pressley expresses his reflections on the teaching described in this book.

Chapter 12

Explicit Teaching and Learning of Strategies and Skills in Whole Language Classrooms

Ellen McIntyre, Diane Kyle,
Ric A. Hovda, and Jean Anne Clyde
University of Louisville

Theresa, a primary grade teacher, sits on the floor with her students gathered around her. It is fall, and the children in her whole language classroom have been writing stories and other texts on topics of their choice since the first day of school. On this day, Theresa chooses to share some of her writing strategies with her students. "Remember when I started writing my poem on leaves?" she begins in a excited tone. "Well, as I was driving to school this morning I was thinking about what else to include. And let me tell you what I saw . . . "

Theresa tells the children that as she was driving by a statue of a man on a horse, she saw a group of leaves "dancing on the street." She described how they were skittering about the curb and made a circle. "You know what it reminded me of? Children playing in the street. It made me think of Ring Around the Rosie, because they were going around in a circle, and the wind stopped, and . . . "

"They all fell down," offers one child, smiling.

"That's right. And I thought of my poem. And I took some notes, and here they are."

Theresa then displays and reads her notes to the children, who are absorbed by her thoughts. Afterwards, she "thinks aloud" as she considers other ideas to include in her poem. She says, "I was excited about this and told Mrs. Graft (another teacher) who talked about how slippery the leaves are when they are wet . . . how they skitter across the road. They *are* slippery. That might be another thing I could add . . . I could warn people. . . . But I might want to do some research first." (Field notes, 10/93)

To teach the skills of a writer, Theresa often demonstrates (Cambourne, 1988; Smith, 1985) her thinking to her students. In the lesson above she demonstrated many important ideas about how writers write: First, writers often take more than one day to compose a text (in this case, a poem). Second, ideas about what to write can come at any time (driving to work) and from many different people (her teacher friend). Third, writers often take notes on their ideas and ponder them later. And fourth, poems often involve description and metaphors, and sometimes have to be researched.

Demonstrations are a vital part of Theresa's daily instruction. When introducing a new concept or strategy, she "walks through" the process herself, making her thinking "visible" to the children. She is careful to let children know that her strategies are just one way to approach any of these kinds of tasks. She often finds other children or adults who can share different ways they engaged in the same task.

To ensure that her students truly learn the skills of writers and readers, Theresa also insists that children make *their* strategies explicit to one another or to her. Her instructional approaches for doing this are not unlike those of nine other teachers with whom she worked on a research project that examined how teachers become effective whole language teachers in nongraded primary settings. This chapter will describe several of the ways that these 10 outstanding whole language teachers teach writing and reading skills in meaningful, authentic ways.

The Context

Ten primary grade teachers participated in an 18-month study of how they created nongraded, multi-age whole language classrooms. These 10 teachers taught low-SES children in four different urban and rural settings. Their primary classrooms were organized differently, but could all be characterized as team-taught multi-age settings that included children with special needs. All 10 teachers considered themselves whole language teachers and were working to better understand teaching and learning from this perspective.

Four university researchers (the authors of this chapter) regularly observed and interviewed the teachers about their instruction. We also held several all-day meetings in which all 10 teachers came together to reflect on their understandings of effective teaching in primary grade classrooms. The teachers discussed their dilemmas and challenges (from dealing with a wide range of students to how to teach phonics). They also reflected on their change processes. During these meetings, the teachers wrote explanations of what they taught and why, and they elaborated on these written reports during discussions. These questions were generated primarily by the researchers through examination of field notes. The data were analyzed in collaboration with the teachers and provided the frame for the patterns of excellent teaching we describe in this chapter. (See McIntyre et al. [1995] for details on data analysis.)

Characteristics of These Whole Language Classrooms

All 10 teachers' instruction focuses on helping children construct meaning through reading and writing. They all use literature to teach children to read and the process approach (Graves, 1983; Calkins, 1986) for the teaching of writing. Their classrooms are highly social communities in which children learn a great deal from one another (Gregory et al., 1995). The classrooms are warm, inviting places for children to learn, and are characterized by risk-taking on the part of teachers and children. The students have many opportunities to choose what to read and write in their classrooms. Small group instruction is guided by what teachers see children need after they have made a careful assessment (Hovda et al., 1995; Gregory et al., 1995), and some of the teachers have children with special needs included in the regular classroom for the entire school day (McIntyre, 1995a; Cron, Spears, & Stottman, 1995). For these teachers, understanding developmentally appropriate literacy instruction has been a constant goal (McIntyre, 1995a; 1995b).

Explicit Teaching in a Whole Language Context

The 10 teachers described in this chapter understand that good whole language teaching is more than immersing children in literature and providing authentic opportunities for writing and reading. The best teaching also makes explicit what children need to know and provides opportunities for children to make their own learning explicit (Roehler & Duffy, 1986; Palincsar, 1986).

Many teachers who move toward a whole language orientation first focus on meaning and fluency in their literacy instruction. The initial awareness of what children can do in these contexts and how instruction differs from more traditional teaching sometimes results in teachers' "hands-off" approaches to teaching. Later, as teachers get a firmer grasp on how to facilitate learning, they move to a focus on more competent reading and writing through explicit instruction (Langer & Applebee, 1987; Bratcher & Stroble, 1994). These 10 teachers all began teaching with a meaning-focus or constructivist orientation. As they developed, they began to understand and apply principles of explicit teaching within these meaningful contexts.

Learning to be a highly effective whole language teacher takes time, and confusions and struggles are common along the way. Vickie, one of the teachers, explained what she learned in the last two years about excellent teaching:

> What I learned is that you need to make it very clear to the children where they are and what the next step is. I don't think I used to do that. I just sort of threw it all out there and those who got it, got it. Those who did not, I feel I didn't help as effectively. The details (about excellent teaching) are starting to get filled in a little more as I go along.

Some of the details of the instruction that occurred within the 10 whole language primary classrooms follows in the next section.

Teacher Explanations

One pattern of interaction common in the 10 classrooms was when teachers explained processes, shared facts, or offered reminders to the children. These occurred in conversation, much like those described by Roehler & Hallenback (this volume). For example, Anna, in an engaging game-like fashion, regularly reminds her students about the rules of decoding as they read charts, notes, and other texts as a class. Teacher explanations were highly varied and served many purposes. However, the telling and explaining was done not so that children would memorize what was said, but rather so that they could move on to more important learning (that is, reading for meaning or writing for a purpose). The following statements were all made in the context of story and chart reading or strategy instruction with literature.

> "O-o in the word 'noodle' gives it that /oo/ sound."
>
> "One way to figure out a word you don't know when reading is to skip it, read to the end of the sentence, and then go back and think of what might make sense in the sentence."
>
> "Barley is a grain, kind of like rice."

"Robert Munsch often uses humor in his stories so that children enjoy them."

"This is a fiction book, a made-up story."

"This is the Table of Contents. It tells you which page the chapters start on."

These teachers agree that at times it is appropriate for them to simply tell or explain things to children, if it helps them move on to more important work. They also agree that at times it helps when teachers direct children to use particular strategies as they read or write.

For example, one of the teachers, Gayle, used a patterned picture book, *Birthdays* by Joy Cowley, to emphasize the use of picture clues for ascertaining words when reading. After seeing a demonstration of how to do this with the first couple of pages, the children began to make predictions and explain them. Gayle supported each as they used the picture clue by saying, "You noticed the tag in the picture, that's a good clue," and "Yes, it's shaped like a bird cage, isn't it?" Later, the children wrote their own birthday books, using the pattern of the book. Gayle supported these efforts, too, and pointed out how one child decided on a modification. She said, "Did you notice how she changed that part to 'Open it, open it' instead? That was a nice difference."

One teacher, Tina, had been working regularly with a group of emergent readers. She wanted them to gain confidence in reading predictable books and gain sight word recognition as they read. They had read Eric Carle's *The Very Hungry Caterpillar* (1980) many times. As she introduced a new book, *Cookie's Week* (Ward, 1988) to a small group, she highlighted its similarities with their old favorite, "This book is just like the *Hungry Caterpillar* in that something happens each day of the week and you can join in on the parts that repeat." As she read to them, she stopped periodically and said, "Here's that part again" so that the children knew when to join her in reading. After the class reading, Tina gave each pair of children their own copy of the book to read for practice. She explained to them, "I know you use the pictures a lot when you read, and that's good. But now I want you to look at the words." She monitored and encouraged them to point to print when they read.

Giving explicit instruction on how and even what to read became a regular feature of Joy's (Tina's teammate) teaching as well. While still honoring students' choices, she also wanted to be sure children read material that was appropriately challenging. When working with a group of emergent readers one day, she explained, "When you choose your books during reading time today, some of your books can be books you really love, with lots of words and pictures. And you might just look at the pictures on those. But some of your books *need* to be those where you can really read the *words*." She then picked up a short, predictable book and showed the group, "Here is one."

Strategies for figuring out unknown words, phonics, and other word analysis skills were also explicitly taught in the context of reading or study of some topic. For example, in Gayle's class the children talk about a different state each day. One morning Gayle pointed to the word Maryland and said, "I wonder what our state is for today."

A child looked at the words and slowly read, "/mary land/."

"That's right, when you take the word apart, it's mary and land. When we say it, it's Maryland. I wonder where it is? Do you think it might be a big state or a little state?"

As in the above examples, the explanations most often occurred incidentally as teachers saw that children needed immediate information or reminders about how to do something. Occasionally, when they saw it was necessary, teachers planned such explanations, but always in the context of reading or writing for authentic purposes. When teachers carefully explain to students what is being learned, why it is being learned, when it will be used, and how it will be used, students learn more (Roehler, Duffy, & Meloth, 1986; Palincsar, 1986; Roehler & Duffy, 1986; Rosenshine, 1986; Smith & Goodman, 1984). Explicit instruction within whole language teaching may help some children construct necessary information that others construct on their own (Delpit, 1991; Harris & Graham, 1993).

Teacher Demonstrations

All 10 teachers say it is not enough to tell or explain things to children; teachers must *show* children how to do what it is they want them to do. Some of the many processes that were demonstrated by these teachers included:

1. A demonstration of thinking (for example, about the connections made while reading, of deciding what to write about).
2. A demonstration of questioning or wondering (for example, about what a book might be about).
3. A demonstration of how to do something (for example, how to take notes like a researcher, how to write a letter, how to write

from experiences, how to share writing, how to decode, how to form letters, how to write number sentences and equations, how to spell a word, how to use the context of the sentence to figure out words, how to choose a book).

When the teachers showed children how to think, wonder, write, or read, they did it carefully and accompanied with explanations, just as Theresa did in the opening example of this chapter and as Tina does below:

> Tina noticed some of her young writers often could not read what they had written the previous day or two. She wanted to demonstrate how they could figure out words they do not know when reading—even when reading their own texts. She stands in front of a group of children at the overhead projector with a copy of her own messy-looking journal entry displayed, in which she had written about how she and her husband have had trouble deciding on their first child's name. She tells the children that she noticed some of them were having difficulty figuring out words as they read, even words they had written themselves. She says, "Watch me as I read." She reads her own text, haltingly because of the handwriting. She stops at one point and says, "Hmmm, I don't know what this word is. What did I write? I was thinking about how Andy and I have been arguing over the baby's name . . . the word can't be baby because that wouldn't make sense in the sentence . . . but it does start with a 'b' . . . " Tina continues "thinking aloud" her processes for figuring out a few more words as she reads through her text. She ends the lesson by saying, "See, you can guess what the word is by remembering what you were writing about, but you should also look at how you might have spelled the word and the sounds that go with it." (Field notes, 10/94)

In another example, Kris explained and demonstrated to her class how to conduct surveys.

> Kris begins, "I am going to tell you the survey question I am interested in." (She writes "Survey Question" on chart paper.) "This is what I wonder, and this has no right or wrong answer. I want your opinion. (She writes, "What do you think is faster, a race horse or a cheetah?") She continues, "This is not a time for 'I know, I know!' This is to help you know how to get your group focused. First, I read the question. Then I count answers. My way of keeping track is by writing initials. Now, how do I record initials?"
>
> A student says, "The first letter of her first name and the first letter of her last name."

"Right, what strategy did I use to write their initials down?" The children explain that she is writing the results in a column, which makes it easier to tally when finished.

As in the above examples, explanations and demonstrations can be about a variety of literacy skills, from figuring out unknown words while reading, to coming up with topic ideas for writing, or recording survey results. As Anna says, "Teachers should show children *everything* they want the children to do independently."

Children's Work as Demonstrations

Some of the teachers use the children's work as demonstrations for other children. For example, Kris has her students conduct original research projects in which they pose a question, gather data, and report results. She demonstrates how to ask questions she is interested in, how to observe or survey, and tally. After Kris had demonstrated to the children how to do a survey (as shown earlier), and many of them attempted their own, she gathered the class to show them how one group of children had proceeded:

> Kris reads the question Abigail (a six-year-old?) posed: "Do you like to take a shower or do you like to take a bath?" She holds up Abigail's survey form and shows how she has organized the information. "This side was for people who like showers and this side was for people who like baths. She wants to find out for people in our class. She made a table, not the kind you sit at, but some columns where she put answers. This is one way to do it, but there are all sorts of ways to do a survey." Kris went on to explain what Abigail and the group of children did in order for the rest of the class to visualize the process. "We talked about why we do a survey, to find out what people like, to find out if people like the same things you do, what people are thinking, or feeling, or doing. Like, you all see each other at school and might do a survey to find out more about each other. What are some things you could find out?"

As in the above example, the following example also shows how teachers can use children's work as models.

Sara and Patty team teach a group of six- to nine-year-olds. In this example, they use one child's work as a demonstration for other children on several writing skills.

> One afternoon Sara decided to conduct a lesson on using vivid words in order to draw readers in. She asks Shawn, an eight-year-old, to share the beginning of his story, knowing his text was an excellent

demonstration for the others. She tells the children to listen to Shawn's story for "words that make pictures in your mind." Shawn reads, "In the deep, deep woods, there was an old, old house. There lived six kids and ten grown-ups. Two of them were scientists . . . " After a few minutes (and several pages) of reading, Sara asks Shawn where he plans to go with the story. The two interact a minute and another child offers a suggestion that Shawn says is a good idea. Then Sara turns to the class and asks, "What good picture words did you hear as Shawn read his story?"

One child says, "Chemical."

"Old, old, man . . . and in the forest."

"Boom."

"Sizzle."

Sara agrees they are all good words that help make readers picture the story. She suggests they look over their own drafts for ways to use more vivid words.

Explanations and demonstrations often go hand in hand. Teachers explain why they do what they do *as* they are demonstrating something. As Anna recalls, "Sometimes you have to show them *and* tell them or they won't understand."

These whole language teachers all understand the place of explanation and demonstration in their teaching, but they also agree that these teaching behaviors are unimportant if teachers do not help children become explicit about what they know and do. The children in these classrooms—where authentic explanations and demonstrations occurred regularly—were systematically encouraged to articulate what they knew and how they knew it. The teachers see this kind of metacognitive knowledge as essential for helping children become self-directed learners.

Metacognitive Learning

Metacognition is the knowledge and control people have over their own thinking and learning activities, including reading and writing (Baker & Brown, 1984). It may involve awareness of what one knows, what it takes to perform effectively to meet the demands of particular situations (for example, writing a letter), or self-regulatory actions such as monitoring comprehension as one reads (Brown, El-Dinary, & Pressley, this volume). Educators have for a long time known the importance of teaching such awareness to young children, particularly those who do not come to metacognitive insights on their own.

However, recently there has been a call for maximizing metacognitive instruction with authentic tasks in social environments (Palincsar et al., 1991), such as in whole language classrooms. In the classrooms described in this chapter, the teachers created contexts in which children were encouraged to articulate what they know. They did this in primarily three ways.

"Explain your thinking." The 10 teachers commonly asked children to explain their thinking. Often this was in reference to how they solved a problem, how they decided on a writing topic, or how they selected a book to read. Inviting children to predict during story reading was a regular part of reading instruction, and the teachers often elicited from children how they came about their predictions. When children completed major projects such as writing a "chapter book," teachers asked children to share how they proceeded and what they struggled with as they made decisions during their writing. Further, these teachers often asked children what their "plan" was or how they might proceed with a particular task even before getting started. When children articulated their thinking, they not only seemed to become more metacognitive about what they knew, but their words served as a demonstration to others.

Kris explained how she gets children to articulate their thinking about how they go about solving academic problems. She said,

> I took them through the steps, and after we had done it a couple of times, we talked about what we did. I said, "If somebody else is going to come in here and you were going to tell them what we did, what would you tell them?" I then wrote it down, made a list, and put it up there [on the board]. But sometimes I would have to stop and demonstrate again.

Prompts and questions. Many of the teachers have been observed prompting children as they struggled for language to explain themselves. They also regularly asked open-ended questions that helped children think about and verbalize what they knew. The common prompts and questions asked daily in these classrooms included:

How do you know?
What do you notice?
Why? Why not?
Can you explain your thinking?
Can you justify your reason?
How could you figure that out?
Why is that important?

What do you think it means?

Tell me more.

Show me.

Draw a picture that shows that.

How could you find that out?

If someone else came in our room and didn't know, what would you tell them?

These questions and directives are at the "tips of the tongues" of the teachers in this study. While some of them have been asking these questions of their students for years, others have had to make a conscious effort to ask children to explain their thinking or articulate what they know. One teacher, Donna, said she had not given children as much credit for what they knew before this study. She said she has learned to encourage children's explanations and she gives more "wait time" to children as they try to find the words they need to express themselves. Donna said that a focus on using these prompts to get children to explain their thinking has certainly helped the children internalize the reading and writing skills and strategies that have been taught.

Reporting. Sharing, publishing, and reporting are integral to the classrooms described here. These teachers value children's products as well as their processes because they know that at times, products drive processes (Routman, 1991). Sharing what has been learned or projects that have been completed gives children opportunities to further articulate what they know in planned, formal ways.

Writing is a key opportunity for children to articulate what they know. Children in all classrooms write extensively every day. Children write to express what they know in journals and logs, but also in more formal ways. For example, many of the teachers have their students write letters periodically explaining what they learned that week. Theresa regularly has children make presentations to the class, and she has them share their learning logs with their parents. In Donna, Tina, and Joy's team-taught class, the children write letters about how their reading and writing are improving (see Figure 12-1).

In Theresa's room, self-assessment is also a regular part of helping children understand what they know. She has developed a rubric which she has shared with the children, along with examples that represent each category of the rubric. (The categories include novice, apprentice, proficient, and distinguished and are based on the statewide assessment system rubric.) She then has children self-assess their

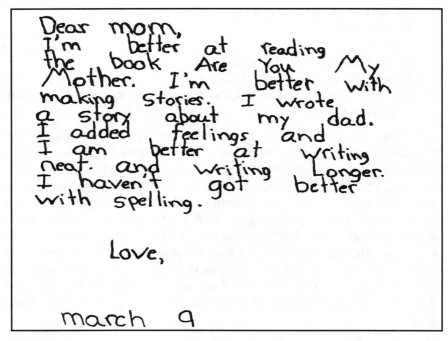

Dear mom,
I'm better at reading the book. Are You My Mother. I'm better with making Stories. I wrote a story about my dad. I added feelings and I am better at writing neat. and writing Longer. I haven't got better with spelling.

Love,

march 9

Figure 12-1.

own writing, based on the rubric. In Figure 12-2, an eight-year-old assesses his nonfiction book about the varieties of transportation.

In these examples, children use language to come to an understanding of their own skills. As in the example above, the children articulate what makes good reading and writing and which of these skills they now have. Some of the other teachers in the study also focused on expanding ways children can articulate what they know. Their strategies included role playing, other drama activities, and art. Creating graphs and K-W-L charts (Ogle, 1986) were also regular features of some of these classrooms.

Development of Metacognition: It Takes Time!

Helping children to explain their thinking was a goal for all the teachers, but not one that was always easily achieved. All the teachers said that it took time for children to get used to justifying their answers, to explain their thinking, and to describe procedures to others. The teachers report that often, early in the year, the children's "thinking" seems

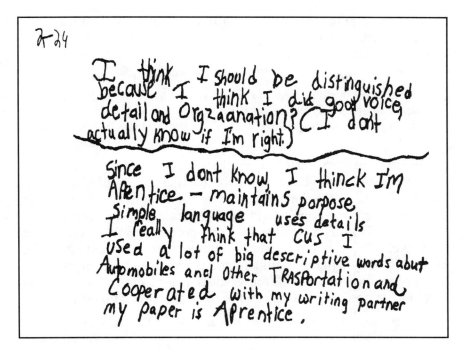

Figure 12-2.

superficial or they simply mimicked what a teacher had said. Children are heard using the teacher's phrases and terminology, such as "I noticed we have new spelling words" in Gayle's classroom where "What do you notice?" is a frequently asked question. Gradually, however, the children learn that they are expected to show their thinking, and they come to understand that their responses will be valued. Eventually, children begin to truly reveal their thinking processes. As Vickie explained,

> In the beginning the responses were very stilted and very much conforming to the demonstrations. But as time went on, after more demonstrations, they begin to discuss things with each other. They actually begin to think about how they feel about things . . . how it relates to their lives.

Children often begin articulating their knowledge after teachers have explained and demonstrated something. For example, Donna explained components of story structure—setting, characters, and plot (problem, climax, conclusion)—and then read a storybook and pointed out the components of story structure as she read. Later, she asked children to point out the elements of story structure in their own writing, much like the teacher in the study by Graham & Harris (this volume). Vickie explained that after she demonstrates something, children often approximate what she has just done:

> When I show them the steps of research and we are doing graphs, theirs don't end up looking like mine. They are similar, but they do it in their own way, like making a graph that is non-standard. It's like invented spelling.

Indeed, teachers must be conscious that mimicking and later approximating (Cambourne, 1988) the teacher are natural first steps toward metacognitive behavior. It may not be until children gain insights into their own cognition that real strategic learning occurs (Baker & Brown, 1984). Thus, children's articulations may at first seem surface level. Children will also approximate their peers' examples, but eventually they will better understand themselves as learners. Gayle further explained how children gradually used their own voices by first following teachers' examples, then their peers', and finally their own:

> The teacher mimicking becomes less and less and . . . one or two of them say something on their own and do not mimic exactly what the teacher has said, and others see that that's OK and they start doing it too. Then they mimic each other, but it's not exactly the same thing, but their own thoughts.

Self-reflection is also a technique that enables children to become more metacognitively aware of their knowledge and processes. As in the earlier examples, Kris shows her students their earliest writings and asks them how their writing has changed. She says at first they couldn't seem to "see" it, and she would help them along, and later they would be able to see specific ways their writing has changed across the year. She also says they begin to get interested in how their peers' writing has changed.

When and With Whom to Be Explicit

In whole language classrooms, children often discover the rules of language as they participate in reading and writing for their own purposes. They often learn conventions by necessity (Graves, 1983; Calkins, 1983). However, these 10 teachers do not leave the learning of these skills to chance. They are planful about determining how to differentiate instruction for the varied learners in their classrooms

(Hovda et al., 1995). Tina described it as a mission to find out who needs what and when.

Assessment plays a key role in knowing when to be explicit and with whom. Sara and Patty use the Kentucky Early Learning Profile (KELP), a tool for the systematic approach to assessment created to document children's progress through the primary school. The KELP uses anecdotal records, checklists, "learning descriptions" (that cue teachers about what behaviors they might see as children develop) and conversations with the children and their parents in order to understand what children know and need. This tool has been instrumental in helping Sara and Patty identify those children with whom they need to be more explicit. One summary or "snapshot" page of the "learning descriptions" that focus on reading is shown in Figure 12-3. Tools like KELP can help teachers know what to look for as they observe children and know what kinds of behaviors lead to fluent reading and writing.

Talking about children with colleagues has also helped these teachers know the skills particular children need. Donna, Joy, and Tina team teach a group of 40 six-, seven-, eight-, and nine-year-olds, 15 of whom are children with learning disabilities. To keep track of their needs and growth, they have a planning meeting every Friday afternoon after school to discuss the children, their needs, and how to plan instruction for each child for the following week. In the following transcript, the three teachers review the work the children completed that week and decide their instruction for the following week.

Joy says, "What about DeJuan?"

Donna shakes her head, "No, I don't know. I'm at a loss."

"What are you talking about!" Tina counters, "I thought he had a good week! He wrote all that . . . "

". . . Yea, he did, you're right, but he was so lost in story group. I think he needs some straight phonics, I mean of the hard core kind."

The teachers all laugh and Joy, the special education teacher, says, "I was planning on doing phonics with several of my kids (those in the class labeled with a learning disability), so he could join my group."

"That would be great, he needs it . . . "

"What are you planning, exactly?" Tina asks.

Joy describes a song she wants to teach the children that has a lot of alliteration in it. She wants to put the song in print and teach decoding from the song sheet.

"Oh, DeJuan will love that. That's perfect," Donna says.

The teachers agree and move on to talking about the next child.

Continuum: BEGINNING →→ DEVELOPING →→ COMPETENT → EXPANDING →→→
EMERGENT →→ EARLY →→→→→ FLUENT →→→

SNAPSHOT
This section provides a quick overview of the reading components listed below. It gives the user of this document a general idea or a starting point when identifying the characteristics a student is exhibiting while learning reading. Few students will exhibit characteristics all at the same point on the continuum. Using the narrative explanations will give you more specific information about the student's reading development.

EMERGENT
- Holds a book correctly and enjoys looking at the pictures.
- Likes to listen to books being read and enjoys repeated reading.
- Begins to exhibit reading behaviors resembling those that parents/guardians and teachers exhibit.
- Enjoys and listens for long periods of time.
- Favors books with rhythmic or predictable text.
- Recalls repeat phrases or rhymes from favorite books.
- Asks "wondering" questions about stories.

EARLY
- Enjoys being read to, but is beginning to select favorite books to "read" and "reread" by himself.
- "Reads" by memorizing the text, the story line, or "reading the pictures."
- Moves his finger left to right when using very simple text.
- Points to known words that are part of sight vocabulary.
- Begins to read signs and TV commercials.
- Reads own name and may know some or all of the letters in it.
- Asks fewer "wondering" questions.
- Uses drawings to support oral interpretations of stories.

DEVELOPING
- Reads text that is rhyming, predictable, has many high frequency words, and has familiar text.
- Retells previously read stories from beginning to end.
- Responds to print in various ways (e.g., diorama, mobile, or puppet play).
- Reads familiar signs and commercials.
- Begins to develop drills and strategies but still needs the support of parents/guardians and teachers.
- Attempts silent reading, although has not acquired the skills to read silently.
- Begins to locate books to find specific information and for enjoyment.

(DEVELOPING → COMPETENT)
- Reads predictable, rhyming, and familiar texts with ease.
- Uses sight vocabulary when reading familiar text using skills and strategies such as letter/sound association syllabification, picture clues, predicting, comparing, and inferring.
- Begins to self-monitor and correct with support from parents/guardians and teachers as more challenging and unfamiliar texts are read.
- Begins to use books for a variety of purposes.
- Understands text structure and reads with an understanding of this structure.
- Responses to literature are more details.

COMPETENT
- Develops a preference of genre and often has to be encouraged to expand reading past this main interest.
- Has a sound understanding of the various purposes for reading and is using text consistently to gain information.
- Begins to read silently.
- Has begun to internalize the skills and strategies necessary to read text, although may still struggle with unfamiliar text and may need the support of parents/guardians and teachers.
- Actively self-monitors and corrects when reading familiar text, but may not be as successful when reading unfamiliar text.
- Responds to literature in a variety of ways, some with more details than others, depending on interest.

FLUENT
- Reads for many purposes, although still has preferences concerning recreational reading.
- Uses skills and strategies regularly that work most successfully regardless of situation.
- Engages in self-monitoring and correcting while reading any text.
- Continues to develop a larger repertoire of strategies to respond to literature, and selectively uses them based on the understanding of the purpose of the genre and/or style.
- Begins using new skills and strategies when old favorites do not help.

EXPANDING
- Actively engages in reading all types of text, although recreational reading may consist of preferred genre.
- Self-monitors and corrects with most texts.
- Uses appropriate support strategies selectively when reading challenging text, but there are no visible signs of this.
- Begins to develop own style for approaching reading.
- Continues to read and respond to literature in a variety of ways based on the purpose, genre and/or style of the text.

Figure 12-3.

Formal, traditional assessments like some of those described by Purcell-Gates (this volume) can also help teachers understand what they need to do. One teacher discovered important information after she had given all of her students the Burns and Roe (1993) Informal Reading Inventory. Kris explained:

> I found out that as long as they had books with a lot of structural language cues and picture cues, they could read. But when it came down to reading black and white, no pictures, they couldn't get a sense of the story. I found out they weren't as good readers as I thought they were, at least in that context. So, we really got to work. We did a lot more teaching of decoding, through stories and poems, and more direct teaching on strategies for figuring out words. This led into more informational reading, or nonfiction, because you don't have that story language to hang on.

These examples show the critical need for teachers to be "kid-watchers" (Goodman, Watson, & Burke, 1987) who also give appropriate formal assessments in order to understand all children's strengths and needs. It also shows the importance of understanding children's literacy development in order to best decide instructional practices that are most appropriate for all learners.

Conclusion

While these 10 teachers have learned the place of explicit instruction within an authentic curriculum, they are often reminded that, without a meaningful context, children will not understand what is taught to them directly. Anna recalls:

> There are times when I've gotten a little bit anxious and felt like, "Oh, oh, we're getting behind on something and I've got to hit this thing and I've got to hit it hard. We've got to get it done." The next thing I know I'm in a panic and I'm up there trying to do direct teaching and I realize I am losing them.

Like Anna, teachers often need reminding of what is most important in literacy instruction—that reading and writing must remain meaningful and whole for children to maintain interest and purpose in what they are doing. Teachers must, above all, remember the principles of whole language teaching outlined in the introduction of this book. Only then can they determine the best instructional approaches for teaching the specific skills children need.

References

Baker, L., & Brown, A. L. (1984). Metacognitive skills and reading. In P. D. Pearson, R. Barr, M. L. Kamil, & P. Mosenthal (Eds.), *Handbook of reading research* (Volume 1, pp. 353–394). White Plains, NY: Longman.

Bratcher, S. & Stroble, E. J. (1994). Determining the progression from comfort to confidence: A longitudinal evaluation of a National Writing Project site based on multiple data sources. *Research in the Teaching of English, 28,* 66–88.

Burns, P. C., & Roe, B. D. (1993). *Burns/Roe informal reading inventory.* Boston: Houghton Mifflin.

Calkins, L. (1986). *The art of teaching writing.* Portsmouth, NH: Heinemann.

Cambourne, B. (1988). *The whole story: Natural learning and the acquisition of literacy in the classroom.* New Zealand: Scholastic, Inc.

Carle, E. (1980). *The very hungry caterpillar.* New York: Scholastic, Inc.

Cron, T., Spears, J., & Stottman, D. (1995). Let the wild rumpus start! A story of a multi-age classroom. In R. A. Hovda, D. W. Kyle, & E. McIntyre (Eds.), *Creating K-3 nongraded primary programs: Teachers' stories and lessons learned.* Corwin Press, Inc.

Delpit, L. D. (1986). Skills and other dilemmas of a progressive black educator. *Harvard Educational Review, 56,* 379–385.

Delpit, L. D. (1991). [Interview with William H. Teale, editor of Language Arts]. *Language Arts, 68,* 541–547.

Duffy, G. D. & Roehler, L. (1987). Improving classroom reading instruction through the use of responsive elaboration. *Reading Teacher, 40,* 514–521.

Goodman, Y., Watson, D., & Burke, C. (1987). *Reading miscue inventory: Alternative procedures.* New York: Richard C. Owen.

Graves, D. H. (1983). *Writing: Teachers and children at work.* Portsmouth, NH: Heinemann.

Gregory, K., Kyle, D. W., Moore, G., Wheatley, V., Clyde, J. A., Hovda, R. A., & McIntyre, E. (1995). *The social nature of learning in nongraded primary programs: What young children learn from each other.* Paper presented at the meeting of the American Educational Research Association, San Francisco, CA.

Harris, K. R. & Graham, S. (1993). Cognitive strategy instruction and whole language: A case study. *Remedial and Special Education, 14,* 30–34.

Hovda, R. A., Davis, S., Monarch, S., McIntyre, E., Kyle, D. W., & Clyde, J. A. (1995). *Differentiated instruction in nongraded primary programs.* Paper presented at the annual meeting of the American Educational Research Association, San Francisco, CA, April.

Langer, J. A. & Applebee, A. N. (1987). *How writing shapes thinking: A study of teaching and learning.* Urbana, IL: National Council of Teachers of English.

McIntyre, E. (1995a). Teaching and learning writing skills in a low-SES urban, primary classroom. *Journal of Reading Behavior: A Journal of Literacy, 27,* 213–242.

McIntyre, E. (1995b). The struggle for developmentally appropriate literacy instruction. *Journal of Research in Early Childhood.*

McIntyre, E., & Freppon, P. (1994). A comparison of children's development of alphabetic knowledge in a skills-based and a whole language classroom. *Research in the Teaching of English, 28,* 391–417.

McIntyre, E., Shell, T., Stottman, D., Kyle, D. W., Clyde, J. A., & Hovda, R. A. (1995). *Explicit instruction within constructivist classrooms.* Paper presented at the annual meeting of the American Educational Research Association, San Francisco, CA, April.

Ogle, D. M. (1986). K-W-L: A teaching model that develops active reading of expository text. *Reading Teacher, 39,* 564–570.

Palincsar, A. M. (1986). The role of dialogue in providing scaffolded instruction. *Educational Psychologist, 2,* 73–98.

Palincsar, A. M., & Brown, A. L. (1984). Reciprocal teaching of comprehension-fostering and comprehension monitoring activities. *Cognition and Instruction, 1,* 117–175.

Palincsar, A. M., & Klenk, L. (1993). Broader visions encompanying literacy, learners, and context. *Remedial and Special Education, 14,* 19–25.

Roehler, L. R., & Duffy, G. D. (1991). Teachers' instructional actions. In R. Barr, M. L. Kamil, P. Mosenthal, & P. D. Pearson (Eds.), *Handbook of reading research, Volume II.* New York: Longman.

Roehler, L. R., & Duffy, G. D. (1986). Why are some teachers better explainers than others? *Journal of Education for Teaching, 12,* 273–284.

Roehler, L., Duffy, G. D., & Meloth, M. (1986). What to be direct about in direct instruction in reading. In T. Raphael & R. Reynolds (Eds.), *Contexts for school-based literacy* (pp. 79–96). New York: Random House.

Rosenshine, B. (1993). *Is direct instruction different than expert scaffolding?* Paper presented at the annual meeting of the American Educational Research Association, April, Atlanta.

Rosenshine, B. (1986). Synthesis of research on explicit teaching. *Educational Leadership, 43,* 60–69.

Routman, R. (1991). *Invitations: Changing as teachers and learners K-12.* Portsmouth, NH: Heinemann.

Smith, E. E., & Goodman, L. (1984). Understanding written communication: The role of explanatory schema. *Cognition and Instruction, 1,* 359–396.

Smith, F. (1985). *Understanding reading.* Portsmouth, NH: Heinemann.

Smith, F. (1988). *Joining the literacy club.* Portsmouth, NH: Heinemann.

Ward, C. (1988). *Cookie's week.* New York: Scholastic, Inc.

Chapter 13

The Nature of Outstanding Primary-Grades Literacy Instruction

Michael Pressley and Ruth Wharton-McDonald,
University at Albany, State University of New York
Joan Rankin, University of Nebraska-Lincoln
Jennifer Mistretta and Linda Yokoi,
University at Albany, State University of New York
Shari Ettenberger, Mohanasen Public Schools, New York

Explicit decoding instruction and whole language make unique contributions to the development of competence in literacy. For example, whole language students understand that writing is for meaning making, whereas students in conventional classrooms may not (see, for example, Boljonis & Hinchman, 1988; Gambrell & Palmer, 1992; Graham & Harris, 1994; Rasinski & DeFord, 1985). Children in whole language classrooms also are learning that the goal of decoding is to gain understanding of the text, rather than sounding out of words (for example, Freppon, 1991; Mills, O'Keefe, & Stephens, 1990). Placing young children in whole language environments that invite and support literacy stimulates children to do things that are literate (for example, Morrow, 1990, 1991; Neuman & Roskos, 1990, 1992). When literature drives instruction, as it does in whole language, there are positive effects on students' autonomous use of literature and attitudes toward reading (for example, Morrow, 1992; Morrow, O'Connor, & Smith, 1990). Consistent experiences with high-quality literature foster growth in understanding the structure of stories, which improves both comprehension and writing, as well as the sophistication of children's language (for example, Feitelson, Kita, & Goldstein, 1986; Morrow, 1992). Just as broad reading expands the knowledge of adults (Stanovich & Cunningham, 1993), extensive experiences with stories expand children's knowledge of the world, for example, as reflected by breadth of vocabulary (for example, Elley, 1989; Robbins & Ehri, 1994). In summary, immersion in authentic reading and writing provides great benefits for young readers and writers.

Even so, whole language may not increase word decoding, vocabulary, and comprehension abilities, at least as measured by standardized tests (Stahl, McKenna, & Pagnucco, 1994; Stahl & Miller, 1989). Development of letter-sound associations and explicit decoding instruction focusing on the sounds of words is definitely associated with later reading success (Adams, 1990) and related competencies, such as spelling (for example, Ball & Blachman, 1991; Lie, 1991; Nelson, 1990; Tangel & Blachman, 1992; Uhry & Shepherd, 1993). Especially with respect to the weakest beginning readers, the case is strong that explicit decoding instruction increases reading competence (see Adams, 1990; Mather, 1992; Pressley & Rankin, 1994).

Given that whole language and explicit decoding approaches produce complementary advantages, it makes sense conceptually to attempt to teach decoding explicitly and systematically in the context of a curriculum filled with reading and exposure to excellent literature and opportunities to construct text, with examples of this balanced approach represented in this volume.

Thus, we set out to find out what excellent primary-level literacy teachers do to promote the literacy development of their students. We are using two very different methodologies in the conduct of this work, with all indications to date that converging outcomes are emerging from our studies. Before summarizing our findings, however, we present an example of outstanding teaching, in a way that will make obvious how challenging it is to understand excellent teaching.

10 January 1995: Morning in Ms. Ettenberger's Grade 1 Class

8:55 A.M.: When students arrive in the room, they begin reading favorite books, working on writing, or spending time in one of the classroom centers. When it is time for the school day to begin, Ms. Ettenberger claps in cadence, the class comes to order, with Ms. Ettenberger assessing the attendance and doing the morning checks (milk, lunch, etc.) in a matter of seconds. Jennifer, a student in the class, shares a book, reading it to her attentive classmates. There is a place in the reading when Jennifer's enthusiasm reflects the emphasis signaled by an exclamation point in the text. Ms. Ettenberger provides a mini-lesson on exclamation points after Jennifer reads the exclamation with enthusiasm.

9:02 A.M.: Jennifer continues reading, telling the class how the main character in the story is like her sister. When Jennifer stumbles over a word, Ms. Ettenberger sneaks in a mini-lesson about all the things that can be done when encountering a difficult word—sounding it out, looking for picture clues, or skipping it. When Jennifer concludes the book, Ms. Ettenberger praises her reading.

9:07 A.M.: Ms. Ettenberger announces she is having a problem filling out the attendance form, pointing out that everyone has problems that must be solved as part of writing. Ms. Ettenberger cannot remember how to spell out the number four, the number of students absent. Many students volunteer to help her. One who is selected to respond, hesitates, and looks at a number-word chart in the room. Ms. Ettenberger praises him for using the classroom's resources to solve the problem. Ms. Ettenberger's problems continue as the students turn to the daily calendar, which needs to be corrected. During the corrections, Ms. Ettenberger cues students to listen to the word "Monday" and points out how the sounds of the word map to its letters. This leads to a discussion of others words that begin with the letter *M*. (Three students exit when they are called out to participate in book reading with an adult.) As part of fixing up the calendar, the remaining students read as a group a set of cards referring to weather conditions (for example, cloudy, warm, etc.), deciding which of the cards should be placed on today's calendar. When it is time to record that it is seven degrees this morning, Ms. Ettenberger asks the class about a "t-word that tells how hot or cold it is." Ms. Ettenberger uses a variety of techniques to make certain all students participate in constructing the morning calendar, for example, asking students to give thumbs up or thumbs down in reaction to the weather-descriptive words that are appropriate to describe this morning.

The morning meeting will continue for about 20 minutes, with lots and lots of opportunities for discussion—for example, how the 10 days in January experienced thus far can be thought of as two groups of five days or as a group of seven days and another group of three days. When the janitor comes in to adjust the thermostat, Ms. Ettenberger talks about the "o-f-f button." She introduces the students to some books she has found about winter, the current theme in the class. When she does so, Ms. Ettenberger points out that every one of the book titles includes one of the weather words that were on the cards considered for placement on the daily calendar (for example, *The Snowy Day*). As books are introduced, the students read the titles as a group. When the book *White Snow, Bright Snow* is introduced, there is a mini-lesson on rhyming words, in this case rhyming words that are also "descriptive words." This discussion of what snow is like—that is, *white* and *bright*—leads to reading a chart poem about snowy days, a chart poem that just happened to be on the easel next to the class meeting rug. This version of the chart poem has some blanks in it, which are to be filled with weather description words. The students are to figure out which words should be placed in each blank as they read the poem. Reading of the poem permits some discussion about when capital letters should occur in poems and the placement of punctuation in poems . . . It is only 9:35 A.M. . . .

There will be many, many literacy and numeracy tasks as the day continues, with many, many mini-lessons. Bossy *r*s will be discussed as a student attempts to sound out *stair.* There will be student guesses about why words that begin with vowels require *an* rather than *a.* The kids will be into these discussions because they occur as part of interesting readings and related writing. Much is planned somewhat in advance by Ms. Ettenberger, such as the 15 minutes taken up discussing how to correct the morning letter, which had some errors planted in it by Ms. Ettenberger. The corrections are necessary for the students to read the letter, and they do so once they have revised it so that the reading makes sense. The morning letter activity leads to the journal activity of the day, which involves revising, with Ms. Ettenberger having planned this reading-writing connection. The specific mini-lessons that individual students receive as they revise journals were not planned in advance, however, but rather were reactions as Ms. Ettenberger monitored student progress in revision. These mini-lessons covered spelling, punctuation, intertextual connections, and the communicative nature of good writing, depending on the needs of the moment for the particular student receiving the mini-lesson. And it goes on and on . . . on this day . . . and every day. Each day involves new literacy tasks, ones connected to current content themes, ones connecting reading and writing (for example, storywriting involving the creation of alternative endings for a story read by the entire class).

Whole language and skill instruction are embedded in one another in Ms. Ettenberger's classroom. Much reading of real literature and daily composing occurs along with teaching of phonics. There are in-the-context mini-lessons about sounding out words and situationally appropriate discussions about how a final *e* makes a vowel long, a final *r* makes the vowel short, and two vowels together result in the first having a long vowel sound. These in-context remarks follow from short, formal lessons on phonics that had occurred days, weeks, and months before in whole group. Literacy instruction is certainly balanced in Ms. Ettenberger's classroom. It is also very, very busy, with many elements of instruction contributing to her teaching. Ms. Ettenberger's teaching reflects her commitment to balance, which came through in an interview in spring 1995.

Ms. Ettenberger Talks About Her Teaching

Ruth Wharton-McDonald: Do you have a philosophy of how reading should be taught, how reading develops?

Shari Ettenberger: I think that . . . being able to read stems from a lot of things: Exposure to print, being talked to . . . it definitely starts with being talked to. You can tell what . . . a student receives at home—and what experiences are provided by the parents. Being immersed in print, and in different kinds of print, whether it be on cereal boxes, street signs . . . McDonald's symbols . . . whatever it is. It's just that the child is exposed to it. And the exposure is authentic.

RW: Mm hmm . . .

SE: And I think when you go to teach a child, you have to continue the exposure. I think it's a fine balance—between immersing the child in whole language and teaching through . . . sounds, going back to using skills.

RW: Right.

SE: Um, teaching them the sounds but not doing it in complete isolation; teaching sounds . . . through their literature. What you see every day in their poetry and their books. And it actually just happens to come up. And teaching them to see, and write . . . so they can get it in more than one way. I think that the teacher is the facilitator. They (the students) are working with what they have. And you just take them from there and provide them with what they need . . .

RW: So, within your framework, you said you needed a balance between literature and skills . . . what do you see as the essential components to a reading program?

SE: First, I don't think you can separate reading and writing. I think that there is definitely a connection there. They go along with each other. If you can recognize words, you can write words. If you know your sounds, you can write—I don't think you can separate the two. I think there is a definite connection and it needs to be taught that way—holistically. But you do have to make sure the kids have the basics . . . to do that. And encourage them to do that . . . using their sounds so they can decode a word when they get to a word they don't know. The word starts with a "d" and they know "d" sounds /d/. And you take it from there. And I think you have to reinforce the skills that the kids already have.

RW: Mm hmm . . .

SE: So they can expand on them. And tying it in with all the good literature—the literature that the kids pick, the literature that you pick, making sure that there's a variety so that the kids don't get bored—or frustrated—with what they're doing. You need to provide the kids with the strategies that they need to be good readers. Be certain that they know what those strategies are, and how to use them. For example, if they do get to a word they don't know, they have to know their options. What am I going to do next? Can I skip over the word? Can I use the picture clues to help me figure out what this word is? Can I know the words around it to help me figure out what the word is? So, you have to provide them with all those . . . it's like a problem-solving ability almost—in math. But geared toward reading. And I, I think that's where it all stems from.

RW: In discussing reading groups for instruction . . .

SE: I try to get away from ability grouping because I find that the kids know. Even if you're not using a basal series that points out, "these are the star readers, these are the bottom readers." It's known. I find that it's intuitive . . . with them.

RW: Yes.

SE: So I mix it up. Sometimes I'll count off by fives and if you're a one, you come meet with me now. If you're a two, come meet with me now. And it works out, where the stronger readers are helping the weaker readers, and the weaker readers are finding out that I'm not the only person who can help them. They have resources in the room that they can use. So, it's just always varied. I don't have the same groups because I do find that the kids know

... when they're not the strong readers. And I don't want them to be discouraged. Because they tend ... this group anyway, tends to get the idea in their head that, "Well, I'm the low one. So I can't do it." And then they don't put forth as much effort.

RW: Right.

SE: And I do paired reading with the kids. The kids buddy up and read together. There's another form of dynamic grouping. Always changing.

RW: When you pair them, do you pair them, strong with weak?

SE: They pair themselves. And I was worried that the strong reader would always be with a strong reader, but that hasn't been the case. They do it by who's their friend, who's reading a book that they're interested in. So ... it works out. It really seems to work out. Give children choice and responsibility and they will work to their ability.

RW: Yes.

SE: Next year, it might not work the same. So I'll have to revamp. I think that's an important thing to remember, too. You've got to ... work with the clientele that you have. Something might not always work twice. And you have to take a look at what the kids have. And go from there. You cater your program to the kids. Not the kids to the program. And I think that's why it always seems to work. Because I'm looking out for their best interest. Not what's always easiest for me.

RW: In discussing a classroom reading program ...

SE: Nothing can be narrowed down to one thing, I don't think, at all. If you don't have a balance of many components, it's kind of like trying to fit a square through a circle. It doesn't work. You don't connect with everyone if you don't use a variety of strategies ... I think that's important. I really do. You know, that there's not one right way to do anything.

RW: Right.

SE: There's lots of different components. You know? Just like, when you're wearing an outfit. It's not one piece of clothing. It's lots of little parts that go with it. I think that's with everything.

RW: Right, yeah.

SE: That's what makes a car run. Lots of little parts, you know.

RW: I wonder if you could talk a little bit about what you intend as the purpose of read aloud. When you read-aloud to the kids, what do you see as the purpose of that?

SE: Actually, there are many purposes in the read-aloud. The child is learning to become a good listener. They listen for many things. And often you forget that listening is part of the language parts arena. It's the communication: listening, speaking . . . and, in the beginning of the year, that's one of my main intentions: To sit and be a good listener. And we go over what a good listener is. And the kids actually define it. So, it's the expectation according to what they know is a good listener.

RW: What kinds of things do kids say in the beginning of the year?

SE: Don't talk. Sit still. And, they . . . they can't sit still at this age. So, we talk about sitting still, but it's really just so you're not disruptive.

RW: Right.

SE: But mainly, it's just to be focused on the person that's talking. And show them the respect that you'd like to have when you were up in the chair reading or sharing something. And, that goes with everything—not just reading, obviously. If you're presenting something that you brought from home . . . or whatever. And then, that's reinforced in the Morning Program. So, that's one thing. I would also want them to be able to derive meaning from the stories. You introduce a lot of your literary elements right here: Who were the characters? What was the plot? What was the main idea?

RW: Right.

SE: The kids don't have to be reading the text to pick it out.

RW: Sure.

SE: Um, read-alouds—I have them predict. I show them the cover of the book and ask them, "What do you think the story is going to be about?" Or, "What's going to happen?" I'll tell them the title, and they'll have to do the same thing. I'll read a few pages, and have them predict. I'll read most of the book and have them create their own ending. Then go back . . . there's lots of strategies you can use read-aloud for. But, initially, it is just to become attuned to listening and what I would expect from a good listener. But qualified by how . . .

RW: Right. And what about, how about when kids read to each other? Like, read aloud to each other. Or, do you ever have students get up in front of the group?

SE: Oh, always.

RW: O.K.

SE: Of course, when I'm reading aloud, I'm modeling. But I think the kids view that as so out of their reach that, "Wow. The teacher's perfect. I can't do that." But then they see their peers doing it, and they realize, "Oh, that's something that I can achieve." And, so the kids are acting as a peer model. And I find, that they relate better. And they're more helpful to one another . . . if someone's stuck, is stumbling over a word, I'll have five or six kids letting them know different things, strategies they can use to figure out the word.

RW: Right.

SE: So, it's kind of a tutoring session, too. It's a whole bunch of things. And, it's strange how the kids seem to pair off, if it's just a read-aloud between two people, they don't pair off highest to highest, or highest to lowest—they find a comfortable niche. And, whether it be just because of a friendship, or some other reason, but they're always acting as tutors. You can hear them sounding out, decoding. You can hear it going on, and you can see the little lips . . .

RW: (laughs)

SE: (laughs) So, it serves many purposes. Getting down the basic reading strategies—basic skills that they need—to become a reader.

RW: O.K. How about, journal writing? What do you see as the purpose of journal writing?

SE: Journal writing, I do mainly . . . I use it for a lot of diagnostic purposes, where are they in their writing? I use it so they can express themselves freely. I don't give them topics to write in their journal about. It's free choice. It's used mainly as a tool for expression. And they can write about anything, and they illustrate. In the beginning, a lot of kids would just start their journal with a picture, and possibly a word or a sentence underneath the picture . . .

RW: Right.

SE: Now, it's this big contest: Who can write a whole page? Who can write two pages? And, I've used it . . . I've attached skills to it as skills come up when they're reading to me. It's used for editing. They'll be reading their sentence, and I'll notice that their sentence didn't start with a capital. And, I'll tell them, "Oh, I love what your sentence is about, and this and that." And I'll say, "But, I always know that a sentence starts a spe-

cial way." And, they'll pick right up on it. Then, when I give
them a clue like that, they know to look at their punctuation, too.

RW: Right.

SE: So, it's used for writing skills, too . . . (skills) that don't have to
be taught whole class, up on the board. "This is where we put
the period. This is where . . . "

RW: Right.

SE: So, it's very personalized that way. So I use the journal for
personalized instruction. I know exactly where a child's at.

RW: Do you ever use instruction like that in a group?

SE: In a big group like that? Not generally, no. I find that the kids
tune out. I only have five percent of the class with me. So, why
waste that whole block of time . . . some kids need it. Some
kids don't need it. And here, everything's pretty personalized
to where they're at. And, it meets their needs better. I think.
Personalization is the key in attempting to meet the many needs
in a classroom.

(new topic)

RW: So, what percentage of time do you think the kids are actively
reading—as opposed to, say, listening or writing . . . ?

SE: I would say with everything we do in here . . . how everything
is so integrated . . . that, to do any activity in here, they need to
read something. So, I would say for everything we do in here
there is a reading portion. So most of the day.

RW: So most of the day they are actively reading.

SE: They are . . . immersed in that text! So—well, you just find
ways to incorporate it. It can't be separate. You can't be driving along and say, "Oh! I've got to read that sign. So, I better
stop, read the sign, and then go on." It's just there. It's part of your
day. And that's how it is in here, too. I don't . . . have the reading
groups say, from 9 to 10:30 we're having reading. And then read
them all the directions for everything else the rest of the day.

RW: Right.

SE: It's an all-day event in here.

RW: In discussing centers . . .

SE: Most kids make it full circuit (around to each of the centers
over the course of the week). Some research says that you
shouldn't have "have to's" when you're doing things like center time. But I found that this particular group needs that
structure—or I would have that problem that they'd always be

at the art center. Once they get done with the reading and the writing, they have the extras, like going to the art center. And things like that. Again, though, I'm trying to meet the needs of the particular group.

RW: So you try to get them to do the other ones—the reading and writing centers—first.

SE: The other ones. Yeah. And then they have the option of the art, and games, and like that. But sometimes I worry about that too. Because art isn't less important than the reading and writing. So I do make sure that we have other opportunities to do art. With projects and things. So . . . there's a lot involved. Sometimes teachers don't see it that way. "Art center's a waste of time. Well . . . it's not as important." But it really is, because it's another form of expression for the kids. And some of them strive that way. So, you can't take it away. So . . . I'm kind of having my own battle with that right now. I haven't come to any conclusions. Which is terrible. But, what I've done is I've left it open so there is enough time . . . for all the kids to get through. And if for some reason, a child is through the whole circuit way before anyone else, then I'll add something else. Or they can go back to their favorite center . . . It's pretty flexible. Pretty free. And, it's directed by them. So, like, in the math center, there are endless possibilities of things they can do. So they can go back there and do a different activity.

RW: At the end of the school year—as they go from first grade to second grade—what do you see as your students' greatest strengths? You know, "Oh, those kids left Ms. Ettenberger's room . . . "

SE: Um . . .being independent, I think. Being able to do for themselves. And discover on their own. And have the know-how to discover on their own—which I think is all tied back to independence.

RW: Yes . . . so independence is important?

SE: In the beginning of the year, I always write the parents a letter about, "My goals are to help your child become more independent." Because I think being independent fosters everything else. It's the basis for everything. And to love learning. They'll have a good attitude about school. They'll enjoy coming to school. And I think that with the atmosphere I provide, that's what they'll leave with.

RW: That's a lot.

SE: Along with all the skills. You know, everything that goes along with it.

RW: What do you like best about teaching first grade?

SE: The kids. They make my day. (beams) They really do. Not that they need me, but . . . I feel good knowing that I'm a facilitator: That I can give them a lot of tools to help them learn. I don't do the learning for them. I don't dispense the information. But I've got the tools to help them . . . discover the information on their own. And I like that. I like the relationship that I build with kids. I mean, I don't ever wake up saying, "Oh, God, I've got to go into work." I just don't. And I like that it changes. It doesn't allow you to be stagnant. I like that about teaching. It's always something new. You never get bored.

RW: Thank you.

Based on observations of SE's balanced teaching, we also have concluded that SE's students never get bored. Based on other data collected by us, we have concluded as well that her balanced teaching is consistent with the balanced teaching of many other literacy teachers who are outstanding in developing their students' reading and writing abilities.

Surveys of Teaching Practices

We have conducted two surveys of the practices of teachers who are considered by their supervisors to be excellent in developing primary-level literacy competencies in their students, both involving teachers from across the United States. One study focused on regular education kindergarten, first grade, and second grade teachers (Pressley, Rankin, & Yokoi, in press); the other involved special education teachers (Rankin & Pressley, in preparation). The starting point in each were teacher responses to an open-ended question requesting a list of the 10 most important elements of their literacy instruction. The many elements of instruction cited in response to this question were then tapped in a questionnaire, with the responses to the questions on this instrument quantifiable (that is, involving mostly Likert-scaled responses or quantitative estimates). For example, the following questions appeared on the instrument:

- Do you use "big books"? (answered on a "never" to "several times a day" scale)
- After a story, do you ask students "comprehension questions"? (answered on a "not at all" to "all stories" scale)
- What percentage of the material read by your students is outstanding children's literature? . . . written at a "controlled" reading level? . . . written to provide practice in phonetic elements and/or patterns . . . high interest, low vocabulary materials?
- Which of the following extension activities do you use regularly, occasionally, or never: arts/crafts with print attached, cooking activities, dramatics or puppet plays, drawing or illustrating stories, movement activities, field trips, games?
- Are home/parents involved in your reading instruction for good readers? . . . average readers? . . . weaker readers?

The many instructional practices reported by the 89 regular-education teachers and 34 special education teachers in this study are summarized in Figure 13-1, on page 271. In short, they reported classrooms filled with authentic and diverse literacy opportunities. The school days in these classrooms were portrayed as jam-packed with all types of reading and writing. Most critically, from the perspective of this volume, great balance was reported in the instruction offered to students. Consistent with the recommendation of a number of educators and theorists (for example, Adams, 1990; Cazden, 1992; Delpit, 1986; Duffy, 1991; Fisher & Hiebert, 1990; McCaslin, 1989; Pressley, 1994; Stahl et al., 1994), the teachers in this study depicted their classrooms as integrating explicit skill instruction within their whole language classrooms. Although there was reported immersion in literacy experiences, extensive explicit teaching through modeling, explanation, and mini-lesson re-explanations was also reported, especially with respect to decoding and other skills (for example, punctuation mechanics, comprehension strategies).

The special education teachers especially reported explicit teaching of letter-level and decoding skills as well as elementary writing skills. This outcome was consistent with the regular education teachers' reports as a function of student ability, with consistent reporting of more explicit and extensive lower-order (that is, letter-level and word-level) with weaker compared to stronger students. Most critically, however, both the special education and regular education teachers reported that, for the most part, they offered instruction to weaker readers that was very similar to the instruction offered to stronger readers. The differences in instruction for weaker versus stronger students were more quantitative ones than qualitative ones, with teachers recommending more of some types of instruction for some students than others, rather than one type of instruction for weaker and another type for stronger readers. Especially important in the context of this volume, the instruction reported by special education teachers and by regular education teachers for weaker students was balanced, involving both explicit instruction of decoding and other skills in the context of rich authentic reading and writing.

There were many reasons for confidence in the survey data. One was that there was little variability in the opinions offered, despite the fact that the data came from teachers across the nation. Another was that the data were orderly in ways that would be expected (Harris & Sipay, 1990) if the teachers were being honest in their reports. Thus, teachers who claimed to be exclusively whole language were, in fact, less likely to endorse practices not endorsed by pure whole language theorists, such as out-of-context decoding instruction. Also, there were reported decreases in instructional practices that should decrease between kindergarten and second grade, and there were reported increases in instructional practices that should increase between kindergarten and second grade, as depicted in Figures 13-2 and 13-3, found on pages 275 and 276.

Nonetheless, such survey data are a step removed from actual teaching, and many behavioral scientists have more confidence in observational data. Thus, it made sense to obtain some, especially given the commitment of our group to multi-method study of literacy (see Pressley et al., 1992).

Qualitative Study of Outstanding First Grade Literacy Instruction

As this chapter is being written, Wharton-McDonald, Pressley, and Mistretta are in the midst of a study in which we are observing the teaching of five first grade teachers in the Albany, NY area who are outstanding in promoting the literacy of their students. All five were nominated by their supervisors. We are also carrying out in-depth interviews with these teachers to understand the backgrounds they bring to teaching and their reasons for teaching as they do. In order to understand the unique qualities of the outstanding teachers, a sample of more typical teachers is also being studied, with these teachers selected by supervisors as very solid representatives of the teaching in their districts, teaching certainly consistent with district expectations and standards for first grade. The project is far enough along that some conclusions can be offered confidently, although not so far along that a definitive, complete summary of the results is possible.

First, one reaction that we encountered to the long list of instructional practices summarized in Figure 13-1 was that no classroom could include so much. Thus, one issue for us was to determine if the list in Figure 13-1 was overly inclusive—that surveyed teachers were claiming to do more than they possibly could do. It is clear that all of the outstanding first grade classrooms we are watching this year include most of the elements summarized in Figure 13-1. One of the most striking characteristics of the outstanding classrooms relative to the more typical ones is the intensity of the literacy instruction, with school days definitely filled with high-quality reading and writing experiences. In contrast, more typical classrooms have large portions of time that is not nearly as intense or literacy-relevant. For example, in one comparison classroom, there is a great deal of copying, something almost never observed in the classrooms constructed by the outstanding teachers. In another, much of the literacy instruction is devoted to communications activities that occur in a sharing circle, with much of the discussion during this sharing not relating to what the children are reading or to other academic content. In general, there is less real reading and writing in the more typical, compared to the outstanding, classrooms.

There are several characteristics of outstanding classrooms that are being detected through observations and face-to-face interviewing that did not come through in the survey studies. First, there is a great deal of connection in the instruction offered by the outstanding teachers, with students writing about what they have read, and the outstanding teachers often relating concepts encountered today to ones encountered previously. It is much easier to observe disjointedness in the comparison classrooms than in the outstanding classrooms. Second, the outstanding teachers are terrific managers. Their behavior management of students is superb and always positively toned. Moreover, their management of resources is striking. Thus, when resource teachers are available to an outstanding teacher, the resource teacher's time is well spent. In contrast, we have frequently seen resource teachers underused by the more typical teachers. Third, the engagement of students is very high in outstanding classrooms. In our observations we try to note every few minutes the percentage of students who seem to be attentive and gainfully involved. In outstanding classrooms, this is typically most or all students and never less than half of the students. In contrast, inattention is much more commonly observed in the more typical classrooms. In summary, as the qualitative study now in progress is providing data convergent with the outcomes in the survey research, it is also producing some unique insights.

Conclusion

As we carry out our current observational research, we are in awe of the complexity of balanced teaching. If we have a frustration at this point, however, it is that we do not know, nor do we believe others know, how to develop teachers who are so expertly balanced. How can teachers be educated so that they know children's literature well enough to direct every child to an interesting story matched to his or her reading and conceptual competence, who understand the structure of words so well that they can provide a mini-lesson responsive to any of the infinity of decoding problems that occur daily during beginning reading lessons, and who grasp people management well enough to create a positive classroom experience for every child and a productive teaching day every day for every resource teacher and parent volunteer in their classroom. We admire the high energy level of outstanding primary-level literacy teachers and wonder if it is an energy level within reach of most primary teachers. We also admire how much the excellent teachers we have been observing care about their students, a caring that comes through in both how they act every day and their interviews. We are not sure that all who are primary-level teachers or who aspire to the role have it in them to be so committed to other people's children.

On a more positive note, there are some certainties that emerge from our analyses. Teachers should not be educated to be parochial in their teaching, adhering strongly to one theoretical perspective or another (for example, explicit decoding or whole language). Rather, excellent teachers more often blend perspectives, intermeshing a variety of methods and contents (Duffy, 1991).

Further, we close by noting that every first grade classroom that we have studied has its own personality, with that personality largely determined by the instruction and environment offered by the teacher to students. Thus, Figure 13-1 is no more than a skeleton of instructional elements that are found in excellent primary-level classrooms. We are becoming more convinced as we work on the observational/ interview study that there is no prototypical, excellent primary-level classroom. In every case, however, excellent classrooms have warm, busy, attractive personalities, and are the kinds of balanced and engaging places that we would like every primary-level student to have a chance to experience.

This chapter is dedicated with affection to Miss Lindley McKinney, who was Michael Pressley's first grade teacher during school year 1957-58. In April 1995, she wrote to him, "This might be the time for me to confess a long-held secret. As I taught the Scott-Foresman whole word basal approach, I also worked in plenty of phonics while keeping an eye out for the principal to appear in the doorway . . . Neither whole word or phonics could stand alone." Excellent teachers have been balancing complementary models of beginning reading instruction for a very long time.

The research reported in this chapter was supported in part by the National Reading Research Center, sponsored by the U.S. Department of Education, and University at Albany (that is, through financial support to Wharton-McDonald, Mistretta, and Yokoi). The opinions expressed here, however, are not those of the funding agencies. Correspondence regarding this chapter can be sent to Mr. Pressley, Department of Educational Psychology and Statistics, University at Albany, SUNY, Albany NY 12222.

References

Adams, M. J. (1990). *Beginning to read.* Cambridge MA: Harvard University Press.

Ball, E. W., & Blachman, B. A. (1991). Does phoneme awareness training in kindergarten make a difference in early word recognition and developmental spelling? *Reading Research Quarterly, 26,* 49–66.

Boljonis, A., & Hinchman, K. (1988). First graders' perceptions of reading and writing. In J. E. Readence & R. S. Baldwin (Eds.), *Dialogues in reading research, Thirty-seventh yearbook of the National Reading Conference* (pp. 107–114). Chicago IL: National Reading Conference.

Cazden, C. (1992). *Whole language plus: Essays on literacy in the United States and New Zealand.* New York: Teachers College Press.

Delpit, L. D. (1986). Skills and other dilemmas of a progressive black educator. *Harvard Educational Review, 56,* 379–385.

Duffy, G. G. (1991). What counts in teacher education? Dilemmas in educating empowered teachers. In J. Zutell & S. McCormick (Eds.), *Learner factors/teacher factors: Issues in literacy research and instruction: Fortieth yearbook of the National Reading Conference* (pp. 1–18). Chicago: National Reading Conference.

Elley, W. B. (1989). Vocabulary acquisition from listening to stories. *Reading Research Quarterly, 24,* 174–187.

Feitelson, D., Kita, B., & Goldstein, Z. (1986). Effects of listening to series stories on first graders' comprehension and use of language. *Research in the Teaching of English, 20,* 339–356.

Fisher, C. W., & Hiebert, E. H. (1990). Characteristics of tasks in two approaches to literacy instruction. *Elementary School Journal, 91,* 3–18.

Freppon, P. A. (1991). Children's concepts of the nature and purpose of reading in different instructional settings. *Journal of Reading Behavior, 23,* 139–163.

Gambrell, L. B., & Palmer, B. M. (1992). Children's metacognitive knowledge about reading and writing in literature-based and conventional classrooms. In C. Kinzer & D. Leu (Eds.), *Literacy research, theory, and practice, Forty-first yearbook of the National Reading Conference* (pp. 215–223). Chicago: National Reading Conference.

Graham, S. & Harris, K. R. (1994). The effects of whole language on children's writing: A review of literature. *Educational Psychologist, 29,* 187–192.

Harris, A. J., & Sipay, E. R. (1990). *How to increase reading ability: A guide to developmental and remedial methods.* New York: Longman.

Lie, A. (1991). Effects of a training program for stimulating skills in word analysis in first-grade children. *Reading Research Quarterly, 26,* 234–250.

Mather, N. (1992). Whole language reading instruction for students with learning disabilities: Caught in the cross fire. *Learning Disabilities Research & Practice, 7,* 87–95.

McCaslin, M. M. (1989). Whole language: Theory, instruction, and future implementation. *Elementary School Journal, 90,* 223–229.

Mills, H., O'Keefe, T., & Stephens, D. (1990). Looking closer: *The role of phonics in a whole language classroom.* Urbana IL: National Council of Teachers of English.

Morrow, L. M. (1990). Preparing the classroom environment to promote literacy during play. *Early Childhood Research Quarterly,* 5, 537–554.

Morrow, L. M. (1991). Relationships among physical designs of play centers, teachers' emphasis on literacy in play, and children's literacy behavior during play. In J. Zutell & S. McCormick (Eds.), *Learner factors/teacher factors: Issues in literacy research and instruction: Fortieth yearbook of the National Reading Conference* (pp. 127–140). Chicago: National Reading Conference.

Morrow, L. M. (1992). The impact of a literature-based program on literacy achievement, use of literature, and attitudes of children from minority backgrounds. *Reading Research Quarterly,* 27, 251–275.

Morrow, L. M., O'Connor, E. M., & Smith, J. K. (1990). Effects of a story reading program on the literacy development of at-risk kindergarten children. *Journal of Reading Behavior,* 22, 255–275.

Nelson, L. (1990). The influence of phonics instruction on spelling progress. In J. Zutell & S. McCormick (Eds.), *Literacy theory and research: Analyses from multiple paradigms* (pp. 241–247). Chicago: National Reading Conference.

Neuman, S. B., & Roskos, K. (1990). The influence of literacy-enriched play settings on preschoolers' engagement with written language. In J. Zutell & S. McCormick (Eds.), *Literacy theory and research: Analyses from multiple paradigms* (pp. 179–188). Chicago: National Reading Conference.

Neuman, S. B., & Roskos, K. (1992). Literacy objects as cultural tools: Effects on children's literacy behaviors in play. *Reading Research Quarterly,* 27, 203–225.

Pressley, M. (1994). Commentary on the ERIC whole language debate. In C. B. Smith (Moderator), *Whole language: The debate* (pp. 155–178). Bloomington, IN: ERIC/REC.

Pressley, M., El-Dinary, P. B., Gaskins, I., Schuder, T., Bergman, J., Almasi, L., & Brown, R. (1992). Beyond direct explanation: Transactional instruction of reading comprehension strategies. *Elementary School Journal,* 92, 511–554.

Pressley, M., & Rankin, J. (1994). More about whole language methods of reading instruction for students at risk for early reading failure. *Learning Disabilities Research & Practice,* 9, 156–167.

Pressley, M., Rankin, J., & Yokoi, L. (in press). A survey of instructional practices of primary teachers nominated as effective in promoting literacy. *Elementary School Journal.*

Rankin, J. & Pressley, M. (in preparation). *A survey of instructional practices of primary-level special education teachers nominated as effective in promoting literacy.*

Rasinski, T., & DeFord, D. (1985). *Learning within a classroom context: First graders' conceptions of literacy.* (ERIC Document Reproduction Service, No. ED 262 393).

Robbins, C., & Ehri, L. C. (1994). Reading storybooks to kindergartners helps them learn new vocabulary words. *Journal of Educational Psychology, 86,* 54–64.

Stahl, S. A., McKenna, M. C., & Pagnucco, J. R. (1994). The effects of whole language instruction: An update and reappraisal. *Educational Psychologist, 29,* 175–186.

Stahl, S. A., & Miller, P. D. (1989). Whole language and language experience approaches for beginning reading: A quantitative research synthesis. *Review of Educational Research, 59,* 87–116.

Stanovich, K. E., & Cunningham, A. E. (1993). Where does knowledge come from? Specific associations between print exposure and information acquisition. *Journal of Educational Psychology, 85,* 211–229.

Tangel, D. M., & Blachman, B. A. (1992). Effect of phoneme awareness instruction on kindergarten children's invented spelling. *Journal of Reading Behavior, 24,* 233–261.

Uhry, J. K., & Shepherd, M. J. (1993). Segmentation/spelling instruction as part of a first-grade reading program: Effects on several measures of reading. *Reading Research Quarterly, 28,* 218–233.

Figure 13-1. Classroom Characteristics and Instructional Practices Often Reported by Effective Primary Literacy Teachers

---

General Characteristics of the Learning Environments

Teacher creates a literate environment in the classroom, including in-class library, displays of student work, chart stories/poems displayed, posting of word lists

Classroom rich with stories: stories read, reread, and told; audio-taped stories

Learning centers: listening, reading, and writing centers

Teacher identifies with language experience/whole language approach, at least somewhat

General Teaching Processes

Overt teacher modeling of literacy skills and strategies as well as modeling of positive attitudes toward literacy

Daily practice of reading and writing with limited practice of skills in isolation

Repetition of unmastered skills, including of phonics, letter recognition, and spelling (often in the context of other reading and writing activities)

Limited use of workbooks and worksheets

Cooperative grouping used

Different approaches to instructional grouping used, with more whole group than small group instruction, more small group than individual instruction, and more individual instruction than individual seatwork

Limited use of ability grouping and round-robin reading

Monitoring of student needs, with mini-lessons as needed, reteaching as needed

Concern with individual achievement and participation: leadership opportunities, students permitted to make progress at their own pace, assessment of student learning styles and adjustment of teaching according to learning style, individually guided reading instruction, individually guided writing instruction

Literacy instruction integrated with the rest of the curriculum

Extension experiences (for example, arts & crafts, illustration, games, etc.)

Figure 13-1. continued

Teaching of Reading

What is Taught

Teaching of skills prerequisite to reading (for example, auditory and visual discrimination; attending and listening skills), both in the context of other reading and writing activities and in isolation (for example, with games)

Teaching concepts of print (for example, concept of a word, parts of a book)

Teaching of letter recognition, both in the context of other reading and writing activities and in isolation

Songs conveying literacy knowledge (for example, "The Alphabet Song")

Teaching the alphabetic principle, both in the context of other reading and writing activities and in isolation (for example, with games)

Activities focusing on the sounds of words

Teaching of letter-sound associations, both in the context of other reading and writing activities and in isolation

Limited use of the letter of the day or week approach

Limited copying and tracing of letters

Teaching of punctuation, mostly in the context of other reading and writing activities

Teaching of decoding strategies, including using context and picture clues as well as sounding out words using letter-sound knowledge

Teaching of phonics, in the context of other reading and writing activities, with respect to invented spellings, and sometimes using decontextualized approaches (for example, worksheets, drills)

Development of new vocaulary and sight vocabulary, often in the context of other reading and writing

Invented spelling encouraged

Teaching of spelling, including with spelling tests

Teaching reading as meaning making

Teaching of text elements (for example, cause-and-effect relations, theme/main idea, character analysis, etc.)

Teaching of comprehension strategies, especially prediction and visualization

Teaching of critical thinking skills, including brainstorming, categorization, and recalling details

Development of background knowledge before reading stories, especially through prereading discussion and reading of related books

Figure 13-1. continued

Types of Reading

Students reading along with teacher

Echo and choral reading

Shared reading (besides big book reading)

Students reading aloud with others

Daily silent reading daily (USSR: uninterrupted sustained, silent reading; DEAR: drop everything and read)

Student rereading of books, stories

Discussion of stories and literature read

Student book sharing (for example, via book reports)

Teacher involves parents in reading instruction by sending books home and asking parents to listen to the child read

Reading homework

What is Read

Reading of outstanding children's literature

Shared reading of big books

At least some reading of chart poems and stories

Reading of picture, patterned, and predictable books

Limited reading of basals, although highly variable depending on the teacher

Limited reading of chapter books, poems, and expository materials

Limited reading of materials at a controlled reading level

More reading of instructional level than either easy or frustration level materials

Reading aloud by students, especially of stories written by them and classmates, with these readings most frequently to peers or the teacher

Author studies, with coverage of illustrators as well

Figure 13-1. continued

Teaching of Writing

Types of Writing

Student story, book, and journal writing, with teachers responding to writing

Writing in response to pictures, wordless picture books, and stories read

Student dictations of stories (sometimes group dictations) to teacher as scribe

Shared writing

Students are asked to write at home

Infrequent copying of other people's writing

Teaching of the Writing Process

Writer's workshop in some classrooms

Teaching of planning, drafting, and revising as part of writing

Publishing of student writing

Use of computers during writing instruction, although not yet in the majority of classrooms

Explicitness/Extensiveness of Instruction as a Function of Reader Ability

Same elements of reading and writing instruction for good versus weaker readers

More explicit/extensive teaching of some prereading, letter-, and word-level skills with weaker readers

More guided reading and writing instruction and individualized instruction with weaker compared to good readers

Making Literacy and Literacy Instruction Motivating

Teachers attempt to motivate literacy by reducing risks for attempting literate activities, positive feedback, setting an exciting mood, encouraging students to believe they can be readers and writers, and so on

Accountability

Comprehension checks, including questions following a reading and student retelling of stories heard and/or read

Use of sentence strips and/or illustrations to reconstruct poems, stories heard and/or read

Frequent monitoring of students progress in literacy

Writing portfolios, and, to a lesser extent, reading portfolios

Regular conferences with parents and communications to home

Figure 13-2. Classroom Characteristics and Instructional Practices Reported Less Often with Increasing Grade Level

---

Learning Environment

Signs and labels
Learning centers
General teaching processes
Letter recognition drills
Small group work and instruction
Songs (for example, "The Alphabet Song")

Teaching of Reading

Teaching letter recognition
Copying/tracing letters
Teaching alphabetic principle with good and average readers
Teaching focusing on sounds of words
Teaching concepts of print, including the concepts of "letter" and "directions of print"
Phonics drills
Teaching of phonics using games and puzzles
Letter of day/week
Decoding strategies instruction to weaker readers
Explicit attempts to develop sight word vocabulary with good and average readers
Teacher rereading of stories
Shared big book reading
Rereading of big books by good and average readers
Chart stories and poems
Picture books
Patterned books
Reading aloud of patterned books
Controlled reading-level materials
Materials providing practice reading specific phonetic elements
"Easy" reading
"Frustration"-level reading with good and average readers

Teaching of Writing

Student dictation of stories to adults (including whole class dictation to teacher)
Shared writing

Accountability

Parent conferences

Note: $P < .05$ for each effect summarized in this figure.

Figure 13-3. Classroom Characteristics and Instructional Practices Reported More Often with Increasing Grade Level

---

General Teaching Processes

Round-robin reading

Individually guided reading for weaker readers

Teaching of Reading

Teaching decoding strategies to weaker readers

Teaching use of syntax cues for decoding

Teaching common phonics rules

Teaching morphemic-structural analysis for decoding

Teaching syllabification rules for decoding

Spelling drills

Spelling tests

Sight word drills

Teaching comprehension strategies, including activating prior knowledge, question generation, finding main ideas, summarization, and using story grammar cues

Teaching of critical thinking skills, including webbing and identification of causes and effects

Preteaching of vocabulary

Choral reading

Homework

Student reading aloud to other people

Student reading aloud of poetry, trade books, and basal stories

Silent reading

Chapter books

Basal use

Controlled reading-level materials

Materials providing practice with specific phonetic elements

"Instructional"-level reading for average and weaker readers

Teaching of Writing

Student storywriting

Writing in response to reading

Planning before writing

Revising during writing

Publishing story collections

Teaching punctuation, including out-of-context teaching

Accountability

Writing portfolios

Note: $P < .05$ for each effect summarized in this figure.

Chapter 14

Concluding Reflections

℘ ———— ℅

Michael Pressley
University at Albany, State University of New York

During the course of co-editing this book, I was impressed with the conceptual attractiveness of the teaching described in each of the contributions. I had some recurring thoughts, and even doubts, as this project proceeded, however. I offer them here because I know that this book will inspire some readers to try balanced teaching. I also know that teachers who do so should be aware that there are many issues about balanced literacy instruction yet to be resolved. That is, some of the envisionments of teaching presented in this book have not been tested in ways that permit high confidence that the instruction they describe really does work better than potential alternatives. The chapters present more a set of hypotheses than a set of tested, true principles—appealing ones, but hypotheses nonetheless.

A New Set of Hypotheses About Teaching

These conceptions of teaching are neither conventional whole language nor conventional explicit instruction, but something quite different. Having seen many elementary classrooms, including those advertised as whole language as well as ones described as explicit instruction by teachers, I know that the balanced teaching featured in this volume is anything but commonplace. Balanced teaching requires *constant* monitoring of students and *continuous* responding to them. What are some teachers' best moments are typical moments in the day of the balanced teacher, who is teaching and reteaching constantly, hinting and prompting continuously, all day anticipating a problem that Jennifer is going to have in the next moment as she assists Johnny in this moment. Balanced teaching is as intensely interactive all day as the many snippets of teaching reported in this volume.

I do not know if day-in, day-out, day-long balanced teaching will ever become commonplace. Such balanced teaching is very difficult to do. First, teachers must know a great deal about children's literature and be committed to learning much more. They must also understand decoding, comprehension, and composition processes well enough that they can explain these processes and model them for students. More than that, however, they must be able to re-explain and re-model the processes in light of particular student difficulties and misconceptions . . . difficulties and misconceptions that often will be apparent only after teachers have been immersed for some time in the world of student misunderstandings (that is, teachers experienced in teaching reading and writing to students). Awareness of student difficulties to the degree necessary to permit sensitive re-explanations and support requires vigilant monitoring of individual students and their progress. Moreover, third, fourth, and fifth attempts to explain simple ideas can require great patience . . . and faith, as well, that such scaffolding can make a difference. To provide excellent balanced teaching to even a single student who experiences difficulties in reading and writing requires high teacher motivation. Of course, few teachers are so lucky as to have only one student who needs heavy doses of explicit teaching and reteaching of reading and writing processes in order to make progress. (See Pressley, Hogan, Wharton-McDonald, Mistretta, & Ettenberger, et al., in press, for extensive commentary about all the reasons teaching like that described in this volume is difficult to do.)

In the best classrooms, scenes like the ones portrayed in this book continue all day. I have seen such classrooms and if this volume inspires more of them, I will be delighted, for there is a good chance that reading instruction will be vastly improved. Whether it is or not will be known only if great commitments are made to doing additional research about such teaching.

Need for Research

Much research is needed on the hypothesized benefits of the teaching portrayed in this book. Many readers undoubtedly noted that there was little discussion of formal research and data in this volume, something rare in the great debates surrounding elementary reading. One reason is that there is nothing in the extant research literature to permit data-based conclusions about the relative efficacy of the alternative approaches to balance reviewed in this volume.

Moreover, the models of balance presented in this volume do not exhaust the possibilities. For example, I know of at least one first grade curriculum that balances authentic reading and writing with systematic phonics instruction for all students, instruction covering the full scope of phonics skills in a hypothesized optimal sequence. The authors of that program believe, based on their interpretation of the scientific evidence relating to decoding instruction, that exhaustive systematicity in decoding instruction is desirable for all students, with students receiving such systematic instruction much better able to benefit from the rich literature and writing experiences included in the program. Having observed some first grade classrooms in which their program is being piloted, I was struck that the students were making great progress, with students enthusiastically engaged in wonderful literature and writing experiences. I favor formal comparisons between a variety of approaches, such as the ones presented in this volume, but also including comparisons with even more instructionally intensive approaches, such as the program just described. Such comparative evaluations would yield a great deal of information with respect to whether some mixes of explicit instruction and more natural reading and writing experiences are more potent than other mixes. My hypothesis is that students require quite a bit of explicit instruction, teaching sensitive to student needs as it covers the full scope of what they need to know. As I advance that hypothesis here, even more forcefully than in my earlier chapters in this volume, I do so to make the point that my chapters were advocacy chapters. My perspectives on balanced instruction, like the perspectives of the other contributors to this volume, reflect hypotheses about effective instruction. My ideas about balance require more empirical scrutiny, as do the ideas of many of the other contributors to this volume. If there is serious research analyzing and comparing the alternatives presented here, a lot more will be known about balanced teaching than is known now.

A Range of Potential Impacts

I hope, as researchers turn their attention to evaluation of the various versions of balanced teaching presented in this volume, that much thought is given to the dependent measures in these studies. What must be remembered is that excellent literacy instruction potentially produces a range of impacts and, thus, requires a range of dependent variables to study it. Excellent instruction produces readers who understand well the varied purposes for reading and writing and many strategies for achieving diverse perspectives. Excellent literacy instruction also should result in students with extensive cultural and world knowledge, developed in part through extensive, thoughtful reading and writing. Credible evaluations of balanced instruction must tap these diverse outcomes. One reason the great debates of the past have been so unconvincing to many is that only very limited measurement (that is, standardized measures) occurred in many of the studies cited prominently by the debaters.

Potential Individual Differences With Respect to Instructional Needs

As research evaluations of balanced instruction occur, I also hope that they will be more intelligent in another way than have the evaluations contributing to the great debates of the past. It may be that there really is something to aptitude by treatment interactions (Cronbach & Snow, 1977) for weaker readers, that there is no one best model of literacy instruction for students experiencing difficulties. Rather, to paraphrase Sly and the Family Stone, different folks who are weaker readers need different instructional strokes. For example, maybe some students require extremely systematic, explicit instruction for them to learn to decode, instruction supported by a variety of materials, whereas for others, decoding lessons can be more *ad hoc,* more driven by the specific difficulties the student is experiencing.

There is considerable evidence that American students in general are reading and writing less well than they could and should. I am continually confronted with unsatisfactory performances of American students (for example, National Assessment of Educational Progress—NAEP), especially with respect to higher-order comprehension processes, such as those that can be stimulated by explicit comprehension strategies instruction, and composition skills, such as those that can be stimulated by explicit writing strategies instruction. The NAEP has also documented that American students know less about literature and history than they should, in part because they read too little. At a conceptual level, it makes sense that all of these perceived shortcomings of American students should be alleviated by balanced instruction—instruction immersing students in literature and content-area reading that permit extensive opportunities for students to practice applying the literacy competencies emphasized during explicit instruction.

More positively, there are classrooms in which balanced teaching is provided to a wide range of students (for example, see Pressley et al. chapters in this volume). It is not known, however, whether balanced instruction makes a difference in the achievements of average and better-than-average students, but it may make quite a difference. I fear that the benefits for students who are not at risk may go unstudied if balanced teaching comes to be viewed as critical only for weaker readers and writers. Much work remains to be done to understand the benefits of balanced teaching for students of all ability levels. This, by the way is a critical theoretical point. There are many models of instruction that specify the need for more instruction and more explicit instruction for weaker students. If that is all the balanced instruction perspective is, it is not theoretically innovative. Alternatively, if it turns out that more explicit instruction has benefits for all students, and perhaps different benefits as a function of ability level, that is a much more unique and interesting situation theoretically.

What Goes on When the Student Is Not With the Teacher?

In balanced classrooms, even students who receive disproportionate amounts of one-to-one (or a few-to-one) attention from the teacher actually spend only a very little bit of their school day in one-to-one or few-to-one interactions with a teacher. Many teachers believe that the rest of the school day goes better largely because of this small amount of highly individualized instruction that students in need of instruction receive. But does it? Is it the case that the little bit of one-to-one or few-to-one interaction that is possible in a classroom of 20 to 25 children has a noticable impact on students' abilities to operate on their own the rest of the time? Is the whole school day better for weaker readers if they get a few minutes of intensive explicit instruction? If it is better, how and why is it better? As conceptualization about and research on teaching continues, there needs to be a focus on students and learning, rather than on teaching. We need to look at how children fare when reading and writing on their own.

Student Self-Regulation

I think that if future thinking about teaching is student-centric, the power of balanced teaching might be ever more obvious. The examples of scaffolding presented in this volume are impressive in terms of reflecting how skilled teachers can cast and recast mini-lessons for struggling students on a one-to-one basis. Even more impressive to me is that these dialogues with individual students are occurring while everyone else in the class is productively busy, highly engaged in literacy experiences. When I am in these classrooms, I am always impressed by the high degree of student self-regulation. Students are off reading and writing as they are supposed to be, sometimes on their own and sometimes collaboratively. There is always so much going on!! That is what all of us involved in the great debates about literacy instruction want, classrooms of self-regulated, engaged readers. Much of the secret to such engagement may be in scaffolded teaching—and of course that is implied throughout this book.

More emphasis on the student in conceptualizations of balanced teaching is reasonable from both whole language and explicit instruction perspectives, for both models embrace student self-regulation as a high ideal. Whole language activities are highly meaningful and motivating to students. Explicit instruction attempts to provide tools that make reading and writing more do-able and, hence, less frustrating. Good explicit instruction also aims to develop students' ability to decode words in any context, be active comprehenders from the beginning to the end of readings, and tackle all aspects of composing, from planning through final revisions (that is, provide students with tactics for self-regulated control of all of decoding, comprehension, and composition). One reason I am so high on balanced teaching is that I have memories of engaged children, working away even when the teacher seems totally consumed in scaffolding one student in particular. Students know what to do and want to do it in these classrooms. They are motivated.

Student Motivation

All of the presenters in this volume were concerned about student motivation, that instruction be grabbing for students. Why their concern with motivation? Although the reasons are beyond the scope of this discussion, it is indisputable that motivation to do things academic declines precipitously as a function of attendance in conventional American schools, with the declines particularly pronounced among students experiencing difficulties in school (Nicholls, 1989). Good teachers attempt to prevent declining motivation in struggling students by providing additional support and instruction before failure overwhelms students. By explicitly teaching powerful decoding, comprehension, and composition strategies, they are providing at-risk students not only with powerful tools, but also with opportunities to see that they can decode, comprehend, and compose if they exert effort to use tools that are within reach of them. That is, struggling students experience opportunities to learn that what happens to them academically is somewhat within their control, with such knowledge highly motivating. When students understand that their academic efforts can make a difference in achievement, they are more likely to exert efforts in the future than if they believe academic achievement is out of personal control (Borkowski, Carr, Rellinger, & Pressley, 1990).

Beyond the explicit instruction, however, the immersion in meaningful literacy tasks is intended to motivate as well. At least since Dewey (1913), it has been understood that experiencing interesting and meaningful academic tasks is motivating to students, consistent with the contemporary whole language emphasis on student interest and personal meaning as driving forces in effective literacy instruction. Balanced instruction, which is rich in whole language opportunities, has great potential for motivating students and, thus, as balanced instruction is evaluated, much effort should go into determining what difference it makes in both short-term and long-term motivation.

In my visits to classrooms, I also have been struck that they are happy places. Students read materials they like and write about topics that interest them. Moreover, because students are getting the help they need, intellectually isolated, frustrated, and depressed students are rare in these classrooms. Balanced teachers believe that all students can learn, but some need more support than others. They convey to their students the attitude that that is an all right state of affairs and what is important is that students improve in their reading and writing. The contributors to this volume believe that students are improving and feel good about themselves as a result. This possibility deserves careful study, for if it is true, it is powerful evidence in favor of balance as an approach to beginning literacy instruction, an approach that keeps struggling students academically oriented rather than increasingly cynical about participation in a schooling situation in which they have no chance of succeeding.

Active Learning

All of the instruction discussed in this volume is intended to stimulate active student learning and knowledge construction rather than passive learning. This is particularly important to emphasize with respect to the explicit instructional input that students receive in balanced classrooms, because explicit instruction is often represented as rote rather than constructivist by its critics, including critics who identify with whole language philosophy. Explicit instruction in balanced classrooms is not mindless, rote teaching, but rather intended to stimulate students to connect new information they are learning to what they know already—to come to understand decoding, comprehension, and composition processes—to approach decoding, comprehension, and composition as active problem-solving processes requiring reflection and decision making. The illustrative dialogues in this book are filled with instruction intended as a starting point for student reflection. The dialogues are of teachers explaining decoding, comprehension, and writing rather than of teachers specifying a set of rules that students should apply mechanically as they read and write. See Pressley, Harris, and Marks (1992) and Harris and Pressley (1991) for elaboration about how explicit instruction about cognitive processing provides a good start for student construction of understandings about the processes taught.

Diversity in Implementation of Balanced Teaching

Although in my own work I have been able to detect similarities in balanced classrooms (for example, there is systematic instruction of decoding in formal lessons and in mini-lessons provided on an as-needed basis; there are large doses of authentic literature; writing occurs daily, often in reaction to what has been read), no two balanced classrooms are identical. Even teachers with similar philosophies and intentions will translate balance differently. Deciding to be balanced in no way stifles teacher creativity and ingenuity. Some teachers do more whole group than small group, and some are comfortable with whole days of small group. Some make formal spelling instruction a centerpiece of their explicit decoding instruction, and others do not. Some encourage as much reading of expository material as narratives, and others immerse their students in the worlds of great narrative authors. Some classrooms are polite and relatively quiet; others are filled with students who strongly and loudly assert their beliefs as they react to texts they read, as they reflect on what might go into their compositions, and as they argue with one another about the possible spelling of a word one youngster wants to use in an essay. Even relatively explicit models of balance will be implemented very differently in different classrooms.

Balanced Teaching as a General Model of Instruction

Teaching literacy skills is much like teaching children to play baseball (Klenk & Palincsar, this volume; Pressley & Rankin, 1994). Coaching baseball involves balancing explicit skills instruction and actual playing of baseball. Every late spring and early summer night, at diamonds all over the country, little leaguers will spend the first 45 minutes of practice on batting, infield and outfield practice, followed by an hour intrateam scrimmage. On game night, the half hour of warm up will be devoted to exercising skills before the kids play six innings of baseball. During both scrimmages and games, the coaches will be constantly reminding players about how to incorporate skills drilled during practice into actual play. The shortstop who makes an anemic toss to first will hear, "Billy, remember to make one step when you throw," with the coach mimicking the motion as he gives the reminder. When a big hitter comes to the plate, a coach may cue, "Outfielders, back up and remember, two hands." These during-the-game remarks from the coaches make sense because they are tied to previous skills practice, albeit skills practice that does not at first transfer certainly or directly into the game without reminders.

That is, I believe balancing skill instruction and in-context learning opportunities is more of a general approach to teaching than simply an approach to the teaching of reading. Balance is not a new idea, but similar to proposals offered throughout this century, from Vygotsky's pre-World War II proposals (1978 translation) that formally taught concepts are really understood if they are related to naturally acquired ones to Elbow's (1986) major thesis in *Embracing Contraries*, that effective teaching involves both knowledge transmission and discovery. It is conceptually sensible from a variety of perspectives to balance instruction of skills and whole learning opportunities.

The Promise of Balanced Instruction

This book on balanced elementary literacy instruction is only a beginning. The promise is great, but, for that promise to be fulfilled, many more teachers must try to implement a balanced approach in their classrooms. In addition, researchers must expend great effort to document the effects of this kind of teaching. This volume is but a set of first hypotheses. I look forward to witnessing progress in the implementation of balanced instruction in many more classrooms and watching it evolve, informed both by the experiences of teachers and the insights of the researchers who work with teachers to better understand teaching and learning.

References

Borkowski, J. G., Carr, M., Rellinger, E. A., & Pressley, M. (1990). Self-regulated strategy use: Interdependence of metacognition, attributions, and self-esteem. In B. F. Jones (Ed.), *Dimensions of thinking: Review of research* (pp. 53–92). Hillsdale NJ: Erlbaum & Associates.

Brown, R., & Pressley, M. (1994). Self-regulated reading and getting meaning from text: The transactional strategies instruction model and its ongoing evaluation. In D. Schunk & B. Zimmerman (Eds.), *Self-regulation of learning and performance: Issues and educational applications.* Hillsdale NJ: Erlbaum & Associates.

Brown, R., Pressley, M., Schuder, T., & Van Meter, P. (1995). *A quasi-experimental validation of transactional strategies instruction with previously low-achieving grade-2 readers.* College Park, MD: University of Maryland, National Reading Research Center.

Cronbach, L. J., & Snow, R. E. (1977). *Aptitudes and instructional methods: A handbook for research on interactions.* New York: Irvington.

Dewey, J. (1913). *Interest and effort in education.* Boston: Riverside.

Elbow, P. (1986). *Embracing contraries: Explorations in learning and teaching.* NY: Oxford University Press.

Harris, K. R., & Pressley, M. (1991). The nature of cognitive strategy instruction: Interactive strategy construction. *Exceptional Children, 57,* 392–404.

Nicholls, J. G. (1989). *The competitive ethos and democratic education.* Cambridge MA: Harvard University Press.

Pressley, M., Harris, K. R., & Marks, M. B. (1992). But good strategy instructors are constructivists!! *Educational Psychology Review, 4,* 1–32.

Pressley, M., Hogan, K., Wharton-McDonald, R., Mistretta, K., & Ettenberger, S. (in press). The challenges of instructional scaffolding . . . the challenges of fuller instruction that supports student thinking. *Learning Disabilities Research and Practice.*

Pressley, M. & Rankin, J. (1994). More about whole language methods of reading instruction for students at risk for early reading failure. *Learning Disabilities Research and Practices, 9,* 156–167.

Vygotsky, L. S. (1978). *Mind in society: The development of higher psychological processes.* M. Cole, V. John-Steiner, S. Scribner, & E. Sonberman (Eds. and Trans.). Cambridge: Harvard University Press.

Epilogue

In December 1995, the editors and many of the contributors of this book held an informal session at the National Reading Conference in New Orleans to discuss the instruction espoused in this book. The session was packed, and nearly one hundred people stood outside in the hall unable to get in, demonstrating the interest the field has in this topic. Three contributors presented vignettes that typified the kind of instruction found in this book. Lesley Mandel Morrow then described patterns found across all chapters, and Victoria Purcell-Gates discussed what we still need to know and where the field needs to go next regarding this kind of instruction.

Then, for about 40 minutes, groups of 20 to 30 people discussed the following questions: (1) What do we know about the role of strategies and skills in whole language instruction? (2) What do we still need to know? and (3) Where do we go from here? Answers varied greatly as different perspectives and philosophical stances were shared. Common patterns were found as well. Some of the ideas explored that day include the following:

- A few NRC members had problems with using the term "balance" to describe this teaching. Many agreed that we should not back away from the term whole language, because what we are describing is exemplary whole language teaching. It is not eclectic instruction in which teachers try a little of this and a little of that, but thoughtful, planned practice based on what children know and need to know and in which direct and explicit instruction is part of the authentic tasks that interest children. It is a powerful model of instruction that seems to many of us a step forward for the field. This instructional model is not unlike what Lisa Delpit called for over 10 years ago in her now famous article, "Skills and Other Dilemmas of a Professional Black Educator." When she received a standing ovation as keynote speaker at the 1995 NRC conference, I was struck by how long it had taken the field (not individual teachers and researchers) to recognize the need for a balance of strategies and skills within authentic tasks.

- A second theme that emerged was the need for improved teacher education in the area of literacy. Students benefit from understanding research from all perspectives in order to understand the value different perspectives bring. Students must know what is behind the controversy in order to be empowered to make the best instructional decisions. One of the tasks of teacher educators is to show respect for all research that contributed to our understanding of literacy learning and teaching, not just research from our own paradigm. And of course, if we want our education students to truly understand the kind of teaching we espouse, we must demonstrate it to our students as we teach children in schools.

- Finally, we all agreed that our field needs to communicate better with the public and with policymakers. It seems that the public sees reading and writing instruction as an either/or choice between either phonics or whole language, between either a traditional or a progressive approach. The media love to play up the differences, the debates, the controversies, with little attention to reason and civility. This does not help our field or the many teachers trying to help children learn to read, write, and think. It is my hope that this book will be only a beginning of the discussion among teachers, teacher educators, researchers, and community members about strategies and skill instruction in whole language classrooms.

—Ellen McIntyre

Biographical Sketches

Ellen McIntyre received her Ed.D. in Literacy Education from the University of Cincinnati. She is currently an Associate Professor at the University of Louisville. Her research interests focus on early literacy and social contexts for learning, and she is currently working on research in children's academic and social development in nongraded primary programs, funded by the Center for Cultural Diversity and Second Language Learners. Dr. McIntyre has published widely in the *Journal of*
Literacy Research, Research in the Teaching of English, and the *American Educational Research Journal,* and is co-editor of *Creating K–3 Nongraded primary Programs: Teachers' Stories and Lessons Learned* (1991).

Michael Pressley is a Professor in the Department of Educational Psychology and Statistics, University at Albany, State University of New York. He is also a principal investigator of the National Reading Research Center, headquartered at the Universities of Maryland and Georgia. He has conducted extensive research on the nature of effective reading instruction throughout the elementary years, in both regular and special education settings. His most recent books are *Verbal Protocols of Reading* (with Peter Afflerbach) and *Advanced Educational Psychology for Educators, Researchers, and Policymakers* (with Christine B. McCormick). He is a Fellow of the American Psychological Association and the American Psychological Society. As of January 1996, Dr. Pressley is the Incoming Editor of the *Journal of Educational Psychology.*

Kathryn H. Au is an Associate Professor of Education at the University of Hawaii at Manoa. She is currently developing a teacher education program aimed at increasing the number of Native Hawaiian teachers in classrooms in their own communities. Her research interest is the school literacy development of students of diverse cultural and linguistic backgrounds. She has published over 50 articles on this topic, as well as a textbook, *Literacy Instruction in Multicultural Settings.* For a number of years, she was head of a team responsible for development of a K–6 whole literacy curriculum used by about 150 public school teachers affiliated with the Kamehameha Elementary Education Program (KEEP) throughout the state of Hawaii.

Pamela Beard El-Dinary is Senior Research Analyst for the National Foreign Language Resource Center at Georgetown University/Center for Applied Linguistics. Her current research focus is on strategies use and strategies instruction for foreign language learning at the elementary school through college levels. She received her Ph.D. at the University of Maryland, College Park, with a focus on strategies instruction.

Rachel Brown is a faculty member in the Department of Counseling and Educational Psychology, Graduate School of Education, State University of New York at Buffalo. She received her Ph.D. in curriculum and instruction from the University of Maryland. Her research interests include reading strategies instructional self-regulated learning, sociocognition, and the use of technology to enhance reading comprehension.

Jacquelin M. Carroll received her M.Ed. from the University of Hawaii at Manoa. She is currently a curriculum developer at the Cultural Learning Center at Ka'ala Wai'anae, Hawaii, on an anthropology curriculum and Hawaiian studies program for high school students designed to link course work across academic disciplines with field work in the community. Previously, she was a curriculum researcher and developer for the Kamehameha Elementary Education Program (KEEP). Her research interests are in the areas of literacy instruction, students with special needs, and authentic assessment.

Jean Anne Clyde is an Associate Professor at the University of Louisville. Her current interests include inquiry-based learning, early literacy, and multiple ways of knowing. She is coauthor/coeditor of the January 1996 issue of *Primary Voices K–6: Reimagining Collaboration to Support Inquiry.*

Curt Dudley-Marling is Professor of Education at York University. He received his Ph.D. from the University of Wisconsin—Madison. His interests include the reading and writing development of struggling students, the politics of language and literacy, teacher development, teacher identity, and the effects of school "failure" on parents. His current writing projects include an edited book with Carole Edelsky which examines the fate of progressive language practices. He has authored or coauthored numerous books and articles.

Shari Ettenberger is a Language Project Leader for the Mohanasen Central School District, New York. She had taught grades 1–2 and is currently working on a multiage developmental team. She received her Bachelor's of Science in Education at The State University of New York at Oneonta and is working towards her Masters in Reading at the State University of New York at Albany.

Penny A. Freppon is an Associate Professor and Director of the Manney Literacy Center at the University of Cincinnati. She is working on children's interpretations of their instruction. She received her Ed.D. from the University of Cincinnati.

Steve Graham is Professor at the University of Maryland, College Park, in the Department of Special Education. His work focuses on children's writing, particularly children who struggle with learning to write. He has been involved in a variety of research projects investigating strategy and self-regulation instruction in writing, the process approach to writing, the teaching of the mechanics of writing, and alternatives modes to writing. Much of his recent work has focused on the integration of more explicit teaching procedures within the context of process writing classrooms. He received his Ed.D. in Special Education from the University of Kansas.

Mark J. Hallenbeck has taught high school English and for the past 15 years has been a junior/senior high resource room teacher. He is a doctoral candidate in the Department of Counseling, Educational Psychology, and Special Education at Michigan State University and received his M.A.T. in special education from Augustana College in Sioux Falls, SD. His current research interests include writing instruction and classroom discourse.

Karen P. Harris received her Ed.D. from Auburn University in Special Education. She is a Professor of Special Education at the University of Maryland, College Park. She has taught kindergarten and fourth grade, as well as elementary students with learning disabilities, adolescents with severe learning and emotional problems, and young deaf children. Her research focuses on the integration of knowledge from affective, behavioral cognitive, developmental and social-ecological viewpoints in the development of instructional philosophy and practices for diverse classrooms.

Linda Headings taught inner-city kindergarten and first-grade children for over 13 years, She is currently on maternity leave with her son Jake as she awaits the birth of a second son. She received her M.Ed. from the University of Cincinnati.

Ric Hovda is a Professor in the Department of Early and Middle Childhood Education at the University of Louisville and Director of the Center for the Collaborative Advancement of the Teaching Profession. He teaches courses in literacy, children's literature, and action research. He is co-editor of *Creating Nongraded Primary Programs: Teachers' Stories and Lessons Learned.* His current research focuses on nongraded primary programs and interdisciplinary preprofessional and professional development.

Laura Klenk is an Assistant Professor in the Department of Learning and Instruction at the State University of New York at Buffalo. She is currently looking at early literacy acquisition in children with special needs and the role of play in language and literacy acquisition in kindergarten classrooms with diverse language and ethnic populations. She received her Ph.D. from the University of Michigan.

Diane Kyle is Professor and Chair of the Department of Early and Middle Childhood at the University of Louisville where she teaches courses on elementary curriculum and action research. She has co-authored *Reflective Teaching for Student Empowerment: Elementary Curriculum and Methods* and is co-editor of *Creating Nongraded Primary Programs: Teachers' Stories and Lessons Learned.* Her current research focuses on nongraded primary programs.

Meredith McLellan teaches English as a Second Language at Spartan Village School, an international, multicultural elementary school in East Lansing, Michigan. She has been involved in educational research projects for the past six years, collaborating with Michigan State University professors and graduate students. Her experience in second language teaching and learning outside the United States includes both teaching and traveling. She has taught and lived in Monterrey, Mexico; Tapei, Republic of China; and Junja, Uganda.

Jennifer Mistretta is currently a doctoral student at the State University of New York at Albany in Educational Psychology and Statistics with a research focus on parents' influences on children's school interest and achievement. Her dissertation is a study of parents' beliefs and practices regarding literacy development in first grade.

Lesley Mandel Morrow is a full Professor at Rutgers University's Graduate School of Education, where she is coordinator of the Graduate Literacy Programs. She began her career as a classroom teacher, then became a reading specialist and later received her Ph.D. from Fordham University. Her area of research, with children from diverse backgrounds, deals with physical and social contexts that motivate reading and writing, early literacy development, and family literacy. She has more than 100 publications including journal articles, book chapters, monographs, and 10 books.

Annemarie S. Palincsar received her Ph.D. from the University of Illinois at Urbana-Champaign. The Jean and Charles Walgreen Jr. Professor of Reading and Literacy at the University of Michigan, she is currently collaborating with teachers exploring the teaching of Language as a tool for making sense of and communicating ones understanding across subject matters.

Muriel K. Rand is an Assistant Professor at Jersey City State College in the Administration, Curriculum, and Instruction Department. A specialist in early childhood curriculum and literacy development, she received her doctorate from Rutgers University. Dr. Rand has written other book chapters and journal articles on children's play in early literacy development and using thematic instruction in language arts. She is currently researching the differences in language usage using dramatic play with and without adult guidance.

Joan Rankin is an Associate Professor in the Department of Special Education and Communication Disorders, University of Nebraska—Lincoln. Her primary interests are related to the literacy development of individuals with diverse learning needs and improving educational practices used with special education and high-risk students, including the use of technology to support developing literacy skills.

Laura R. Roehler is a Professor in the Department of Teacher Education at Michigan State University. As part of her responsibilities, she conducts oral discourse research at Spartan Village Elementary School. Currently with a team of University and school faculty, she is exploring performance assessment in ESL classrooms. Her teaching includes university literacy courses taught in over twenty different countries. Her publications include many journal articles, book chapters, and books about literary teaching and learning.

Nancy Svoboda teaches English as a Second Language to students who come from over 40 countries and speak over 30 different languages at Spartan Village School on the campus of Michigan State University. She is involved with projects in which Spartan Village School teachers collaborate with MSU professors, student teachers, and graduate students.

Ruth Wharton-McDonald *is* completing her doctorate in educational psychology at the State University of New York at Albany. She has worked with a variety of student populations as a reading specialist and as a school psychologist. Her current research interests are in the area of school learning and in particular, literacy. Her current research investigates the nature of outstanding literacy instruction at the primary level.

Roberta A. Wilson is Project Co-ordinator, PATTER (Parents and Teachers Together Encouraging Reading) at the Ha'aheo School, Hilo, Hawaii. She received her degree in Elementary Education from the University of Hawaii. Before coming to the Ha'aheo School she was involved in the Whole Literacy Program in the Demonstration Teacher Project for KEEP.

Linda S. Wold is a Doctoral candidate in Reading at Northern Illinois University and a Chapter I Reading Resource Teacher for Grade One at Palos East School, Palos Heights, Illinois. Her dissertation research is on understanding emergent literacy in Grade One. Her special interests include poetry in context, children's literature, parent literacy partnerships, the fragility of second language learners, and reading strategies.

Linda Yokoi is a doctoral student in the Department of Educational Psychology and Statistics and the State University of New York at Albany where she is conducting work on developmental aspects of strategy use in both children and adults.

Index

෴ ─── ෴

Abigail (student), 238
Achievement, 56, 283
    evaluation of, 41, 54
    tests, 125
Adapted Word Chains, 214–225
Alba (student), 98
Alesha (student), 1–2
Allyson (student), 55
Alphabet, 68–70, 122, 130, 136.
    See also Letters
*Amelia Bedelia's Family
    Album*, 29
Analytical Reading Inventory,
    112, 115, 117
Andy (student), 54
Animals,
    stories about, 98–99,
        188–189, 216–218
    study of, 83–84, 94–96,
        98–99
    stuffed, 83, 91, 95, 98, 188
Anna (teacher), 234, 238–239,
    247
Anthropology, 4
Art, 67, 242, 261
    center, 87, 90, 94–95, 261

Articles, 27, 44, 196
Assessment, 2, 13–14, 22, 28,
    44, 54, 110, 123, 125,
    132, 137, 167, 172, 229,
    233, 245
    intelligence, 117
    learning new ways of, 69
    notebook, 1
    objectives in, 69–70
    self-, 161–172, 241–242
    speech, 134
    tests, 122
    through portfolios, 41
    traditional, 133, 247
Attention disorders, 106, 112,
    134
Au, Kathryn, 22, 39
Audiotapes,
    for feedback, 26, 41, 98
    of books, 68
    of classes, 135, 148
    of stories, 30, 92, 98
Author's Chair, 49, 131, 133,
    135, 140, 148, 196–197,
    258
    in literacy center, 93, 96

Autonomy,
  in classroom instruction, 22,
    50, 90, 99, 161, 180,
    186, 238, 282
  as goal of education, 7, 96,
    98, 153, 157, 239, 261
  in reading, 28, 30, 39, 67,
    115, 122, 214, 223, 225,
    251
  in writing, 39, 76, 122, 148,
    164–165, 171–172

B

Barbara (student), 27, 29
Bedtime for Frances, 91
Benchmarks, 22, 41, 57
  reading, 41, 43–44, 47–48
  vocabulary, 45
  writing, 41, 50, 52–56
Benizar (student), 32
Bill (student), 56
Birthdays, 235
The Big Enormous Turnip, 29
Blocks, 87, 90, 95, 99
Bloome, Judy, 109, 114
Books, 27, 30, 67, 69, 71, 75,
    122–123, 154, 187, 196,
    198, 247, 253, 255
  big, 73–74, 78, 263
  comic, 27
  discussions of, 40, 43, 48,
    68, 213
  (*see also* Literature circles)
  Hardy Boy, 29
    in literacy center, 91–94,
    96–98
  love of, 49
    in readers' workshops,
    39, 44, 46, 57
  selection of, 28–29, 215,
    236–237, 240, 252

  by students, 76, 95, 240
  on tape, 68
  titles, use of, 214–221, 258
  in writers' workshops, 54
Brown, Rachel, 154, 177

C

Capitalization, 10, 41, 95, 254,
  259
"Caps for Sale," 84
Carle, Eric, 235
Carroll, Jacquelin, 22, 39
Catherine (student), 27
Charles (student), 26–28, 30–34
Charts, 26, 237, 242, 254
  interactive, 67, 69–72, 90,
    234, 253
  song, 94
  strategy, 153, 164–165,
    169–170
  word, 45–46
The Chick and the Duckling,
  221
Children,
  acquisition of knowledge by,
    4–7, 68–69, 72, 74,
    90–91, 98, 244
  collaboration between (*see*
    Learning, cooperative;
    Reading, collaborative;
    Writing, collaborative)
  development of, 14
  display of work by, 92–93
  guidance of, 3, 7
  involvement of, 91
  with learning disabilities or
    special needs, 26, 109–124,
    130–151, 158–161,
    167–168, 170–171,
    232–233, 245
  of low-income families, 66, 232

Children, (cont.)
  motivation of, 4, 56–57, 68,
    84, 99, 215–216,
    282–283
  names of, 71, 78, 138
  needs of,
    individual, 21, 171, 177
    instruction as response
      to, 2–3, 5, 50, 66,
      70, 72–73, 75, 105,
      158, 180, 190, 218,
      245
    skill, 14, 27, 52, 90, 154,
      247
  respect for, 2, 5, 7–8,
    12–13, 57, 77–79, 202
Christopher, Matt, 119
Classroom,
  changes in, 3, 156
  as community, 2, 43, 53, 57,
    71, 76, 78, 156, 158,
    189, 233
  library, 29, 50, 68, 76,
    91–92, 100
  literacy-rich, 90–91
  peer groups in (*see* Learn-
    -ing, cooperative;
    Reading, collabora-
    tive; riting,
    collaborative)
  setting, 22, 26, 52, 66–68,
    71, 83–96, 100, 154,
    213, 252, 260
  special needs, 124
  whole language, 2–14,
    21–22, 66, 213
    explicit instruction in,
      28, 35, 56–57,
      231–234, 240, 244,
      263, 288

  learning conversations
    in, 195, 197
  reading practices in, 225,
    251
  transactional strategies
    in, 189–190
  writing strategies in,
    155–156, 160, 171
Clifford the Big Red Dog, 31
Cloze tasks, 33, 73
Clyde, Jean Anne, 229, 231
Coaching, 53, 119–120, 125,
  180, 183–185, 215, 223
Community Circle, 52, 55–56
Computers, 83, 93, 120–121
Conferences,
  with parents, 69–70
  peer, 39, 53
  teacher-student, 50, 52–55,
    160–161, 165, 168, 170
    benchmark, 54
    record sheets of, 50–51
    spot, 52–53
    table at, 90
  writing, 42, 49, 131, 155
Constructivism, 4, 40, 66, 68,
  77, 79, 148, 155, 172, 234,
  284
Context clues, 31, 46, 106, 112,
  114, 237
Cookie's Week, 235
Count!, 95
Cowley, Joy, 235
Cues, 24–25, 35, 69, 75, 111,
  114–115, 186–187, 194,
  247, 253
  graphophonic, 24, 28, 31–
    32, 65, 70–71, 73, 76,
    78–79, 110–112, 123–124
  pragmatic, 24, 110, 124

Cues, (cont.)
    semantic, 24, 28, 31–33,
        110, 120, 122–124, 169
    syntactic, 24, 28, 31–33, 74,
        110, 112, 122–124
Curious George Rides a Bike,
    136

D

Dahl, Roald, 116, 119
Damien (student), 84, 98
Dane (student), 46
Daniel (student), 46
Danoff, Barbara (teacher),
    160–170
David (student), 105, 117–121
Decoding, 76, 137, 234, 237,
        245, 247, 251–252, 256,
        263–264, 266, 278–280,
        282–284
    at Harvard Literacy Lab,
        106, 109, 112, 114–118
DeJuan (student), 245
Demonstration, 10, 14–15,
        25–28, 32, 42, 44, 47, 52,
        57, 89, 132–133, 154, 229,
        232, 235–240, 243–244
Dew Drop Dead, 57
Donna (teacher), 241, 243, 245
Drafting, 40, 49–50, 52, 55,
        163, 195–196
Drama, 68, 83–84, 94, 98, 242
    center, 87, 90, 95, 263
Drawing, 76, 141, 263
Dudley-Marling, Curt, 21, 23
Dustin (student), 47

E

Editing, 39, 49–50, 120, 259
Education, 4
    changes in, 8, 40
    goals of, 7

El-Dinary, Pamela Beard, 154, 177
Emily (student), 84
Environment. *See* Classroom,
    setting
Erin (student), 39
Ettenberger, Sherrie, 230,
    251–262
Explanation, 10, 12, 21, 25–26,
        28, 41, 44, 48, 52–53,
        57, 154, 160, 164, 181,
        183–186, 229, 234–239,
        263, 278, 284
    by students, 240–243
Explicit instruction, 78, 90, 108,
        149, 233–236, 247,
        251–252, 263–264, 277,
        279–284, 287.
        See also Skill instruc-
        tion; Strategies, teaching
    at Harvard Literacy Lab,
        111, 114, 123
    in learning conversations,
        209–210
    need for, 27
    of reading skills, 25,
        214–215, 218, 221,
        223–224
    of transactional strategies,
        179, 181, 184, 190
    in workshops, 39, 42, 57,
        153–154
    of writing skills, 159

F

Fantastic Mr. Fox, 116
Fatima (student), 30
The Fight on the Hill, 216–217,
    219, 221
Films, 196
Finders Keepers, 30
Freppon, Penny, 22, 65

G

Games, 71, 74, 123, 234, 261, 263,
Gayle (teacher), 235–236, 243–244
Graham, Steve, 153, 155
Grammar, 6, 156, 160, 162, 166, 167
Graphic organizer, 53
Graphs, 162, 164–165, 242, 244
Gravois, Mr. (teacher), 94–95, 98, 99

H

Hallenback, Mark, 154, 193
Handwriting, 133, 156, 237
Harris, Karen, 153, 155
Harvard Literacy Lab, 105, 107–125
The Haunting of Grade Three, 26
Hawaii State Department of Education, 41
Headings, Linda, 22, 65–78
Helen (teacher), 1–3
Holiday Inn, 57
Homework, 67, 71–72
Hovda, Ric, 229, 231

I

I Know an Old Lady, 33
Ikaika (student), 55
Independence. *See* Autonomy
Informal Reading Inventory, 247
Instruction,
    authentic, 2, 4, 7, 22, 56, 68, 72, 85, 107, 110, 124, 150, 229, 239–240, 247, 252, 263–264, 279
    in reading, 2, 255
    in writing, 155–156,

direct (*see* Explicit instruction)
effective, 8, 77
as exchange of ideas, 40
holistic approach in, 3, 12, 28, 40, 49, 65, 77, 107, 110–111, 124–125, 133, 202, 256
individual, 22, 53, 69, 73, 75–77, 89–90, 97, 99, 109, 144, 160, 162, 164, 170, 213, 281
literature–based, 42, 233, 251, 281
on–line, 187, 190
skill (*see* Skill instruction)
small group, 2, 22, 43–44, 46, 52–54, 69, 74–76, 87–90, 96–99, 160, 162, 169, 178, 213, 233, 260, 284
for weaker vs. stronger students, 264
whole group, 22, 44, 69, 73–75, 89, 133, 168, 178, 213, 284
Instructional actions, 2–3, 195, 247, 263–265.
    See also Demonstration; Explanation; Mediation; Modeling
Ivory (student), 98

J

Jacob (student), 39
Jacques, Brian, 119
Jarena (student), 45
Jennifer (student), 27
Jennifer (student), 252–253
Jessie (student), 47
Jim (student), 98
Jonnell (student), 84

Joseph (student), 98
Journals,
    class, 99
    research, 44
    students', 43, 68–69, 73–75,
        94, 110, 113, 120, 135,
        160, 166, 169–170, 196,
        241, 254, 259–260
    teachers', 42, 48, 52, 57,
        237
Journey to Jo'burg, 48
Jovanna (student), 99
Joy (teacher), 235, 241, 245

K

Kamehameha Elementary
    Education Program (KEEP),
    40–43, 49, 56
Kamuela (student), 56
Kaniela (student), 53–54
Katie (student), 84
Katya (student), 99
Kawika (student), 45, 47, 57
KEEP. *See* Kamehameha El-
    ementary Education
    Program
Keith (student), 47
Kentucky Early Learning Profile
    (KELP), 245
Kevin (student), 106, 130–151
Klenk, Laura, 106, 129–130,
    132–133, 140–142,
    144–148, 150
Kris (teacher), 237–238, 240,
    244, 247
Kristin (student), 39, 56
Kyle, Diane, 229, 231

L

Language, 45, 68, 78, 87, 123,
    198, 240, 247, 258, 277

English as Second, 109,
    154, 194–196, 211
learning, 5–6, 124, 132,
    156–157
and literacy, 40
meaning of, 24
native, 5
oral, 27, 66, 86, 91, 93–94,
    194, 198, 200
power of, 71
rules of, 244
use of, 2, 6, 24, 53–54, 67,
    193–194, 242, 251
whole (*see* Whole language)
written, 66, 69, 71, 74, 94,
    117, 130, 136, 194
Lauren (student), 105, 111–117,
    121
Leads, 2–3, 41, 53, 55
Learning,
    as active, 40, 43, 172
    by children (*see* Children,
        acquisition of knowledge
        by)
    conversations, 48, 194–211
    cooperative, 96–99
        (*see also* Reading,
        collaborative; Writing,
        collaborative)
    environment, 100
    experiential, 2, 22, 107–108,
        130 (*see also* Instruc-
        tion, authentic)
    love of, 99
    theories, 4
    through conflict, 98–99
Letters, 69–75, 77–78, 91, 95,
    114, 116, 123–124,
    134–151, 215, 237,
    252–253, 263 (*see also*
    Alphabet)

Lila (student), 28–30, 32–33
Linguistics, 4, 35, 110
Literacy, 13, 99, 194, 251, 264
  activities, 6, 39, 56, 68, 73,
      84, 86–87, 96, 117–118,
      132, 136–137, 196, 254,
      263, 282
  center, 86–87, 89, 91–94,
      96, 98
  cycle, 196–197
  development, 27, 57, 85–86,
      93, 97, 100, 106, 115,
      122, 136–137, 149, 151,
      157, 249, 252
  environment, 85, 90–91, 93,
      99, 107, 122
  expectations, 77
  instruction, 3, 8, 13, 49, 65,
      124–125, 131, 137, 193,
      233, 247, 254, 262, 265,
      277, 280, 282–283, 286
  learning, 7, 78, 96, 106, 110,
      132, 158–159, 288
  research, 131
  six aspects of, 40–41
  skills, 14–15, 22, 25, 35,
      84–87, 94–96, 98,
      100, 135, 149, 154,
      238, 285
  as social practice, 25
Literature. *See* Books; Instruction, literature-based;
  Reading; Stories
Literature circles, 43–44, 47–48
The Little Red Hen, 98

M

Magazines, 27, 92, 95–96, 122,
  196
  National Geographic, 99
Mahy, Margaret, 216

Malani (student), 46
Malia (student), 39
Mapping, 120–121, 198–199,
  201–202, 204
Marcel (student), 98
Marcia (student), 2
Martin (student), 28, 30, 33
Math, 68, 179, 256
  center, 83, 87, 90, 95
McIntyre, Ellen, 1, 229, 288
McKinney, Lindley, 267
Meaning, 74, 110, 131, 233
  construction of, 3, 6–9, 35,
      68, 75, 149, 181, 187,
      189–190, 207, 213, 233,
      251
  understanding, 42–43, 112,
      119 (*see also* Reading,
      comprehension)
Mediation, 41–42, 44, 46–48,
  52–53, 57, 85
Memory, 106, 112, 122–123,
      134, 144, 150, 157, 164,
      169–170, 178–179, 182,
      203, 210, 234
  mnemonic aid to, 162,
      164–165, 170
Message Board, 93
Metacognition, 13–14, 159,
  204, 223, 239–240, 244
Metropolitan Reading Test, 195,
  210
Michael (student), 46
Millions of Cats, 113
Millson, Mrs. (teacher), 83–84
Mini-lessons, 3, 34, 43–45, 50,
  52–53, 72, 76, 155, 158,
  161–163, 166–167,
  253–254, 263, 266, 282,
  284
Mistretta, Jennifer, 230, 251, 264

"The Mitten," 187–188
Modeling, 12, 14, 42, 84, 97–98,
    180, 197–199, 209–211,
    223–224, 263, 278
  peer, 238, 259
  of reading strategies, 48, 75,
    119, 124, 182–184
  of writing strategies, 148,
    155, 160, 163–164, 170
Monitoring, 178, 180
Morrow, Lesley, 22, 83, 287
Multidisciplinary Evaluation
    Team (MET), 134
"Mushroom in the Rain,"
    180–182, 184
Music. See also Songs
  center, 89, 94, 99

N

Nader (student), 26, 29, 30, 34
National Assessment of Educa-
    tional Progress, 41, 280
National Public Radio, 9
National Reading Conference,
    287
Neurological Impress Method,
    118
News. See Reports, news
Newspaper, 2, 25, 27, 122,
    132–133, 151, 166, 196
Nicholas (student), 27, 32–33

O

Of Mice and Men, 122
Okamoto, Nora (teacher),
    39–42, 49–57
On My Honor, 45, 47–48, 57
One, Two, Three to the Zoo, 95
Orthography. See Spelling
Ownership, 40, 48, 55, 57, 79,
    155–157, 198–204, 206, 210

P

Pahoa Elementary School, 42,
    49
Palincsar, Annemarie, 106, 129
Patrick (student), 98
Patty (teacher), 238, 245
Pen pal program, 93
Phonetics, 11, 24, 122,
    136–137, 140, 142,
    147–148, 150, 263
Phonics, 8–9, 21–22, 65, 76–79,
    106, 110, 112, 114, 123,
    137, 172, 233, 236, 245,
    254–255, 267, 279, 288
  constructivist-based teach-
    ing of, 68–74
Phonology, 136
Pictures, 2, 26, 71–73, 75, 92,
    94, 208
  children's illustrations, 40,
    141, 259, 263
  mental (see Visualization)
  photography, 26, 120
    as story clues, 136, 154,
      178, 184, 188, 214,
      216–218, 223,
      235–236, 247, 253,
      256
Planning, 49–50, 156, 158–160,
    163–165, 169–170, 172,
    240, 282
Poetry, 1, 27, 29, 45, 52, 71, 74,
    92, 137, 196, 215, 231–232,
    247, 254–255
Post Traumatic Stress Disorder,
    121
Prediction, 6, 31, 47–48, 74,
    154, 178, 184–189, 235,
    258
  with word chains, 214–224,
    240

Pressley, Michael, 154, 177, 229–230, 251, 264, 267, 277

Print, 21, 70–71, 74–75, 98, 105, 122, 130–131, 135–137, 144, 148–151, 218, 235, 245

environmental, 26–27, 66–67, 71, 90–91, 95, 142, 255

visual processing of, 112, 116–118, 121

Prompts, 240–241

Psychology, 4, 35

developmental, 190

educational, 40

Publishing, 40, 49–50, 67, 76–77, 160, 241

Punctuation, 10, 23, 41, 73, 95, 109, 118, 122, 135, 149, 254, 260, 263

Puppets, 92, 98, 263

Purcell-Gates, Victoria, 105, 107, 287

Q

Quarterback Walk-On, 57

Question-Answer Relationships (QARs), 53, 119

Questioning,

demonstration of, 236, 238

by students, 53, 119, 208, 224

by teachers, 42, 44, 46, 54, 184, 199, 203, 209, 240–241

R

Ralph S. Mouse, 32

Rand, Muriel, 22, 83

Ranger Rick, 98

Rankin, Joan, 230, 251

Read-alouds, 14, 43, 48, 68, 219–221, 257–259

Reading, 2, 5, 13, 85, 163, 167, 172, 196–198, 207, 241, 252, 254, 260, 262–266

activities, 68, 71, 85, 106, 111, 113, 122, 137, 150, 177, 179

assisted, 21, 29–30, 75, 118–119

center, 261

collaborative, 43, 97, 114, 120, 187, 282

comprehension, 6, 105, 109, 111, 115, 119, 124, 160, 209, 263, 278, 282–284

articulation of, 8, 11,

benchmarks, 41, 44, 47

improvement of, 27, 98, 114, 154, 213–225, 251–252

monitoring, 31–32, 106, 239

strategies, 35, 177–190

tests, 117, 121

effective, 6, 57, 113, 177, 181, 183, 185, 215–217, 221, 223–224, 242

enjoyment of, 43, 48–49, 69, 86, 92, 115

fluency, 28–30, 76, 112–114, 119, 245

functional, 14, 67, 125, 244

groups, 75, 184–185, 187, 189–190, 235, 256–257, 260

at home, 85, 92, 222, 255, 263

and literacy, 7, 40, 157

Reading, groups (cont.)
  in literacy center, 91–94
  materials, 22, 27–29, 68, 99,
    197, 235, 263, 283
  motivation for, 84, 87, 93
  Recovery Program, 70
  recreational, 57
  remedial, 109, 112,
    115–124, 149
  repeated, 21, 29–30,
    112–113
  response theory, 42, 44–45,
    189
  silent, 40, 43, 48, 105, 112,
    115, 119
  skills (see Skills, reading)
  socio-psycholinguistic model
    of, 23–25, 35–36
  strategies (see Strategies,
    reading)
  teaching, 3, 70, 108, 132,
    156, 233–236, 240,
    255–256, 272–273, 278,
    288
  voluntary, 40,
  workshops (see Workshops,
    reading)
Reciprocal Questioning
  (ReQuest), 119
Reports, 2, 153, 166–171, 241
  book, 160, 163
  news, 1–3, 138, 140–141
  research, 53,
Responsive elaboration, 154,
  183
Reston, Mrs. (teacher), 180–188
Revising, 49–50, 140, 156,
  158–160, 170, 172, 254,
  282
Roehler, Laura, 154, 193
Roya (student), 28–29, 34

S
Sabrina (student), 47
Sam (student), 105, 121–124
Sara (teacher), 238–239, 245
Saram (student), 199–200,
  204–207
Scaffolding,
  definition of, 4, 108, 133
  methods of, 12, 22, 53, 114,
    154, 183–184
  need for, 21, 218
  practice of, 14, 42, 46–47,
    54, 98, 106, 113, 142,
    144, 148, 150, 164,
    214–215, 223, 278, 282
Science, 179, 186, 198, 209
  center, 87, 90, 94, 99
Self-Monitoring Approach to
  Reading (SMART), 119
Self-Regulated Strategy Devel-
  opment, 161
Self-regulation. See Autonomy
Self-statements, 163–166, 170
Seuss, Dr., 109, 122
Shanna (student), 46
Shawn (student), 238–239
Sina (student) 205, 207
Skill instruction, 3, 21–22, 39,
    44, 65–66, 72, 76–77,
    105, 154, 229, 247,
    254–255, 263, 285.
  See also Explicit instruction
  role of, 8–12, 288
  traditional, 35, 67
  in writing, 52
Skills, 27, 39, 41, 57, 78–79,
    99, 106, 229, 232, 241,
    262–264
  development of, 89–90, 98
  isolation of, 7, 40, 49, 106,
    110–111, 255

Skills, (cont.)
    literacy (see Literacy, skills)
    perceptual and motor, 137
    reading, 23, 25, 43, 73, 236,
        256, 259
    speech and language, 134,
        198, 242
    thinking, 43
    writing, 2, 50, 70, 76, 91,
        95, 123, 156–158, 238,
        260, 263
Skinnybones, 29
The Snowy Day, 254
Social studies, 109, 167
    center, 87, 90, 94, 98, 169,
        171, 179
Songs, 26–27, 68, 71, 74, 90,
    94, 99, 215, 245
Sounder, 122
Spelling, 98, 106, 109, 115,
        132, 136, 148, 157, 243,
        253–254, 284, 285
    invented, 70, 76, 113, 244
    practice, 133, 156
    problems, 118, 120–121,
        140–143, 147, 149
    regularities of, 34
    role of, 9, 23
    strategies, 21, 122, 137,
        158, 237
    tests, 117
Stanford Diagnostic Reading
    Test, 112, 115, 117, 121
Stone Fox, 46
Stories, 1, 10, 26–27, 29, 34,
        45, 54–55, 75, 78, 87,
        123–124, 136, 140, 151,
        196, 239, 247, 252, 263.
    See also Books
    acting out, 68
    audiotaped, 30, 92, 98

    elements of, 161–163,
        165–166, 258
    characters, 48, 89, 92,
        98, 164
    events, 42, 44, 46, 221
    ideas for, 44, 132, 163
    invention of, 219–220
    reading, 219–220, 240
    understanding, 42–43, 46,
        57, 76, 243–244, 251
    writing, 91, 93, 96, 98, 113,
        132–133, 136, 148, 150,
        153, 160–166, 231, 254,
        258, 266
Strategies, 6, 57, 194, 235, 241,
    256, 283
    oral discourse, 197–211
    reading, 23, 35–36, 40–41,
        43, 70, 74–75,
        153–154, 166,
        213–225, 247,
        258–259
    at Harvard Literacy Lab,
        110, 114–116, 118,
        122, 124–125
    sense-making, 14, 28,
        31–32, 36, 69, 72,
        119, 214, 225
    in special education
        class, 137
    role of, 8–12
    teaching, 3, 21, 44, 74–76,
        90, 105–106, 160, 172,
        197, 213, 229, 232, 247,
        280, 288 (see also
        Explicit instruction)
    transactional, 177–190
    writing, 2, 53, 76, 116, 118,
    125, 153–172, 209, 231,
    238, 280
Students. See Children

Summarization, 154, 178, 185–186, 197, 205–206, 208–209
Summer of the Swans, 45
Surveys, 237–238

T

Tales of a Fourth Grade Nothing, 114
Tamar (student), 99
Tanioka, Chris, 39–49, 52, 56–57
A Taste of Blackberries, 45, 67
Teachable moments, 44, 48, 52, 7
Teachers,
approaches of, 3, 11–14, 72, 233–234
decision-making of, 22, 69, 79, 190, 229
dilemmas of, 133, 232–233
discouragement of, 49
empowerment of, 66
example of, 42, 47–48 (*see also* Modeling)
expectations of, 74
goals of, 14, 21, 25, 43
intervention by, 39
mimicking, 244
qualities of outstanding, 264–266
release of responsibility by, 46, 53–54, 56, 180, 183
role of, 10–11, 27, 97, 110–111, 159, 213
as facilitators, 4, 7, 29, 35, 57, 68, 89, 97, 100, 108, 119, 125, 131, 144, 151, 155, 197, 234, 255, 262
as participants, 47, 57, 84, 195

as time managers, 22
special education, 153, 160, 167, 262–264
thinking of, 65–66, 69
views of students by, 5, 40, 66
Teaching. *See* Instruction
Television, 2–3, 132
Tests, standardized, 110, 116–117, 122, 125, 134–135, 149. *See also individual names*
Theresa (teacher), 231–232, 237, 241
Think-alouds, 12, 154, 163, 170, 180–182, 185–187, 215–216, 218–219, 223–224, 231
Three Billy Goats Gruff, 98
Tiajun (student), 204–205
Tiana (student), 55
Tiffany (student), 98
Tina (student), 199, 204, 206
Tina (teacher), 235, 237, 241, 245
Tough to Tackle, 57
Troy (student), 29
Tyshell (student), 98

V

The Velveteen Rabbit, 119
Verification, 154, 178, 198, 206, 209–210
The Very Hungry Caterpillar, 235
Vickie (teacher), 234, 243–244
Videos, 1–2
Visualization, 44–45, 53–55, 154, 178, 182–184, 186–187, 217–218, 220–222, 239

Vocabulary, 27, 54, 94, 109,
    111, 123–124, 221, 163
  breadth of, 252
  development, 94
  knowledge, 117
  and literacy, 40
  new, 221
  sight, 91, 114
  strategies, 45–46, 123, 214
  (*see also* Context clues)
  word collections, 93–94

W

Wharton-McDonald, Ruth, 230,
  251, 255–262, 264
Where the Wild Things Are, 32
White Snow, Bright Snow, 254
Whole language, 197, 252–252,
    254
  background of, 4
  classroom (*see* Classroom,
  whole language)
  teaching, 2–4, 7–14, 67, 69,
    72, 140, 153–157, 171,
    229–230, 232–234, 239,
    255, 283
  theory and philosophy, 5–9,
    27, 40, 57, 65–66,
    96, 105, 156, 193,
    209
    role of explicit/skill
      instruction in, 10–11,
      23, 27, 35–36, 77,
      158–159, 172, 247,
      264, 266, 282, 284,
      287–288
Wide Range Achievement Test,
  117
Wilson, Roberta, 22, 39, 53
Wold, Linda, 154, 213

Word recognition, 8, 11, 21,
    32–33, 76, 98–99, 109,
    112–116, 119, 135, 147,
    149, 214, 218, 224, 235,
    256
Workbooks, worksheets, 43,67,
    109, 137, 149
Workshops,
  reading, 40, 42–49, 56
  writing, 39, 42, 49–56, 68,
    73–74, 76, 153, 160,
    164, 166–167
Writing, 1–2, 4–5, 13, 35, 86,
    91, 196–198, 251–252,
    254, 262–265
  activities, 68, 71, 85, 106,
    111, 113, 120, 122–123,
    132, 137, 150, 177
  center, 261
  checklist, 170
  collaborative, 97, 120, 155,
    157, 161, 164, 167–168,
    170–171, 196, 282
  detail in, 54–55
  effective, 3, 6, 49, 57,
    158–159, 195, 242
  enjoyment of, 56, 92, 161
  as expression of knowledge,
    241–242
  feedback on, 49–50, 55 (*see
    also* Author's Chair)
  functional, 14, 67, 125, 244
  improvement of, 54, 113,
    116, 121, 124, 241, 244
  and literacy, 7, 40, 157
  in literacy center, 91–94
  materials, 93, 95, 99
  motivation for, 84, 87,
    93–94, 161
  organizing, 53–54, 117,
    120–121

Writing, (cont.)
  process approach to, 42,
    49–50, 130, 155–172,
    233
  remedial, 109, 112–114,
    116–118, 120–124,
    130–151
  requirements for, 49
  as response to reading, 1,
    43, 48, 113, 265
  samples, 41, 93
  skills (*see* Skills, writing)
  strategies (*see* Strategies,
    writing)
  teaching, 3, 50, 70, 108,
    130, 233–234, 256, 278,
    288
  topics, 1, 22, 68, 133, 140,
    149, 155, 238, 240, 283
  use of paragraphs in, 50
  workshops (see Workshops,
    writing)

Y

Yokoi, Linda, 230, 251
Yolanda (student), 99

A Handbook for
Wilderness Survival

A Handbook for Wilderness Survival

Bob Harris

Illustrations by Benjamin Morehouse

M. Evans and Company, Inc.
New York

M. Evans and Company, Inc.
216 East 49th Street
New York, NY 10017

Library of Congress Cataloging-In-Publication Data
Harris, Bob (Robert)
    A handbook for wilderness survival / Bob Harris.
        p.   cm.
    Includes index.
    ISBN 0-87131-786-9. — ISBN 0-87131-787-7 (pbk.)
    1. Wilderness survival—Handbooks, manuals, etc.   I. Title.
GV200.5.H37   1995
613.6'9—dc20   95-31009
                                                                        CIP

Text design by Charles de Kay

Manufactured in the United States of America

9   8   7   6   5   4   3   2   1

For Mary,

who taught me what

a mother should be.

Contents

Preface   9

Chapter I
If You Are Lost   13

Chapter II
Emergency Kit   21

Chapter III
Direction Finding   25

Chapter IV
Maps   37

Chapter V
"Getting Out"   45

Chapter VI
Hypothermia   47

Chapter VII
Clothing   55

Chapter VIII
Winter Shelters   61

Chapter IX
Shelter Living   73

Chapter X
Fire Making 77

Chapter XI
Fire Know-How 91

Chapter XII
Dehydration 97

Chapter XIII
Water 103

Chapter XIV
Basic Food Needs 113

Chapter XV
Food from Animals 115

Chapter XVI
Trapping Know-How 137

Chapter XVII
Improvisations 143

Chapter XVIII
Food from Fish 153

Chapter XIX
Food from Plants 157

Chapter XX
Winter Problems 217

Chapter XXI
Making Do 229

Preface

It makes no difference what your preferred form of outdoor recreation is: if you pursue it long enough in primitive surroundings, you are likely to become lost or stranded at some time. In many such situations, only a knowledge of the basic elements of survival, your ingenuity, and your own common sense would then stand between you and the ultimate disaster.

Do not then allow yourself to think that you are facing a hostile environment or that the weather is trying to do you in. Nature is never hostile, only indifferent. Whether you live or die makes no real difference in the scheme of things, and you will neither be helped nor hindered in your struggle to survive. The wind will blow at the same speed and the temperature will be exactly the same whether you are adequately sheltered and clothed or completely exposed, and snow will fall as gently or as softly on your frozen body as upon your snug and cozy shelter.

Of the many dangers that may seem to threaten, most are either groundless or grossly exaggerated. You will not be attacked by wild animals, with the exception of biting and stinging insects. Rattlesnakes are a minor hazard in some areas and at some times, but will avoid you if they can. Black bears may raid your camp, but are normally no threat to you. None of these are present in winter. The single biggest threat is always fear itself, and most such fears are baseless.

You will not starve to death, you will not freeze to death, and you will not suffer undue hardship unless you are both careless and stupid. Regardless of what the coroner may choose to list as the cause of death when a stranded or lost adult is found dead, the actual cause is ignorance or carelessness.

The necessities of life will be everywhere around you, but they are not there for your benefit. They are not packaged and labeled for your convenience, and no sheet of instructions comes with them. You will have to find and procure what you need by your own unaided effort, and you must adapt it to your use on the basis of your own knowledge.

The information contained in this book should enable you to survive almost any situation in the wild, but it should be used primarily as a guide in seeking firsthand information on your own. The book will tell you much of what you need to know, but any additional knowledge will be invaluable in a survival situation.

To gain full value from the instructions contained herein, test each one before your life becomes dependent upon it. Try to build a fire by each of the primitive methods outlined in Chapter VII. Make the attempt in vile weather, but in your own backyard, so you can retreat to the safety of your home when the attempt fails. Once you have learned for yourself how difficult and uncertain such methods are, you will be doubly sure to equip yourself with a more dependable means of starting fire when you again venture afield.

Make each and every trip into the field an imaginary survival test. Learn to identify the plants you might someday need and gather some of them to be sampled as food. Set up an emergency camp, perhaps only a few feet from your comfortable camper, tent, or trailer, and spend a night in it. You will then probably be able to think of additional ways to ensure a reasonable degree of comfort if forced to remain out overnight.

Practice using a map and compass, even if you are in country you know well. Practice the other means of determining direction, too, and learn to identify the North Star at a glance. Practice making snares, deadfalls, and traps, using sticks as "animals" in any devices that would injure or kill. Learn to identify the tracks, droppings, and other signs left by birds and animals and study their habits.

Remember always that under that pampered, scrubbed, comfort-loving exterior, you are the exact counterpart of the first members of our species, and you have inherited each and every one of the instincts and abilities that have brought that species to dominion over the earth. You are also the rightful heir to the accumulated knowledge of many cultures over many centuries.

Under that sleek and helpless-appearing surface, then, lies the toughest and most adaptable animal this world has yet known. Your ability to survive in a desperate situation depends to a large degree upon how quickly and completely you can shed that surface veneer of culture and revert back to the omnivorous, opportunistic, no-holds-barred ways of your remote forebears.

Your life is important only to you in a survival situation, and you alone will decide by the actions you take whether you will live or die. This book is intended to help you tip the scales toward life. Good luck!

Chapter I

If You Are Lost

Your first reaction when you suddenly realize that you are lost is apt to be blind, unreasoning panic. You will have an almost irresistible urge to run, as if mere speed would get you out, even though you haven't the faintest idea where "out" is. Searchers have often found the bodies of lost persons who have run themselves to exhaustion and death or have run blindly off cliffs or into disabling or bone-breaking obstacles in this first panicked rush.

When you first become aware that you are at a complete loss as to direction or location (this awareness strikes suddenly and without warning), stop! Clear a space of flammable material and build a fire. Make a cup of cocoa, coffee, tea, or plain hot water if you are equipped to do so. Light up a pipe or cigarette if you smoke. The human mind is so conditioned that a fire means security, and panic is unlikely to persist in the light of a cheerful blaze. The hot drink will give you a lift and the pipe or cigarette will add to your sense of well-being. Reason will return, and you can assess the situation calmly and rationally.

When you first realize that you are lost, you are usually not very far from a known point. Draw a sketch map in the bare soil near your fire. Sketch in visible topographical features and mark your present location in relation to them. Try to trace in the route you took in getting here. You can often determine where you took the wrong fork in the trail, followed the wrong ridge, or crossed one too many draws.

13

You should pinpoint on your map the last point where you definitely knew where you were. You will find, in most cases, that you are fairly close to that spot and can remember your way back to it. Alternatively, you may be able to recognize some feature of the visible landscape as a known landmark seen from a different angle.

Unless you reestablish your orientation to the point that you are positive you know where your car or camp is, and unless you are reasonably sure that you can reach it before dark, make an overnight camp and settle down to wait for morning. If you are merely "mislaid" and the weather is mild, your problems will be solved with the return of daylight, especially in well-roaded country. In any case, once you are camped you can make your decisions calmly and sensibly, basing them on your reasoned assessment of the situation that confronts you.

Never allow yourself to be influenced in your decisions by the need to keep others from worrying. Your life is more important than anyone's peace of mind. Don't fret about being late for work or missing an appointment, no matter how important that job or appointment might normally be. Don't worry about the hazing or ridicule you may later face from your hunting or fishing buddies or the nicknames of "Old Pathfinder," "Dan'l Boone," "Davy Crockett," or such that they may call you. To survive is the only imperative, and all decisions must be made with that one objective in mind. All else is trivia.

If, once you have settled down, you think you can find your way back to a known point, *be very sure to mark your present location before setting out to see if you are right!* Remember, this spot is at least fairly close to a known point. Tie a piece of brightly-colored material to a tree or stake, build a conspicuous tripod or a cairn of stones, or simply bank the fire (in damp or wet weather, but not in fire season!) with long-lasting materials that will make it smoke profusely. Mark your trail as you leave this point by breaking brush or branch tips, by leaning poles against trees, or by setting stakes or piling stones as markers. You can then return to your fire if your new-found sense of direction should prove to be misplaced, and can set up an overnight camp nearby.

If in really wild country or if the weather is severe, and you can't decide with reasonable certainty where you are in relation to some reachable objective, stay where you are! Don't compound your problems by striking out blindly. You will exhaust your energy to no purpose if you allow yourself to blunder about with no real idea of where you are going. You may also leave the search area of possible rescue parties. These people will be better equipped both in knowledge of the area and in actual equipment than you are, so let them do the moving while you remain in one place to give them a stationary target.

Help such searchers by building a smudge fire if weather conditions are such that smoke can be seen from a distance. Green boughs or damp leaves thrown on a hot fire or on a bed of live coals will produce a dense white smoke. Motor oil, animal dung, or pitchy wood will produce darker smoke. The white smoke is hard to distinguish from rising wisps of fog or against low, light-colored clouds, but is otherwise highly visible. Keep a good supply of smoke-producing materials near the fire, ready to be tossed on if a plane passes over.

Aim the beam of a flashlight or sunlight reflected by a mirror at passing planes (a polished piece of tin or an unwrinkled piece of tinfoil will serve as a makeshift mirror) or sweep the horizon with random but more or less regularly-timed flashes. Such a heliograph flash is visible and eye-catching from miles away and will hold the attention of anyone who sees it. If that person knows, or later learns, that someone is lost in the area, he will either investigate its source himself or report it to someone who will.

Spell out *SOS* or *HELP* by spreading ashes from a fire, by sweeping the letters free of snow, or by laying green boughs or other dark-colored material in a snowy clearing. Such messages must be as large as you can reasonably make them, with letters five feet thick and twenty-five feet tall being the bare minimum and twenty by one hundred feet being much better. You can make contrasting lines in any area of more or less uniform coloration, such as a sandy beach or dune, an alkali flat, a meadow clothed with either green or dry grass, or a bare hillside. Make the lines by stacking vegetation, by wetting or disturbing the soil, by tearing up the grass to expose the dark soil beneath, or by controlled burning of vegetation. The more marked the difference in color between message and background, the more easily it will be seen from the air.

Shadows are easily seen from a plane, and letters stamped or dug into deep snow will show up black from above whenever the sun is at a sharp angle to the depressed letters. Even a thin screen of any opaque material or a raised bank of snow along the sunward side of a letter will cast visible shadows. If the sun is not shining brightly enough to cast dark shadows, then you must use dark-colored materials to make the letters visible.

An emergency code of signals designed to facilitate ground-to-air communication is simple, easy to learn, and well worth knowing. The code is most widely understood and works best in areas where pilots are most familiar with search and rescue, but these are the very areas where an emergency calling for such knowledge is most likely to occur.

If you are injured or sick and in need of medical assistance including a doctor, make a cross or a single straight line. If you need medical supplies only, make two parallel straight lines. Make a capital *F* to ask for food and water, and a simple square to ask for map and compass. (See Figure 1.)

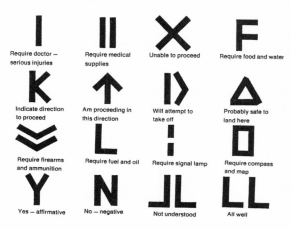

Figure 1: Emergency signal code

When a pilot has spotted your distress signal, he will generally circle closer, either to observe you or to direct ground parties to your location. This is the proper time to use your body as a signalling device. Lying flat on your back with arms stretched out to the sides means you are injured or sick, as does standing with your arms crossed in front of your body so that the right palm is in front of the left hip and vice versa. Standing with arms stretched over your head means you want to be picked up. If you don't remember these standardized signals, simply kneel and assume an attitude of prayer. This will be instantly recognized by anyone as a plea for help; and in this day of the helicopter, help will arrive in a short time.

Three fires in a row, three equally-spaced puffs of smoke, three spaced blasts on a whistle, three shots fired in a timed sequence—all are universally recognized as distress signals. If in hunting season, the shots should be fired shortly after full dark to prevent their being mistaken for ordinary hunting shots. Don't waste ammunition by repeating often, unless you hear answers.

In summer, a large smudge fire will bring help in a very short time, as a fire watch is kept in most timbered and brushy areas then; anyone seeing smoke will quickly report it. You must make sure that the fire is built in such fashion and so located that it cannot possibly spread. If the site is timbered or brushy, you must be alert to the risk of being bombed with fire retardant.

You owe it to yourself and to the public to take certain precautions before entering areas where you might conceivably become lost or stranded. Always inform someone as to where you plan to go and when you intend to return, so that a search can be made if you fail to turn up. Ideally, this should be a relative or friend who will be concerned enough to take action when you are overdue. It must not be another hunter or other person casually encountered, as he has no personal interest in your welfare and may forget or move on before your scheduled return. If no suitable person is available, leave a large note in your car, weighting it in such a position that it can be read from outside the car. Spell out exactly where you have gone, when you plan to return, and add any other details you think pertinent. This might result in thefts from your car, but it might also result in saving your life!

Once you have told others where you will be, *do not go elsewhere without notifying them of the change in plan, and don't fail to let them know when you return!* Both mistakes are frequently made, and they sometimes result in a full-scale search being made for no reason or in the wrong area.

Many persons have been lost, some of them fatally so, when they spotted game while puttering around in camp, snatched up bows or rifles, and ran in pursuit. A similar situation often occurs when game is seen from a car. The hunter quickly parks the vehicle, grabs his weapon, and takes off after the quarry. Under either circumstance, the hunter is likely to be poorly prepared, often being hatless, coatless, or without gloves. He rarely has matches or a lighter unless he smokes, and has none of the other items necessary if he is to spend a night in the woods in relative comfort and safety. Incidents such as this tend to occur late in the day, and, if the weather is severe, the hunter is headed for a night of misery at best, and possibly for death.

Carry an emergency kit at all times when afield, and make this so much a part of your gear that you feel naked without it. The best-planned and most efficient emergency kit is totally worthless when left in camp or car, so make it an unvarying habit to carry it at all times. When you arrive in camp or get into a car, fasten the kit to your bow, rifle, or fishing rod so you cannot take one without the other. *Never be caught without an emergency kit!*

Chapter II

Emergency Kit

An emergency kit to be carried on the person should be totally waterproof, unsinkable, and rip resistant. It should contain waterproof matches in a waterproof container with a self-contained striker; tinder; aluminum foil; fishhooks and fishline; a coil of light, strong wire such as brass or copper picture-hanging wire; a large square of transparent plastic film; a magnifying glass; a spare compass; a double-face signal mirror; and a police-type whistle for emergency signaling. (A whistle's blast can be heard several times as far as the loudest shout; blowing one consumes far less energy than shouting, and the sound cannot be confused with any of the normal background noises.)

If you need corrective glasses, place a second set in its own protective case in the kit. In winter, carry snow goggles or polarized sunglasses with close-fitting side shields and add extra "fire insurance" in the form of a butane-fueled lighter. In summer, add iodized salt tablets, insect repellent and a face net, and a snakebite kit.

Include a first aid kit containing tincture of iodine, bandages, tweezers, a soothing eye ointment, headache pills, a mild laxative, and three feet of surgical rubber tubing. (This can be used as a tourniquet, but it is useful in many non-medical ways as well.)

The kit should contain some means of boiling water, as many foods that you could not otherwise use are made edible or palatable by boiling. Drinking heated liquid will restore deep body heat faster than any other method. Pack the smaller items in an army canteen cup, which can also do duty as a kettle. Add several plastic bags of the type used for boiling or roasting. These take up little room and weigh almost nothing, yet they will work as boiling kettles if the flames are kept from touching them above the water level.

Although you will probably have either a sheath knife on your belt or a pocketknife in your pocket, you should also put a good-quality Boy Scout knife, a Swiss Army knife, or a "Leatherman Tool" in the kit. These have a number of useful tools in addition to their cutting blades. A pair of four-inch vise-grip pliers is almost indispensable, as is one of the compact knife, fork, and spoon sets designed for campers.

One item that should always be included, especially when cold or wet weather is a possibility, is one or more of the tiny "space blankets" that weigh only two ounces. These are folded to be only slightly larger than a cigarette package when purchased (like a road map, it is hard to refold one to that size!) and are made of a super-reflective material that will reflect more than 90 percent of incident heat. This is a poor substitute for a regular blanket, but it will serve as a splendid shelter top or liner, a water catcher when it rains, a windbreak, an emergency poncho, liners for wet boots, or a radar-reflecting signal.

Another almost indispensable item is a small flashlight of some kind. Even a penlight is a great deal better than nothing. To be on the safe side, put a snippet of tape between the battery and bulb to prevent an accidental discharge of the batteries. It is also good practice to have an extra set of alkaline batteries and a spare bulb.

This list sounds formidable, but all items listed can be contained in a package not more than six inches in any dimension; and the pack when filled will weigh less than two pounds. If an emergency ever arises when you need its contents, you will agree that it is worth more than its weight in diamonds!

A much larger list of equipment can be carried in a small backpack, since the bulk can be considerably increased and the weight can be raised to five or even ten pounds without a problem. The cooking gear can then be increased by the addition of an aluminum mess kit, a nested set of backpack kettles, a small roll of aluminum foil, and perhaps a cooking grid. The tiny space blankets can then be supplemented by one of the twelve-ounce space blankets, which are actually useful as blankets and are so brightly colored that they are also useful as signal devices. These are very valuable as emergency equipment. Don't substitute this for the smaller type; carry both. Both are useful, and two ounces is too little weight to be of concern.

When traveling in cold weather, you should carry a two-pound down sleeping bag (as a minimum) or its equivalent, as well as an extra suit of down or fiber-filled underwear. When used as pajamas, these add the equivalent of several pounds to your sleeping bag; and when worn under the outer clothing, they nearly "cold-proof" your body. You should then also carry an extra set of mittens or gloves, at least two pairs of heavy wool or thermal socks, an extra set of felt liners if you are wearing packs, and a knitted wool cap or balaclava helmet. Worn as a nightcap, one of these again adds considerably to the warmth of the sleeping bag.

In dry country, you will want to carry a sizable canteen in addition to your emergency pack.

A much larger emergency pack should be carried in any vehicle venturing into unpopulated or infrequently traveled areas. Any vehicle can strand you, either through mechanical failure or by becoming stuck. For an auto or plane, the list of items carried should include sleeping bags for all passengers, a small tent, nested cooking gear, at least five gallons of fresh, potable water (much more if in arid country in summer or if more than two passengers are along), a supply of basic foodstuffs, an axe, a shovel, and a bucket. (The last three items are required by the U.S. Forest Service when a vehicle enters one of the national forests during fire season.)

A boat needs the same basic supplies already packed in a watertight container that is securely fastened to the life raft or dinghy.

Signal flares or rockets should be carried on a boat or plane, and the red signal flares carried in cars and used to warn traffic of stalled vehicle or other hazard can be used to signal aircraft or other potential rescuers as well. They are also useful as emergency fire starters.

One of the most useful items in any emergency pack is a contour or topographical map of the area you are entering. This is especially useful if you are traveling on foot. When traveling by car, you will need a larger map or several maps, as topographical maps do not cover large areas.

The map is most useful, of course, when "square with the world" or properly oriented by compass.

Chapter III

Direction Finding

Carry a good-quality, liquid-filled or mechanically or induction-damped compass attached to your clothing or to a cord around your neck. *Use it to take bearings before leaving known territory!*

You can't use a compass to find a road, a power line, or a stream unless you first know the general trend of its course, and you can't locate your camp by taking bearings on a landmark unless you first know the bearing from the camp to the landmark. *You cannot "follow a compass needle" anywhere!*

To demonstrate this, hold a compass in your hand and let the needle settle on the *N*, but without sighting on an object. Now move well to one side and try the compass again. No matter how far or how often you move, the compass will always find Magnetic North, but the sighting lines will be a series of parallel tracks. They would allow you to travel in a generally northward direction and nothing more! You might be well to the east or west of your original sight line on each successive sighting. You can only follow a bearing to, from, or based on some object or mark.

Such a bearing or azimuth line is unique. If you establish bearings to two separate landmarks, then you have established a unique point. *At no other spot in the universe will those lines intersect!* Given those azimuths and an adequate description of the landmarks, anyone could easily find that exact spot.

You must believe the compass! This seems so basic, so elemental, as to need no stating; but the compass reading often seems so totally at variance with the evidence of your senses that you will be tempted to disregard it, to think the compass defective. Check it with the spare from your kit if you must verify it, keeping the two well away from each other, and from iron or steel or any operating electrical device. A gun barrel, a knife, or even a steel belt buckle will cause a grossly inaccurate reading if the compass is held near them; and a flashlight when turned on is one of the worst culprits. *Lacking such proof, believe the compass, not your senses!* Experience proves that human senses often lie, but a good compass seldom does. When one does, the cause is interference.

The discrepancy caused by iron or steel or by other anomalies is known as "magnetic interference," "magnetic deviation," or "magnetic deflection." To check whether or not some part of your clothing or equipment is deflecting the needle and giving a false reading, place the compass face up on a level surface and slowly back away from it. If the needle moves as you move toward or away from it, something on your person is the cause of the movement. There is no certain field test for magnetic ore deposits or other such anomalies, however. Remember that an electric watch, the light meter of a camera, a flashlight bulb, or any other electrical device creates a magnetic field when energized, and the compass needle will react. A nearby power line will render a compass unusable. The magnetized needle of a spare compass will also cause a grossly inaccurate reading when the two compasses are in close proximity.

To use a compass with confidence, you must understand that the needle is magnetized and will therefore be attracted by ("point to") any magnet of opposite polarity or will align itself with the lines of force when in a magnetic field. In real-

ity, then, the magnetized needle of the compass aligns itself
with the magnetic field of the earth, and the north-seeking
end of that needle (actually its own southern pole) is said to
"point" to the magnetic north pole of the earth. A magnetized sewing needle thrust through a cork and floated in a
bowl of water will act as a primitive compass. Any magnetic compass is merely an updated and improved version of
this, and with the cheap, snap-top, pocketwatch types of
compasses, the only improvement is their portability. Just as
with the cork and needle, they will indicate Magnetic North
in a general sense, but offer little other useful information.
They are notoriously undependable.

Because the magnetic pole is actually a 50-mile-wide area
located at approximately 75 degrees north latitude and 100
degrees west longitude, and because the Geographic North
Pole is at 90 degrees north latitude and is common to all lon-
gitudes, compass needles do not "point" to or indicate True
North. The needle can automatically point to True North
on only one line, called "the agonic or no-angle line." This
line enters the United States in the Great Lakes area, cuts
through Lake Michigan, runs down to Florida, then out to
sea. This line (and the whole magnetic field of the earth)
shifts westward by seven minutes of longitude per year.

As you move away from this line, a discrepancy develops
between a true north-south line and a magnetic north-south
line. The amount of this discrepancy, known as "magnetic
declination," increases rapidly with distance and even
more rapidly as one moves north. As you will note on the
isogonic chart shown in Figure 2 (on the next page), the
declination varies widely and without apparent reason. The
isogonic lines are numbered outward from the agonic or
zero line and are represented by a number and a letter. The
number indicates the degree of declination, and the letter
indicates whether it is to the east or west. The compass nee-

dle does not lie along the line, which merely connects all points having a common degree of declination. ("Isogonic" means equal angle, see Figure 2.)

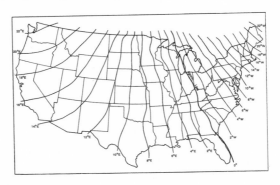

Figure 2: Isogonic chart

The amount of declination is usually marked on maps. Most maps have a small triangle drawn to represent true north-south and magnetic north-south lines. The lines are marked *TN* (although the letters are often replaced with a star) for True North, *GN* for Grid North, and *MN* for Magnetic North. You can safely ignore the Grid North line, but you must take the declination into account when trying to establish bearings. It is often said that you subtract (from the compass reading) for west declination and add for east, *but this is true only on a dial numbered in a clockwise fashion.* The Cruiser- and Forester-type compasses are numbered counterclockwise, and some compasses have both clockwise and counterclockwise numbering. The simplest way is just to remember that anywhere west of the agonic line (in most of the continent, therefore), Magnetic North lies to the east of True North. Remember the westward drift of seven minutes per year. If the map is dated, multiply the number of years since it was printed by seven minutes to get a correct declination figure. (See the next chapter for information on longitude.)

If you have no map, you can determine the degree of declination for your area whenever you can see the North Star, Polaris. Sight over two sharpened stakes, moving one as necessary to get them in proper alignment. The stakes must be needle-pointed and you must sight with your dominant eye, just as you would with a rifle. When so aligned, the stakes represent a true north-south line; and your compass will give you a magnetic north-south line. The difference in degrees between these two bearings is the declination for that area.

Magnetic declination reaches a value of 150 degrees and higher in the far north, and each degree represents a variance of more than one hundred feet per mile of travel! The computation is simple: Forty-five degrees of deflection would equal one foot of deflection for every foot of forward progress. Five thousand, two hundred and eighty divided by forty five yields well over one hundred feet per degree. You cannot afford to ignore this factor when traveling by map. You can safely ignore it, however, when you have taken a bearing on a visible objective.

Compasses come in many styles and price ranges, but the best one for ordinary use, in my opinion, is the Cruiser or Forester style. In this type, usually rather expensive, the degrees are marked counterclockwise, with the letters E and W transposed. This allows the "North" end of the needle to point directly at the proper azimuth number. To go due east, for example, simply turn the compass until the "North" end of the needle points at the E or 90 degrees. The sighting line will then point directly east. Declination for the area can be preset with an adjustment screw.

Another feature of this and other good-quality, mechanically or induction-damped compasses is a number of turns of fine copper or brass wire on one end of the needle. This feature is an adjustment for "magnetic inclination" or "magnetic dip." The wire winding is slid inward or outward to compensate for the tendency of the needle to dip toward the earth when near the magnetic poles. This feature is not found on liquid-damped compasses, as you could not gain access to the needle.

The Swedish Orienteering Compass is another good choice for the nonprofessional user. This consists of a rectangular plate of transparent plastic, often with one long and one short edge ruled for use as a ruler. The narrow ruled end is usually beveled as well, and the unruled end normally has a hole for the attachment of a lanyard or cord. An engraved and painted "way-to-go" arrow, sometimes interrupted by a small magnifying bubble, leads from the raised housing to the center of the narrow ruled end. These configurations vary slightly in different brands, but the basic elements remain the same.

Around the top of the housing, or on an internal or external flange on some models, is a circle divided into 360 degrees numbered clockwise and divided into quarters by the letters *N-E-S-W*. Intermediate directions are normally indicated by dots called "ticks." The housing is so mounted that it is free to rotate on the base plate, but will remain fixed until some pressure is exerted to turn it. Its top is transparent so you can see both the needle (this is contained in an oil bath to prevent or "damp" excessive vibration) and a broad arrow engraved or painted on the housing floor. The tip of this arrow points at the *N* mark and turns with it.

Let us suppose you want to travel due east. Simply hold the base plate firmly and rotate the housing until the base of the way-to-go arrow is at *E* or 90 degrees, plus or minus the declination allowance for the area, then rotate your body until the compass needle and the arrow beneath it are perfectly aligned. The way-to-go arrow will then point due east. To reverse your course exactly, rotate the housing 180 degrees so the way-to-go arrow is at the *W* or 270 degrees, plus or minus the allowance.

Always remember that it is physically impossible to "follow a compass needle" anywhere! You must take a sighting on some object to establish a bearing. Then, as long as you can see that object, you can hold to that bearing or return to it if forced to detour. If the object will be obscured during part of your travel, you must establish a line of intermediate targets and proceed from one to another. Remember that a reverse or reciprocal bearing is just as useful as a forward one, as you can travel as directly away from a bearing point as toward one. To determine the proper back bearing so that you can retrace your course, simply point one end of the compass needle (either end) at your original azimuth. The other end will then point at the reciprocal bearing. You can also figure this by adding or subtracting 180 to or from the bearing, adding if the bearing is less than 180, subtracting if it is more. If you wind up with impossible figures such as more than 360 or less than one, you added when you should have subtracted or vice versa.

It is good practice when in strange country to take cross bearings from prominent landmarks to your camp or to a salient point near it. Do not try to commit these to memory; write them down. As long as one of those landmarks is visible and recognizable, you can always locate your camp. If you can see two such points, the task is easy. At no other spot in the universe will those two bearings from those two landmarks intersect.

It is almost impossible to go away from and return directly to a single spot, such as a car or camp; but it is easy to return to a baseline such as a road, a power line, or a stream.

The problem often is to know which way to turn once you reach the baseline. The easiest way to solve this problem is to deliberately bear to one side of your original course when returning, with the outward and inward courses forming a definite **V**. The amount of deliberate error should be determined by the distance to be traveled. Remember the formula: one degree equals one hundred feet per mile. For the **V** to be wide enough to be useful, you must veer off from the reciprocal bearing by ten or more degrees for short distances, much smaller amounts for long distances. When you reach the baseline, you then know which way to turn.

A map must be "square with the world" to be very useful. To properly orient a map, you must turn it so that the north-south lines on it are in alignment with the north-south axis of the earth. You can most easily do this by aligning your compass needle with the magnetic north-south line on the map if this is indicated. If it isn't, you must place the compass on the map with the *N* and *S* on one of the north-south map lines, then rotate the map until the compass needle points to the proper azimuth to allow for declination.

You can use a watch as a compass if the sun is bright

enough to cast a shadow and if the watch is properly set for the time zone. Remember to allow one hour for daylight savings time. Point the hour hand at the sun while holding the watch face up. Due south then lies at the point midway of the shortest route between the hour hand and noon (1:00 P.M. DST). If it is before 6:00 A.M. or after 6:00 P.M., you must use 6:00 instead of noon. A digital watch is useless for this purpose. (See Figure 3.)

Figure 3:
Watch as compass

Even on thinly overcast days, it is often possible to locate the sun by standing a twig on a watch face, a mirror, or a spectacle lens. Such a polished surface tends to reflect even faint light, and the twig will cast a faint shadow directly opposite to the position of the sun.

The North Star, Polaris, actually rotates around a circle two degrees in diameter, so is exactly in line with True North at two points of this circle, but is never more than one degree from it. Polaris is directly overhead or at ninety degrees to the surface at the North Pole and is just on the northern horizon or at near zero degrees near the equator. The degree of angle to the ground is thus the exact latitude at any point north of the equator. Polaris can be most easily found by drawing an imaginary line from the bottom of the Big Dipper, *Ursa Major*, outward through the two stars that form its pouring lip. The first bright star just off this line is the North Star. It actually is the last star in the handle of the Little Dipper, *Ursa Minor*. (See Figure 4.)

Figure 4: North Star

If you cannot see the North Star, you can determine direction by observing any other star or star pattern for a period of time. Locate the star or star group in relation to some fixed reference point such as the tip of a tree (if the wind is blowing, use a sharpened stake instead of a tree) or between two reference points. If the stars seem to be rising, you are facing east; if they are sinking, you are looking west. When you are facing north, stars will appear to be moving from your right to your left; and stars moving from left to right indicate you are facing south. The movement is slow, but it is easily seen over a period of half an hour.

Most of us have no trouble in knowing which direction is which in a general sense whenever the sun is shining. If a general idea of direction is not enough, however, as when you want to orient a map or reset a watch, you can use the shadow method. This was the original principle that allowed for the construction of sun dials. There are several variants, but the most accurate, easy-to-use, and least time-consuming of all is the shadow stake method. It has become the standard technique described and recommended in all U.S. military survival manuals. It will enable you to determine direction with a plus or minus error of less than five degrees.

Drive a tall stake into the ground and mark where the shadow of its tip strikes the ground. Wait ten minutes or so, then mark the new spot where the shadow of the tip strikes. A line drawn through these two points is a true east-west line. To determine time, simply draw a short line at right angles to the east-west line and plant a stake at the junction. You can use this stick as one point of a compass (dividers), using a stick on a string to inscribe a circle that will represent a twenty-four hour clock. In any case, when the shadow of the stake is parallel with and completely covers the short northward side line, it is exactly noon in standard time.

Do not attempt to tell direction by which side of a tree has the most moss, by the relative width of growth rings in tree stumps, by watching so-called "compass plants," or by noting which way trees have fallen. All are subject to so many variables that any reliance on them is foolish.

When you read such instructions on route or direction finding, you should check them out by trying to make them work when you are not under the pressure of really needing them, and when no life is at stake when they fail. You will find that such systems are undependable at best and are totally unworkable in most instances.

Do not, in any circumstance, depend upon "a sense of direction!" The U.S. army has proved, by repeated experiments, that no such sense exists in human beings. When blindfolded, all persons tended to walk in circles; and the same was true of persons tested in a dense fog, "whiteouts," or snowstorms where visibility was sharply restricted.

Both sides of a mountain often look the same when visibility is limited, and you might easily find yourself in the wrong watershed. A blanket of snow will make familiar country look completely strange, and people have been known to cross good roads, paved highways, or frozen streams (in level country) on fresh, untracked snow without realizing they had done so. They may then have based their plans on knowing the road or stream was safely reachable in front of them when it was, in fact, already behind them. Such misunderstandings have often led to tragedy.

Always carry a compass, no matter how well you know the country and even if you are fully confident of your ability to navigate!

Being lost is the result of not knowing your own location, the lay of the country, or the direction to go to reach your destination. You can solve each of these problems with a map.

Chapter IV

Maps

The first maps were probably lines sketched with a stick in the soil or sand and were undoubtedly accompanied by verbal instructions to "go down the creek until you reach the big rock, turn right up the hill to the big pine, turn left there—," or something to that effect. This is still used extensively and works very well when both the mapper and his listener are familiar with the area.

When man began to leave his home territory, it became necessary for him to make more complicated maps, and these became more complicated still when mariners stopped visually following coastlines and began to cross large bodies of water. It is in ocean navigation, in fact, that mapping or chart making has reached its ultimate level. The finest nautical charts now show depth of water, prevailing wind and tidal currents, underwater formations or obstructions, navigational aids such as buoys, and hundreds of other bits of useful information.

To chart or map large areas, it was necessary to grid the whole world. This was done by establishing lateral lines (parallel with the equator) known as "parallels" or "lines of latitude," and vertical lines (running from pole to pole) called "meridians" or "lines of longitude." There is an infinite number of meridians, as a meridian by definition is any line intersecting both poles. The line on which one happens to be is known as "The Observer's Meridian." Longitudinal lines, however, are limited in number and in definite and fixed positions.

The lines of latitude begin at the equator, which is zero, and are numbered in both directions to 90 degrees at the poles. The latitude is expressed as either north or south latitude, with north often being represented by a plus sign (+) and south by a minus sign (-). A degree of latitude equals 69.4 miles.

It was necessary to establish an arbitrary starting point for measuring longitude. There was some dispute as to which was the proper starting point, with the French using "The Paris Meridian" that runs through their capital, and everyone else using "The Greenwich Meridian" that runs through Greenwich, England, and is now generally known as "The Prime Meridian." The lines of longitude are numbered outward in both directions to 180 degrees (the international dateline) and are known as east and west longitude.

One can divide a degree of latitude and a degree of longitude into sixty minutes, and each minute into sixty seconds. (One minute of longitude at the equator is one nautical mile, or 6,080.27 feet.) Even finer measurement is by hundredths of a second. Minutes are often denoted by a single mark (') and seconds by a double mark (") immediately following the given figure. Using latitude and longitude, then, it is possible to pinpoint any spot or mark off any area on the earth's surface, or to compute the airline or map distance between any two points.

Land maps in common use are U.S. Forest Service, BLM, proprietary (Metsker, Pittmon, Rand-McNally, et al.), state and U.S. Geological Survey maps. Each of these is gridded, too, but not on the basis of latitude and longitude, although these are given to locate the map in relation to the world as a whole. Most of these maps are gridded on the basis of townships.

When surveying a new area to establish boundaries for future land ownership division, the surveyors first estab-

lished a base meridian (always named) and an east-west baseline as starting points. All land within the area to be surveyed was then measured and described in relation to these
two lines. When Oregon and Washington were surveyed, for
example, the starting point was in the hills just west of
Portland, in what is now known as the Willamette Stone
Park. The meridian that cuts through the center of that
stone is known as the Willamette Meridian. Running parallel to this at six-mile intervals are other north-south lines
called "range lines." These are numbered outward in either
direction in ordinary sequence, and the land between range
line number one and the Willamette Meridian is described as
"Range 1 East" or "Range 1 West of the Willamette
Meridian."

The baseline that runs east and west through the
Willamette Stone is not named, as far as I know. Running
parallel to this line, again at six-mile intervals, are east-west
lines known as "township lines." These, too, are numbered
in ordinary sequence in both directions from the baseline;
and the land lying between that baseline and township line
one is referred to as "Township 1 South" or "Township 1
North."

One of these blocks bounded by range and township lines
is known as "a township"; and the one lying in the southeast
angle of the Willamette Stone would be described as follows:
"Township 1 South, Range 1 East of the Willamette
Meridian." Range lines are numbered on top and bottom of
maps, and township lines are numbered down both sides.
Simple arithmetic will tell you exactly how far you are in airline distance from the Willamette Stone.

As a township is six miles in each direction, it contains
thirty-six square miles of territory. Each square mile is
known as "a section" and is said to contain 640 acres of land.
As all land measure is considered as if the land were level,

steep land has a much larger surface area than the official acreage, however. The method of numbering sections within a township is shown in Figure 5, and the Cruiser or Forester compass has the numbered sections engraved on the inside of the lid.

For dividing the land into smaller parcels, a section is broken into quarter sections of 160 acres, and each of these is broken into 40-acre quarters. This division can go on and on. (See Figure 5.)

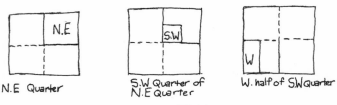

N.E Quarter   S.W Quarter of   W. half of S.W Quarter
                     N.E Quarter

Figure 5: Land division

The original surveys govern in any dispute as to boundaries. As the original surveys were made with magnetic compasses and by several survey parties operating independently of each other, certain discrepancies exist. In southern Oregon, for instance, there is a whole series of "long sections," some of which are a nearly a quarter of a mile too long. This resulted when two survey parties met, found that their surveys were that much out of whack, and simply added enough footage to a strip of sections to bring the surveys into accord.

Absolute chaos prevails where two survey areas with different starting points meet! Along the California-Oregon border the range lines and the township lines are off between a third and a half mile! This results in a jumbled series of fractured townships and sections along each side of the border.

Other methods of gridding exist, as in military maps, platted townsites, etc., but the principle remains the same. In each case there are numbered or named north-south and east-west lines intersecting each other at regular intervals. Either the points of intersection or any point within (or any part of) the block enclosed and bounded by grid lines can be readily and positively located and identified by reference to these lines, known as "coordinates." You can also use these lines to compute the distance between any two spots on the map. On steep land, distances between points are greater than map measurements would indicate, however.

The most useful of all maps for the ordinary person entering or traveling in relatively unknown territory is the topographical map made by the U.S. Geological Survey. These maps were made from airplane photos and give you an uncannily accurate picture of the terrain. They show the actual topography of the country by the use of contour lines at stated intervals (40 feet, 80 feet, etc.) of elevation, with every fifth line being darker in color and labeled as to the elevation at frequent intervals. The steeper and more rugged the country, the more valuable these maps become, as they will show all topographic features that are large enough to reach any two contour lines.

To more easily understand the contour principle, gradually submerge an irregular rock in a container of water, tracing the new "shoreline" at each successive half-inch depth. You will quickly see the resemblance between the tracings and the contour lines on the map. You will see that you could actually build a three-dimensional replica of the rock by using the contour lines alone, with only those features less than one-half inch high not represented. (See Figure 6.)

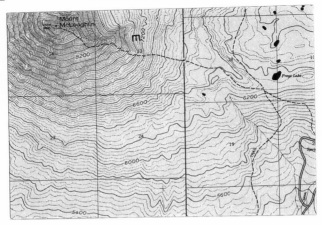

Figure 6: Contour principle

Any good map will indicate the date it was printed. Multiply the intervening years by seven to update the magnetic deviation for the area. Every nine years will yield one degree and three minutes of change (9 x 7 = 63). In any area west of the zero or Agonic Line, you must *subtract* this figure from the declination given on the map, as that line has moved toward you by that much. (In reality, it is almost or quite impossible to read within one degree of accuracy on a hand-held compass, but you might as well be as accurate as possible.)

Forest Service and Bureau of Land Management maps, as well as those produced by other federal and state agencies, are moderately priced and of good quality. Proprietary or commercial maps sold in most sporting goods and hardware stores are generally poorly reproduced copies of one or more of these government maps and are sold at more or less reasonable prices. Their only virtue, in my opinion, is their availability.

Any map will be of some help, but don't bet your life on its being absolutely accurate! Maps often show intermittent streams (as a series of blue dashes) where no surface water does or can exist, show roads that may have been planned but were never built, and show a road or trail where time has effectively eliminated all traces of one.

If you have no map (and you always should!), it is often helpful to note the courses you have traveled and the estimated distances or the time it took to travel each course, and to draw in or establish the salient features or landmarks in their proper places. Make the map by drawing the information on a piece of paper or scratching it on a piece of wood or, in a real emergency, into the stock of a rifle. Each bit of information can spell the difference between success or failure when attempting to establish or maintain location or to retrace a course. A rifle stock can be replaced; your life can't!

To stay found, you must know where you are. It does you no good to know you are in North America, in the United States, in Oregon, or even in Baker County, for example. Each of these geographic divisions is so immense that knowing you are somewhere within its boundaries gives you little help in knowing where you are. If you know, on the other hand, that you are in the Blue Mountains northeast of Granite, Oregon, and if you can see a landmark such as Gray's Peak or Mt. Ireland, then you will have no difficulty in locating yourself in relation to the country.

Remember always that *to know where you are, you must know where you are in relation to some specific landmark or place!* Only when you know where you are can you get "out" as easily as you got "in."

Chapter V

"Getting Out"

When trying to make your way out of unknown territory, it is always best to follow any road you may come upon, no matter how old or overgrown it may be. Old logging roads, tote roads, and abandoned railroad rights-of-way offer far easier travel than a cross-country course, even when vanished trestles and bridges make for frequent detours; and all such roads eventually lead to better roads and to civilization.

When you first strike such a road, you may be puzzled as to which way is out. If the land is level, just choose one of two directions and start walking; but if the land is sloping, then go down the hill. When you come to the first junction, study it carefully. Most such intersections are in the form of the letter **Y**, and the odds greatly favor the main stem as being the way to go. If the angle between the forks is such that a truck could not go from one to the other without difficulty, then probability becomes almost certainty.

Not only roads, but power lines, survey lines, abandoned mining ditches, and Forest Service trails will lead you to sites of human activity, past or present; and roads or better trails will connect these to civilization. When lost, do not abandon such well-marked routes to return to the brush and timber or to pursue a "shortcut." Hundreds of cases are on record where lost people have reached such areas of comparative safety, followed them for a short distance, then plunged back into the brush. When they have survived, most have said they abandoned the marked route because it did not go where they wanted to go!

Don't worry as to whether or not the road is the "right" one. Finding any inhabited area is better than being lost, and you can always return to your car or camp by your original routing. Once you have reached even one inhabited home or made contact with even one person who definitely knows where he or she is, you are found!

Be on the alert for signs of human habitation or activity. Watch for rising columns of smoke and listen for man-made noises. You can hear the sounds of truck traffic for great distances, and gunshots, a dog's bark, or even the crowing of a rooster can be heard from a mile or two away if conditions are right. All of these sounds indicate human presence.

The old maxim that when lost you should always go downhill or follow the water is excellent advice if tempered with judgment. In some parts of the continent, however, streams are at the bottom of impassable canyons, wander back and forth through almost impenetrable brush, or are bordered by treacherous bogs and swamps. Streams in some parts of the western United States lead only to salty or alkaline sinks, where they disappear. In parts of Canada and Alaska, following the streams would take you away from settled areas and into the almost uninhabited Arctic. At other times, common sense would tell you to climb to a nearby crest or high point that would let you overlook the whole area.

The problem of getting out is complicated by the risk of hypothermia and dehydration.

Chapter VI

Hypothermia

The human body is a heat engine that requires four basic supplies to function: air, food, heat, and water. Air is a problem only at extreme altitudes or in tightly enclosed spaces, and food needs are rarely urgent. Given the other supplies, the body can generate its own heat. Only dehydration (water loss) and hypothermia (heat loss) normally present immediate threats to life.

The rapid and uncontrolled loss of body heat, commonly referred to in coroners' reports as "hypothermia" or "exposure," annually kills more people than any other outdoor hazard except drowning. It is so deadly because many people do not know, or refuse to believe, that a threat to life can exist "when it's not even cold"!

Hypothermia-producing weather is not necessarily cold. What matter is the degree of heat loss, and dampness and wind can raise this to deadly levels when the actual temperature is mild. The majority of deaths from exposure occur at temperatures between thirty and fifty degrees Fahrenheit and many of these fatalities take place within less than twelve hours after exposure begins!

Dampness will kill you in cold or windy weather, and it makes no difference whether that dampness is caused by external conditions or by sweating. Each droplet of water that is in contact or near contact with your skin will gradually warm to the vaporization point. As it evaporates, it will take with it the heat it took to raise it to that temperature;

A Handbook for Wilderness Survival

and it will also steal the much greater latent heat required to vaporize it. All of this heat can come only from your body.

The vapor will travel outward through the layers of clothing until it reaches a layer cold enough to recondense it. It will turn back to water, wetting and further chilling the cold layer; and all the heat given up during condensation will be lost to the surrounding environment. The fibers of cloth then act as wicks to draw the water back into contact with the skin, and the whole cycle begins anew. Wind greatly speeds these actions by increasing the speed and the amount of evaporation.

This is classic refrigeration, quite similar to the process in your home refrigerator or freezer; but the object now subjected to cooling is your body. With wet clothing made of cotton, down, or some of the synthetics, you will lose heat from your body up to two hundred and forty times as fast as you would if the same clothes were dry! Wool and Orlon fabrics have less tendency to wick and retain heat much better, and the insulation value of some of the nonabsorbent synthetics is little affected by moisture.

Windy conditions can cause hypothermia even when all clothing is completely dry because of the "wind-chill factor." At an actual ambient temperature of forty degrees Fahrenheit, a forty-mile-per-hour wind gives an effective

Wind Speed		COOLING POWER OF WIND EXPRESSED AS "EQIVALENT CHILL TEMPERATURE"																				
Knots	M.P.H.	TEMPERATURE (FAHRENHEIT)																				
Calm	Calm	40	35	30	25	20	15	10	5	0	-5	-10	-15	-20	-25	-30	-35	-40	-45	-50	-55	-60
		EQUIVALENT CHILL TEMPERATURE																				
3-6	5	35	30	25	20	15	10	5	0	-5	-10	-15	-20	-25	-30	-35	-40	-45	-50	-55	-65	-70
7-10	10	30	20	15	10	5	0	-10	-15	-20	-25	-35	-40	-45	-50	-60	-65	-70	-75	-80	-90	-95
11-15	15	25	15	10	0	-5	-10	-20	-25	-30	-40	-45	-50	-60	-65	-70	-80	-85	-90	-100	-105	-110
16-19	20	20	10	5	0	-10	-15	-25	-30	-35	-45	-50	-60	-65	-75	-80	-85	-95	-100	-110	-115	-120
20-23	25	15	10	0	-5	-15	-20	-30	-35	-45	-50	-60	-65	-75	-80	-90	-95	-105	-110	-120	-125	-135
24-28	30	10	5	0	-10	-20	-25	-30	-40	-50	-55	-65	-70	-80	-85	-95	-100	-110	-115	-125	-130	-140
29-32	35	10	5	-5	-10	-20	-30	-35	-40	-50	-60	-65	-75	-80	-90	-100	-105	-115	-120	-130	-135	-145
33-36	40	10	0	-5	-15	-20	-30	-35	-45	-55	-60	-70	-75	-85	-95	-100	-110	-115	-125	-130	-140	-150
LITTLE DANGER							INCREASING DANGER							GREAT DANGER								
Winds above 40 have little additional effect							Flesh may freeze within one minute							Flesh may freeze within 30 seconds								

Figure 7: Wind chill chart

temperature of ten degrees; and a true temperature of zero with the same wind is equal to fifty-three below with no wind! You would not be foolish enough to venture out at fifty-three below, but you might chance it if the thermometer reads zero. If a wind is blowing, don't! (See Figure 7.)

When it is cold and windy or wet and windy, then, you must have adequate protection or you will die. The exact danger point will depend upon the temperature and wind velocity, whether it is raining or snowing, and the type and amount of clothing available.

Think of body temperature as a balancing act between production and loss. A temporary and minor imbalance is not ordinarily dangerous; but over any considerable time the two must be exactly equal. *Internal body temperature cannot vary by more than two or three degrees plus or minus without serious consequences!*

The body generates heat by burning fuel in the form of calories. (The calorie, as the term is used in nutrition, is the large calorie or kilocalorie, equal to 1,000 small calories.) It also absorbs heat when in a warm environment and gets some heat by direct radiation from the sun or from a fire, although radiation is of little value when heavy clothing is worn. The body also absorbs heat by conduction when in direct contact with an object warmer than itself. Heated fluids or foods taken into the stomach are in direct and total contact with the internal surfaces of the body, and transfer of the surplus heat is very rapid and complete.

If production is larger than loss, you must produce less or lose more. Lower heat production by slowing your rate of exertion and get rid of surplus heat by ventilation, especially of the head and torso. If you do neither, you will sweat; and this will dampen your clothing. If no food is available (in cold weather), you cannot afford the second option, as each calorie of heat vented to the environment is a calorie withdrawn from your reserves and wasted.

Unintentional heat loss is accomplished through respiration (cold air in, warm air out); through insensible perspiration (your body exudes warmed moisture through the skin even when you aren't sweating); by evaporation of that moisture from the skin; through heat transfer between skin and air; by conduction between the body and any colder surface in contact with it; and by the voiding of heated body waste.

If loss is larger than production, you must lose less or produce more. If you do neither, you will begin to shiver and lose a measure of control over your movements. *If the loss remains larger than production for very long, you will die!*

Reduce heat loss by putting on more and heavier clothing, by seeking shelter, or by creating a warm or heated environment (as in a shelter).

For the body to produce more heat, it must burn more fuel. Muscular activity can increase heat production by a factor of eight or more, but you must then consume high-caloric foods or draw heavily on your body's energy reserves. You will burn as much as seven hundred calories an hour during such extremes of exertion.

To deliberately produce more heat, you must fully exert your strength without accomplishing any work. Strain one muscle against another by "Indian wrestling" with yourself or attempting to move an immovable object. Try to pull up a large tree or brace your back against one large tree or rock and try to push another away with your feet or hands. When no motion is produced by the effort, all energy used will be converted directly into heat and kept within the body. No heat will be transformed into mechanical energy and wasted in useless work.

Newton's famous third law—"To every action there is always opposed an equal reaction"—explains why you should not attempt to warm yourself by stamping your feet, running in place, or flailing your arms. Exactly 50 percent of the energy used up in such actions is expended in making dents in the snow or ground or in moving quantities of air, and neither of these help you in any way.

Continue your exercise for at least fifteen minutes to produce useful quantities of heat. This is often the only way to prevent violent, convulsive shivering when you stop to find shelter and build a fire.

This is the most dangerous time of all! Heat production will drop by 50 percent or more when you stop walking; and if you have allowed yourself to become thoroughly chilled or overly tired before stopping, internal body heat may fall to dangerously low levels.

When temperature of the blood begins to drop, the first casualty is the ability to think clearly. You will begin to make poor or even silly decisions. As the process continues, you will become more or less groggy or fall into a complete stupor, and you will not realize this is happening. As deep body heat continues to fall, the body's ability to produce heat falls still faster, and this feed-back cycle leads to death when the temperature of the vital organs falls below seventy-five degrees.

The victim of hypothermia becomes unable either to recognize the situation or to remedy it when his core temperature reaches the low nineties. He is then so apathetic or nearly unconscious as to be totally unaware of his desperate situation. This is the point of no return for a person who is alone.

Never eat snow or ice or drink cold water when body heat is marginal! It takes as much heat to melt enough snow or ice to make a cupful of water and to then bring that water to body temperature as it would take to bring a cup of cold water to a boil! Drinking cold water robs the body of less heat than the snow or ice would, but the sudden and severe heat drain may still be sufficient to cause instant hypothermia.

Watch for hypothermia symptoms when out in cold and windy or in wet and windy weather. If alone, be especially vigilant and err on the side of excessive caution. If in a group, assign the person who has the best protection to maintain a constant observation of those other members who are poorly or less well protected.

Indicators to watch for are chattering teeth or shivering (both of which are attempts by the body to warm itself by involuntary exercise), stiff and clumsy hands, a stumbling or lurching gait, slurred or incoherent speech, or a generalized appearance of drowsiness or lassitude.

When one of a party shows such signs, the others should get him to the nearest temporary shelter, strip him of any wet clothing, and cover him with whatever dry clothing or bedding may be available. If a sleeping bag is handy, they should get him into it without delay. If he is so far gone in hypothermia that his body will not generate sufficient heat to warm the bag's interior, then another person will have to strip off all clothing and join the victim in the bag. The warmth from the second body will both warm the bag and transfer heat to the patient by body-to-body contact.

Don't allow modesty to kill a companion! It may lead to later embarrassment if two people of the opposite sex must spend some time in a sleeping bag while both are nude, but it will also allow both to remain alive to be embarrassed.

Once a victim is in dry clothing or bedding, build a fire to heat the shelter area. Heat some liquid and force the victim to drink as much as he can, at as high a temperature as he can stand. Heat some rocks (never from a stream bed or other permanently wet area!), wrap them in several layers of cloth, then pack them around the patient's body and especially the feet. Feed him some high-calorie food if you have it. Continue the treatment until all symptoms have disappeared and full alertness has been restored.

If alone when you realize that hypothermia threatens, begin to exercise right then. Seek out the nearest sheltered site and build a fire. Exercise some more while the fire is growing large enough to heat the sheltered area, and eat some high-calorie food if you have it. Heat and drink liquids to help restore deep body heat. *Do not relax until all symptoms are gone,* as to do so may be to die.

Once the shelter area is warm, remove and dry any items of clothing that show the slightest trace of dampness. Woolen articles must be dried very slowly and carefully or they will be scorched or shrunk to the point of becoming completely worthless. Many of the synthetics are highly flammable or meltable, so dry them carefully as well.

Do not attempt to dry leather boots or shoes by direct heat, as this will crack, deform, or harden leather to make footgear unwearable. If you have plastic or other thin water-proof material, put on dry socks and wrap the sock-clad feet with pieces of this. You can then use damp or even saturated boots without drying them at all, unless the weather is so cold they will freeze. If you must dry boots and shoes, stuff them with heated, dry, absorbent material; let this absorb all the moisture it can, then remove and dry the stuffing material. Repeat the procedure as often as necessary.

When you are warm and comfortable and all of your clothing is dry, you may feel tempted to continue on your way. *You must not do so if the weather conditions that caused your problems still prevail!* Move only as far as you must to find a better campsite, one that will furnish adequate supplies of fuel for a longer stay, possibly for several days.

Make a better camp and settle down to wait for an improvement in the weather. Don't fret about those who may be expecting you in camp or at home, or about the worry they will feel when you fail to arrive on schedule. Worrying is always preferable to mourning, and it is much better to be late than dead.

If you cannot stay warm and dry with the clothing available, do not risk further exposure!

Chapter VII

Clothing

Man is essentially a tropical animal that exists in other climates only by virtue of the artificial climates he creates in his dwellings and his clothing. By these devices, he prevents heat from being lost faster than his body can generate it.

In his shelters, man creates a heated environment by the use of external energy sources; but the heat within his clothing must normally come from within the body itself. As the body generates heat at a low rate, the clothing must be an effective insulator if man is to live and function in cold surroundings.

The insulative capacity of clothing depends primarily upon the amount of dead air it will hold, the "loft." Any low-density material that will increase the thickness will thus serve to enhance the insulation value. This allows the use of all sorts of natural substances to improve the heat-retentive ability of your clothing.

Natural materials vary widely in their value as insulation. Down from waterfowl is nearly the ultimate insulator, and the whole skins of such birds are nearly as good. Pin or tie such skins or those of smaller birds between the layers of clothing or use plucked feathers as stuffing.

The hair of members of the deer family is hollow and usually somewhat crinkly, and is one of the finest thermal insulators to be found. Caribou, elk, and moose hair is exceptionally high in insulation value. Wear a whole hide hair-side in or scrape loose hair from an old carcass and pour it inside the clothes.

The pelts of fur-bearing animals are well known insulators and are used by the Innuit (Eskimos) in preference to caribou skins or waterfowl down.

Down from cattails, fireweed, silkweed (milkweed), and thistles is very high in insulation value but tends to lose this quality rather quickly as it mats or packs. Use such plant-derived down with harsher and more mat-resistant materials for best results. Dead grasses, dry leaves, moss, and dead pine needles are good for this when used alone if they are first thoroughly dried and then crumpled to make them occupy more space.

Green bushy twigs from evergreen trees are much less effective than the materials already mentioned, but they are a great deal better than nothing. Remember that it is the dead air a material holds and not the material itself that provides the insulation.

The easiest way to insulate the legs is to tie the bottoms of your pantlegs around the tops of your boots or shoes, and then pour or stuff loose insulating material into the sacks thus created. The same technique works very well for the arms and torso.

Wind greatly complicates the problem of keeping warm. It removes heat from the unprotected skin and from the surface of the clothing; it enters the clothing itself to set up convection currents and to stir up the dead air that serves as insulation; and it greatly speeds the evaporation of moisture. You need an outer covering of windproof material to prevent these effects, and this covering must be waterproof to protect against rain or snow driven by wind. Make an emergency poncho from a sheet of plastic, a space blanket, a tarp, a large animal skin, or any wind and waterproof material. *If you can arrange no such covering, then end the exposure to wind!*

The head is the body's most effective radiator of heat, as the veins of the head will not restrict to reduce heat loss, as do all other surface veins; and it has often been said that "to keep your feet warm, cover your head." You must make every effort to prevent excessive loss from this area. A parka-type hood is more effective than any other head covering, but a piece of fabric or other soft material wound turban fashion will serve. The skin of a rabbit or other small animal or the whole skin of a large fowl turned hair- or feather-side in will make a warm and comfortable cap. A piece of cloth tied as a handkerchief and stuffed with loose insulation will do a good job, too, but is apt to cause considerable itching. Discomfort is infinitely preferable to frostbite, however; and such a makeshift will greatly increase your ability to withstand cold weather and wind. *If you cannot adequately protect the head, end the exposure!*

The effect of wind on the bare face often limits the amount of wind you can tolerate, even when the rest of the head and body are adequately protected. Wear a balaclava helmet or ski mask if you have one, or tie a handkerchief or other fabric loosely over the face. Make a face mask from an opened-up spare sock or the skin of a bird or animal. *If you cannot protect your face, end the exposure!*

Your hands are especially sensitive to cold, and you must make every effort to keep them from becoming so stiff and clumsy that you will be rendered helpless, unable to handle matches and tinder. Ski gloves or windproof mittens over a wool or foam-rubber inner glove are best, but you can use wool socks for liners and pieces of plastic for mittens. You can also use the skins of birds or small animals as both mittens and liners by turning them wrong-side out so the fur or feathers will be on the inside. In very frigid weather or when there is snow, gloves or mittens should be tied to the clothing or to the opposite ends of a string that is threaded in one sleeve and out the other. This will prevent loss and ensuing misery. *If you cannot protect your hands, end the exposure!*

Your feet are also highly vulnerable to cold, being both far removed from the torso where heat is generated and in contact with the ground or snow. There are a number of types of footgear on the market that are guaranteed to keep you warmly shod under any conceivable circumstance; and if you are lucky enough (or foresighted enough) to be wearing such boots, then keeping your feet warm will present no problem. With normal footgear, the problems can range from mild to severe and desperate.

A satisfactory substitute for thermal boots can be made by wrapping the bare feet in plastic, pieces of space blanket, or other thin, waterproof material, putting on one or more pairs of heavy socks, then wrapping these with another waterproof covering. Moisture cannot penetrate the socks to destroy their ability to insulate, and the waterproofing barriers add some insulation value as well. This is the famous "Korean" or "Mickey Mouse" boot in crude form.

The "Mormon moccasins" of pioneer days were opened-up burlap sacks wrapped in multiple layers and tied around the boots or shoes. The skin of an animal or the seatcovers or headliner of a car will serve as well; and you can even wind or tie evergreen twigs, twisted bundles of dead grass, rushes, or plaited cattail leaves in a layer several inches thick. This cover will pack full of snow and will furnish a high degree of insulation. These will quickly wear out if worn on bare ground, but will last well in snow, where they will also leave monstrous tracks that would convince an observer that he has stumbled on the trail of Bigfoot!

The skins of small animals such as rabbits make splendid lounging moccasins for use around camp and are near-perfect substitutes for socks if the footgear is roomy enough to permit their use. They are too fragile to wear as boots unless protected by more durable material.

You can make moccasins from blankets, from carpets or floor mats from a car, from rawhide from animals such as deer, or even from a cut section of tire. With all but the tire, you can cut the material and sew it (using electrical wire from the car, perhaps) in conventional pattern; or you can simply place your foot in the middle of a piece of material at least eighteen inches square, then fold and tie this around the foot and ankle. With the section of tire, you must insulate the foot with other materials (grass, rabbit skin, blanket moccasins, etc.) and slip the trough-shaped piece of tire over this.

The Thule Innuit (Eskimos), who live within nine hundred miles of the North Pole, use sealskin outer boots or "kamiks" with bearskin soles, and inside these they wear inner boots made of rabbit skin with the hair turned in. To improve insulation of the feet, they place a thick pad of dry grass (collected and stored in summer) between the soles of the inner and outer boots. While you are not likely to have sealskin or polar bear skin available, the grass will work as well for you as for them, especially as you are not going to be walking on ice at sub-zero temperatures.

If stranded by a stalled or disabled car in severe weather and you find your clothing inadequate, the appointments of the car itself can be life savers. Most car seats today are padded with rubber or plastic foam, and this is splendid insulation. Cut through the seatcover (save and use this also) and remove the padding in large pieces. Use these to insulate your clothing. Don't forget that many cars have padded dashboards, many engine compartments are insulated with fiberglass, and many carpets are underlaid with sound-absorbing pads.

Seat belts can be used as belts, suspenders, or pack straps; and carpets, floor mats, headliners, and seatcovers can be used in many ways not already mentioned. Improvisation is the name of the game in a survival situation, so use your imagination. *Don't hesitate to salvage these items if you need them. A car is expendable, but your life is not!*

If your clothing will still not keep you dry and warm despite such improvisations, end the exposure. Remember that no other objective can be as important as staying alive and in possession of your ears, fingers, toes, and limbs. *If you cannot stay dry and warm with the clothing and materials available, build a shelter to protect against further exposure!*

Chapter VIII

Winter Shelters

A winter survival shelter has only one purpose: to enclose an environment more suitable to human requirements than that which prevails outside its walls. This being so, it follows that the smaller and more tightly enclosed the shelter, the easier it will be to create and maintain such an environment within it.

The type of shelter you choose to build should be determined by the area in which you find yourself, the weather conditions prevailing there, and the materials available without excessive expenditure of energy.

A shelter site must meet certain criteria: a shelter must not be built in an area subject to flooding, in the pathway of possible snow or rock avalanches, in the lee of an obstruction where drifting snow would bury it, or within reach of standing dead trees or large dead limbs. It does little good to take shelter from the weather in places where one of these hazards is every bit as threatening. The sites must have (if possible) an easily obtainable supply of fuel large enough to last for some time without skimping, suitable materials for constructing the shelter and a source of water. Snow makes water available everywhere, but melting snow is a slow and irksome process, and is next to impossible without suitable pans or kettles. If food animals and/or plants are in evidence, so much the better; but these are not absolutely required in the short term.

If you are caught out at night in cold but not stormy weather, you can make a reasonably comfortable bed against or alongside a large log. Clear a space seven or eight feet long and two or three feet wide alongside the log, digging clear down to the mineral dirt to prevent fire from spreading. Bank some of this dirt against the log to prevent its catching fire. Build a fire, of hardwood or heavy bark if possible, to cover the cleared area. Keep it burning for at least an hour to thoroughly heat the ground, then rake the fire out of its bed, moving it from four to six feet outward from the cleared area. The new fire site should also be cleared of all burnable material before the fire is moved. Make sure no burning material is left behind.

Cover the heated area of ground with a thin layer of dirt for safety. Place a small log or a wall of rocks along its outer edge and fill the space between it and the large log with small evergreen boughs, dry grass, moss, dead pine needles, or any other resilient material. Make this mat a foot or more thick and tuck all stiff stems or twigs well down inside. This is to be your mattress, so take some pains to make it a comfortable one.

Lay rafter poles across the large log in such fashion that the projecting "eaves" overhang your bed, and roof this overhang with bark or boughs. This will catch and reflect the heat from your fire, especially if you make a suitable reflector on the far side of the fire.

Be sure to collect enough wood to last the night, remembering as you do that the fire is as long as your bed and will consume a great deal of fuel. Gather as much as you think you'll need, then add twice that much more! Late-season nights are long, and they often get very cold; and it is far better to have more than enough wood than to run out before morning.

If you wish to do so, it is easy enough to contrive a coverlet or comforter of sorts. Simply lay two slender poles parallel to the side logs and sixteen to eighteen inches apart atop your mattress. Lay some small sticks across these and heap on small boughs, dry grass, dead leaves, or pine needles in as thick a layer as you think necessary. (All of these materials should be assembled before dark.) Carefully lift one end of both poles and wriggle into the cavity thus created, then allow the covering material to settle over you. This will block off the reflected heat of the fire, but it will help retain the heat from the ground. A much smaller fire will then serve.

If in treeless country, build your fire in the lee of a large rock or ledge and surround it with an embankment of sand or dirt topped with a row of fist-sized or larger rocks. (These must not come from creek beds or other seasonally wet areas!) When the sand and these rocks have been thoroughly heated, move the fire to a new location several feet away. Cover the old fire site with the heated rocks and completely bury these with the heated sand or dirt. Cover this with a thick layer of dry grass or similar vegetation, or with a thin layer of cooler sand or dirt. This is your bed, and the heated rocks and sand beneath it will retain heat for several hours.

If you get cold because of the cooling of your bed, transfer the fire back to its first location and bed down on the newly vacated site. You should then be able to sleep the rest of the night.

You should have no trouble building a decent shelter in timbered country. Many evergreen trees have boughs that droop almost or quite to the ground to form ready-made huts, and a heavy snow cover makes these even more suitable as shelters. Strip a few boughs to make headroom and use these and others procured from nearby trees to make an insulating floor cover at least a foot deep. Weave still more boughs into the walls and overhead or use slabs of bark if these are easily obtained. You can use plastic film or a space blanket for further weatherproofing if you have them.

An alternate of this is to dig a pit around the straight trunk of a tree, digging clear down to bare dirt. Roof this pit with cross poles covered with branches or bark. Again cover the floor with a mat of vegetation a foot or more thick. Make a shield of rocks or dirt against the base of the trunk to protect it from damage and build your fire against this. The tree will actually serve as a primitive chimney, as the smoke will tend to follow it up and out of the shelter through a hole left for the purpose.

In timbered country, you can also often find a large uprooted tree, and there will usually be a large vertical wall of dirt covering the roots. Deepen or square the hole left by the uprooting and use the dirt to build an embankment on the side opposite the root wall. Lay rafter poles over these two walls and cover them with boughs or bark. Build your fire against the root wall and make a smoke hole in the roof directly above it. Fill the bottom of the hole with flooring material a foot or more thick. The wall of dirt covering the roots makes a splendid fire reflector, so build a bed at the lower or opposite end of the shelter.

Find a dense young evergreen tree that is fifteen to twenty feet tall. Use a pole to shake snow off its branches. Chop or shoot into the tree trunk at a point five or six feet above the snow level. Use the pole to push the tree over so that its tip is resting on the snow. The butt will still be hooked to the stump, and the tree will slant steeply downward to the tip. Trim out all bottom branches and dig the snow from beneath the trunk to make a trench to ground level. Floor this with a layer of boughs or other vegetation at least a foot thick. Cut into all branches on the top and sides and break them down to rest on the snow. Stack other loose boughs over the top to make this brushpile a foot or more thick.

Heap snow over this to provide additional insulation. Build a fire shield and reflector against the stump and make your fire against this. This "den" will protect you against anything but warm rain or a sudden, massive thaw.

Lean a pole and bough roof against a large log or lay one over two parallel logs. Make a combination floor and bed of boughs and bark or of boughs alone. Cover one end with a slab of bark or with a woven mat of boughs to serve as a door. Cover the roof with dirt and leaves or with snow to insulate it. Build a fire three feet or so from the open end and make a reflector behind it. Place a plentiful supply of wood within easy reach, leaning some of it against the logs that form your walls. The heat of the fire will dry your wood as it warms the shelter, and you can refuel the fire without leaving the shelter. Don't be alarmed if the side logs catch fire, as you can easily prevent the flames from progressing too far by plastering them with dirt or snow.

Make a teepee by jamming the tips of several poles into the bark of a tree and spreading the butts in a circle. Half a teepee is often all the room you need, and you can spread the poles in a half circle only. Cut or break branches on top of these poles to leave stubs several inches long. Hang the forks of the first thatching boughs over these stubs. Thatch heavily and cover the floor with insulating material. Use large boughs to cover the open side of a half teepee and to provide access. Make a fire shield and reflector against the tree trunk.

In treeless country you can make a wickiup by lashing the tips of tall bushes together and weaving other brush into the framework thus formed. A framework of slender willow saplings with cattail leaves woven as walls is splendid, but you can use twisted bunches of grass as thatching instead. Leave a smoke vent in the top center of your wickiup and build your fire in the center of the floor space. If you cannot find a clump of saplings that can be used in place, you can add others by driving stakes and lashing the butts of gathered poles to them.

Build a lean-to by placing a ridgepole between supports or by using one large rock as a ridgepole. Place smaller poles with one end on this and the other end on a small log parallel to it. Lay still smaller poles over these to form thatch supports. Thatch heavily and cover with snow or with dirt and leaves. Make a thick floor covering and build a bough bed against the smaller log. Cover the open sides with slabs of bark or with large boughs. Build a fire at the high end and make a smoke hole directly above it. This is especially good when the ridgepole is a large boulder, as the rock not only holds up your roof but serves as an ideal fire reflector. You can even lean poles at a steep angle against a cliff to create a very steep-roofed shelter that looks like half of an A-frame structure.

Make a snow cave by tunneling into a compacted drift or under a heavy crust. Make an open semicave by heaping snow walls or by digging or stamping a triangular trench. Floor with boughs or bark and build a raised bed between two points of the triangle. Roof this area, but leave the third corner uncovered. Build a **V**-shaped fire reflector in the unroofed angle and make your fire there. With the dug cave, place the fire and reflector just outside the cave mouth.

Make a snow hut by rolling and stacking snowballs or by breaking thick crusts of snow to serve as building blocks. You cannot build a proper igloo without a snow knife or machete and a great deal of specialized expertise. It is far easier just to build snow walls and roof the hut by using poles or skis covered with brush or with large chunks of frozen crust than it is to make a self-supporting dome out of snow blocks.

In open country where poles and brush are not at hand, you can hollow out a chamber beneath a crusted drift. Make the lid resemble that of a jack-o-lantern, sharply slanted so that its taper will hold it in place. This type shelter is especially valuable when seeking shelter from a snow storm or blizzard in treeless terrain or when the only source of heat is a candle or primus stove. Be sure to poke a stick through the crust to make a ventilation hole, and keep the stick with you so you can use it to keep the hole unclogged. Line the chamber with whatever vegetation may be at hand or with floor mats or carpets from your car.

The Mandan, Navaho, Pawnee, Pima, and Mojave Indians used mound- or loaf-shaped huts made of timbers and brush covered with a thick layer of dirt. The Thule Innuit used dirt and rock igloos, as did prehistoric Aleuts. Such a shelter is unexcelled for warmth in cold weather, but will take considerable effort to build. If you decide to make one (as for a long stay), look for an existing depression that can be deepened to form the lower part of the hut, and use the material removed to cover the top. If the ground is frozen, build a fire to thaw the ground so you can work it.

Desert streams tend to cut very deep channels, and the dirt and rock walls of such miniature gorges are often pocked with shallow caves. This is especially true just below the rim. When the ground is frozen, you can safely deepen such holes to make a room large enough to crawl into. If you can find some suitable material for shoring up the roof, you can make a much larger room and dig a fireplace at the inner end. If possible, use rocks and dirt to build a short chimney around the smoke hole, extending it somewhat above ground level to make it draw better. Use a mat of brush as a door, but don't make it airtight. Don't use such sites when the weather is such that thunderstorms can possibly dump large amounts of rain on the headwaters of the stream, as dry or almost dry watercourses can be filled up to their banks in a matter of minutes.

You will rarely find a true rock cave when you need an emergency shelter, but you will often find large rocks leaning against each other to form cavelike niches. You may even find such a crevice that has a chink or hole ideally placed to let smoke out. Fill other cracks with snow, dirt, gravel, or vegetation to prevent drafts, lay a thick floor of boughs or brush, and make a door from dense young evergreens, a slab of bark, or a woven mat of brush. Build your fire against one of the interior walls if there is a good way for smoke to escape. If there is no smoke vent, build a fire just outside or just inside the entrance if the entrance is wide enough to let you pass the fire to go in and out, make a reflector behind it, and omit the door.

An overhanging rock ledge or a large undercut boulder offers splendid shelter potential. Lean poles against the ledge or boulder and thatch these poles to cover the three open sides. Alternatively, you can stack rocks to make a wall several feet from the fixed rock and make a pole-and-thatch roof. A fire built against a boulder or rockface will heat the shelter almost as well as a stove.

Old abandoned mine shafts and even prospect holes offer marvelous opportunities for shelter building. The mine tunnels must not be used unless they seem solid and not at all likely to cave in. Even then, it is best to make a wall to block off the entrance and another to partition off a small room, rather than to go deeper into the tunnel. You can store your fuel supply against this wall or use it as part of the wall to help block escape of your heated atmosphere.

A stick and wattle shelter takes considerable effort to build, but is well worth the effort if materials are readily at hand and you expect a somewhat lengthy stay. Drive a double row of stakes (use standing small saplings when properly placed) and fill the space between the stakes with tamped brush or boughs, or with brush plastered with mud. This was the type of house built by the first English immigrants to this country, despite the pictures showing neat log cabins. Make a roof of thatch or whatever you can find.

A combination dugout and sod house is another splendid shelter. Simply dig a shallow cave in a steep sidehill and cover the entry with a wall constructed of cut sod or rammed earth. A rammed earth wall is very similar to the stick and wattle wall, except that the sticks are tied to make forms that are then filled with tamped dirt.

All sorts of teepees, lean-tos, and shed-type structures can be made from plastic sheets or space blankets. Remember that these will condense so badly as to be worse than useless unless adequate ventilation is provided and maintained. Leave at least one side open to permit enough air circulation to carry the moisture away.

The interior walls of any shelter built of snow or of any material that will either leak or condense moisture must be made as smooth as possible, as any projections will serve as drip points. When such a point is unavoidable, it is often possible to hang a slanting trough of bark or a smooth stick beneath the point to catch the water and drain it away. It is also advisable to dig a shallow trench around the inside base of such walls to safely channel all water away.

In nearly airtight or meltable shelters, you can use a few heated rocks as a heat source. Build a fire just outside and heat a number of softball-sized rocks (never gather these from a permanently wet area!) in it. Use green stick tongs to transfer the heated rocks to a dug pit or dirt-covered platform inside the shelter. A heated rock will radiate heat for a considerable time, and two or three such rocks will furnish as much heat as a small fire.

The Chinese in colder parts of Asia use hollow beds made of baked clay. They place burning charcoal in these "kangs" to furnish heat throughout the night. You can make a crude substitute by digging a trench across the floor of the shelter, roofing this with flat rocks plastered with mud, and building a stick-and-mud or rock-and-mud chimney at one end. Build a fire in a covered pit at the other end to heat both the shelter and your bed.

A stove is vastly superior to the best possible fireplace, and you can make a crude stove out of pieces of flat rock such as granite, sandstone, shale, or slate. You can make an even better one with metal salvaged from a car or plane. If you have tools to remove them, be sure to salvage the hood or trunk lid if stranded by a broken-down car. Use one of these for the lid of a rock stove or a dug fire pit, first burning the paint off by laying it on a hot fire outside the shelter. If you neglect this, your shelter will be filled with noxious fumes as the paint burns. You can also use the metal as the inner wall of a fireplace chimney by blocking it a short distance from a dirt or rock backwall. When heated by the rising smoke, such a chimney will radiate a lot of heat. You can also use a hood or trunk lid as part of the external wall, with the fire built outside the shelter.

The best roofing material is bark, and you can easily strip this from rotting logs without the use of tools. It is so heavy that you do not need to weight it, sheds water very well if properly laid, and is an efficient insulator. Best of all, you do not have to expend much energy to get it.

Evergreen, coniferous boughs make good thatch, but you must use them properly. You must lay them at a steep pitch to make them shed water at all well, lay them in thick masses to provide much insulation value, and weight them with other material to prevent wind motion. You must take care to lay them with the butts up and the tips down, and turned right-side up, just as they grew on the tree. Laid in this fashion, the needles are so pointed that water will drain down and off.

Bundles of grass, cattail leaves, rushes, reeds, etc., make splendid thatch, provided only that the bundles are laid in several thicknesses and in such a fashion that each layer of bundles overlaps and covers the gaps between lower layers. If you have a sheet of plastic, you can throw thatching material on without tying it in bundles or taking any great pains to orient the stems or the leaves, covering the whole with the plastic held just off the thatch. Vapor from inside the shelter will pass through the thatch and condense on the plastic; and this condensation will then drain down and off.

Many of the shelters described are for long-term use, and it is most unlikely that you will need anything so elaborate. Cases abound where people were downed in a plane, wrecked in a ship or boat, or simply became hopelessly lost for considerable periods, however; and a fancier or more comfortable shelter would have eased their misery. You alone must decide the type of shelter needed in light of the situation.

Remember that it is vital that you not work at a pace that will cause sweating when you are building an emergency shelter or gathering building materials or fuel. This will dampen your clothing and rob you of a great deal of body heat; and it will also waste a large quantity of stored energy. You have a limited supply of energy in reserve, so husband it as if your life depended on it. It well may!

As important as knowing how to build a shelter might be, it is just as important to know how to live in one.

Chapter IX

Shelter Living

Conduction is the transference of heat from a warmer to a colder object by direct contact, and the speed and amount of the transfer depend upon both the temperature difference and the nature (texture and content) of the surfaces involved. A smooth surface will obviously allow a much greater area of actual contact than a rough surface of the same size, and it is more likely to be very hot or very cold. Metal and stone feel much colder than wood, and smooth wood feels colder than a rough piece of bark. The coldest of all, of course, is a smooth sheet of ice.

It is vitally important, then, that you prevent direct body contact with ice, snow, frozen ground, or the surfaces of rocks. It is for this reason that I have repeatedly stressed the need to make a floor of bark, boughs, pine needles, dead grass, or other insulating material laid in considerable depth.

It is the danger of conduction, too, that makes a car an attractive hazard as a shelter. The car is made of metal, is poorly insulated, and is very unlikely to be stalled or stuck at or near a good supply of fuel or in a sheltered area. During a howling blizzard or in wide-open, treeless country, you should stay with the car at all costs. In most circumstances, however, you should seek out the nearest site that offers the essentials for shelter making and living. *Do not leave the car without leaving a message for a rescue party, telling them which direction you went, when, and why.*

If there should be an adequate fuel supply near the car, then you might well choose to stay there. In that case, build a fire near the car but far enough away to reduce fire or explosion hazard, heat some rocks (never from a wet area!) in it, and use them to heat the car. A hub cap placed on a pile of rocks or in the center of a spare wheel will serve to keep hot rocks off flammable or meltable carpets.

Do not attempt to live in (or to build) a snow shelter when the temperature is at or above the freezing point. Handling snow under such conditions will wet your clothing and rob you of a great deal of heat. When living in such shelters, your body heat alone will raise the temperature significantly; and if the raised temperature is then above freezing, you will have damp and drippy quarters.

If in colder temperatures you find the heat of your fire beginning to melt the interior surfaces of your shelter, there are several useful steps you can take. Lining the structure with bark or boughs will help insulate it, and will let you use somewhat higher heat levels. Enlargement of the smoke vent or roofless area will let more heat escape, and enlargement of the doorway or thinning or removal of the door material will let more cold air enter.

With reasonably adequate clothing and complete protection from the wind, you can stay relatively comfortable with the temperature somewhat below freezing. It is much better to be chilly and dry than to be warm and wet.

A very real problem in severe weather is the elimination of body wastes. The single largest cause of death among the German troops outside Moscow in the winter of 1941 was officially listed as "congelation of the anus." This translates as freezing of the bowel or colon and was brought about by the combination of widespread dysentery and unprotected and unheated latrine areas. If the weather is only moderately cold, you can use a well-protected spot near your shelter as a latrine. If the temperature is very low or if it is both cold and windy, you must either build a latrine shelter you can heat or make a "chamber pot" you can use in your shelter. This can be a slab of bark or other material that can be carried out and buried with its contents.

Remember when selecting a latrine area or a dumping ground for your chamber pot that the wastes may remain frozen until the main thaw, but will then be released to the environment. Be careful to select an area that will not allow them to be carried into a watercourse or otherwise create a pollution threat when spring comes.

Snow is a great thief, and any article left outside the shelter in winter is apt to be buried and lost. Take everything but a firearm into the shelter with you. The chilled metal of a gun will sweat (condense moisture from warm air) if taken into a heated atmosphere; and ice may then form in the barrel when you take it outside again, dangerously restricting the bore. Other metal parts may be effectively welded into a single immovable block by freezing. Leave the weapon outside the shelter, perhaps hanging it upside down from a lower branch of a dense young evergreen. If you are unwilling to be separated from your gun, then first warm it to room temperature and then thoroughly dry it, taking special pains with the bore.

Snow plus heat equals water. Whenever you leave your shelter in snowy conditions, your boots and possibly your clothing will pick up some snow. If you enter your shelter without first removing this snow, it will melt, dampening both your clothing and the shelter floor. Use a small evergreen bough or a bunch of dried grass as a whisk to brush all snow off clothing while still outside. If falling or blowing snow tends to replace it as fast as you can brush it off, then you must make some sort of porch or anteroom that is unheated but offers some protection.

Extra clothing and all bedding material should be kept as dry and as clean as possible. Dry such items at the first sign of dampness and fluff them at every opportunity. This will both help to retain the bulk or "loft" of the material and prevent the buildup of insulation-robbing moisture.

Keep a supply of drinking water at hand if at all possible, and keep it heated to well above body temperature. Use it with or without flavoring, such as one of the vegetable teas mentioned in Chapter XIX if you have no regular tea or coffee. Drink the equivalent of a large glass of it at frequent intervals, whether or not you are thirsty. The water will prevent dehydration and the heat will help maintain your core temperature without burning any of your reserve energy.

Living in a winter shelter requires the maintenance of an adequate fire.

Chapter X

Fire Making

Heat means fire and fires must be started. This requires a means of ignition, tinder to be ignited, and fuel to burn. It also helps immensely to have some sort of dry and heat-reflective material such as aluminum foil to build a fire on.

The best and surest means of ignition is the common wooden or kitchen match. Dip some of these in melted wax to make them waterproof, after first testing them for dryness or drying them in a slow oven to make sure you are sealing dampness out, not in. The wax will completely protect the match from moisture, will not hinder striking, and will make the match burn much more hotly when lit. Carry some of these in each of several pockets and at least a few in a watertight container with a sandpaper striker glued to it or in a commercial match safe, in addition to a plentiful supply in your emergency kit. Matches are cheap and easily water-proofed, so always carry more than an adequate supply.

Almost as effective and only slightly more costly are the butane-fueled lighters now on the market. Include one of these in your fishing or hunting gear and perhaps another in your pocket in addition to the one in your emergency kit. Other types of cigarette lighters are valuable, too; but most require that you refill them with fluid and replace the flints occasionally, where the cheaper butane models are simply replaced. *Butane will freeze and the gas will not flow at near-freezing temperatures, so you must transfer one of these to an inner pocket when the weather is cold.*

Make tinder by soaking blocks of absorbent, burnable material in hot wax. Cardboard, paperboard, acoustic tile, cotton rope, and folded cotton cloths are excellent, and loosely rolled or folded paper towel or toilet paper will serve. Cut into short lengths or small blocks and drop these in a container of melted wax. Hold them under the surface with a fork until all air bubbles cease, then lift them to a rack or screen to let them harden. These blocks will be totally waterproof and easy to light under most conditions, and will burn long enough and hotly enough to ignite even ice-coated twigs. Best of all, one of these blocks will furnish enough heat to restore a measure of dexterity to cold-numbed hands.

A small can or two of Sterno is very good "life insurance" if the time and locale are such that sudden blizzards might occur. You can pry the lid off one of these cans or puncture the can or lid even when your hands are almost clubs, and even a spark will then ignite the alcohol. This will burn hotly enough to ignite other fuels even in windy or rainy conditions. You can often slide the can from beneath the blazing fuel, recap it, and save part of its contents for future need.

You are often told how valuable birchbark is for starting fires, but you are seldom told that this is true only of the paperbark birches; and you are never told that these do not even exist in two-thirds of the country. This bark exfoliates (peels) in very thin sheets that are like oiled paper (although the bark looks solid on the tree); and these thin sheets will burn much like oil- or grease-soaked paper. It takes an actual flame, not a spark, to ignite it. Water has little effect on this quality. Most species of birch do not have this useful feature.

Other tinders that can be lighted easily with a flame are animal fat; camera film; dry, shredded pinecones; pitch shavings; paper; wispy dead wood left by termites; and resinous dead conifer twigs. Good pitch shavings will light even when wet. Film from a camera will light and burn almost explosively.

Tinders that can be lighted with a spark are dry, powdered bird droppings; dry manure from grass-eating animals; downy feathers or plant down; human or other hair, pounded and wadded; dry grass or pine needles rubbed to a fibrous pulp; and fine, rotted wood powder. The fine dust left by termites, carpenter ants, or wood-boring beetles is also very good. Each of these must be perfectly dry to be usable.

Make emergency tinder from cotton cloth. Pound a piece of handkerchief between rocks to reduce it a pulpy, linty mass. The tiniest spark will start a smoldering fire in this lint, and you can easily blow this into flame. If you have no other tinder on hand and expect to build up more than one fire, tear your cotton handkerchief into three equal strips, roll each of these into a several-walled tube, then plait these together to make a crude rope. Pulp one end by pounding. When a spark has landed in the lint, grasp the other end of the rope and twirl it rapidly to fan the fire. Extinguish it by pounding the burning end between rocks or by smothering it with the sole of your boot after starting a fire with it. The partly charred end will be even easier to light the next time you use it.

You can make sparks with a "metal match," a patented item available in stores and by mail order. Scrape it with a knife edge or with the scraper furnished with it. Scrape slowly to produce burnable particles to mix with other tinder, or rapidly to produce a shower of superheated, long-lived sparks. Being made of metal, this igniter is totally impervious to water. It is a valuable piece of emergency gear.

Even an out-of-fuel cigarette lighter can be used to send a shower of hot sparks into a bed of tinder. Some people carry a lantern, stove, or cutting-torch lighter. The torch lighter consists of a wire bent into a long, narrow **U**-shape, with one end fastened to a metal cup that contains a piece of file, and with the other end bent in a right angle and tipped with a piece of commercial flint. The bent wire serves as a spring, and the cup serves to focus and direct the sparks produced by grating the flint against the file. The stove lighter works like a pair of spring-loaded pliers, and the lantern lighter spins a serrated steel wheel against flint. All three produce showers of superhot and long-lasting sparks.

You can make sparks by stroking a piece of steel such as your knife blade or a sharpening steel against a very hard rock such as agate, chrysolite, feldspar, flint, garnet, hematite, iron pyrites (fool's gold), jasper, magnetite, quartz, or any other rock that is too hard for your knife to scratch easily. You can even make sparks by striking two chunks of iron pyrites or magnetite together, although you are more likely to wind up with smashed fingers than with fire. Look for suitable rocks in the gravel bars along streams or where ledges protrude through snow or forest duff.

When using a smallish rock and steel, it is best to hold the tinder cupped in the palm of your weaker hand, with the fingers of the same hand holding the rock in position just above the tinder. The steel is grasped with the other hand and stroked briskly and repeatedly against the rock in such fashion that all sparks are driven into the tinder.

When using two rocks or one large rock and a large piece of steel such as a hatchet, the best technique is to put the tinder on a piece of bark or tinfoil placed on a large rock or piece of wood. Kneel beside this and hold one rock in the weaker hand just above the tinder. Take the other rock or the steel in the stronger hand and strike it in a glancing downward fashion against the stationary rock. Do this repeatedly and as rapidly as you can manage.

When a spark catches and "holds," the signal will be a fine thread of smoke. Pick up the bundle of tinder and either blow gently on the spark or wave the bundle back and forth to fan the spark to greater life.

Any tinder is vastly improved by being charred, and many natural tinders that you could not otherwise use are rendered useful by this process. Among these are: the shreddy outer bark of cedar, cliff rose, cypress, grape, honeysuckle, juniper, and sagebrush, all of them excellent. The inner bark of dead aspen, cottonwood, poplar, and willow are good. Fair to good charred timbers can be made from the pith of such weeds as fireweed, mullein, and sunflowers, or from that of shrubs such as elderberry, mock orange, or ocean spray. Dried fungi such as puffballs found on oak trees, the "conks" on diseased coniferous trees, and dry mushrooms such as puffballs and bracket fungi found on dead trees and logs are excellent.

Any nonresinous softwood, either green or dry, can be used as charred tinder. Scrape with the edge of a knife, a sea shell, a sharp-edged rock, or a piece of broken glass to produce very thin scrapings. *Do not whittle.* Scrape, as in paint removal. Burn or char these scrapings in the absence of oxygen and rub or grind into a powder.

Prepare any charred timber by heating the material in an airtight container or by smothering burning material in very dry dust or ashes. Carry or store the material in an empty shotgun shell or cartridge case with a whittled plug for a stopper. You can also carry it in a section of elderberry or other pithy stem with the pith punched out or in a hollow bone plugged at both ends. *Once you have started a fire by primitive means, do not neglect the making of some charred tinder to make future fire starts easier and more certain.* The best of all charred tinders is cotton or linen cloth.

These are makeshifts at best and should be reserved for playtime. You should not bet your life on them! *Carry matches and tinder!*

You can start a fire with a firearm. Pry out the wadding of a shotgun shell or remove the bullet from a metal cartridge. With a blunt-nosed bullet, you will have to lay the neck of the cartridge on a rock and tap all around it with the back of a knife blade or a sharp-edged rock, unless you have pliers, a Leatherman Tool, or similar device. With a pointed bullet, you can use the gun muzzle for a vise. Insert the bullet in the muzzle as far as it will go, then wiggle the cartridge to stretch the case neck slightly to loosen the bullet. Try the cartridge in the chamber, as wiggling or tapping may have enlarged or deformed the neck to the point that you must grind it to make it fit. Remember, though, that you can safely use very considerable force on the action, especially with a bolt action gun. The removal of the bullet will have removed the danger of damage to the gun or to you, even if the cartridge fires.

Discard the bullet or the shot. Dump all but a small part of the powder into a prepared base of tinder and fuel. Tear a small piece of cotton cloth, pulp this by pounding or fraying, and twist it loosely into the cartridge or shell. Chamber the cartridge or shell, point the gun muzzle straight up, and pull the trigger. The cloth will be ignited and blown into the air, and its flight will fan the flames. Scoop up the blazing cloth and use it to light the powder mixed with the tinder. Repeat the process if necessary, this time twisting a little powder into the cloth.

This often works very well with a shotgun or large-caliber rifle or pistol, but it will not work dependably with a small-caliber weapon. It will not work at all if it is raining, snowing, or very windy, or when your hands are too stiff and clumsy from cold to do all this. *Carry matches and tinder!*

You can start a fire with a bow and drill. You need a bow, a fireboard, a drill, and a socket. You will also need an uncommon lot of luck! The wood for the drill must be nonresinous and bone-dry softwood such as aspen, cedar, cottonwood, juniper, larch, tamarack, willow, or yucca. You must find it when you need it and you must have enough remaining energy and manual dexterity to do the tedious and time-consuming work. One drop of water or one vagrant gust of wind will spell defeat and possible death. *Carry waterproof matches and tinder!*

Make a fireboard from a piece of one of the woods listed above that can be split or whittled to make a flat spot near one end. It must be at least two or three inches wide, an inch or more thick after being shaped, and at least eighteen inches long. Use the point of a knife or a pointed stone to start a half-inch-wide hole an inch or so from one edge. Cut an undercut, **V**-shaped notch in and through the edge of the board, with the point of the **V** cutting the side of the hole. The hole needs to be just deep enough to house the taper of the drill. Finish the hole by grinding with the drill, shaping both at the same time. The notch and hole will look much like a keyhole for a skeleton key.

Make the drill about one-half to three-quarters of an inch in diameter and a foot or more long. Taper the small end to not more than a quarter inch in size, round it, and polish it as smoothly as you can. Make a blunt and shallow taper on the other end. Make the drill six- or eight-faceted where the string is to run and remove all projections or rough spots that might fray or damage the string.

Make a socket from a knot, a chunk of wood, or a smooth rock that has an indentation on one side. This is used as a bearing to hold the top of the spinning drill, and you should lubricate it if at all possible. The graphite (lead) of a pencil is perfect for this, and you can rub it with a lead-tipped bullet, instead. A bit of animal fat or the wax from your ear will serve. Even the oil obtained by rubbing the drill tip against the side of your nose or through your hair will help, and a bit of pine gum rubbed into the upper drill tip will form a glaze that will help reduce friction. *Do not use water as a lubricant!*

You can make a bow from a springy green branch, making it in conventional bow shape and not less than two feet long, but it is far better to make a more or less triangular bow from the trunk and limb of a bush or sapling. Either cut grooves for the string or drill holes for it if you have a knife with a reamer. The hole is far superior to a groove, especially on the handle end.

Use a bootlace, fishline, raveled threads twisted into string, or any other flexible cord for a bowstring. You cannot use wire, as it would quickly break from metal fatigue. As the string will often stretch during use, a means of tightening it is essential; several methods are shown in Figure 8.

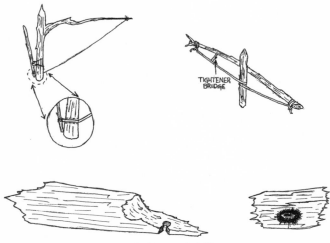

Figure 8: Bow and drill

Tie the bowstring to one end of the bow, loop it once around the drill, and tie it to the other end, keeping it as tight as you can. Kneel on the right knee and plant the left foot firmly and solidly on the fireboard to keep it from moving about. Place a wad of tinder under the notch, putting it on a piece of foil, plastic, bark, or wood so the tinder can be moved without being scattered. Drop a few grains of sand or gritty charcoal from a burned log or stump into the hole to increase friction. (This is helpful, but not necessary.) Set the large end of the drill in the hole and put the socket atop the drill, holding it in your left hand and resting the left forearm on the bent left knee to steady your hand. Take the bow in your right hand and start moving it in steady, back-and-forth sweeps that are as long as the string will permit. (You must reverse these directions if left handed.)

Once begun, the motion must be maintained at a steady pace; and the pressure on the socket must be as high as you can make it without slowing the speed of the drill. As the drill spins, its lower end will generate a great deal of heat, and both the drill end and the surface of the hole will begin to blacken. Heat will continue to build up as the friction continues, and carbonized dust will spill through the notch onto the tinder below. When the friction area and the tinder pile are smoking, speed up the bow action, increase the pressure on the socket, or both. A few seconds of this and you should see an actual glow of fire in the blackened dust heaped on the tinder.

When you are certain that such a glow is real and not just a wishful thought, lay the bow and drill aside, move the fireboard, and pick up the chip or whatever with its load of tinder. Gently fold the tinder over and around the smoldering area and carefully blow on it or fan it into flame. Use it to light your prepared fuel.

This will work very well if all goes right, but you may die if it doesn't! *Carry matches and tinder!*

Another friction fire starter is the fire plough. Make a fireboard as before, but somewhat longer and with no notch or drill hole. Using a knife or a pointed rock, make a long, straight, longitudinal, shallow groove in the flattened area. This groove must be eight to twelve inches long and about half an inch deep, and it must run to the end of the fireboard. Select and shape a stick of one of the listed materials. It must be ten to twelve inches long and half an inch or more in diameter. Cut the small end at a near forty-five degree angle, round the large end, and cover it with a cloth pad to protect your hand.

To use, kneel on both knees with the fireboard clamped between the knees with the grooved end projecting forward. Grasp the plough in your left hand (if right handed) with the thumb and forefinger encircling it just below the pad. Cup the palm of the right hand over the pad and your left hand. Bearing down firmly with both hands, start sliding the beveled end of the plough back and forth in the groove with as much speed as you think you can maintain.

The sliding plough will generate enough heat to blacken and carbonize its own end and the surface of the groove. The toe will then begin to grind out a blackened powder and deposit it on tinder placed beneath the open end of the groove. Continued friction will produce sufficient heat to start a glowing spark in the dust.

Carefully add tiny shreds of tinder to this dust pile and carefully and gently fan or blow the fire to greater life. You can do this without moving from your position, and this enables you to resume the friction process without delay if you fail to achieve fire on your first attempt.

You can start a fire with an electrical spark if stranded by a broken-down or disabled gasoline-powered vehicle.

With a battery, simply touch a wire that leads from one battery post to a wire leading to the other post, or touch any hot wire to vehicle metal. *Do not short directly from post to post!* Batteries produce hydrogen gas, and you could touch off an explosion.

You can also use a spark plug or spark plug wire to generate sparks. Brace or block a wire so that it is nearly but not quite in touch with the vehicle metal. Lay the metal body of a spark plug in solid contact with such metal. With a magneto-fired or electronic ignition system, you must then turn on the ignition and crank the engine to produce sparks. With a distributor, you can remove the cap, pull the secondary (large) coil wire from its central turret, and hold the end of the wire near the metal. Remove the distributor rotor and work the ignition points by hand. Each time you open the points (with the ignition on), the wire will produce a tremendously hot spark. This will work even if the battery is too weak to crank the engine.

For tinder in such a situation, use a rag tied to a stiff wire or a slender wand. Dip it in the fuel tank to soak it with gasoline. Be careful when you light it, as it will light almost explosively. If you are planning to leave the car to set up camp, take some gasoline with you if at all possible, as you cannot find or devise any tinder as good.

A car's cigarette lighter will light anything flammable, and is almost as good as a match. Any fire lighted by one of these emergency methods will then have to be carried to your campsite if you leave the vehicle. Matches are still your best choice!

You can easily start a fire with a burning or magnifying glass when the sun is shining, and such glasses are easily improvised from binocular, camera, or telescopic sight lenses. A single lens reflex (SLR) camera can also be used. Open the back of the camera and remove the film, then turn the shutter speed selection to the bulb setting. When you trip the shutter, it will remain open; and you can use the whole camera as a burning glass. Most SLR cameras have a lens that can be removed without damaging either camera or lens, however; and detaching the lens does not risk damaging the film.

It is also possible to cut a piece of crystal-clear ice to proper shape (flat or concave on one side, strongly convex on the other), and to polish it by melting or smoothing with the hands. The sun in winter is so low in the sky that the lens must be held far to one side of the tinder, and any melt water produced by your "glass" will not drip on that tinder.

The problem with depending on a burning glass is that the sun is seldom shining when you most need fire. A burning glass will help you conserve your matches, but is no real substitute for them. *Carry matches and tinder!*

You can actually start a fire with two flashlight batteries and a steel wool pad, such as the Brillo pad you might carry to clean cooking gear. Hold the two batteries firmly in series, just as they fit in a flashlight. Tease a thin strip of steel wool by pulling gently. Hold one end of the strip firmly against the base of the bottom battery and stroke the other end against the top battery post. When a spark glows brightly, blow briskly on it to give it much greater life. The spark will expand to a red-hot mass that will give off intense heat. This will not last long, but long enough to enable you to light a prepared fire stack with it.

Each of these emergency means of starting fires will work when conditions are exactly right, but none is certain to work when you most need fire. It is often very difficult to build a fire in stormy situations, even with adequate tinder and matches. Try each of these methods of fire starting in your own back yard when the weather is bad, so you can retreat to safety when they fail to work. You will then never again venture afield without more certain means of starting fires! *Always carry matches!*

As with matches, so it is with tinder. You can find usable tinder of many kinds in summer when everything is dry. You might also find some in winter; but you might not. Unless you are in paperbark birch country, you are most unlikely to find any when you need it and when you have neither the time nor the energy to waste searching for it. Having a supply of instantly available tinder in a pocket or emergency kit might then spell the difference between life and death. *Carry tinder!*

If you have no prepared tinder and everything is covered with snow or is dripping wet, don't give up. There are always a few places where dry materials can be found. Packrat and woodrat nests may look like ungainly mounds of twigs, cones, and other forest debris dumped haphazardly, but the lower parts of these mounds are always dry. Somewhere near the center of the dry area is a nest of dried grass or other soft, fibrous material, and this is highly flammable. You are also likely to find a goodly store of nuts, seeds, or other such food secreted in a snug pantry chamber.

Other spots likely to produce dry tinder in all weathers are burned or rotted hollows in the base of trees, the undersides of partially rotted or burned logs where these are free of contact with the ground, conifer needles or deciduous leaves where these have been protected by an overhanging ledge, and the inner surfaces of hollow logs. It is also possible to find "fat pine" or pitchy wood in stumps, logs, or the knots of rotted logs.

It is vitally important that you not attempt to start a fire until the fuel necessary to maintain that fire has been assembled. You often see would-be outdoor types assemble the necessary tinder, ignite it by whatever means, and only then begin a frantic search for fuel. All too often the fire expires before the fuel is found and brought to it. Always make it a point to have everything in readiness before striking a match or making any further attempt to ignite the tinder. The sole exception to this would be when you need to use tinder alone to warm cold-numbed hands.

The *Boy Scout Handbook* and most books on outdoor skills list a number of different types of "fire lay." The most useful of these, in my opinion, for warming fires or for starting fires in bad weather is the "teepee lay." The kindling is stacked in teepee fashion with an opening on one side, and the tinder is placed inside. Larger and larger pieces of fuel are leaned around the outside. When the tinder is ignited, the flames rise up through the narrowing cone; and the teepee walls both protect against drafts and reflect the heat back and forth, just as in a furnace combustion chamber. Once the fire has reached respectable size, you can lean damp or green wood against the stack to be dried and to form a heat reflector.

Whatever the tinder and the means of ignition, and no matter what fire lay you choose, a blowpipe will be of help. This can be anything from a soda straw to a large grass or weed stem, but you can also use the rubber tubing from your emergency kit. I use a four-inch piece of quarter-inch copper tubing, flattened on one end, on the fire end of this rubber blowpipe. By blowing through such a tube, you can concentrate oxygen exactly where it is needed and can nicely regulate the force at the point of delivery. This is especially valuable when blowing a spark into a flame. Another advantage to using a blowpipe is that you can keep your face well out of the smoke.

The well-prepared user of the outdoors should also know more about fires than simply how to start them.

Chapter XI

Fire Know-How

You must not build your fire where snow from a tree, a bank, or an overhanging ledge can fall or slide to bury it, or where its heat will cause melt water to drip on or run under it at any volume. A little dripping is sometimes unavoidable and will do no damage if the fire is of a good size before the melting starts.

It is nearly impossible to build a fire on a really wet surface, and this is especially so if this is an absorbent material such as dirt or wood. If you have a piece of foil in your emergency kit (and you should!), spread this over the wet surface. The foil will both reflect heat upward through the wood of the fire stack and prevent steam from rising through that stack. If you have no foil, use the driest and least absorbent material you can find for a base.

A fire built directly on snow or ice will quickly melt its way down and drown itself in the melt water produced. Build a fire on a rock or stump that projects above snow level if possible, or make a platform of green or dry logs or bark covered with dirt. Do not use a layer of small rocks, as these will heat quickly and melt their way down. If the ground is bare but frozen, make a platform of either green or dry wood and build the fire on this. The wood will be wetted by the thawing ground and will not burn until both it and the ground under it are dry.

Wood burns only when it is heated to its kindling point, and this differs with each kind of wood and with its condition.

Moisture in or on the wood serves both to raise the kindling point and to absorb and carry off much of the heat you are trying to concentrate on that wood. It matters not whether this moisture is sap naturally contained in green wood or is water absorbed by dead wood. Damp or green wood is useful only on a very hot fire or when used to keep a fire burning slowly over an extended time. Ash, birch, cassiope, and certain other species of trees and shrubs burn as well when green as when dry; but these are exceptions to the norm.

Use standing dead wood and the dead limbs that grow from the bottoms of evergreen trees when you can. The bark from most dead evergreen trees and logs makes splendid fuel once you have a good fire going, but it is not good for starting fires. The thin, hard bark from dead hemlock or from white fir logs is almost as good as charcoal for producing a lot of heat and little flame; and the thicker bark from Douglas fir has actually been used in place of charcoal in forges.

It does little good to list the comparative values of different trees or shrubs for fuel. You will have to make do with those found in your area. Suffice it to say that most hardwoods burn hotter and produce more lasting coals than most softwoods (these are botanical terms and do not denote actual texture or density of wood); that resinous softwoods such as pines, firs, Douglas fir, etc., produce more soot and throw more sparks than other woods; and that the slower-growing and harder the wood, the better it normally is for fuel.

Sagebrush, chaparral, and greasewood found in arid areas of the West make splendid fuel, but the fire must be kept tiny if one person is to keep it supplied with fuel. The sagebrush is one of those woods that "keep one man chopping, two men toting, and one man stoking" to keep a good-sized fire going. Most other brushwood is nearly as bad, for the small-diameter pieces of dry hardwood burn very rapidly.

The easiest way to collect wood for fuel is to gather "squaw wood." This consists of dead limbs attached to standing trees or downed logs and of whatever bark, small logs, limbs, wood chunks, or other burnable wood product that is both readily at hand and obtainable without the use of tools. Remember that wood that has been lying directly on the ground is probably damp, at least in all but midsummer.

Do not waste energy by trying to break limbs or poles into burnable lengths if your fire is built outside a shelter where space is no problem. Instead, lay the pole or limb across the fire so that it will be burned into two pieces, repeating as necessary. An alternative to this is the so-called "Indian fire." In this method, poles are placed with one end in the fire and with the other pointing outward, the outward ends radiating to form a half or three-quarter circle. The missing quadrant allows access. These poles are then shoved inward as the tips burn off.

It is often possible to build a fire against a large stump or log that will itself burn, and by judicious use of smaller fuel to keep this burning for several days. If you use your shelter only at night, such a fire can be the center of your daytime activities, and it can serve to keep a fire going while you are out checking traps, building signals, and so forth.

Animal dung (from grass eaters), twisted grass, peat moss, dry cattail leaves—are all burnable. Animal fat makes a usable fuel, too, although use of it can make a camp smell like Dogpatch's Skonk Rendering Works! You can burn this fat by placing it in a shallow container with a wick (a slush lamp) or by draping thin strips over a pyramid of bones or an open fretwork of rocks and building a hot fire under this. The melted fat will run down over the bones or rocks and will burn, producing some heat, a great deal of sputtering, and still more stench.

A fire for cooking and a fire for heating a shelter should both be as small as they can be and still accomplish their purpose. Do not build a roaring bonfire unless you are on the verge of hypothermia and need to develop a great deal of heat in the shortest possible time or unless you are using the fire as a signal. Such fires are wasteful both of fuel and the energy used to gather it. Some long-ago Indian is reported to have said, "White man build heap big fire, stand way back. Injun build small fire, get heap close." The Indian was the wiser man; emulate him!

A rock-lined firepit will help both to contain a fire and to concentrate the heat where it is most needed or wanted. *Do not use streambed or other wet-area rocks to build this!* You can make all sorts of arrangements for cooking over this, can use one end for a fireless cooker, and can bank live coals under a heavy blanket of ashes to preserve fire-starting coals for a considerable time.

The coastal Indians of the Pacific Northwest used cedar bark torches to light their cabins and maintain fire over a long period of time. Bark from cypress, juniper, yew, sagebrush, and cliffrose will work as well; and grasses, peat moss, tree moss, and other similar material can be used. The Indians used finely shredded or pounded cedar bark as the central core of the torch, surrounding this with parallel splints to form a tube, and wrapping this with thinner bark laid in overlapping, helically-wound layers. When the shredded bark was lit, it would burn with a low, flickering flame that would last for twenty-four to forty-eight hours, depending upon the size of the torch. Most were made in a diameter of four to six inches, were from two to more than four feet long, and weighed as much as fifty pounds. Such a torch is too heavy to be easily portable.

Another traditional way of preserving fire over a long period is by the use of punk. This can be fluffy rotted wood, the dried pith of weeds or shrubs, dried or powdered manure, or the dust left by wood-boring insects. To use punk, you must burn it in a tightly enclosed space, allowing just enough air to keep the fire slowly smoldering. A hollow bone, a seashell, or even a hollow piece of wood will work; but you'll have to line the wood with mud to keep it from burning. You can even mold a hollow ball out of mud, then cradle this in a sling made of cloth, woven vegetation, or animal skin for carrying or hanging.

Another way to preserve your fire-making ability is to take steps to protect an ample supply of dry wood and kindling. *Do not neglect this!* Nothing can be more discouraging and disheartening than to wake to find the immediate environment, including all available fuel, has been sheathed in a layer of ice by a freezing rain or is buried under a fresh blanket of snow. A supply of dry wood and of bone-dry prepared tinder and kindling can then literally be a lifesaver.

Use a sled to transport fuel whenever possible, as this uses less energy than carrying it. When you have exhausted the readily available fuel within the area, move the camp to a new supply rather than transport the fuel to your existing camp. Do not build a too-elaborate camp at the new location if the fuel supply there is again inadequate for an extended stay.

You must not build a fire where the fire or its coals can fall or slide into contact with your bedding, your clothing, or any part of your shelter if this is constructed of flammable materials. Everyone knows how flammable dry grasses, dead leaves, or dry pine needles are. Few seem to know that evergreen boughs are also highly flammable after several days of drying and become almost explosively so after a week or two. Fire is the largest single cause of injury in wintertime camping, and an emergency camp is no less vulnerable than a recreational one. Be extremely careful unless your shelter is constructed of flameproof or hard-to-ignite materials.

Carbon monoxide is an ever-present and deadly threat whenever a fire burns in an enclosed area! The gas is produced when a fire is deprived of sufficient oxygen or is smothered in its own by-products. It is prevented by adequate ventilation. *Let fresh air in; let smoke out!*

Carbon monoxide (CO) is colorless, odorless, tasteless, and non-irritating, and cannot be detected by human senses. Its victims normally remain unaware of the threat until they are helpless, unable to take any remedial action. Indeed, most victims die without a struggle, without ever realizing that a problem exists.

The CO molecules combine with hemoglobin, the oxygen transporter of the blood, in the exact same proportion as would oxygen. (Actually, the hemoglobin shows a distinct preference for the carbon monoxide, choosing it over equally available oxygen.) This creates a stable compound known as carboxyhemoglobin, and this compound causes the bright-red blood and the dark-red skin color that is diagnostic in its victims. The effect is cumulative and death results when a total of one and a half quarts of the pure gas has been inhaled in a brief period. Lesser amounts can cause severe and lasting brain damage.

Take no chances with this insidious killer! Maintain adequate ventilation at all times. If in doubt, over-ventilate. It is much better to be chilled than killed! If you even suspect that the shelter atmosphere has become dangerous, get outside, fast! Breathe deeply of fresh, clean air for a period of not less than fifteen minutes. When you feel completely alert, take steps to purge the shelter of its noxious atmosphere and to improve the ventilation. Most of this work can be done from outside the shelter.

Chapter XII

Dehydration

The need for water is greatest when the air is very dry and the ambient temperature is high, but you must have water even in the wettest and coldest of weather. You lose water every time you exhale (dry air in, moist air out); moisture is lost through the skin even when you aren't sweating (insensible perspiration); and approximately one and a half quarts are excreted on a daily basis. The total daily loss amounts to a minimum of two and a half quarts, and this loss is greatly increased by high temperatures and exertion.

The body manufactures a quart or so of water by digesting food, but this still leaves a daily deficit of one to one and a half quarts that must be made up by drinking fluids or by eating water-containing foods. These amounts will suffice only if you stay out of the direct sunlight and stay as quiet and relaxed as you can. Failure to supply these demands will bring on dehydration. Wind will hasten its onset by speeding evaporation.

The earliest sign of dehydration is an intense and growing thirst, caused by a drying of the inner surfaces of the mouth and throat. The discomfort of this can be somewhat to largely alleviated by holding a small pebble or even a button in the mouth or by chewing gum. You can also reduce the drying of these surfaces by keeping the mouth closed. These expedients will relieve the symptoms but will do nothing to eliminate the underlying cause.

A Handbook for Wilderness Survival

If ambient temperatures are high or if you are exerting yourself, your body must rid itself of the heat being absorbed or generated. The external veins will dilate so excess heat can be exchanged with the atmosphere. If air temperature is above 99 degrees Fahrenheit (body temperature is 98.6 degrees), no heat can be exchanged and body temperature will rise. When internal body temperature rises to 99 degrees, you will begin to perspire profusely. This is an effort by the body to cool itself by evaporation, and it is highly effective when the air is very dry or when the wind is blowing. The problem is that this mechanism is venting water to the atmosphere and increasing dehydration.

If internal temperature still continues to rise, your heart will accelerate and the rate of perspiration will increase. Your face will become flushed, your pulse rate will become rapid and erratic, and your breathing will become labored and harsh. Unless the lost water is then replaced, you will begin to make silly and irrational decisions, just as in hypothermia.

The water contained within the cells will begin to migrate through the cell walls to the area between the cells and all bodily processes will begin to slow down. The blood will begin to thicken and the kidneys will attempt to compensate for the lack of water by concentrating the urine, which will become very thick and cloudy. Water will be withdrawn from the contents of the stomach and intestines and all digestive functions will cease. Toxic by-products of life processes will accumulate.

If the lost water is still not replaced, you will become dizzy and begin to lose muscular control, and you will become nauseated. Vomiting, if successful, will increase water loss. You will then be very close to heat exhaustion and death, and the danger of a heart attack will be very real. You will have almost reached the point of no return, where you become unable to help yourself in any way. *If the body is not then cooled and the lost water replaced, you will soon die!*

It is possible to reach this point in one day! The air temperature of many of the drier parts of our continent regularly reaches between one hundred and one hundred and ten degrees in summer, and much higher temperatures are sometimes encountered. These temperatures are recorded in the shade, and it is much hotter in direct sunlight. An egg will fry on a rock under such conditions!

Water loss can be held to a minimum if you seek shelter from the sun and heat during the hottest part of the day. Take a lesson from the Arabs, who keep themselves fully covered with loose-fitting clothing to prevent both sunburn and evaporation of skin moisture. The shade of a rock, a bush, or a cutbank is often adequate as shelter, but you can make a parasol of brush, cloth, or grass if you must.

When stranded by a stalled or stuck vehicle and no shade is available within reachable distance, use the car as shade. The shadow under the car will be total, and the roof and seats will prevent the floor of the car from becoming hot enough to radiate significant heat. Open all windows and doors and the hood and the trunk lid to allow for maximum air circulation, then get under the car if you can.

You can increase clearance by either removing dirt to make a trench or by jacking the car up. If you use a jack, do not then get under the car without securely blocking the car in raised position, using a spare tire, rocks, mounded dirt, or anything else solid enough to keep the car from crushing you if the jack is displaced. If you cannot create enough clearance, stay on the shady side of the car. *Never stay in the car itself!* The air in the car will be much hotter than the air outside, even with the windows and doors open.

The temperature at the surface of the ground is much hotter than the temperature a foot below it, and the bottom of a two-foot-deep trench will be as much as fifty degrees cooler. Dig a trench in an east-west direction and heap the sand or dirt along the south side. Use a hub cap to dig a trench if stranded by a car. Do not attempt to dig during the heat of the day or under direct sunlight, as the extra heat caused by the exertion might well be enough to cause prostration and death. Instead, dig the trench well after sundown or before sunup and only when the dirt or sand is loose and easy to move. In sand, of course, you must be alert to the danger of a cave-in.

If lost or stranded, be sure to leave a conspicuous marker of some kind in a prominent place near your ditch! If you neglect this, a searcher might pass near by without either of you knowing the other is near.

Do not eat during periods of critical water shortage, as the food will absorb water from the system and will not be digested in any case. Make an exception to this rule for foods such as soups or canned foods with a high water content.

Do not attempt to severely ration a limited supply of water. Water in the canteen does not prevent dehydration. Only water taken into the body can do that. Many persons have died of dehydration with water still in their canteens! Use water sparingly, but drink what you need when you need it. Your life will not depend solely on rationing water, but upon being found, making your way out, or finding water.

The body of an average man, weighing approximately one hundred fifty pounds, contains about ninety pounds of water. You must lose only slightly more than one tenth of your total water to die of dehydration, and for this man this amounts to only a little more than a gallon! The normal daily water deficit, with neither high temperatures nor excessive sweating, is about one and a half quarts; and if you do not manufacture water by the digestion of food, it is about two and a half quarts! The difference between the actual and the maximum sustainable loss represents your margin of survival, and you must make every effort to prevent excessive loss.

You must also replace that basic loss and make up that deficit by consuming at least that amount of water daily.

Chapter XIII

Water

You will have little trouble finding safe water in the mountains in winter and spring. You may find water in the summer or fall as well, but you will generally not know whether or not that water is fit to drink. Water is seldom poisonous, but it may be so grossly polluted as to be just as dangerous; and it is often so full of minerals that it causes severe digestive upset to those not accustomed to it. Some waters harbor harmful parasites. Water found in desert country is almost always of doubtful quality, quite regardless of season.

Never drink water if you are doubtful of its purity! This must be understood to apply with equal force to the use of water in any way that might allow it to enter your body. Don't use it to wash your hands before handling food unless that food is to be thoroughly cooked. Don't use it to wash dishes or cooking utensils unless those are to then be immersed in boiling water for several minutes, not just wiped dry. Don't use it for making tea or coffee unless you allow it to cook at a rolling boil for at least five minutes. Improper use of impure water may make you gravely ill, may cause your death directly, or may render you helpless so you may die of other and unrelated causes. *If in doubt, purify!*

Make germ-polluted or parasite-infested water safe by boiling it for at least five minutes (at really high altitudes, boiling will not reliably purify water unless a pressure cooker is used; but water found there is less likely to be contaminated), by the use of halzone or iodine tablets, or by distillation. Of these methods, only distillation will significantly change the mineral content of the water.

When using halzone or iodine tablets, follow the directions on the label. Double the number of tablets, the time before drinking, or both if the water is obviously polluted. Two drops of tincture of iodine will replace one iodine tablet. When using such chemicals to purify water, make sure to wet all parts that may come into contact with either the water or the mouth (canteen cap, threads, cup, etc.) with the treated water and do not then use for the prescribed time.

You can completely purify water with a solar still. Such a still will even "create" water by extracting it from seemingly dry soils. You need a square of transparent, wettable plastic film such as polyethylene to make a still. You should have such a piece in your emergency kit. It folds almost as small as a cigarette package and weighs little more, yet has a hundred uses. Use it as a windbreak, a waterproof lean-to, a blanket, a water catcher, a shelter liner, a ground sheet, or even as an emergency poncho or raincoat. Its greatest potential value, however, is as a solar still that will either supply water where no water exists or purify and demineralize bad water.

Dig a conical hole about eighteen inches deep and three feet or so in diameter. The site should be in the lowest spot available, as that is most likely to be damp. The sandy or muddy bottom of a recently dried up watercourse or pond is ideal. Place a catchment container in the bottom center of this hole, or line a bowl-shaped depression with plastic if you have no container. Place one end of the surgical tubing from your emergency kit in the container and anchor the other end well out of the pit. Lay the plastic sheet loosely over the pit, then push the center down to form a cone-shaped depression with its bottom just above the container. Weight the

edges with dirt and rocks to make an airtight seal. Place a
fist-sized smooth rock in the center of the cone to keep the
plastic stretched tight. This cone will also trap small mammals and lizards. (See Figure 9.)

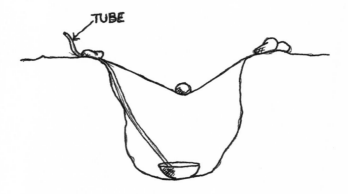

Figure 9: Solar still

The sun shining through the transparent plastic will heat
the air beneath it by its greenhouse effect, and this superheated air will suck moisture from the soil. As the then
moist and heated air comes in contact with the cooler plastic
film, it will deposit part of its moisture in a fine layer of condensation. With a wettable surface, this condensate will run
down the plastic and drip from the point of the cone into the
waiting container.

It takes from one to as many as three hours for a still to
begin producing water, this depending on the angle of the
sun, the temperature of the air, and the amount of moisture
in the soil. Each time you break into the still to procure its
collected water, you break the seal; and all of the super-

heated atmosphere escapes. It will then take nearly as long for the still to resume production as it took to first start it. With a tube running from the container to a point outside the still, you can suck water from it without in any way disturbing the seal.

One such still will produce several pints of water a day from a seemingly dry soil, and you can greatly increase this amount by lining or partially filling the pit with chunks of cactus, succulent, nontoxic weeds, or green grasses and leaves. You can even soak the soil of the pit with poisonous, polluted, or highly mineralized water, and will then recover pure distilled water in almost the original volume. *Do not allow even one drop of dangerous water to touch the inner surface of the plastic or the inside of the catchment container!*

Do not attempt to distill water from body wastes, from car radiator or battery water, or from unknown plants. Each of these either does or may contain poisonous or harmful substances that are more volatile than water, and distillation would only concentrate these substances.

If you have no plastic but need to purify poisonous or mineralized water, you can do so by boiling the water and collecting the steam. Boil the water by fencing off or digging a small pool if you have no pot. Dump enough hot rocks (do not heat rocks that have been in or near the water!) in it to bring it to a boil. Cover your "pot" with a thick pad of cloth, dry grass, or any other absorbent and nontoxic material held well clear of the water. As this material collects steam, wring it into a container or into your mouth.

Water is polluted by animals, by man, and by decay of vegetation, but only pollution by man and, to a lesser extent, by animals is dangerous. An exception to this is any species of water hemlock, *Cicuta,* which can actually poison animals or men when its underwater parts are injured as by livestock trampling and release their toxins to the water. Rotting plant material will discolor water and will render that water more or less distasteful and malodorous, but it will not ordinarily make the water unsafe for use.

If the water is unpleasantly colored or strong smelling, you can largely eliminate these objectional qualities by filtering the water through layers of charcoal. Pick out the blackest chunks of charcoal from a campfire and use these. *Do not use ashes!* Water and ashes together make lye, a strong caustic solution. You can strain out large particles or organisms by making a cone-shaped filter of grass or similar vegetation, or by filtering the water through a layer of sand. *None of these makeshifts will purify germ-polluted water or significantly affect its mineral content!*

Rain is distilled water and is perfectly safe to use *if the catchment surface or container is not contaminated.* Snow is also distilled water and is safe to use if not visibly contaminated. Crusty or long-compacted snow contains much more water by volume than fresh or fluffy snow. Do not eat snow when low on food or when body heat conditions are marginal because of its chilling effect. Melt it instead and take the chill off the resulting water. Snow makes water available throughout the area of the snowfall and ends all questions of water purity until the last drift has melted.

When melting snow for water, do not put fluffy snow into a pot and place this over high heat, as you can actually scorch the pot! Put a small quantity of snow in the pot and place this near but not on the fire. When the pot's bottom is covered with liquid water, you can then fill it with snow and expose it to direct flame.

Ice normally contains every impurity that was in the water before it froze, although sea ice tends to lose salt as it ages. If you have ever nibbled or sucked on an icicle after breaking it from the eaves of a house, you have noticed the distinct flavor of tar that permeates it. That this flavor may have owed some of its tang to bird droppings and other such exotic elements never seemed to perturb me or my compatriots when I was a child. Ice, like snow, should not be used to quench thirst. Melt, heat, and treat as you would water from the same source.

Many cacti contain juices that can be squeezed or sucked from the pulp, but this is by no means the equivalent of spring water! No cactus is toxic, but taste ranges from almost good to nauseating. Most cactus plants dehydrate to some extent in continued drought conditions, too, and this source is vastly overrated in most books. Don't count on finding sufficient water to supply your needs by chopping up cactus in summer or early fall unless you are using a solar still to extract it. Cactus plants from a low, damp area will be both extremely large and very succulent; and they will indeed yield useful quantities of glue-like juice that will sustain life. I have no experience with *Bisnaga*s, the several types of barrel cactus, which are most often cited as emergency sources of water.

You are often told how to extract water from grapevines, but you are never told how limited is the range of wild grapes or how unlikely you are to find them in arid or waterless areas. The only advantage grapevines offer is that the juice is perfectly safe to use even when all of the surface water is contaminated, stagnant, or highly mineralized. Extract the juice by cutting a deep notch in a thick vine as high up as you can reach. When you then sever the vine at ground level, all of the sap in the section below the notch will drain out. Stand the cut ends of several such sections in a trough of bark and put your container under the low end. An alternate method in spring is to cut off the tips of some of the new canes and bring the cut ends into a bundle above your container. This is less destructive of the vines than cutting the older trunks.

The body fluids of temperate zone fish are drinkable, but this source will be of use to you only if stranded on a boat or island surrounded by salt water. Even then, if the means were at hand, distillation of the salt water would be a better choice than using the juices of raw fish. If you have to use such juices, put pieces of cut fish into a shirt sleeve or a pant leg and wring it as tightly as you can.

You are often told how to locate water by digging. You must not try this unless you find a spot that is very damp or wet or find an obvious catchment basin in the bottom of a recently dried up watercourse. If such spots are sandy and are very damp or wet within a foot of the surface, then water will be found within two or three feet. In gravel, the water is far more apt to be at a depth of ten feet than two, and digging to such a depth, especially without tools, would probably kill you from increased water loss long before you reached it.

Bees of any kind (this includes yellow jackets, hornets, and wasps) indicate nearby water, usually within less than a mile. To find their source of water, "line" the bees, just as you would to find a honey tree. Simply follow the flight of a bee as long as you can, then go to the spot where you last saw it and repeat the process with the next bee. If the bee is flying a straight course rather than bumbling about in apparent aimlessness, it is flying either to its nest or to water. If you find the hive instead of water, simply line the largest number of outbound bees to find their waterhole.

Deer, antelope, cattle, wild horses, and other large animals must have water to live, and in hot weather these animals like to drink every day. Fortunately for the waterless survivor, these animals are all creatures of habit, tending to follow definite trails as they go to or return from their watering places. These trails will merge into larger and larger trails as they near water, and the junctions will be **Y**-shaped, just as with roads. Again as with roads, the main stem will be the way to go; for the trails branch as the animals go away from water and come together as they go to water.

Quail and chukar indicate water within a mile or two. In some cases this water will be a "guzzler" provided by the wildlife agency of the state or province. These underground tanks or cisterns are fed by a catchment apron and so arranged that the birds can reach the water but large animals cannot.

Small desert-dwelling animals from mice to jackrabbits do not need water to survive, and their presence does not indicate water. These plant-eating animals manufacture water by digesting the carbohydrates they use as food, and the small carnivores that prey on them get all necessary fluids by eating their flesh and drinking their blood. That blood is a useful substitute for water for you as well.

Watch the weather! Desert areas are sometimes drenched by torrential thunder showers, and you can often see such storms for many miles. *Stay out of deep gullies or canyons when such storms are visible!* A storm miles away can fill such depressions in a matter of minutes, and nothing could be more ridiculous than to drown while seeking water!

If it looks as as if it might rain in your area, prepare some means of catching water. Lay out a sheet of plastic or other material to make a pool or a trough to channel water into any containers you have. Dam a gully with dirt to hold runoff water. Knot a shirt around a rock or a tree trunk in such fashion that water running down the trunk will drip from one point only. Lay out cloth to be soaked so you can wring it over a container. Don't wait until the rain starts to make your preparations. Desert storms are soon over and desert soil is thirsty. Have everything in readiness when the first drops fall.

Water tends to flow downhill, of course, and in doing so it cuts and carves the hardest rock. That distant thunderstorm will have filled numerous depressions if in rocky country, and some of these "tanks" will retain water for days or even weeks. In such cases, it is wise to ignore the usual rule for finding water and to even go uphill to the area of the storm.

Nights are usually cool to actually cold in the desert, even in midsummer, and the metal surfaces of a car, some rocks, and smooth-surfaced vegetation such as grasses become chilled to the dewpoint on some occasions. You can collect this moisture by wiping it off these surfaces (you should have wiped them clean earlier) or by mopping it off the grass. To mop efficiently, tie floppy rags or twisted bundles of dry grass around your feet and shuffle through the grass to saturate the material. Wring the water into a container. Continue until the sun has risen and the dew has largely evaporated.

Conspicuous green vegetation in an otherwise arid landscape is almost a sure sign of water either on or very close to the surface. Very large cottonwood trees in such areas are certain indicators of water. Greasewood is much greener than sagebrush but is not as vivid a green as cottonwood, and it only indicates alkaline water fairly close to the surface. A twisting line of green vegetation along a canyon floor indicates a stream course, but the vegetation will continue to thrive after surface water has dried up. Following such streambeds for any considerable distance downstream will usually lead to small pools or to still wet places where water can be obtained with a minimum of digging or with a solar still.

The tailings or abandoned buildings of worked-out mines normally (but not invariably) indicate water, either in the tunnels themselves or somewhere nearby. The water will often be so full of drowned insects, lizards, snakes, and small mammals as to be undrinkable, but it will still be wet; and you can purify it by one of the methods described. A search of such sites will often turn up bottles or other usable containers that can be used to carry a supply of water if you choose to take the mine access road.

Be in no hurry to do so! If in desert or largely waterless country, it is not always wise to leave a water source you have found. You can obviously be rescued from that spot as easily as from any other, and you are far more likely to survive to be rescued if you remain by a dependable water supply. In addition to the water itself, such spots also provide a source of food, as both plants and animals will be more concentrated there.

When you find or reach a plentiful supply of water after a period of dehydration, do not drink all the water you want immediately. Stop after a few sips, wait for a time, then sip some more. Too-rapid intake of water will cause violent nausea, and in some cases will bring on what amounts to a severe case of heat prostration.

It takes hours or even days for the contents of the stomach and intestines to absorb enough water for normal function to resume, and you should not be alarmed by a temporary lack of bowel activity. Indeed, it is often found that attempted bowel movement during the first twenty-four to thirty-six hours results in the passage of large quantities of almost-clear water. Do not take medicines or laxatives, as the problem will cure itself when the water balance of the body is fully restored.

Do not camp at the waterhole! Animals and birds of the area will be totally dependent upon its water, and your presence there would deprive them of access to it. Camp some distance away.

Chapter XIV

Basic Food Needs

You will not die of starvation for a very long time even if you do not eat at all. The body at rest, in warm surroundings, uses energy at a low rate. It has been determined that a man of average size, weighing approximately one hundred fifty pounds, requires about fourteen hundred calories a day to maintain his bodily functions. To these must be added those calories required to provide the energy for whatever activities he performs and to offset heat loss caused by low temperatures.

[It must be noted that the term "calorie" as used in nutrition refers to the large calorie or kilocalorie, which is equal to one thousand small calories. A kilocalorie is the amount of heat required to raise the temperature of one kilogram (2.2 pounds) of water by one degree Centigrade.]

The total daily requirement at moderate temperatures is about sixteen calories for each pound of body weight at a low level of activity, increasing to twenty-one for moderate activity, and twenty-five for strenuous activity or hard work. Low temperatures or poor protection from the weather will vastly increase these requirements.

If less than the required amount of calories is consumed as food, the deficit will be made up by the consumption of fat and protein from the body itself. This catabolism (autocannibalism) will continue until almost all of the fat and more than half of the protein has been consumed, at which time death from starvation will occur. During this period, the body will grow progressively weaker as protein is withdrawn from the muscles, but this weakening results in lessened activity and a correspondingly lowered demand for energy. Also, each pound of weight lost reduces energy demand.

If this same one-hundred-fifty-pound man referred to earlier is in reasonably good condition, his body will contain approximately twenty-eight pounds each of fat and protein. (Most people have at least some excess fat, and their health will actually improve during the first two or three days without food!) Each ounce of fat will produce about two hundred sixty calories when catabolized, so the twenty-eight pounds of fat would provide needed energy for more than thirty days of moderate activity. Each ounce of protein yields one hundred fifteen calories, so half of his total protein would keep him going for another five or six days.

These figures are approximations only, and can vary by as much as five percent plus or minus, even in the same person. Then, too, metabolisms are different, and no two people will operate these mechanisms with the same efficiency. The somewhat overweight person would have a distinct advantage over a thinner, more muscular one. These figures prove, however, that the average human body can subsist on its own reserves, with no food intake at all, for nearly forty days if those reserves are not squandered by reckless expenditures of energy.

When seeking food, then, you must first of all determine whether the possible gain in calories exceeds the amount of energy you must expend to get it. An additional factor in this equation is the very real psychological advantage of having a full stomach. A good mental attitude is vital to long-term survival, and constant, unsatisfied hunger is destructive to this.

Emergency food supplies are available from two sources: animal life and plants.

Chapter XV

Food from Animals

Forget food and taste preferences! Forget the code of fair chase! Eat anything you know to be edible and take food birds, animals, and other creatures by any and all means available. Don't wait until you are weakened by hunger and in poor physical shape before giving up the luxury of being squeamish or selective in what you eat and how to get it.

Any mammal or bird found on the North American continent is edible in all of its parts, with the exception of the livers of polar bears, some seals, and all canines. These livers are toxic because of excessive vitamin A content. The skins of some frogs, toads, and salamanders are toxic because of toxin-filled glands. The heads of poisonous lizards and snakes are also dangerously toxic. Some Pacific shellfish are toxic because of organisms they ingest at certain times. With these exceptions, you can safely eat all of the parts of any amphibian, mammal, bird, fish, reptile, or crustacean you can catch, club, shoot, snare, or trap. You can also eat many insects, but not all.

Animal flesh is generally the most nutritious food you are likely to find, and the flesh you are most likely to secure is that of one of the rabbits or hares. These animals are almost universal in distribution, do not hibernate, and are so predictable in their habits, so lacking in common sense, that they are easily trapped or snared. Their meat is very tasty in most cases (some taste rather strongly of sage), and is nutritious as well; but it must be supplemented with edible fat from other sources.

You can starve to death on a diet of lean meat alone! You can eat all you can hold of rabbit meat or winter-poor venison, yet still die of starvation! An exclusive diet of lean meat will soon cause a severe diarrhea that will quickly drain your energy. You can live for forty days or more with no food intake, but you are not likely to live half that long on lean meat alone. *You must have fat in your diet!*

You can obtain edible fat from insects, from most animals and birds, and from seeds and nuts. Bone marrow is a very rich source. Crack the larger bones to get the marrow, then cook only as much as you must to make it edible. Crush and boil smaller bones to extract the fat. Even large bones left by predators in cold weather are valuable if not too old. Crush these between rocks and boil the fragments to extract nourishment and to kill harmful organisms. Use as soup.

Cicadas, crickets, dragonflies, grasshoppers, katydids, and locusts are considered delicacies in North Africa, the Middle East, and Asia. Do not waste time and energy by chasing such flying or hopping insects, but, instead, look for them on grass blades or other vegetation immediately after dawn, when they are still sluggish or torpid from the chill of night. Earthworms, caterpillars (don't use brightly colored caterpillars), and even ants and termites are edible, as are periwinkles, helgramites, and other nymphs found in water. None of these will be available in winter.

With the large hopping or flying insects, remove the sawtoothed portion of the legs and the harsh, membraneous wings. You can then thread them on a wire and toast them over coals, or bake, boil, fry, or roast them on hot rocks. The caterpillars and worms can be cooked directly in hot ashes or by boiling. This is a food source you are unlikely to exploit except in real emergency, but some people find them tasty, and they are real life savers. Most such insects contain more than 50 percent fat! Bears remain fat and healthy on a diet made up largely of insects (mostly ants and termites), and you can do the same.

A large caliber or high-velocity bullet will completely destroy a grouse-sized bird or a squirrel-sized animal, leaving little or nothing that is edible. Unless you have a bow, a .22 rifle or pistol, or a pellet gun, the best way to secure such animals and birds for the pot is to use deadfalls, snares, or traps.

These devices can be made in almost endless variety, but the ones listed and described here are the best of those that can be made with only a knife or hatchet as tools. If you have neither of these, don't give up. Sticks can be cut with sharp-edged rocks, and notches (when needed) can be worn or ground rather than whittled or carved. Snares will require wire or cord, but even a bootlace will serve in a pinch. Once you have captured the first animal, you can use instestines, strips of skin, or sinews and tendons for cord. You can also make usable cords out of vegetation as explained in Chapter 21.

Box traps are widely used for pot animals and birds, but should not be used for animals likely to dig or gnaw their way out unless you plan to wait nearby. Make such boxes by stacking notched sticks in log-cabin style, vertically to make a square-sided box, or with every layer or second layer indented to make an A-frame or a square-based pyramid. Place a heavy weight on top to hold the sticks tightly locked together.

To make such boxes portable, lay a stick across the top logs and tie its ends to the bottom logs. This will form a convenient carrying handle and will hold the logs securely locked even if the structure is used as a movable drop box.

For fowl such as quail or pheasant, place a box with one corner projecting slightly over a low bank, or dig a trench or ditch from well outside to just inside the box. A fowl enticed into the box by a baited trail laid in the trench will try to find an escape route at or above its normal eye level and will not normally find the hole beneath its feet. To make sure that it doesn't, heap some loose dry grass or leaves in the box and scatter bait through this. In looking for this bait, birds will scratch loose material into the escape hole, blocking their only way out.

Make a trigger to drop a box over an animal or bird by balancing the box so delicately on a propping stick that the slightest touch will upset it. Prop the box on a stick and wait in ambush to jerk the stick with a string or to nudge the box with a pole at the proper moment. You can also use a trigger such as the "figure four," the "toggle stick," or the "post and wedge." Each of these will work as well with a deadfall. (See Figure 10.)

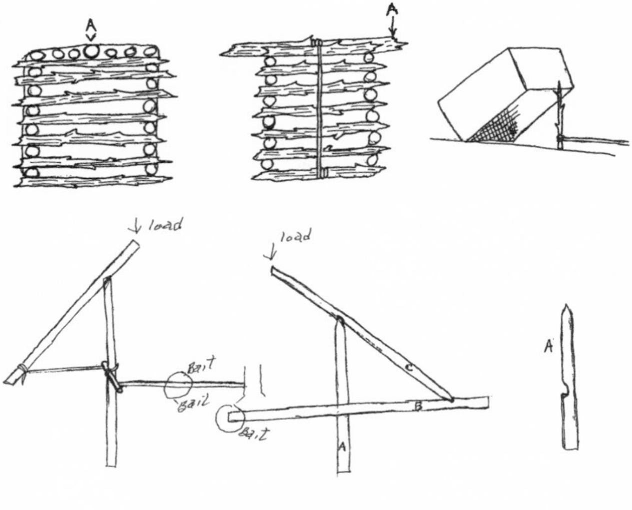

Figure 10: Box traps & triggers

Make a stake box by driving sharpened stakes to form a three-sided palisade pen. Roof it and make a drop gate at the open end or lay a roof of logs parallel to the long sides and hinged at the closed end so that it will fall to close off the open end. Use a stick and toggle trigger.

Make an open-ended stake pen with drop gates at both ends. As this resembles a tunnel rather than a closed box, animals will enter it more readily than a closed-end pen. Lay a solid roof of logs and pivot or hinge a door at each end. These doors must be somewhat wider than the openings. Drive two slanted stakes at each end, locating them two inches or so from the outer and lower edges of the closed doors and far enough apart to let the falling doors pass freely between them. Cut two jam logs considerably longer than the span between the stakes and two inches or so in diameter. These must be almost perfectly straight and you must trim them smoothly. Lay short logs three inches or so in diameter across the roof logs a foot or so in from each end to serve as pivots or fulcrums. Cut two long, stiff sticks to serve as levers. Tie one end of stick to the bottom of the door, raise the door and prop it in position, then lay the lever stick across its fulcrum. Cut a trigger stick an inch or more in diameter and long enough to reach from a foot above the roof to within a foot or less of the ground. Cut a deep notch in the center of this, with the square side of the notch at the bottom. Cut two notches on opposite sides of this stick, one about five and the other about seven inches above the lower notch, with one of them being oriented to match the lower one, and both of them having the square side at the top. With the doors propped in raised position, cut the lever sticks to length and carefully shape their ends to fit these last notches.

Remove the roof log that lies directly below the lever ends, cut a square-sided notch in one side of it that is deep

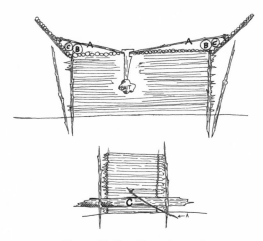

Figure 11: Double-end tunnel trap

enough to let the largest girth of the trigger stick lie loosely
in it, then carefully square its bottom surface to match the
square side of the deep notch on the trigger stick. Return the
log to the roof and tie it firmly into position. Slide the trigger stick through its hole and engage the notch with the
squared surface. Place bait of some kind on its lower end.
Place the shaped end of each door's lever in the appropriate
notch. Once this is done, lay a jam log in poisition on each
door and remove the props that have held them open.
When the bait stick is moved, its notch will slip off the
squared log, and the weight of the doors will jerk it upward,
releasing the levers. The doors will fall to close off the openings and the jam logs will roll down the doors to wedge
themselves firmly between the doors and the slanting
stakes. (See Figure 11.)

A deadfall is essentially a heavy weight so suspended or
propped over a bait or a trail or runway that it will fall upon

and disable or kill anything attempting to get that bait or travel that trail or runway. Its effectiveness depends upon the amount of weight involved, the length of stroke, the type of backstop, and the nature of the striking object. Each of these can be modified to fit the circumstances.

Increase the weight by adding heavy objects to the deadfall after it is set or create a compounding effect by placing a second rock or log in such a position that it will increase both the speed and the weight of the stroke. Raise the deadfall higher, or add a *coup de grace* stroke by making a second and heavier deadfall to deliver a second and harder blow when it is triggered by the fall of the first.

A suitable backstop is a log or rock so placed that the target animal (if it is a fairly large one) must be standing with its front feet on one side and its back feet on the other when it trips the deadfall. If you cannot so arrange matters, drive stakes in the ground beneath the deadfall and sharpen their upper ends. For long-necked animals such as antelope, deer, or elk, make one stretch its neck across a waist-high pole or log to reach the bait or bump the trip lever.

Arm the striking log by sharpening branch stubs on its lower side or lash spears to it. Let the sharpened forks of a compounding log project below the striker. The object is to ensure the speedy death of the animal sought, so suit the method to the target.

With smaller animals, the deadfall can simply catch and hold the animal against the ground or between the deadfall and a backstop pole. It is better to have the deadfall deliver a killing blow even with such animals, but it is not absolutely necessary; and it is neither necessary nor advisable to leave sharpened projections to spear the animal. For such small animals, a figure four, post and cam, or a stick and toggle trigger work best.

The simplest of all deadfalls involving bait is one involving a weight suspended by a wire or cord that is interrupted by a section that is either part of, or is held in place by, the bait itself. Lead the wire or cord upward from the high end of the deadfall and over a limb or other "pulley." Bring the free end back down nearly to ground level and pass it under some sort of hold-down, then lead the edible section across the area directly under the deadfall and secure it at a point opposite the hold-down. If cord or wire is limited, use a slender pole as a lever, tying it by a short length of cord to the deadfall, passing the lever over the limb, and bringing the end of the lever down almost to ground level. You can then tie the lever tip with bait, but the lever must have room to complete its arc without striking anything. For a porcupine, the bait can be a salt-impregnated cord or stick. Porcupines are always salt-starved and will eat anything containing salt. Use meat or a piece of fresh skin or intestine for meat-eating animals. The bait must in any case be something that will entice the target animal into eating it.

The Indians made a trap for otter and coon that is one of the easiest to make and the deadliest to use for beaver, coon, opossum, porcupine, or any animal of similar size. Drive a forked stake and a somewhat shorter unforked stake on each side of a well-used trail. Both the forks should be about three feet from the ground and so oriented that a support pole laid in the forks will span the trail. The gap between a forked stake and its unforked companion should not be more than two inches. Cut two sticks an inch or so in diameter and lay them between the paired stakes so they, too, span the trail. Tie a stout thong or cord to the middle of one of these sticks and to the end of the trigger stick thirty inches or so long. Bring this trigger stick up and over the supporting pole and bring its end down until it parallels the stakes. One of the cross sticks will then be suspended just slightly lower (six inches or so) than the support pole. Raise the second of the cross sticks until it holds the trigger stick in position. Lay the ends of two heavy logs on the suspended cross stick (it will be necessary to brace one end up until the second log can balance the first) to provide the necessary killing power. If logs are not available, lash rocks to the ends of the killing bar. When an animal attempts to scamper over the lower cross stick, it will dislodge the trigger, and the upper stick will fall like a dull guillotine. (See Figure 12.)

Figure 12: Indian otter trap

To make a large-animal deadfall built between two guide trees, raise a good-sized pole between two trees so that the smaller end lies on the ground and the heavier, raised end projects several feet beyond the guide trees. Tie it in raised position well above where your resting log is to be. Cut a pole two inches or so in diameter and long enough to reach from a supporting branch on the rear side of one tree to a point six inches beyond the second tree. This will be the resting log. Cut a second pole with an upward-pointing fork near its base and an inch and a half thick above the fork. Hang this fork over a branch two feet or more above the planned height of the resting log and mark it where the resting log is to be. Cut a similar stick and notch and bind the two together so that the two crotches face each other, are rotated ninety degrees, and are the proper distance apart. Hang one fork over its branch and lay the resting log in the other. One end of the resting log should be resting solidly on a branch, and it should be level or nearly so.

Cut a trigger pole two inches or so in diameter, with an upward-pointing fork near its base. Hang this fork over the resting log just inside the suspending fork and bring the small end down and forward alongside the second tree. Tie this trigger pole to the trunk of the tree at a point somewhere near its middle to form a pivot or fulcrum. Secure bait of some kind to its lower end and fasten it so firmly that an animal must really jerk to get it free. Fence the bait so a bear can get at it from one direction only and must be standing under the deadfall when it tugs at the bait. If your target is a grass-eating animal rather than a meat eater, you must use a snare to entrap it and tie the snare wire to the trigger pole. Release the tied deadfall log and lower it to rest on the resting log. (See Figure 13.)

Figure 13: Deadfall

A hard pull on the trigger pole will either pull the resting log off its supporting branch or lever the fork of the hanging pole off its end, and the deadfall will come crashing down.

A smaller and more sensitive version of this can be made for smaller animals by using a trigger cam between the mating surfaces of a slightly different trigger mechanism.

A basic or blunder snare is a noose so placed in a runway or trail that an animal using it will run its head through the loop. An animal so caught will usually try to escape by lunging ahead, and this will draw the noose tight. The cord or wire can be secured to a stake, a convenient tree, or a bush. When the ground is covered with snow, use a drag stick.

Don't use this type of snare for large and powerful animals, as they are likely to break the strongest cord or wire you could have with you. Cord is unsuitable for carnivorous animals other than cats, as they will bite or chew their way through it.

To make a multiple blunder snare for rabbits or for quail or other fowl on one trail, lay a small evergreen tree across the trail. Cut out lower branches to make a series of openings and put a snare in each one. You will rarely catch more than one bird out of a covey, as the frightened struggle of one bird is apt to frighten the others away. A rabbit will quickly choke itself to death, however; and another rabbit will not be frightened by finding its way blocked by a dead rabbit in a snare. It will normally just move to another opening. Neither rabbits nor fowls will abandon use of a trail because one of their number has been caught there.

Make a similar set for tree squirrels by propping a pole at an angle against a tree that shows squirrel sign. Place a series of snares along the pole. Squirrels will often use the pole as a shortcut. The first to do so will run its head through a noose, struggle, and fall off the pole. Once it has ceased to struggle, its dangling dead body will not deter other squirrels from using the pole and being caught.

You can use a small pole covered with fine snares to catch perching or roosting birds. Place such a pole in a horizontal position in a bush or tree either frequented by or used as a roost by the birds you are after, or allow it to project well beyond all foliage to resemble a horizontal dead limb. Use a series of snares tied to a long wire or cord laid across a sand bar or on a log where waterfowl either roost or congregate, and trigger it by a good strong jerk on its free end.

Make a snare that will either lift an animal off the ground or place so much upward tension on the animal as to render it helpless. Use a bent-over sapling as a springpole or use a balance pole or a counterweight to provide the lifting force. Each of these has advantages and disadvantages when measured against the others.

A springpole is easy to make and needs little wire or cord beyond that used for the noose itself. You must find a sapling in the right location, however, and this is sometimes difficult. The sapling also tends to lose resiliency if left bent too long or in freezing weather; and you could not possibly bend a tree large enough to be really useful against large animals.

To test a sapling for use as a springpole, bend it into an inverted **U**-shape, then release it. Unless its return to an upright position is sudden, violent, and complete, it is not suitable for any but the lightest and weakest of animals. If you decide that it will serve, trim off all branches, as these would tend to slow or impede rebound and might also serve to warn wary or suspicious animals. Carry the branches some distance away.

A balance pole also requires little cord beyond that used for the noose. It is little affected by weather (deep snow will shorten its fall and its lift) and can be left set for extended periods without losing its effectiveness. You will have to find or build a pivot or fulcrum at the appropriate spot, however; will have to move the heavy pole to that location; and will have to use sheer poles or a windlass to lift a large pole into position.

The balance pole is essentially a pole so pivoted that most of its weight is on one side of the fulcrum. The heavy end is high in the air so that its weight will provide leverage to jerk the victim off the ground when the set is sprung, and the small end is held down by the trigger mechanism. Trees or driven stakes must prevent the heavy end from being moved about by the frantic struggles of the victim after it has fallen, and it must be heavy enough to prevent that victim from getting decent purchase or traction on the ground if it is too heavy to be lifted bodily. It is possible to make springy "hold-downs" to keep the heavy end from being raised again.

A counterweight is useful in treeless country, is little affected by any weather but deep snow, and can be left set indefinitely. It consists of a heavy rock or other object so placed on a stump, log, boulder, or sidehill that only the tension of the snare keeps it from falling or rolling. It can also be a heavy object suspended in midair by the cord or wire. Its only disadvantage is that it requires much more cord or wire than either the springpole or the balance pole.

The cord or wire must pass through the fork of a tree, across a limb, a crossbar, a tripod, or a large log or boulder. The wire or cord must be so placed on these primitive pulleys that it cannot be pulled off the side, as this would create enough slack for the victim to regain full contact with the ground. Unless the snareward side of the log, rock, or other such object used is so overhanging that the animal could not possibly climb when against it, you must either provide a hold-down for the animal to be jerked against or for a hold-off to hold the snare wire away from its surface. Neither of these is necessary if the animal will be suspended out of reach of any solid surface. (See Figure 14.)

Figure 14: Springpole, balance pole, counterweight

One other version of the counterweight works with very little cord or wire and does not actually lift the animal at all, but is useful only on a steep slope or bank. In this set, a large rock or log chunk is chocked or braced in position just downhill from two saplings that grow close together or from two closely-set and deeply-embedded rocks. The cord or wire is fastened to the boulder or chunk and the free end is passed between the bases of the saplings or through the gaps between the rocks. The wire is fastened to a trigger mechanism and a noose is placed in position. The final action in setting the snare is to remove the chocks so the rock or chunk is free to roll down the hill, being restrained only by the snare wire. When the set is triggered, the snare will jerk the animal against the trees or rocks and will hold it helpless or strangle it. The steeper the hill, the more effective the set.

Triggers for unbaited hoisting snares are easily made. One of the simplest is the double notch. For a springpole, bend the sapling until the tip nearly touches the side of a rabbit trail. Cut off the top and whittle a groove to hold the wire or cord. (If you cut it above a side branch or fork, no groove will be needed.) Cut a stick three or four inches long and an inch or more in diameter. Make a notch with its square side an inch or so from one end and make a groove around the other end. Cut a matching notch in a cut-off stub beside the trail or drive a prenotched stake, this time with the square side of the notch toward the top. Tie one end of the wire or cord to the springpole tip and tie the notched stick at two or three inches from that tip. Make a snare noose in the free end of the wire.

Bend the springpole over and hook the two notches together. Place the noose in the trail, holding it open by bending thin grass stems or pine needles around the wire or cord and sticking the ends in slits made in fencing branches placed around the noose. Trip the snare to make sure it doesn't hang up and to test the sensitivity. Adjust this by varying the angles and the depths of the trigger surfaces. This will work just as well with a balance pole or a counterweight. If the springpole tip is large enough, you can omit the notched stick and carve the notch in the springpole itself.

A variation of this that works splendidly with a balance pole is to drive a three-foot-tall forked stake beside a rabbit trail. Cut a second forked stake, cut one side of it to two or three inches long, and leave the other eighteen to twenty-four inches long. Sharpen this long side and drive the stake, this time crotch downward, on the opposite side of the trail. The smaller limb of this fork should be on the trail side. Lay a balance pole in the first fork and put its flattened tip under the downward-pointing side of the second fork. Attach a snare noose to the pole at a point near its tip, then hang a heavy rock or any other weight to the raised end.

Make another trigger by hooking a flattened branch stub on an angled trigger stick under the flattened end of a projecting branch stub on a trailside tree. Tie the wire or cord in a groove cut into this trigger stick, then lead one free end of the wire out to the longer end of the stick and hang the noose there. The other end of the wire is then tied to the force provider.

Make a trigger by placing a flattened trigger stick under the flattened ends of two branch stubs near the base of a trailside tree. Tie the wire or cord in a groove cut into this stick, leaving enough of it free to make a noose on one end and to connect to the force provider on the other. Place the noose in the trail as before. A hard yank should free the trigger stick from the stubs. Govern the sensitivity by shaping the contact surfaces. The wire leading from the noose and the force provider should form a very shallow **V**, with the trigger at its apex. This will pull the trigger stick out, not up.

Make another trigger by cutting a straight stick an inch or so in diameter and eighteen inches or more long. Make a noose in the wire or cord and secure it to the small end of this trigger stick at a point not more than inch from the noose. Lead the wire down the length of the stick and tie it firmly about two inches from the large end. Set it by placing this stub end against one side of a driven stake or a trailside stub, and run the wire or cord around the other side of this and under the projecting stub end. When an animal is caught in the noose, the trigger stick becomes a lever transmitting the force of its struggle along its length, and the butt of this lever will quickly free itself of the wire or cord that restrains it. The upward pull of the cord or wire will hold the trigger stick securely in place until or unless it is dislodged by such force.

Another excellent trigger is made by driving a prenotched stake (growing saplings are always preferred if you can find them properly located) on each side of the trail. The notches must be square at their upper edge, and must be at least sixteen to eighteen inches above ground level. Cut a green stick an inch or more in diameter and long enough to reach between the stakes with room to spare, and having a side branch running at near right angles somewhere near its middle. Cut this limb to sixteen inches or so. Then, holding the stick with the limb parallel to the ground, square the top and the side opposite to the limb where they are to fit the notches. Tie the cord or wire around the main stick at its junction with the limb, run one end out to the tip of the side branch and hang a noose there. Tie the other free end to the force provider. To set, place the stick in the stake notches. When an animal is captured, its movements will twist the stick out of the notches.

Make snares for baitable animals almost as easily, using the same systems to provided lifting force. Fence the bait to make sure an animal can get to it from one side only and place the bait and the snare so that the animal must be within the grasp of the noose to touch the bait. When you find fencing impractical or when wire or cord is plentiful, simply place additional nooses to cover all avenues of approach.

The most sensitive trigger for baited snares are the stick and toggle, the double fork, the notch and squared face, and the notch and chisel. Each of these has several variants and can be modified to fit the situation and the materials at hand.

The stick and toggle consists of a short stick with a wire leading to the force provider tied to one end. The other, much longer end is passed under a horizontal bar or around a vertical bar (a stake, the base of a sapling or bush) and a bait stick or trigger is braced against the very end of it to hold it in position.

The double fork trigger is even more sensitive and can be set to spring as easily as a mouse trap. Cut two forked stakes, leaving one side of each fork sixteen inches or more long but cutting the other side to two or three inches. Cut the main stem of one fork short but leave that of the other five or six inches long. Drive the long side of this second fork into the ground until the short side nearly touches the ground. If the target is large or the ground is soft and loose, lash this fork to the base or stump of a sapling to prevent its being pulled up by the tension of the snare. Hook the fork of the second piece through the fork of the first in such fashion that its long side roughly parallels the upward-pointing main stem of the first. Mark and carve facing notches and whittle and shape a stick to fit between them. Make a groove around the at the center of this stick and tie the wire or cord there at a suitable distance from the noose.

To use, bend the springpole or lift the balance pole or counterweight into position and carefully fit the trigger stick into its notches. Bait the long side of the movable fork and place the noose around or under the bait so the animal must be within reach of the noose to reach the bait. Trip the device to test it. Govern the sensitivity by changing the angle and depth of the mating surfaces. (See Figure 15.)

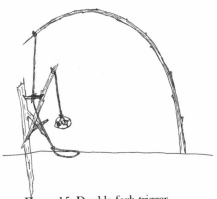

Figure 15: Double fork trigger

The notch and squared face is made by squaring off two adjacent sides of a horizontal bar placed two or more feet from the ground. A bait stick of equal length is then cut and a groove is made around its larger end. Carve a deep notch within two or three inches of the wire groove, with the square side of the notch to fit the bottom of the squared crossbar and the belly to fit its squared side. The bait is fixed to the long end of the bait stick, which is near the ground. Sensitivity is governed by the relative lengths of the two sections above and below the crossbar and by the depth of the notch.

The notch and chisel involves a bait stick exactly like that just used and described. In this trigger, you must drive a forked stake so the fork is aimed downward and the tip of its short side branch left eighteen inches or more from the ground. Shape this point to a chisel edge and hook the notch on this.

You can make each and every one of these triggers in any size and in any plane, and a trigger stick can be tripped or activated by a wire or cord. This allows you to make club, flail, spear, or catapult traps suitable for large animals.

It can never be too strongly emphasized that these larger traps are potential man killers. *NEVER SET SUCH TRAPS ALONG A TRAIL OR PATH WITHOUT PLACING ADEQUATE WARNING SIGNS WHERE ANYONE USING THAT TRAIL CANNOT FAIL TO SEE THEM!* Remember always that no matter how isolated you may consider yourself to be, other persons may come there at any time, perhaps even looking for you. You do not want to greet a rescue party by killing or maiming one of its members!

Use a large balance pole as a club by using a fulcrum or pivot at one side of a trail. There should be trees or other barriers on the other side so the animal cannot sidestep the blow. You can substitute a version of the suspended booby trap or spear-armed hanging platform used by the Viet Cong for the balance pole if you have rope heavy enough to suspend it. Use any one of the triggers for baited snares, running a trip wire across the trail instead of using bait. An alternate method is to use a very large version of the double fork trigger.

Make a club or flail trap that operates in a horizontal plane. Lash the tips of several limber poles (it is easier to bend several, one at a time, than to bend a large one) between trees on one side of a game trail in such fashion that the butts rest with considerable tension against a backstop on the far side of the trail. This can be a log end, a stump, a large rock, or a good-sized tree. Leave several branch stubs a foot or so long on the backstop side of these butts and sharpen them as spears. Spears can also be lashed to the butts. Bend the poles one at a time and tie them securely to a standing tree (remember that you are in front of some bent ones until all are back!), then lash them into a bundle. Run a trip wire across the trail and fasten it to one of the triggers already described. An alternate trigger, in case you have no wire, is a double fork made entirely of small poles. Once the trigger mechanism is in place, release the ties that hold the poles in bent position, letting the trigger hold them. This trap is highly effective against large animals.

Make a small spear trap by lashing a springy pole vertically to the side of a tree and bending the lower or spear-bearing end away from the trunk. When sprung, the trap will catch the animal between spear pole and tree.

Make a flail set to catch small birds and animals. Weave sticks to form a fly-swatter–type flail, put the end of its "handle" under a log or rock, and bend the swatter end away from the ground. Use any of the described triggers to hold it in position. When sprung, it will hit the victim a considerable blow and will hold it between flail and ground. This is highly effective, especially against small rodents.

You can easily make a set bow, using a stick and toggle for a trigger and running a trip wire to it. This is a deadly trap that was used by wartime survivors downed in enemy territory. Use this device only over bait or to take a bear as it emerges from its den, perhaps forced to do so by fire or smoke. *Do not use it on a trail, unless you are prepared to face a charge of manslaughter!*

Catch birds by digging a pit (the hole left by an uprooted tree will often do) or by heaping walls of snow or logs to form a pitlike enclosure. Either one must be a foot or more deep and the sides must be vertical. Lay slender poles or wands across the pit to form a slatted grating, lashing or bracing the ends to hold them in place. Space them four inches apart for jay- or magpie-sized birds, somewhat wider for birds such as ducks, ravens, or crows. Bait liberally. Birds will enter the pit by hopping down through the grating, but they cannot get out without flying; their spread wings are too wide to pass through the grating.

Catch ducks and geese or other large birds by digging a deep and narrow trench with one sloping end. When birds have followed a baited trail into the trench, rush at them from the entry end to startle them into attempted flight. Unable to spread their wings, they are helpless before someone with a club. A narrow, three-sided pen made of sticks will serve as well.

Catch "glutton birds" such as camprobbers, crows, gulls, jays, and magpies by placing fishhooks in bait and attaching these by a short line to a weight too heavy for the bird to lift. If you have no hooks, make gorge hooks of wood or bone, sharpening an inch-long splinter at both ends and securing the line to a groove in the middle. Turn this parallel to the line and insert it in the bait. When a bird swallows the bait, the pull of the line will turn the gorge crosswise. This works very well for grain-eating birds, too, but you will have to use a nut or a very large seed softened by boiling.

An alternative way of catching such birds is to thread one end of a cord such as fishline through a piece of bait, then bring the end back to tie around the standing cord, forming a slip noose with the bait on one side. Tie the cord to a suitable weight. When a bird picks up and attempts to swallow the bait, the noose will encircle one half of the beak, and its struggle will keep the noose tight.

For birds such as ducks, geese, and swans, place a baited hook on a rock protruding from shallow water (not less than eighteen inches or more than three feet deep) or on a floating chunk of log anchored there. Tie the hook to a line not more than a foot long and tie this to rock weighing two or more pounds. When the bird picks up the bait, it will jerk the weight into the water, and the weight will hold its head under water until it drowns. This will work for gulls or crows, too; and a live minnow or frog tethered to the weight and allowed to swim around will catch fish-eating birds. If the water is deep, attach a float to a longer line and tie this to the weight, as this will let you locate a bird that is completely submerged.

It cannot be too strongly emphasized that these methods are for emergency use only and are both repugnant to most people and unlawful. Some of the deadfalls, snares, and traps described here were and are now being used by trappers engaged in lawful trapping for fur-bearing animals, but no state or province allows their use for any large or small game animal or bird.

With your life at stake, of course, you would ignore such considerations, and most agencies would overlook violations made under such circumstances. In any case, you could not be punished for the violation until you have been found or restored to civilization; it would be far better to subject yourself to a fine than to starve!

You should also know more about traps than simply how to set them.

Chapter XVI

Trapping Know-How

The key to successful deadfalls, snares, or traps is proper placement. It obviously does no good to set a trap for an animal that does not frequent the area. Knowing where to set the trap is therefore fully as important as knowing how to make it. Only a study of the creature's habits, either through direct observation or by careful examination of the signs it leaves, will enable you to take advantage of those habits.

Not only birds of prey (hawks, owls, eagles, etc.) but carrion eaters and smaller birds like to perch on a dead snag or stub. A pole thrust up from a patch of low brush or from the middle of a glade or meadow will provide such a perch, and snares set at the tip and on any projecting branch stubs near the top will catch such birds fairly reliably.

Rabbits or hares tend to use regular patterns of movement, and they create regularly used trails. These trails are easily seen in snow and can usually be located when there is no snow. If no trails are seen but rabbit droppings are in evidence, use a stiffly branched dead limb as a crude harrow to stir up the soil in a grid pattern to so their trails will show. Place your snare or trap at the point of greatest traffic.

Numerous species (ground squirrels, true rabbits, marmots, woodchucks, etc.) live in dens or burrows, and the entrance to such dens are perfect sites for traps. The temporary dens of badgers, coyotes, and even bears are also good locations.

Many animals reside in hollow trees, usually hardwood species; and many of these trees lean slightly or strongly off the vertical. An examination of the high side of such trees will show clawmarks and discoloration if the tree is regularly used. Lean a log against this high side and place a snare on it in such a position that any animal going up or down the tree will be caught. With straight trunks, use several poles.

Other animals such as packrats, woodrats, tree squirrels, muskrats, and beaver build conspicuous nests, and the entrances to most such nests are ideal trap sites. Tree squirrels usually build their nests so high off the ground that it entails a dangerous climb to reach them. For beaver, you may have to knock away part of the dam to lower the water low enough to reach the entry. If that is not practical, tear a small hole in the dam and set traps or snares to catch the beaver as it comes to make repairs. Some of these will catch only chunks of wood, so set several.

Beavers often dig canals in order to transport logs or limbs for construction or food, and such canals offer splendid locations for traps. You must first make sure to drive all beavers from the cutting area back to their pond, so the trap will take only an animal going to the work area. If you neglect this, your snare may catch only a log or limb, leaving a dazed and toothless beaver to wonder where his log has gone!

Most big game and many smaller animals follow regular trails, and well-used trails are readily recognized. Most such game litters the trail with its droppings, and an examination of this gives a fair idea of when and how often the trail is used. Following such trails for a short distance will often lead you to an intersection with a larger trail, and you can set a trap or snare on both branches.

In desert country, a waterhole is an ideal place to set snares and traps, but you can rarely find the necessary materials there. Simply set blunder snares secured to heavy drags and rely on the animals' escape attempts to tighten nooses. Such country often has lava rims that extend for miles, with only infrequent breaks or gaps. All animals that wish to go up or down such walls (except those that can climb) must do so through these gaps, and such sites are also good locations for traps.

Remember always that you must first study the situation to determine what an animal does, and then arrange your deadfall, snare, or trap to catch him in the act. Baits and lures are also highly effective when suited to the animal sought.

Salt will entice antelope, deer, elk, goat, moose, porcupine, rabbit, and sheep. Fish, meat, or blood will attract all types of flesh eaters, ranging from shrews to badgers, bears, bobcats, coons, cougars, coyotes, foxes, lynxes, possums, and wolves. These will also attract both predatory and carrion-eating birds, including buzzards, crows, eagles, gulls, jays, magpies, and ravens.

Crumbs, grass or weed seeds, and smaller nut kernels will attract most birds and fowl such as quail or pheasant. These and larger nuts such as acorns will attract ducks, geese, and turkeys as well as mice, rats, and squirrels. Insects, grubs, and worms will attract many of the smaller birds and some of the smaller animals. Fish, frogs, and salamanders (these killed and skinned) are excellent bait for many of the wading birds and for some of the flesh eaters. A tethered bird, lizard, or snake will lure hawks, owls, and eagles.

Honey is outstanding bait for bears, coons, martens, and skunks; but you would have to find a bee tree to get it. A consideration here is that no natural food exceeds honey in nutritional value, and you might better simply eat it than use it as bait. Another consideration, of course, is that robbing a bee tree is not without hazard! If you find a bee tree and decide to rob it (assuming that the honey is accessible), burn spongy, punky wood in an almost airtight container to produce dense smoke. You can make such a container of baked clay if you have nothing else suitable. Set this smoking container within the hive itself to stupefy the bees, or rig a homemade bellows to puff smoke into the hive.

Most lures used by trappers are scents made from the glands or urine of the animals sought. Many and exotic were the ingredients and methods of culture used by old-time trappers, and most such recipes went to the grave with their creators. To those who have been privileged to smell some of these concoctions, the permanent loss of the formulae is not a matter of regret! One old trapper I knew made a coyote lure comprised in part of fish heads, coyote urine, and anise oil mixed with other ingredients unknown to me in a bottle and set aside in warm place to "ripen." After several months, it was either adjudged "jest right" or "spiled," with the former to be saved for use and the latter to be buried in unopened condition. To my unsophisticated nose, they were both spoiled beyond redemption; and I think even the coyotes approached with extreme caution and from upwind, possibly with paws held over their noses! They did approach, however, as he always caught a good many.

Under survival conditions you will have neither the time nor the inclination to make such lures, but fresh lures will work. If you catch and kill a coyote, for example, save the bladder full of urine to sprinkle on bushes at trap or snare sites. This is especially effective if the animal providing the urine is an adult female; but male urine sprinkled on a rock, stump, or bush will cause any passing coyote to stop to inspect this "sign post." Beaver castor, the musky exudeate from a beaver's anal glands, will attract most carnivores as well as other beavers.

Other lures can be bright and shiny objects such as a ring, a piece of mirror, or perhaps a polished dime or quarter. Animals such as packrats and coons, and birds such as jays, magpies, and crows are possessed of an insatiable curiosity and a strong acquisitive instinct; they will try to carry such objects away.

Porcupines, hares and rabbits, skunks, ground squirrels, woodrats, etc. are notoriously stupid and unsuspicious, and disturbances of the environment or the lingering scent of man will not normally deter them from approaching a baited set or blundering into a trail set. This applies to most birds as well. Most other animals are much more sensitive to such disturbances or odors, and you must be as careful as you can be when setting traps for them.

Be careful not to be caught in or injured by a trap of your own devising! Remember always to work from behind the sweep of a flail, outside the grasp of a snare, and out of the path of a falling deadfall. A snare noose will catch a human arm, head, or leg as readily as an animal, and a deadfall or flail will be no more gentle with you than it would be with your intended victim. The old movie shot of the bumbling tenderfoot dangling head down from a springpole is always good for a belly laugh, but there is nothing laughable about the real thing, especially when there is no one to help you get free.

A long toggle stick as used in the Indian otter trap described in Chapter 15 describes a wide arc when released, and this motion is both sudden and violent. Many old-time trappers, in fact, call these devices "fly poles." Be careful, then to allow for this motion when you trip a trap to test it, and be alert to the possibility of being struck by such trigger parts.

Remember always that under survival conditions you cannot afford even trivial injuries. As the body's energy reserves dwindle, its ability to resist infection, blood loss, or shock, as well as its ability to regenerate or repair lost or damaged tissue, is sharply reduced. Injuries so minor that they would normally be ignored or treated with a dab of merthiolate can actually be life threatening under survival conditions. *Be extremely careful to avoid injury!*

Many of the books that deal with camping or with wood-craft show forked stakes in the form of a letter **Y**, and would have you believe that these stakes can be driven. Don't believe it! It is impossible to drive such stakes without split-ting the crotch. Instead, you must choose stakes in which the main stem is straight or nearly so, with the side branch com-ing off at a narrow angle. Such a stake can be easily driven, as the force of the blows will be in direct line with the point. Even so, the tip of the main stem receiving the blows will itself split unless it is beveled at the edges or "sniped."

When setting traps in winter, remember the snow! It does no good at all to set a deadfall, snare, or trap where it will be buried or made inoperative by falling or blowing snow. Protect the trap by a bough or bark shelter, by building it on poles well above the probable snow level, or by setting it under a densely-canopied tree.

Remember, too, that even the bloody snow or ground where you have killed or dressed out an animal can serve as bait. Use any unwanted portions of your kills as additional bait. Any carniverous animal will investigate the smell of blood.

Be aware that most animals are very powerful for their size, and that desperation tends to multiply strength. When choosing counterweights or when adding weight to a balance pole or deadfall, then, it is wise to follow the advise of a trap-per friend of mine who used to trap bear, which was a law-ful activity then. He always said to "make your deadfall heavy enough to hold or kill any bear, then add at least twice that much more!"

Animals, birds, or other living creatures can also be taken by more direct means.

Chapter XVII

Improvisations

You can sometimes approach a roosting owl closely enough to be able to knock it down with a thrown stick or rock. You can often secure grouse or other "fool hens" in the same way, and they will sometimes allow you to get close enough to hit them with a hand-held stick.

Capture these birds, or lizards, snakes, turtles, or crayfish, with a wire noose fastened to the end of a long stick or wand. Use the stick to extend the noose, slip it over the head (or the claw of a crayfish), and jerk it tight. A noose formed in the end of a long grass stem works admirably for small lizards. If the movement is very slow, the target creature will rarely take alarm.

You can often kill a porcupine with a club, but this may entail some dangerous climbing. In winter a porcupine will climb an evergreen tree and stay there, living off the bark of the topmost trunk and branches. As this deforms and ruins the tree, these animals are poisoned and shot on sight by foresters. You can recognize a home tree in winter by its threadbare look, by the litter of droppings, needles, and bark fragments beneath the tree, and by snow that is stained or discolored by urine.

In summer these animals feed on tender herbs and forbs, generally at night, and spend their days resting in a tree. They are normally solitary, but communal groups sometimes share a resting tree, and I have seen as many as eight in one small juniper. The ground under such a tree will be covered several inches deep with their droppings. In treeless country, they will often live in a cluster of large boulders.

You will often see them waddling to and from their feeding grounds in late evening or early morning. They are not very fast, and you can easily overtake one on the ground. They are notoriously hard to kill, however, and you might have quite a struggle before you have one certifiably dead.

Once this is accomplished, you should have no difficulty skinning the animal, despite the fearsome quills. Start at the center of the belly (which has no quills) and fold the skin back over itself as you go. These animals are unbelievably rich in fat, both the entire carcass and all of the "innards" being encased in a layer of fat often as much as two inches thick. This fat and the ease of taking make the "porky" an excellent source of survival food. The meat ranges from very good to pretty bad in taste, this apparently largely dependent upon its choice of food.

A club is also useful against mice in their runways or any small animal or bird you can bring within its reach. For really small animals, a woven "swatter" is even more effective, as it requires less precision in aim and is less destructive of tissue. Geese and ducks are flightless when molting, and this makes them especially vulnerable to a club. Some seals are helpless on land, but adult animals are so large that a spiked club or a spear must be used to take them. They are not too dangerous to tackle with a club, just too hard to kill.

A throwing stick is very effective when used at short range against densely congregated birds, and you can quickly become so proficient with practice that you can use it against single animals or birds. Select a straight stick eighteen to twenty-four inches long and two inches or so in diameter. Throw it in such a manner that it will spin horizontally as it travels. You can refine this by choosing an angled piece and carving it to make a crude boomerang, but most of us cannot use this any more effectively than the unshaped stick.

Use the surgical tubing from your emergency kit, a **Y**-shaped forked stick, and a piece of leather (from a shoe tongue, perhaps) to make a slingshot. Use marble-sized pebbles as projectiles. A minimum amount of practice will enable you to make occasional hits, and skill will quickly return if you used one in your youth. This is deadly against small birds and animals.

For an even deadlier weapon, whittle out a rifle stock and barrel with the top of the barrel grooved to receive an arrow. Use the surgical tubing and a leather thong to propel the arrow.

The sling that David is reported to have used so effectively against Goliath consists of two long leather thongs secured to opposite sides of a leather pouch. Such a device is easily made and is just as deadly today as it was reported to be then. One thong should be tied into a nonslip noose of a size to fit snugly over the middle finger of the throwing hand, and the other should have a large thumbknot tied in its free end.

To use, put an egg-sized rock in the pouch and stand with your feet somewhat apart and the left shoulder (if right-handed) pointed at the target. The knotted string should be held between the thumb and forefinger of the throwing hand, and the loaded sling should be dangling to barely clear the ground beside your right foot. Still keeping the arm fully extended, whip the sling up and around the body (only once) and release your grip on the knot when the sling has returned to the starting position. The rock will be lobbed to an incredible distance and at considerable speed, and the impact is capable of killing or disabling almost any animal.

For shots at closer range, the sling must be whirled in a more horizontal plane, but the technique is otherwise the same. Do not whirl the sling more than once in an attempt to build velocity, as this is determined by the length of the strings used, and it is nearly impossible to achieve even moderate accuracy when more than one whirl is made.

It will require considerable practice to achieve a high degree of accuracy, but the sling is deadly when used against a dense congregation of birds or animals, where a miss is unlikely. *If part of a group, do not practice your first throws until all other members of the group are behind solid objects such as trees!* Your first few throws are apt to be uncontrolled, and anyone near you is apt to be at considerable risk! As the center of the circle the sling describes, you will be in no danger yourself.

A variant of the sling is a single string tied to a rock. Tie a thumbknot in the free end of the string and grip this between thumb and finger as before. The string is thrown with the rock.

Bolas consist of two or three weighted strings radiating from a common center. Cast it at a bird or animal in such fashion as to make it spin horizontally as it flies. The strings will wrap themselves tightly around any object struck and will secure themselves against unwinding. An even simpler version is a three-foot string with weighted ends. Grasp one weight and whirl the other around, then throw it at your target. It, too, will wrap around anything it strikes.

The bow and arrow is a highly effective weapon in the hands of someone skilled in its use, but is little more than a toy when a crude version is used by a novice. Even so, a bow that is fairly effective against fish or frogs can be made and used by almost anyone; and you might be able to make one suitable for use against animals and birds. The bow itself is not particularly hard to make, but good arrows are hard to come by.

If you want to use a bow against birds or animals but are unskilled in archery, make a crossbow. The bow is then held in a stock and is pointed and shot like a rifle. The arrows or quarrels are then very short, only ten to fourteen inches long, and are easy to make. The only problem with a cross-bow is to make a trigger sensitive enough to be released without jerking (this would deflect the aim), yet positive enough to hold the bow at full draw until you trigger it.

The most practical trigger you can make under primitive conditions involves a notch and lock-stick catch with a thumb latch release. Groove the top of the "barrel" to make a guide slot for the arrow. Cut a deep transverse notch where the gun action would be. This must be not less than three quarters of an inch deep, and it must be cut with a square shoulder at the front end, a flat bottom an inch long, and a concave ramp at the back end.

Cut a lock-stick an inch or so thick and an inch and a half longer than the bow is wide at the notch. Square the stick on two adjoining sides and whittle a string groove around each end. Tie short cords in these grooves and tie their free ends to the bowstring. The end result should look like a child's swing. The distance between the cords must be sufficient to let them move freely along the sides of the barrel.

To use, pull the bowstring to full draw position and drop the lock-stick into its notch. It should be positioned with one squared face against the forward end of the notch and with the other on the bottom of the lock-stick but at least one quarter inch above the floor of the notch.

Cut a thumb latch stick at least six inches long and half an inch thick, and shape the large end to fit snugly between the lock-stick and notch bottom. The forward quarter of the latch should be free of contact with the concave portion of the ramp, and the latch should rest on the angled corner where notch and stock meet. This point will serve as a pivot or fulcrum. The other three quarters should extend back more or less parallel to the top of the stock. The maximum spread between stock and latch should not be more than two inches, and somewhat less is better. Press downward on the latch to pry the lock-stick up and out of the notch. Sensitivity is governed by the relative distances fore and aft of the pivot point, not by the strength of the bow.

Place the quarrel or bolt (arrow) in the barrel slot with the bowstring resting in a shallow groove cut in its base. Hold it in position by running at least two pine needles or thin grass stems across it and securing their ends in splits cut into the side of the barrel. This will allow you to hold the crossbow in almost any position without the arrow falling off.

Drive burrowing animals or tree dwellers from their dens or hollows with smoke. With den users, you will have to use a thin cover of some kind to force the smoke into the den rather than into the open air. You must also be at pains to locate each of the two or more entrances such dens often have and to set traps at or block these extra escape doors securely.

Flood animals out of their dens if they are near enough to a source of water. Drive packrats from their nests or log dwellers from their lairs by firing the nest or log if there is no chance of the fire spreading. Use a long, slender, barbed wand to spear an animal in its den or hollow if the curves in den or hollow are not too radical or acute. Leave a short fork at the tip of such a wand and thrust it into a shallow den to twist the fork into an animal's hide tightly enough to drag the animal within reach of a club.

You will quickly think of other on-the-spot methods of securing small creatures you have spotted. If necessity is the mother of invention, then hunger is the parent of ingenuity!

You may be able to drive a predator from its prey while it is still intact enough, and fresh enough, to be useful as food. Before appropriating this for your own use, ask yourself if you might better use all or part of it as bait for a trap to catch the returning predator, thus gaining a larger supply of fresher meat.

No North American predator is likely to try to defend its prey against a human, with the notable exception of badgers, bears, and wolverines. With a badger, you can quickly make a spear or club that will settle any argument in your favor. With a bear or wolverine, discretion is always wiser than valor!

If you feel that you simply must have the meat on which a bear is feeding, but have no gun or other weapon with which to kill the bear, you must carefully plan and carry out an attack that uses the only available weapon: fire. It is said that even a grizzly will retreat, however reluctantly, when faced with a freely blazing torch. A large fire built near the purloined meat will keep the animal away long enough for you to build a snare, set-bow, or deadfall, or to cut a goodly supply of meat if this is still edible. Most such meat will be so "ripe" or so befouled that you would not dare eat it.

If you take some meat, you should then carry a freely blazing torch of some kind while moving well out of the area. When you think you are far enough from the scene of your theft, stop and make camp. Build a good-sized fire and gather enough wood to keep it going all night.

I would hesitate to try this myself, at least with a grizzly. I have no experience with grizzlies, but both their intelligence and their ferocity is legendary. All that I have read indicates that it would work, but bears don't read!

Never take chances with a bear, especially not where meat is concerned! A dozen bears might flee, even from a fresh kill, for every one that will try to defend its property; but the first one you encounter may be the one that chooses to defend! The black bear is usually timid where man is concerned, but this is by no means a universal trait. A brown bear (from Alaska), a grizzly, or a polar bear is much more

likely to fight for its meat. Polar bears, in fact, are reported
to stalk men as they would prey, apparently mistaking them
for seals! A bear is a creature of uncertain mood and temper,
and you must take no unnecessary chances when dealing
with one.

If you have a gun or other means of killing a bear, then by
all means do so. Bears are heavily encased in fat in all but the
early spring months, and this is one of the finest of all edible
fats. It is also useful for waterproofing leather boots and
shoes, for grooming the hair, as a medical salve, and for fuel.
The hide of a bear is also extremely useful, either as a coat or
a blanket.

Bears do not actually hibernate, they only sleep, and it is
not too unusual to find them up and doing in midwinter
when food is available. When one does sleep, its den is often
revealed by a hole melted in the snow cover by its breath.
You can use fire, smoke, or simple noise to drive a bear from
its winter quarters, but do not do so without rigging a deadfall, a set-bow, or other deadly trap to kill it as it emerges.
Bears are often "as grouchy as a bear" when aroused from
a winter's nap, and a bear's ill-temper is not to be taken
lightly!

*Never eat bear meat without cooking it thoroughly at high
temperatures!* The bears, like the common hog (and humans),
are omnivores; and they can transmit the dreaded *Trichina*
worms to humans who eat infested meat that is rare or under-
cooked. Bears are unlikely to be infested with trichinosis
unless they have had access to garbage containing uncooked
pork scraps, but you should be aware of the potential hazard
anyway. Trichinosis is reported to be one of the most painful
afflictions known to man and has no cure; so take no chances.
Overdone is properly done with bear meat!

A wolverine is said to be so incredibly vicious and vindic-
tive that the wisest course would seem to be to leave him and

his meat alone. Any meat he has been feeding on would be so befouled as to be unusable in any case. If you have a gun, of course, you might kill and try to eat him—that is if your stomach is strong enough to let you even skin him. They are often known as "skunk bears" and are said to be able to give a skunk the first stink in any contest! I have no experience with them and have never even seen one, but I would personally avoid one as I would the plague unless actually starving.

If you harvest more meat than you can quickly use, as with an elk, a moose, a bear, or even an adult deer, you can preserve the meat in several ways. You can freeze it if the weather is cold enough; you can make it into jerky; or you can smoke it. If you choose to make jerky, you can then use some of this to make that famous survival food, pemmican.

To dry or smoke meat, use the rack described in Chapter XVIII. Cut the meat into strips not more than two inches wide nor more than half an inch thick. Skewer these on rods (of nontoxic woods only!), and lay them across the rack. For future use as pemmican, cut the strips across the grain of the meat. To make pemmican, pound the jerky into a meal and mix this with an equal volume of rendered fat. Stuff into casings made from the intestines, and smoke these to shrink and cure them.

All stored food, and especially strong-smelling foods such as meats, should be stored some distance from camp to prevent attracting marauding bears into camp. Hang the food at least ten feet off the ground and well away from a climbable tree. Wrap it in a tight covering to protect it from magpies and ravens, which also eat meat.

Another source of survival food is fish.

Chapter XVIII

Food from Fish

Fish provide food that is very rich in protein, but fresh fish are too low in caloric content to carry you for very long when eaten alone. You would have to eat almost twenty pounds of fresh trout a day to provide energy for vigorous activity! Fresh-caught salmon just out of the ocean, catfish, most ocean fish, and shellfish have about twice as many calories per unit volume as trout.

It is obvious, then, that the calories must be concentrated by smoking or drying the fish, or that the fish must be supplemented with calories from other sources.

You can catch fish with a hook and line (a whittled gorge hook and a homemade line will work), but this is apt to be a slow and uncertain process, as any angler can attest. A set-line with numerous hooks is a great deal better and does not need your constant attention. Better still, make a spear or gig, a clamp, a harpoon (for large fish), a stake trap, or a tide-pool trap. For crabs or crayfish, make a drop-side trap.

To make a spear, cut a long and slender pole or wand and sharpen the larger end. Whittle a backward-pointing barb or use a conveniently located branch stub as a barb. Harden the point by roasting it in a fire. Make a gig by lashing three or more barbed points to a pole.

A clamp was widely used by Indians. Make one by splitting a springy pole for a distance of a foot or more, using tightly wrapped wire or cord to keep it from splitting too far. Wedge the split open and carve cross grooves on the inner surfaces to leave sharp-edged ridges. Then pry the tips apart and brace them open with the smallest and thinnest stick that will hold them. When this brace is driven against the body of a fish, it will become dislodged; and the clamp will spring closed to grip the fish.

Make a harpoon tip from a piece of deer antler, a bone, or a piece of fire-hardened wood. Whittle a long, peglike base that will fit into a socket at the tip of the harpoon pole, and make a groove or hole for the attachment of a cord. Tie the cord to the point and the pole, leaving enough slack to allow several feet of free play when the tip is pulled off the pole. Wrap several turns of this cord on the pole and pull a loop of slack up under this binding to hold the point in place.

Use woven dip nets to scoop up fish from small creeks and rivers. If the fish tend to dodge the net, you can often blind them by throwing quantities of dirt into the water or by stirring up bottom mud. Even a racquetlike scoop woven out of stiff sticks can be used to bat fish ashore.

Make a drop-side net for crabs and crayfish by making a circular, triangular, or square ring of tied-together limbs or sticks. You can use a woven basketwork of rigid sticks for a bottom. Make a second ring the same size and shape as the first. Tie weight rocks to this at intervals. Join the two rings with sides made of cloth or other flexible material. Tie several cords to the top ring to make a bridle attached to your pull-up rope. Tie some bait such as meat or fish in the center of the bottom and lay a fairly heavy rock beside it.

When you sink this contraption, the weighted sides will settle down around the weighted and baited center of the trap. When crabs or crayfish have crawled aboard to reach the bait, pull the trap up. The sides will be pulled up first to form barriers to escape.

A double-funnel trap woven of sticks will catch both fish and crayfish. The advantage of this is that it can be left unattended for long periods while you do something else. (See Figure 16.)

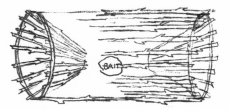

Figure 16: Double funnel fishtrap

No fish found in North America is poisonous (many tropical fish are), but a fish starts to spoil immediately after death in any but freezing temperatures, and spoiled fish is toxic. Prepare and eat fish as soon as caught. To prevent spoilage of any surplus, the best method is to keep the fish alive until needed, using a stake pen, a submerged woven basket, or a fenced-off inlet or dug pond to hold them. Catfish and bullheads will survive for days on a stringer.

The next best method is to freeze the fish if the weather is cold enough to let you do so. If the weather is not cold enough, then you must preserve the fish by drying or smoking if you can't keep them alive.

Dry or smoke small fish by cleaning them and then splitting them from the tail to the head, leaving the head to hold the two halves together. Hang by straddling the split halves over the drying-rack poles. Cut larger fish into strips not more than half an inch thick and skewer these on sharpened, nontoxic sticks, then lay these on the drying rack.

The drying rack should be made of four forked stakes (a tripod will serve as a stake) driven to form a square or rectangle. Lay a crosspole through the two forks on each side and lay a number of slender drying poles across these. This grating should be not less than three feet in height, and five or six feet is better.

Build a fire of alder, aspen, birch, cottonwood, or willow beneath the rack, keeping it low enough that it will not cook the fish and smoky enough to keep flies away. Keep the fire going until a piece of fish will break with a snap and until the center of a broken piece is hard and dry. The fish is dried, rather than smoked.

When smoking fish, dig a trench from the drying rack to a point some distance away on the downhill side. Dig a fire pit there and cover it with a large flat rock to confine the fire. Roof the trench with cut sods or with rocks and dirt to make a smoke pipe. Keep the fire supplied with green, non-resinous, and nontoxic wood to make a dense smoke. Shroud the rack with stacked boughs or slabs of bark to contain and confine the smoke.

The mussels found in great abundance along the Pacific coast are edible, but these and other Pacific shellfish are poisonous at times. You will have heard that they are dangerous in any month without an *R*, but this is simply not true. No one can forecast with any accuracy when, or to what degree, shellfish will be rendered toxic by marine organisms they feed on. These toxins are fortunately as harmful to animals and birds as to man, and an unusual number of dead animals or birds along the shore usually serves as adequate warning. With this one notable exception, shellfish are edible, although freshwater shellfish should be thoroughly cooked to destroy any parasites or bacteria they might harbor.

Periwinkles, helgramites, and most other nymphs of water-hatching insects are edible. So are sea cucumbers, eels, tadpoles, and adult frogs, and turtles. Streams, marshes, and other permanently wet areas also produce numerous edible plants.

Chapter XIX

Food from Plants

Never eat any plant unless you are certain beyond doubt that it is edible! Nonedible plants and their fruits range from mildly irritating to deadly poisonous, and your first mistake may well be your last! Plants of similar appearance may be radically different in chemical makeup, so don't eat a plant just because it looks somewhat like another plant you know to be edible. *If in doubt of identity, do not use!*

There is no such thing as a safe test for edibility! You have probably read that you can test for edibility by holding some part of a plant in the mouth or by chewing it thoroughly without swallowing. If no burning, numbing, or stinging sensation results, you are told, you can then swallow a small portion. Then, if no unpleasant effects are noted after a lapse of one, two, or several hours (this depending on which book you have), you can consider the plant safe to eat, at least in small amounts.

Following such instructions can kill you! The root of any species of the water hemlock, *Cicuta*, apparently tastes and smells good to lots of people. The toxin involved will not burn, numb, or sting the mouth, as children have eaten the raw roots greedily, and adults have often eaten them either cooked or raw. Even so, this is the deadliest native plant found on the North American continent, as a piece of root the size of a marble will kill an adult human being within half an hour of ingestion! The poison involved attacks the nervous system and the process of dying is as painful and unpleasant as can well be imagined, with convulsive seizures so violent that bones are often broken and the tongue is frequently chewed to shreds.

Other plants contain very slow-acting alkaloids that produce no symptoms for twenty-four to thirty-six hours after ingestion, but for which no antidotes or effective means of treatment are known. Still other poisons are cumulative in nature, being dangerous only when eaten in considerable quantity or over a span of time. Any test based on sampling would fail to reveal these hazards.

You must not assume that a plant is safe to use because birds or animals eat it! Squirrels cut and store quantities of the deadliest of mushrooms; bears and hogs eat the deadly death camas with apparent gusto; and birds eat many poisonous berries without apparent harm. Besides, you have no way of knowing that the animal or bird you see eating an unknown plant will not suffer sickness or even death as a result.

There is only one safe way to use wild plants for food: *you must know, positively and beyond doubt, that the plant you propose to eat is edible!* It's a question of being dead certain or of being dead, period. *If you cannot identify a plant as edible beyond all doubt, do not eat it!*

Plant foods vary widely in their nutritional value. Nuts are high in protein and fat content, and are often far richer in calories than most meats. Seeds, inner barks, and roots generally supply starch or carbohydrates. Fruits and edible saps furnish vitamins and calories in the form of sugars, but offer little else. The new leaves and leaf buds of trees and shrubs and the foliage of herbaceous plants are rich in vitamins A and C, but are low in carbohydrates and calories and have almost no protein.

The inner bark or cambian layer of all of the many species of cedar, cypress, fir, hemlock (not the herb!), juniper, pine, and spruce trees is edible and more or less nourishing, if not particularly appetizing.

The only pinelike evergreen tree (not a member of the pine family) that is in any way dangerous is the yew-wood tree, *Taxus brevifolia*. This tree is usually somewhat shrubby in character, with reddish, shreddy bark more or less like juniper bark. The evergreen needles are flattened, an inch or so long, dark green, very glossy. From a distance, the trees often appear rusty-brown. The fruit is a pale red or pink, barrel-shaped berry that is open at the tip, revealing a dark brown or blackish pit or seed. The pulp of the fruit is not known to be seriously poisonous, but the pit or seed is highly toxic. The foliage of all the Asiatic and European members of this genus is among the more dangerous of plant substances; and no part of the plant should be used as food.

The cambian layer of alder, aspen, basswood, birch, cottonwood, elm, maple, sycamore, and willow is edible and, in some cases, even good. Scrape this layer as a pulp to eat raw, or cook it by boiling or roasting. You can also dry it and then grind or pound it to make a flour substitute.

The inner cores or cobs of green fir and pine cones are edible and somewhat nourishing. You should first pound them to a pulp and then roast them. You can also boil them to produce a nourishing soup. As many of these cones take two or more years to mature, the green cones can be found at any time of the year.

The "berries" of all the junipers (these are actually fused cones) are edible either raw or boiled, but they are far too resinous and strong-flavored to be good. These berries are produced so abundantly that distant trees often appear blue, and they usually remain on the tree throughout the winter.

The catkins of alder, aspen, birch, cottonwood, and willow are edible, as are the tiny staminate cones of pine, fir, and spruce.

The seeds or nuts from pine cones are concentrated energy at its best, containing over sixty percent edible fat. They provide more than thirty-two hundred calories per pound, which is almost four times as much as fresh beefsteak! All pine seeds are edible, but those of the Coulter, digger, Jeffrey, limber, piñon, Ponderosa or yellow, and the sugar pine are the largest and therefore the most useful. The seeds of the lodgepole and knobcone pines are smaller, but are retained in the cones throughout the year (the cones do not open until singed by fire), making them available in all seasons.

The seeds of the true firs, the Douglas fir, and the hemlocks and spruces are edible, but are too tiny to be of much value. Many of the species produce seeds that are acrid or resinous to the taste, but roasting or boiling will reduce or eliminate this quality.

To procure the seeds, lay the cone in hot ashes or on a rock beside a hot fire. The scales will gradually open to expose the seeds for easy removal. You can also fire the cones, but this is wasteful of the seeds, as many will be lost and some will be ruined.

The acorns of all the many species of oak, both deciduous and evergreen, are edible, although all are far too bitter to be eaten raw. Shell the acorns, crush them, and place the crushed kernels in rapidly boiling water. Change the water when it becomes tea-colored. Several such changes will leach out much of the bitter tannin to make white oak acorns almost good, and other types will range from slightly to intensely bitter. Repeat the leaching process with the bitter ones or use a slurry of wood ashes and water instead of just water. You will then have to boil them in plain water to eliminate the lye. An alternative method is to crush the shelled acorns and soak them in cold running water for several days. This was the method used by Indians, who had no easy way to boil water. Used the leached fragments as with nuts, pulverize to use as flour, or boil for soup.

Beechnuts, butternuts, chestnuts (most chestnuts have been killed by blight), chinquapins, hazelnuts (wild filberts), hickory nuts, pecans, and walnuts are edible either raw or when cooked with other foods. The seeds of the maples and sycamores are also edible. Crushed kernels of these nuts or seeds will yield a cooking oil. *Horse chestnuts and buckeyes are poisonous!*

You will find that squirrels and other animals and birds have harvested most of these nuts long before winter, but scattered nuts can be found throughout the winter by scratching among fallen leaves, You can also raid squirrel or woodrat nests to obtain larger supplies. In some areas, acorn woodpeckers will have stored large numbers of acorns in shallow holes made in the bark of trees, and you can rob these caches.

The winter leaf buds of alder, aspen, birch, cottonwood, maple, sycamore, and willow are edible either cooked or raw, and the young, unfolding leaves of these trees are richer in vitamin C than fresh orange juice. The tender young twigs of all these trees are edible, either as a nibble or as a boiled dish. The unfolding leaves of the deciduous oaks are edible if boiled in two waters.

The tender new needles of the firs, the Douglas fir, hemlocks (the trees), larches, pines, and spruces are edible if not overly tasty, and these yellowish needles are rich in vitamin C. You can eat them raw, mix them with other cooked greens, or steep them to make a vitamin-rich tea.

The wild rose differs only slightly from the plants in your yard and is therefore instantly and positively identified. The hips or fruits remain on the plant throughout the winter and are often found on stems protruding through deep snow. These fruits are the equal of apples in food value, and they often taste like overripe apples. Three of these hips are said to be the equal of one large orange in vitamin C content, and they were gathered and used in wartime England to replace unavailable citrus fruit. They can be eaten raw or cooked, fresh or dried; but you will need to remove the woolly covering of the seeds in some species.

You can eat both the berries and the young shoots of any of the many species of caneberries. Blackberries, cloudberries, dewberries, lagoon berries, raspberries, salmonberries, thimble berries, and wine berries are included in this category, the genus *Rubus.* These plants are characterized by leaves divided into three to five leaflets and by berries that are made up of many juicy, more or less tasty, one-seeded drupelets. The leaves are edible either as boiled greens or when steeped for tea.

The wild strawberry is identical to the domestic plant but smaller throughout, and the berries are both much smaller and much sweeter. The leaves are very rich in vitamins A and C, and they can be eaten as boiled greens or steeped for tea. The plants are perennial herbs and do not lose their leaves in winter.

Wild cherries are so similar to domestic cherries in all but the size of the fruit that the trees are readily recognized. The seedlings of domestic cherries are widely scattered in wooded and brushy areas and can now be considered "wild." The fruits of seedlings vary widely from tree to tree, with some being almost as good as cultivated varieties. *The fruit of the cherry laurel, widely used for hedges, is not edible!* The chokecherry is a large shrub or small tree that produces small fruits that are astringent or "puckery" when raw, but these are both edible and eatable when cooked. Only the Oregon bitter cherry has small, bright red fruits that are too astringent to be eaten.

Cherries should never be eaten pits and all, and the pits must never be eaten raw! The pits from all members of this genus, including almonds, apricots, cherries, peaches, and plums, contain cyanide compounds in sufficient quantities to make them extremely dangerous. Only the edible almond, and then only when thoroughly ripe and dry, lacks this poison. Cyanide is highly volatile, and the shelled kernels of cherry and plum pits can be rendered safe by long-term drying, by boiling in two or more waters, or by dry-roasting. Do not eat them in significant amounts even then unless you mix them with larger quantities of other foods.

The many species of wild plum indigenous to North America and all seedling plums also produce edible fruits, but the flattish pits are just as dangerous as those of the cherries. Seedling plums are now well established as wildlings. Their fruits vary widely from tree to tree or thicket to thicket, but are as edible as those from domestic varieties. The bark and foliage are poisonous.

The overly-sweet fruits of the hackberry tree are perfectly edible, and the cherrylike pits contain kernels that are both harmless and good. The pits sometimes remain on the tree for considerable periods after the pulp has sloughed off.

The "Indian plum" or oso-berry of the Pacific Northwest is edible but not overly good, and its pits are also harmless.

Wild crabapples and seedling apples and pears are so similar to domestic types in overall appearance that these trees, too, are readily identified. The fruit of all types is edible, although the taste and quality of seedling fruit is different for every tree. Crabapples, of course, are intensely sour. The seeds contain cyanide in significant amount, but this is a hazard only when the seeds are eaten alone, raw, and in considerable quantity, which few would even try. Eaten with the fruit pulp or when cooked, they present no danger.

The hawthorns are tall woody shrubs or small trees with long woody thorns and variously-lobed leaves. The berries are exactly like small red or black apples, and are edible in small amount either raw or cooked. The berries contain a non-toxic heart stimulant and should not be eaten in large amount or without admixture. They are borne in tremendous quantity and remain on the tree all winter.

Red and white mulberries are large forest trees that produce tremendous crops of elongated berries that look like dewberries. These and the tender young leaves are edible raw or boiled. The berries are good when dried, and boiled young twigs are rather tasty. Planted by homesteaders, these trees are now sparingly established in the West.

The mountain ash is found in low-growing shrub and shade tree form. All species produce enormous crops of orange to red berries that are edible when cooked in two or more changes of water. The taste (to me) ranges from mildly awful to downright nasty, slightly less so after heavy frosts; but some people regularly make jelly from them. The pea-sized berries are in dense terminal bunches and remain on the bush or tree until well into winter. Plentiful when found, these berries are too unpalatable to most people to be very useful as emergency food; but you should at least try them. "One man's meat is another man's poison," after all, and you might even like them.

Blue or black elderberries are good either raw or cooked, fresh or dried, although the blue ones have to be washed to free them of a dense white powder that nauseates some people. The flowers are also edible, but the foliage is not. The red elderberry produces bright-red berries that are reputed to be mildly poisonous, although this is frequently disputed; and some Indian tribes are said to have used them for food. Elderberries are found as large, clustered shrubs or as very small trees. The foliage and bark are toxic, but mildly so.

The madrona grows at low to moderate altitudes from California to British Columbia on the west side of the Cascades, and another species grows in Arizona and New

Mexico. The tree is identifies by its polished red or reddish-yellow bark that peels and shreds in rolled tubes and its dark-green evergreen leaves. It produces terminal bunches of urn-shaped, white, sweet-scented flowers and bunches of half-inch orange or reddish-orange berries that look like rough-skinned oranges. Both the flowers and the fruit are edible when cooked, but few would call the berries good. Berries remain on the tree well into winter when not consumed by birds.

The manzanitas are similar to madrona in many ways, but they are always in sprawling or bush form. They are characterized by grayish-green evergreen leaves (two far-northern species are reluctantly deciduous) and brick-red to scarlet bark that is always flaking and peeling. The flat to round berries look exactly like tiny apples (*manzanita* is Spanish for "little apple") and are edible either raw or cooked. The urn-shaped pinkish flowers are also edible.

Kinnikinnic or bearberry manzanita is a sprawling, vine-like shrub with bright-red, round berries growing in clusters beneath the leaves. This is a high-altitude and circumpolar plant (it also grows along the immediate coast) and the berries remain on the plant all winter and well into spring. The dried leaves make a tea that is effective in the treatment of urinary infections or irritations. An interesting but harmless side effect is green urine! Dried leaves have long been used as a replacement for or as an adulterant of tobacco. Berries and flowers are as edible as in the many other species and the berries are valuable emergency food because of the plant's chosen habitat and their longevity.

The service berries (pronounced "sarvice" by many) are large shrubs or small trees with round or oval, bluish-green leaves that are smooth-edged near the leaf stem but sharply toothed near the tips. The berries are round or slightly elongated, blue or purplish, and have five dried-up, petallike projections on the end opposite to the stem. These berries are both edible and good whether raw or boiled, fresh or dried, and the foliage is edible as boiled greens. This was the berry the Indians normally mixed with pemmican or dried in large cakes for winter use.

The Oregon grapes grow as sprawling, prostrate shrubs, as single stems with spreading tops, or as upright, densely clustered shrubs to eight feet tall. All have spined evergreen leaves very similar to Christmas holly. The berries are blue, black, or dull-red, usually covered with a white, waxy powder, in large terminal bunches. These berries are too acidic to be good when raw, but they are perfectly edible when cooked, and they make a splendid additive to nonacid berries or fruits. The red-berried types and the smaller species of the blue-berried types are thought to produce the best-flavored fruit.

The jet-black crowberries are edible either raw or cooked. The plant is a sprawling evergreen shrub with short, needle-like leaves. It is common and abundant in Alaska and Canada, and extends southward along the immediate coast to northern California. The berries have a medicinal flavor, but this is not strong enough to be really unpleasant. The berries remain on the plant throughout the winter and are plentiful enough where found to make it worthwhile to dig through snow to get them.

The eastern blueberries and the western huckleberries are easily identified. The blue, black, and dull-red types are delicious; and the bright-red ones produced on very tall bushes are as good or better than these. The bright-red cranberries borne by a creeping vine in bogs and marshes and the red lingonberries found on low-growing bushes in drier surroundings are much too sour to be enjoyable raw. Cooked with a liberal admixture of sugar (salt reduces the amount of sugar needed) or other sweetener, these berries are very good indeed. These two are the berries of commerce. Both occur in tremendous abundance where found and remain on the plant all winter.

The salal is a low and tangled or thicket-forming shrub that forms dense jungles in coastal areas and grows in forested areas west of the Cascades from Alaska to California. It is characterized by long-oval, shiny-green, evergreen leaves and tough zigzag stems that have earned it the name of "shin tangle." The flowers are urn-shaped, pink or white, in fragile, one-sided clusters at the branch and stem tips; and both these flowers and the soft white flower stem are edible. The berries are bluish-black, barrel-shaped, tough-skinned, hairy, and very juicy, and are edible either raw or cooked, fresh or dried. They occur in tremendous quantity. The foliage is also edible.

Two smaller versions of the salal are found at high altitudes in the western mountains. Both have trailing, zigzag stems that are often buried by forest duff or old grasses, and these put up slender stems to six inches tall or less that are clothed in dense, reddish hair. They are found in thin woods but also grow well and bear prolifically in open alpine meadows where these are damp but not soggy. The leaves are evergreen and the pea-sized berries are red and white, much like tiny Rome Beauty apples. the whole plant is wintergreen scented and both the berries and the foliage are edible.

All of the wild honeysuckles produce berries that are edible in the sense that none are poisonous, but several species have berries that are excessively bitter. These are climbing or trailing vines or densely clustered shrubs, bearing flowers and fruit either in pairs or in terminal clusters.

The viburnums or high-bush cranberries are clustered shrubs with leaves much like shallowly lobed maple leaves. They bear terminal clusters of showy white flowers (the

Figure 17: Viburnums

"Snowball Bush" is a variety with sterile flowers) and enormous numbers of fruits, each containing a single, flattish, plumlike pit. The meat of these "berries" is very thin and has a rather unpleasant odor; but this meat is edible and not at all unpleasant when boiled, and is even good raw when the fruits have been thoroughly frosted or frozen. These fruits remain on the bush all winter, long after the leaves have fallen, often providing a splash of color where the branches protrude through snow. (See Figure 17.)

All of the many species of currant or gooseberry produce edible berries in the sense that none are harmful or poisonous, but some of these are so sticky-glandular, have such an unpleasant odor, or taste so bad that you could not eat them, at least when raw. Don't judge the quality by a single taste, as fruit from bushes a hundred yards apart may vary considerably. These berries are amber, red, black, or greenish, and are characterized by a dried-up tubular flower that clings to the berry. All of the species have shallowly lobed leaves like those of a maple.

The dwarf dogwoods are herbaceous plants with a single whorl of pointed, broad, lance-shaped leaves just below the tip of the six-inch stem. The inconspicuous flowers are surrounded by white bracts that appear to be petals, just as with tree dogwoods. The dense clot of red or purplish-red berries grows at the very tip of the stem. The plants often grow so thickly that they blanket large areas of forest floor, and the berries can be gathered in good quantity. They can be eaten either cooked or raw, but are not overly good when raw.

The cascara or chittum tree produces black, cherrylike fruits with several seeds. These are edible if not overly tasty, but they have a cathartic effect on some people. At least one recently published book lists them as poisonous, but I began eating the raw berries at age fourteen and I am now seventy-two! I don't like them well enough to eat them in quantity, however. The Northwest Indians apparently ate them in large amount. This is the cascara sagrada, the "sacred bark" of the Spanish, and the bark has long been used in the preparation of commercial laxatives. The tree is readily identified by its whitish bark and the deeply impressed parallel veining of the leaves.

The false Solomon's seal is a slender, arching plant rarely over two feet tall, with a double row of lance-shaped, stemless leaves. It bears a terminal raceme (elongate cluster) of small, translucent red berries that are often dotted with darker red. These berries are edible either raw or cooked, but are purgative to some people. The Indians of the Northwest also dug the large root, soaked it in a solution of wood ashes and water for twenty-four hours, then parboiled it to rid it of the lye. They then cooked and ate it as a vegetable.

The roots of the many species of balsamroot are edible when cooked, the young stems are good either raw or as cooked greens, and the seeds are among the most delightful of wild foods. The mule's ear or compass plant is very similar in appearance, and the roots are edible when baked or when boiled in two waters. No one would call them good. (See Figure 18.)

Figure 18: Mules' ears and balsamroots

Figure 19: Mariposas and cat ears

All of the many species of mariposa lilies and cat ears have edible and nutritious bulbs, although some of these are too small to be of much value. The entire above-ground plant, though sparse, is edible as cooked greens. Many of these are dry-area plants, growing in the sagebrush areas of the West and to seven thousand feet in the mountains. Other species grow on the fringes of the Western valleys and in open glades in the forested mountains of the Northwest. Others are found in the deserts of the Southwest. They all have three broad petals and three smaller, straplike sepals that may or may not be brightly colored. The larger and more colorful of these are known as mariposa tulips, and several small species are known as cat ears because of the thickly-haired interiors. (See Figure 19.)

All of the many native species of riceroot lilies have edible bulbs, these thickly covered with fat, ricelike granules that distinguish the bulbs from all others. These plants exist in widely varying habitats and themselves show marked variation within a species. In some species, the features are so inconsistant as to make it nearly impossible to accurately describe them. All species are recognizable either by the shape of their flowers or by the peculiar splotching that is the outstanding feature of all but two of the species. (See Figure 20.)

All of the dogtooth violets, also known as lambtongues, fawn lilies, trout lilies, avalanche lilies, glacier lilies, etc., have edible corms (bulbs), and the stems, leaves, buds, flowers, and seed pods are also edible. These plants have two very long, lance-shaped leaves that are marked with white or brown splotches in some species, unmarked in others. These are fused to the wiry scape (flower stem) below ground level and pull up with it. The flowers are six-petaled (actually three petals and three identical sepals) and come in a variety of

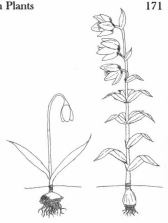

Figure 20: Riceroot lilies

Figure 21: Dogtooth violets

colors. They often grow so profusely that they carpet acres of ground, and one variety or another is found from sea level to well above timberline. (See Figure 21.)

Figure 22: Lilies

The true lilies are tall, stately plants with solitary stems rising from deep-seated, scaly bulbs. The leaves are long and tapering, either in whorls or scattered along the stem. The flowers are deep trumpet-shaped, often spicily scented, very showy, and variously colored. The bulbs and all other parts of the plant are edible either raw or cooked, and the buds and flowers are considered delicacies in Asia. (See Figure 22.)

The cluster lilies have thin, wiry stems springing from very deep-seated, fibrous-coated bulbs. The leaves are few, all at ground level, like flat blades of grass in some species, distinctly **U**-shaped in others, generally withering before the plants bloom. The flowers are papery in texture, six parted, the identical petals and sepals united into a tube for at least half their length in most species, each on a thin stem, these all springing from a common point at the tip of the main stem, but in some cases so short that the flowers are in a ball-like cluster. The flowers are blue, purple, yellow, red and green, two-tone blue, pinkish blue, white, or any off shade of these, with petals often striped with contrasting colors on the midveins. The stems range from six inches to nearly eight feet long in the various species and are sometimes looped or kinked. The bulbs are very deeply buried, often in hard-baked ground, and are very hard to dig. They are delicious either raw or cooked, and are often called "grass nuts." The unripe seed pods are edible when cooked. (See Figure 23.)

The wild onions (and wild garlic) are very similar to cluster lilies in overall appearance, but have the distinctive onion or garlic odor. Anyone with a normal sense of smell cannot fail to identify them by the odor alone. Like their domestic cousins, the entire plants are edible either cooked or raw. (See Figure 23.)

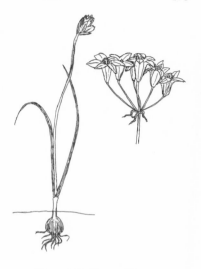

Figure 23: Cluster lilies

The edible camas has single, leafless stems to thirty inches tall (usually twelve to eighteen inches) growing from bulbs as much as two inches in diameter. The leaves are like blades of grass but thicker, flat or nearly so, often powdered, all from the base except for a modified leaf-like bract at the base of each flower branch. The flowers are a flattened bell-shape, from one and a half to more than two inches wide, generally pale blue to deepest blue-violet, but with occasional pure-white specimens. One southern Oregon variety has cream-colored flowers. The plants grow in moist meadows or wherever the ground is very damp or wet until late into spring. The bulbs were one of the most important foods of western Indians, and are still in regular use by some tribes and by some non-Indians. You can cook them by boiling, baking, or roasting, but they taste best (to me) when roasted in the ashes of a fire. (See Figure 24.)

Figure 24: Edible camas   Figure 25: Death camas

Beware the death camas! This deadly member of the lily family shares the range of cluster lilies, the wild onions, and the edible camas; and it has been collected and used in place of all three, often with fatal consequences. There is really no excuse for such carelessness, as the resemblance between these plants and any of the edible threesome is very superficial and the differences are distinctive.

The death camas has grasslike leaves that are sharply keeled or **V**-shaped, and these are very harsh and raspy on the thin edges. Though most leaves are basal, the plants often have two or three definite leaves on the erect stem. These leaves often enclose the stem for a considerable distance in a parchmentlike sheath. The flowers are borne in a dense raceme in which each flower is at the tip of its own threadlike stem, these arising at separate points along the upper end of the main stem. One species has flowers in a panicle, where each of these secondary stems is branched. As with any raceme, the bottom flowers open first, often before the topmost buds change color, and the blooms open in a steady upward progression. The flowers themselves appear to be six-petaled (three identical petals and sepals), and are rarely more than half an inch in diameter. They are saucer-shaped, white with a definite yellowish or greenish tinge that is created by yellow or green claws or glands at the base of each petal. (See Figure 25.)

Both cluster lilies and onions have flowers that terminate in thin stems that rise from a common point, like the ribs of an umbrella. The stems of both are leafless. The flowers of the cluster lilies are more or less in the shape of a tube with a flaring mouth, and no glands are in evidence. The onions have flowers that are trumpet-shaped to bell-shaped and without glands. The onions always have the distinctive odor.

The edible camas bears its flowers in a raceme, as does the death camas; but the flowers are not at all similar. The blooms of the edible camas are shallow-bowl to saucer-shaped, from one and a half to more than two inches across, and would flatten to an even wider diameter. These flowers range from washed-out blue to deepest violet, although one variety in the Umpqua Valley of Oregon is creamy-white. Pure-white specimens occur in all species. The leaves are like thickened blades of grass, flat or nearly so in cross-section, are often powdered, and are smooth edged. As with the cluster lily and onion, the petals are without glands, remaining thin to the base.

Attention to detail is vital! Anyone who uses the death camas by mistake does not die from poison. He dies from ignorance or carelessness! You would not mistake lettuce for cabbage in a store. No more should you confuse death camas with any other plant!

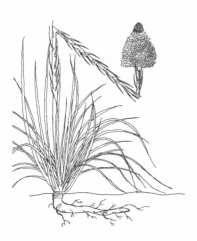

Figure 26: Bear grass

Bear grass is an odd member of the lily family found at moderate to high altitudes in the western mountains. It has tall, erect stems rising from dense mounds of long, thin leaves (one-quarter inch wide and up to eighteen inches long) that often cover large stretches of ground to the near exclusion of other plants. These leaves are extremely strong and were much used by the Indians for basket making. The stem is covered with shorter leaves lying flat against the surface. The flowers are white, tiny, and highly scented, in a dense terminal cluster somewhat to strongly onion-shaped. The rhizomes are much like those of the domestic iris, often partially exposed, and are edible when cooked in two or more changes of water. You can also wash your person or your clothing in the first water, as the saponin extracted by the hot water creates quantities of "suds." The peeled stems are edible when boiled with other greens. The plants are identifiable in winter. (See Figure 26.)

One of the mainstays of the Northwest Indian diet was the "*wokas,*" or yellow pond lily. These plants grow in still water, and the large pads or leaves often completely blanket the surface of ponds or shallow lakes. The large, cylindrical roots are edible when roasted or when ground into meal, but they are not at all tasty to me. The seeds, too, can be ground for flour; but they also make an acceptable substitute for popcorn! Bring the seeds to high heat in a dry or lightly oiled pan, just

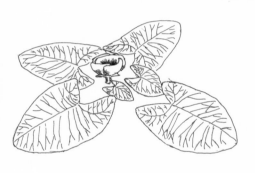

Figure 27: Wokas

as you would with popcorn. They will not explode with the same glorious abandon as popcorn, but they will pop open; and the meat can be winnowed from the cracked shells. To secure the seeds, break open the hard seed pod or soak a mass of them in a container or a pit full of water to soften them. When you extract the seeds, you will find each one firmly attached to a "floater." Simply dump them into a container of water and set it aside. The floaters will all detach themselves from the seeds and allow the seeds to sink, usually within twenty-four hours. (See Figure 27.)

Another highly valued food among the Indians was *"wapatoo,"* or arrowhead tubers. The several species are aquatic plants, growing in water or in oozy mud. They have large, shiny-green, long-stemmed leaves shaped much like arrowheads, and a tall, robust stem with filmy-white, three-petaled flowers in groups of three. The roots are thin and stringlike and bear numerous potatolike tubers. These can be used in any way that potatoes are, but they should be cooked somewhat longer than potatoes of the same size.

Figure 28: Wapatoo

The Indian women gathered the tubers by wading chest deep in the chilly waters of late fall and early winter, hanging on to the sides of an empty canoe. They located and worked the tubers out of the bottom mud with their toes. The detached tubers would bob to the surface, and the women would collect them and toss them into the canoe. A simpler and less Spartan method is to rake the mud to a depth of several inches and to a distance of two to three feet around a plant, stirring vigorously to both dislodge the tubers and free them of clinging mud. Use a stout, well-branched limb or pole as a rake. You can make a miniature log boom by tying floating sticks together to corral the tubers and prevent them from floating beyond your reach. (See Figure 28.)

The common and ubiquitous cattail is a veritable market basket of edible products. The ropelike rootstocks are shallowly buried in a tangled mat in the mud of pond bottoms and in ditches and marshes. Dig or dredge up a number of these roots, peel them of their spongy rind, and crush the cores in a container of water. Work the fibers out of the cores with your fingers and allow the starch to settle. Pour off the water and refill the container, then stir up the starch and let it settle again. Repeat as often as you wish, refining the starch to your own satisfaction. The final result is a fine flour, every bit as good as that ground from grain.

You can also extract this flour, though not in as high a quality, by boiling the peeled roots to a gruel and straining out the fiber; by drying the peeled roots, roasting them, and shaking out the dry starch; or by cooking the peeled roots and chewing them to extract and swallow the starch and spit out the fibers. It is even possible to cut the peeled roots into thin slices or bite-sized chunks, cook them, and eat them, fiber and all, as a vegetable.

Each node of the creeping roots puts forth a sort of sheathed bud that will be next year's plant. Each of these buds contains a delicate, starchy kernel much like a nutmeat, and these are delightful when cooked in a meat stock. They are also good raw, but should not be so eaten if their growth site might be polluted or contaminated.

When the plants are still young (before the stalk emerges), you can grasp the clump of leaves and with one firm yank break the plant away from the root. The inner leaves and the base from which they grow are white, tender, and fragrant, and are among the most delicate and tasty vegetables the wild affords. This product is used nearly throughout the world, and is usually known as "Cossack asparagus." The seed heads of cattails make a very good substitute for corn on the cob when collected before ripening. They tend to be somewhat dry, but are both nourishing and tasty. The pollen stalk that surmounts this head becomes thoroughly coated with fluffy golden pollen during the blooming season, and this pollen is useful as a flavorful and nutritious flour. Even the countless tiny seeds can be used as food in a real emergency. Gather the ripened heads and burn them on a flat rock or other hard and nonflammable surface. The down will be burned away, leaving large numbers of preparched seeds to be sifted from the ashes. No one can go hungry when cattails are available.

Bullrushes or tules also have edible roots. These are marsh plants, ranging from a few inches to more than eighteen feet tall in the various species. The leaves in most species are reduced to pointed sheaths. The plants have stems that are oval, elliptical, or triangular in cross section, and they are easily and positively identified. The roots can be eaten either raw or cooked, but should be thoroughly cooked because of pollution hazards.

The common reed is another marsh plant that produces edible roots, and the whole plant can be eaten. It has stems to twelve feet tall, leaves to one inch wide and eighteen inches long, and great plumy heads like hairy corn tassels. The young stems and leaves are useful as cooked greens and the older stems (before blooming time) can be ground into a very sweet flour.

Even the western skunk cabbage has roots that are edible when properly prepared. This plant has enormous round-oval, shiny-green leaves, giving it the appearance of a tropical plant, although it favors cool bogs and marshy ground. *The leaves are all from the root.* The flowers are tiny and greenish, on a clublike spike held within a flame-yellow cloak or spathe. The whole plant is very rank-scented, and it does indeed smell "skunky." The roots are very thick and fleshy, buried deeply in wet or watery muck. Both these roots and, to a lesser extent, all other parts of the plant contain needlelike crystals of calcium oxalate, a nonsoluble acid. These penetrate the tender tissues of the mouth, tongue, and throat when eaten without proper preparation, and produce a painful burning and choking sensation.

This acid is not water soluble and is unaffected by boiling, no matter how often the water is changed. It is volatile,

Figure 29: False hellebore (left) and Skunk cabbage (right)

although reluctantly so, and either long-term drying or thorough roasting will eliminate all traces of it. When baked in an underground pit for not less than thirty-six hours, the roots are very good indeed; and the air-dried leaves are also good. These plants are readily identified, occur in tremendous abundance where found, are widespread, and are available from early spring till late fall. They are therefore a valuable source of emergency food. (See Figure 29.)

CAUTION: *The tall, leafy-stemmed plant that grows in boggy or wet situations is not skunk cabbage,* although I have seen it so identified in some books. It is instead the poisonous false hellebore, *Veratrum,* and all parts of the plant, especially the blackish roots, are virulently toxic! These plants have boat-shaped leaves with deeply-impressed parallel veins that look like seams in boat planking. These leaves all grow from a common stalk or stem. *Skunk cabbage has no such stem, each leaf having its own stem that comes directly from the root.* (See Figure 29.)

Silverweed, while not a true marsh plant, is still partial to damp soils, especially where these are salty or alkaline. These plants are distinguished by the long, trailing leaves formed of a midstem with as many as twenty-one sharply-toothed, long-oval leaflets that are green on top but silvery on the bottom, these interspersed with tiny leaves that are otherwise identical. The plant spreads by means of red, strawberrylike runners, and the single, hairy-centered, yellow flowers look like strawberry blooms in all but color. The fleshy roots are delicious when fried, only slightly less so when baked or roasted, having a delightful nutty taste. They are also good when boiled, then tasting (to me) more like a sweet potato than a nut. The entire above-ground plant can be used as cooked greens, but the dryish, hemispheric fruit is scarcely edible. The plant grows luxuriantly along the immediate coast, occurs in suitably damp and saline areas in the sagebrush deserts, and reaches very high altitudes in the mountains. It is found nearly throughout the continent, even growing well in the Aleutian Islands. Because of its wide distribution, the ease of identification, and the abundance of the plants where found, this is an ideal emergency food source. The delightful taste is a bonus.

Chufa or nut grass is also partial to damp soils, but it is much less tolerant of salinity or alkalinity than silverweed. It is a sedge, not a grass, and has stout, clustered, triangular stems rising from a clump of grasslike leaves that are usually as long as or longer than the stems. The stems are naked except for a cluster of small leaflike bracts just below the flowers, which are yellowish and tiny, in double rows on the several spikelets. The thin roots produce numerous nutlike tubers, and these are among the tastiest of wild foods. They can be eaten out of hand, roasted and used as a coffee substitute, or cooked by any chosen method to be used as a main dish. The plants have been grown for food throughout the world, and they now occur as escapees almost anywhere from sea level to moderate altitudes in all but

Figure 30: Chufa

the colder and drier parts of the continent. When growing in sandy or loose-soil areas, these are a valuable food source, but digging the tubers from harder soils would expend more energy than you would gain. (See Figure 30.)

Figure 31: Elkweed

Elkweed or deer-tongue is distinguished by its enormous long-oval leaves and its peculiar flowers. The stem is very stout and erect, smooth to faintly scaly/raspy, and grows to seven feet tall, with whorls of leaves like giant willow leaves (narrowly elliptical). These are dwarfed by the basal leaves. These are also shaped like willow leaves but are widest at the tip, are as much as twenty inches long and four inches wide, and have deeply impressed parallel veins. The flowers are greenish-white, edged with purple and dotted with violet, on short stems in the upper leaf-stem junctions. The very large taproot is edible either boiled, roasted, baked, or fried, with those from stemless plants being much the best. The tender young leaves and the younger stems are also edible as cooked greens. These plants are found at high altitudes in the Rocky Mountains and their subsidiary ranges, often forming dense colonies. (See Figure 31.)

The evening primroses all have edible roots. These plants have trumpet or saucer-shaped, four-petaled flowers that are bright yellow, pink, or pure white, large and showy in most species. The unopened buds are conspicuous, usually reddish in color. The plants are stemless or nearly so in some species, but several of the more common types have stems to two feet tall, these densely covered with whitish or reddish hair. The roots are carrot-form, large for plants of this size, and are very tasty either baked, boiled, or fried. The roots of younger plants are best, as older roots become somewhat peppery. The leaves make good greens. (See Figure 32.)

The burdocks have thick/fleshy roots that are edible. These are biennials, the first-year plant being a clump of rhubarblike leaves on long, purplish, **U**-shaped stems. The second-year plant has a large and leafy stem that can be peeled and sliced (before the blooms open) to be boiled or even fried like sliced potatoes. The leaves and their stems can be cooked as greens. All of these products taste best if first parboiled, and a dash of baking soda (you can substitute white wood ash) added to the first water improves taste still further. These roots are sold in produce markets in Asia. (See Figure 33.)

Figure 32: Evening primrose

Figure 33: Burdock

All of the true thistles have edible roots, these generally carrot-form and quite large. The peeled stems are also edible and rather good when boiled, and the despined, unopened buds and the disarmed leaves make good greens. The downy seed heads can be burned and the seeds gathered as with cattails.

Several species of sunflower have edible roots, these either fleshy rootstocks or actual tubers. The Jerusalem artichoke is one of these, and it produces large numbers of knobby tubers as big as potatoes. These are somewhat watery, and they are not very good (to my taste) when fried, but some people like them as well as or even better than potatoes. You can boil them, bake them, or even grate raw tubers and use them raw in a salad. They are nonstarchy but are highly nourishing, and even a few plants will provide a large supply. As with all sunflowers, the seeds are nutritious, and the immature seed heads, or the flower heads before or during blooming, can be boiled and eaten. The leaves, too, are edible when cooked. This is the most valuable species, but check out all of them.

Both the bracken fern and the sword ferns have starchy, fibrous roots that are edible. Boil the roots to a thick gruel, then strain out the fibers. You can also dry the crushed roots and shake the powdery starch into a container, or can even chew the cooked roots to swallow the starch and spit out the fibers. The roots can also be cut into small chunks, boiled, and eaten as a vegetable, but they are hard to digest. The young, coiled fronds of the bracken can also be cooked like asparagus spears, although they more nearly resemble okra in taste and texture.

The common and the alpine bistorts produce edible roots. These are members of the knotweed family. They are found in wet meadows or other damp and unshaded areas at moderately high to very high altitudes. Both produce a single zigzag, reddish stem with a few smallish leaves, but the main leaves are from the base. The leaves are smooth and hairless on top but hairy or fuzzy on the bottom, somewhat brownish, shaped much like blades of grass but normally only three inches or so long. The flowers are tiny, white or pinkish, strong-scented, in a dense terminal spike. The alpine bistort has

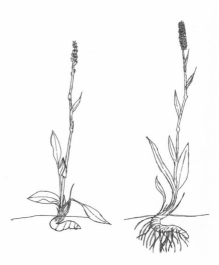

Figure 34: Alpine and meadow bistort

a number of small bulbets clasped against the stem by brownish scales, these occurring just below the spike. (See Figure 34.)

The carrot or parsley family produces some of the finest wild food plants and some of the deadliest plants to be found on this continent. The whole family is characterized by, and is named for, the distinctive flower structure. The flowers are in double or compound umbels, in which a number of primary flower stems (rays) grow from a common point at the tip of the main stem or its branches. Each of these rays bears at its tip a number of smaller branches (pedicels), also arising from a common point, each bearing a single flower. While the entire head and the secondary umbels may be

Figure 35: Compound umbel

domed, saucer-shaped, cup-shaped, or nearly spherical, or may be straggly and disorganized, the basic structure remains the same. In all cases the heads resemble an umbrella with each of the ribs bearing a smaller umbrella at its tip. (See Figure 35.)

The wild carrot is a common and very widespread weedy pest, often taking over unused fields, roadsides, or other uncultivated "waste areas." It is now being found at moderate altitudes and in primitive areas. The plant is a biennial, producing only a clump of finely dissected foliage the first year, flowering, fruiting, and dying the second year. In its first year, it forms the familiar taproot, which makes its cultivated descendant so valuable as a food plant. This root is much smaller and woodier than in the domestic plant and is white rather than yellow; but the taste, odor, and edibility are the same. Use them either cooked or raw, just as you would with the garden-grown ones. The tall second-year stem bears numerous saucer-shaped, white or pinkish heads that are so lacy and delicate that the plant is widely known as "Queen Anne's Lace." An interesting feature of this flower head is a small purple flower, otherwise identical to the rest, at or near its center.

The heads after blooming assume a cup or goblet shape, and the seed heads are then widely known as "birds' nests." This structure clasps the seeds so tightly that some of them

remain with it until the rays disintegrate. These seeds can be
steeped to yield a fragrant, spicy tea that is said to be strongly
antiflatulent, and they can also be used to flavor other foods.

Remember that the wild carrot is distinctively and
strongly carrot-scented throughout, and all of the stems,
including those of the first-year leaves, are solid or almost so,
and are strongly bristly-hairy.

The poison hemlock, *Conium,* is said by many writers to
resemble the wild carrot, but this resemblance is so superficial

Figure 36: Poison hemlock

and the differences so distinctive that it is hard to see how anyone could confuse one for the other. The poison hemlock is much taller than the wild carrot (four to ten feet as opposed to one to four feet), has hollow, thin-walled, purple-splotched stems that are very smooth and polished and covered with a white powder. The first-year plant produces only a clump of lacy, fernlike leaves; but the leaf stems are powdered, polished, and purple splotched. The plant is extensively branched near the top and is roughly shaped like a tall hardwood tree in skeletal structure. (See Figure 36.)

No one with a normal sense of smell could fail to separate them on that basis alone. The carrot is strongly carrot-scented, while the poison hemlock has a distinctly unpleasant musty or "mousy" odor.

The cow parsnip is a tall (to ten feet, but usually four to five feet), stout-stemmed plant. The ridged stems are hairy or woolly, and are often marked with red or purple splotching. The leaves are very large, three-parted, with the leaflets shaped like maple leaves. The heads are white, shaped like and sometimes as large as a dinner plate, with conspicuously larger flowers around the perimeter. The plants grow in dense colonies in permanently damp areas, but are found in stunted form even on the gravel shoulders of highways. They occur from sea level to high altitudes and grow along streams even in some semiarid desert areas. Both the large turnip-shaped roots and the peeled stems are edible when cooked, and some Indians ate the peeled stems raw. I find the taste unpleasant, but tastes differ. I would not hesitate to use them in an emergency.

The desert parsleys are generally low-growing species with dissected, carrotlike leaves, but several species grow to three feet or so tall and some have elliptical or long-oval leaflets. The flowers are white, yellow, pink, salmon-col-

ored, or purplish. These
are mainly dry area
plants, being found from
sagebrush deserts to high,
barren, stony mountain
ridges. All have large,
fleshy roots that are
edible when cooked, and
the foliage is also edible as
cooked greens. One
species, known as Indian
parsnip, pestle parsnip,
or Indian celery, has top-
shaped knobs at the tips
of the main stem and the

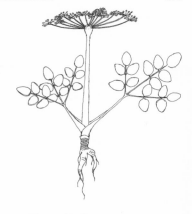

Figure 37: Desert parsley

rays; and these are spicily pungent, more or less like dill. Its
stems, once the seeds have begun to form, have a taste very
similar to that of celery. (See Figure 37.)

The Indian potato, also known as turkey pea, is a small
and low-growing plant with leaves divided into three leaflets
like short grass blades, the whole resembling a turkey track.
The flowers are white, in an irregular head. The radishlike
root is very tasty either raw or cooked, and the foliage is
edible as a cooked green. This, too, is a desert plant, found in
dry sagebrush areas or on barren mountain ridges.

The yampah is a slender plant to two or three feet tall,
with a smooth, hairless stem and leaves divided into narrow
leaflets much like blades of grass (one species has oval
leaflets). The lower leaves die well before blooming time,
leaving the lower stalk naked. The flowers are white, in
more or less dome-shaped umbels, with the secondary
umbels being almost spherical. The roots are carrot-form,
usually two but sometimes one or three, and are among the
most delicious food roots, either wild or cultivated, that are

Figure 38: Yampah

known. They grow in the driest of sagebrush areas but are also found at considerable altitudes in dry mountain meadows. They resemble *Cicuta* in having multiple roots, in having smooth, hairless stems, and in the color of the blooms; but they are never powdered, never marked or spotted with red or purple, and they are never found in marshy or permanently wet areas. (See Figure 38.)

Figure 39: Wild parsnip

Wild parsnip in its first year produces only a clump of leaves and the familiar white, carrot-form root, this differing from the cultivated root only in being somewhat smaller and woodier. The leaves are composed of a midstem with a number of oval or egg-shaped leaflets, these sharply toothed and sometimes cut or lobed. In its second year it is a tall, robust plant (to five feet tall) that has sharp, almost knife-edged vertical ridged on the stem. The flowers are yellow, in flat to dome-shaped heads. You will have heard that this plant is poisonous, but such reports are based on a simple confusion of identity. Dozens of plants in this family have the word "parsnip" as part of their common name and when someone says "wild parsnip" he may actually be referring to any one of several plants. (See Figure 39.)

The roots of the several species of *Cymopterus* are also known as Indian parsnip or wafer parsnip. These plants have no leaf-bearing stem, the lacy, finely dissected leaves all growing from the base, and the short flower stems bear variously shaped heads of white flowers. The root is deeply buried, putting forth an underground stem (a psuedoscape) to reach the surface, and is usually somewhat largest at its lower end. These roots are edible either raw or cooked when very young, and are edible if cooked in two waters when older. The foliage should not be eaten. (See Figure 40.)

Figure 40:
Wafer parsnip

The water hemlocks, *Cicuta,* are the deadliest native wild plants found on the North American continent. This is a wet-area genus, the plants growing either in water or in permanently saturated ground. The stem is hollow, thin-walled, jointed, smooth and polished, powdered, often but not always marked with red or purple, to ten feet tall, but usually four or five feet. The flowers are white or greenish-white, very showy, in dome-shaped to almost spherical heads.

The leaves are to three feet long, compound, composed of a midstem and several branches, each bearing a number of leaflets. The leaflets in all but *C. bulberifera* are like long and narrow willow leaves, but sharply toothed. Its leaves are like blades of grass, sharply but sparingly toothed. In all species but *C. bulberifera* and *C. californica*, the veins run to the notches between the teeth and not to the points as they do in all other members of the parsley or carrot family. A very close examination will show that these veins do not actually reach the notches, but they always appear to do so, and this is diagnostic.

Figure 41: Cicuta

The most distinguishing feature of *Cicuta* is the unique structure of the stem base and rootstock. This underground portion of the stem is greatly enlarged or thickened, and this area contains a number of short air chambers separated by transverse partitions. Very young plants may not have actual chambers, but the future structure will be represented by yellow layers embedded in a white matrix. Cut surfaces of this stem base yield a yellowish exudate that is strongly parsnip-scented. This sap will cause a severe and painful dermatitis on contact with the skin, so wash thoroughly after handling.

The roots number from one to several, and are shaped much like sweet potato or dahlia tubers. They are tender in texture, of good size, smell good (if you like parsnip!), and apparently taste good. They cause numerous human deaths and are one of the worst livestock poisoners. (See Figure 41.)

The best protection until you have learned to recognize members of this genus is simply to avoid use of any member of the carrot family that grows in wet situations unless it has features that clearly distinguish it from *Cicuta*. The cow parsnip, for example, has hairy or woolly stems and large, maplelike leaflets, and many species of *Angelica* have large leaflets that could not possibly be confused with those of the water hemlock. These are the only edible genera listed that grow in such wet areas.

Only Cicuta *has a chambered stem base and rootstock that contains yellow, parsnip-scented sap; smooth, powdered, red or purple splotched stems; dahlia- or sweet potato-like tubers; and veins that run to the notches of the leaflets. No other plant has these features. Be certain of identity or do not use!* There are many other sources of food, but you have only one life!

Wild celery is the domestic plant escaped from cultivation and is now sparingly established to moderate altitudes in some areas. It looks, smells, and tastes exactly as does the commercial plant, but is usually smaller and somewhat less juicy. It is more widely known for the crisp leaf stalks than for its roots, but these are a splendid flavoring agent for soups and stews and can also be eaten as a vegetable if sliced thinly and cooked in two or more waters to reduce the flavor.

The various species of *Angelica* are also known as wild celery, and the stalks are used as celery substitutes. These are tall plants (though one coastal species sprawls) with compound leaves, the leaflets being oblong, egg-shaped, or nearly round, variously toothed, and strongly aromatic. The stems are smooth and hairless to near their tips in most species (one coastal species has hairy stems), but the topmost part of the stems and the flower heads are thinly hairy to strongly woolly. The flowers are white, in rather large heads. Found from seashore to rather high altitudes, these plants offer and excellent survival food during the summer months. *Be careful at first!* You may be allergic to these; many are.

CAUTION: Some species share habitats with the water hemlock, *Cicuta,* or the poison hemlock, *Conium. The veins of the leaflets in Angelica lead directly and obviously to the points of the teeth; the stem is neither marked with red or purple nor powdered; the stem base is not chambered or filled with oily, yellow, parsnip-scented sap; the leaves are not elliptical; and the roots are not clustered tubers. Be certain of identity or do not use!*

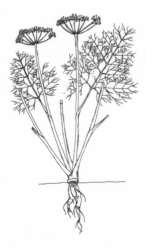

Figure 42: Sweet fennel

Sweet fennel, also known as wild anise or wild licorice, is a densely clustered plant to six feet tall, the individual stems meaty and juicy, almost solid (with a very tiny hollow), bluish-green, densely powdered, very strongly licorice-scented and flavored. The leaves are compound, with numerous threadlike leaflets. The flowers are yellow, in large heads. The odor and taste of licorice is too strong for use as food unless boiled in several changes of water, but the leaves, stems, roots, and seeds are splendid for seasoning other foods. The stems make a pleasant nibble, and a few chopped stems added sparingly to salads will improve flavor. This plant has escaped cultivation to become well established in scattered colonies, and it is now widespread. (See Figure 42.)

Sweet Cicely is a genus of several species, the stems slender to stout, erect, and thinly or not at all hairy. The leaves are compound, the leaflets shaped like short blades of grass or egg-shaped, variously but sparingly toothed, in some species sometimes cut or lobed; all are licorice scented. The primary rays are very long, and the compound umbel is not at all headlike. The flowers are white, sometimes with a greenish or purplish tinge. The seeds are very sharp and bristly, clinging to the clothing and hitching a ride to new locations. One or another of the species may be found from sea level to high altitudes in almost any nondesert area of the continent. Both the roots and the foliage are edible either raw or cooked, but you may find it necessary to cook in two waters to tone down the licorice taste.

Remember! With any member of the parsley family, take special pains to identify before using. *Be positive of identity or do not use!*

Among the many plants with both edible foliage and roots are members of the chicory or dandelion tribe of the Composite family. This group is characterized by certain distinctive features held in common and distinguishing them from other members of the family. Among these features are the typical shape of leaves, the flat "petals" of the flowers, and the bitter, milky latex that exudes when part of the foliage is cut or torn. No member of this group is harmful in normal amounts, but many are so distasteful that you would find it hard to eat them.

Remember that other plants may have leaves shaped somewhat like those of this group, and others may have bitter milky juice (this often indicates poisonous qualities in other families!) or dandelion-like flowers. No plant not a member of this group will have all three of these features, and you can safely assume that any plant that has all three is edible. Don't be deterred by initial bitterness, as both dandelion and common lettuce become excessively bitter with age.

The common dandelion has hollow, thin-walled, leafless flower stems to a foot or so tall, rising from a basal rosette of green leaves that are raggedly cut all the way to the midrib. The flower (actually a large number of ray flowers forming a ligulate head) is bright yellow, and is familiar to all. There are many subspecies and varieties, each of which very closely resembles the others. The leaves, flowers, roots, and stems are edible; and large populations have subsisted almost exclusively on dandelions in time of famine. Boil older plants or roots of any age in two or more waters to reduce bitterness. Dry the roots and slowly roast them until they are brown and crumbly, then pulverize and use as a coffee substitute.

False dandelion resembles dandelion very closely and is even more of a pest, as it has a much longer blooming period. It has smaller heads than the dandelion, and its somewhat taller stems are solid and strongly ribbed. It is both edible and rather good, lacking the bitterness of dandelion.

Wild lettuce is a common and troublesome weed, often protruding from cracks in city sidewalks and completely filling roadside ditches or dominating uncultivated areas. The leafy stems are as much as twelve feet tall in the various species and are smooth and hairless in all but one that has a bristly base. The leaves are short-stemmed or stemless, then tending to clasp the main stem, very long and oblong in shape, cut or lobed, often armed with weak and nearly transparent prickles along the thin edges. The flowers are bright yellow, pale yellow, or pale blue, not more than an inch in diameter, in open, terminal clusters.

These plants are cousins of garden lettuce, and like it they become excessively bitter with age. This quality can be subdued but not eliminated by cooking in two waters. The juice of these plants was formerly collected, coagulated, and used as an opium substitute, but seems to have achieved its effect through the power of suggestion rather than from any intrinsic property. Eaten in large quantity, however, these plants do seem to have a mild tranquilizing effect on some people.

The sow thistles are rank-growing, bushy weeds of widespread distribution. The entire plant is weak-prickly, but the foliage and the flowers are so similar to those of the dandelion that they are instantly recognized as being closely related. The foliage and the roots are edible, but again should be cooked in two waters to improve the taste.

Chicory roots are famous as a coffee substitute or adulterant, and the leaves are widely used in salads. (Endive is a cultivated variety.) The large cluster of basal leaves is blue-green, otherwise much like dandelion leaves. The densely clustered, stiff, much-branched stems have many small, clasping, stemless leaves. The flowers are to two inches wide, a beautiful shade of blue, nearly or quite stemless, and numerous. The stiff, leafless, clustered stems are distinctive even in winter, and will enable you to locate the still edible roots. Dry these roots and roast them until brown and crumbly, then pulverize and use as a coffee substitute. The roots can also be eaten as a vegetable. With either roots or leaves, it is necessary to cook in two or more waters to reduce bitterness.

The oyster plant or the similar goatsbeards have leafy stems to two feet or more tall. The leaves are bluish-green, clasping, long and narrow, tapering regularly, differing from those of other members of their group by being smooth edged and uncut. The purple or bright yellow flowers are cupped in a saucer-shaped involucre (a group of pointed, tapering, modified leaves), the tips of which extend beyond the bloom. The distinctive puffball is at least twice as big as in the dandelion and is "tattletale gray" rather than white. The roots are carrot-form, of good size. The roots of the purple-flowered species are sold in grocery stores as "salsify." They are said to taste like oysters, but they do not taste so to me. In any case, these roots are edible as cooked vegetables and the foliage is edible as cooked greens. Found from sea level to moderately high altitudes and readily identified, these are a valuable source of emergency food.

Other members of this clan abound, but all can be identified by the shared characteristics of notched "petals," milky sap, and dandelion-like leaves. (The sole exception for oyster plant and goatsbeard leaves has already been noted.)

Figure 43: Plantains

Another widespread and ubiquitous genus of edible plants is plantain. Most of these plants have long, narrowly elliptical leaves, but two common species have roundish leaves, all in basal rosettes, with indented, parallel veins. The flower stems are slender, leafless, often minutely hairy or fuzzy, usually strictly erect but occasionally nodding (bent over at the tip), bearing a very dense spike of inconspicuous flowers. The leaves make excellent greens, but should be chopped into short lengths to eliminate stringiness. One coastal species has thickened leaves that snap almost as crisply as green beans and need to be destringed. Bland and tasteless in some species, rather tasty in others, these plants furnish an abundant and easily identified source of food for most of the year. (See Figure 43.)

Another very valuable source of camp or emergency food is the beet family. Its members are among the most salt-tolerant plants known, and can be found in saline or alkaline areas where little else will grow. All but a very few are edible, and most are good. The inedible ones are uneatable because of odor or taste, not because of toxicity.

White pigweed, also known as lamb's quarter, goosefoot, and wild beet, is a common and widespread weed, growing mostly in disturbed soils. It grows to four feet or so tall, is many branched, and has roughly triangular leaves with stepped sides that more or less resemble a goose's foot. All of the foliage, but especially those leaves near the tips, are covered with a white (or sometimes pinkish) mealy powder that gives the plant a grayish-white appearance. The seeds appear in dense spikelets in the axils (leaf-stem junctions) and in ball-like clusters at the stem and branch tips. These seeds remain on the dead plant till midwinter, are highly nutritious, and can be gathered in good quantity. Grind them for flour, cook as mush, or add to soups and stews. The leaves and tender young stems are widely used as cooked greens, and in my opinion are far superior to chard or spinach. My children all shared this opinion. They disliked spinach and tolerated chard, but loved pigweed.

More than a dozen other species of this genus are listed, and one or another may be found anywhere, as they range from coast to coast and from sea level to moderate altitudes. All but one are edible, and most are very good. One

Northern species, known as "Indian strawberry," has pulpy red seed clusters that can be eaten out of hand like a fruit. They are not at all distasteful, but neither are they very good, at least to me. All of the species resemble each other very strongly and are easily identified. You will know the bad one by its strong chemical odor.

Hop sage is a low-growing bushy shrub with brown or grayish, shreddy bark on more or less spiny stems. The leaves are pale green, scaly or mealy, egg-shaped but largest at the outer end, to one and a half inches long. The flowers are inconspicuous, generally unisexual (male or female only on a single plant), but sometimes with both on the same plant, in terminal spikes. The developing seeds are encased in an open-mouthed pouch formed by the fusion of two fleshy red or pink bracts, and the female plants become somewhat showy when in fruit. The leaves, seeds, bracts, and the tender young twigs are all edible when boiled as greens. The plants grow in slightly salty or alkaline soils and from low desert areas to moderate altitudes.

Winterfat is a semisprawling shrub that is densely covered with woolly white hair, and this gives the bushes a distinctive whitish appearance. The leaves are long-oval, to two inches long, with the long edges rolled tightly inward. The flowers are inconspicuous and the seeds appear to be balls of cotton in the axils (leaf-stem junctions). The plants then appear to be completely filled with cotton. They grow in salty or alkaline soils, mostly in the sagebrush communities of the West. The leaves and the tender twigs are edible when boiled.

Greasewood is a tall, bushy shrub with whitish bark and with most of the twigs ending in sharp, hardened spines. The leaves are dark green, to an inch and a half long, fleshy, and triangular to almost round in cross section. The male or staminate flowers look much like small fir cones at the twig tips, and the separate, inconspicuous female flowers are almost hidden in the axils. These shrubs grow in dense colonies on strongly salty or alkaline soils in the arid areas of the West. The leaves, the tender young twigs, and the staminate "cones" are all edible when boiled, but they must not be eaten in large quantity unless boiled in two waters to remove excessive salt and acid concentrations.

Orach or saltbush species form a large group of annual and perennial plants, some of which are even shrubby in character. The foliage is usually mealy or scaly, the stems are often strongly angled, and the outline of the plant is usually rounded or pyramidal, although two species are sprawlers. The foliage bears a marked resemblance to that of the goosefoots, and the plants are readily recognized, regardless of species. The various species are found in alkaline inland areas and in saline soils along the immediate coast, and they are common in almost the entire continent to moderate altitudes. One species is commonly cultivated as a vegetable garden favorite, and the others are just as edible. Cook the leaves and the tender stems as greens, boiling in two waters if necessary to eliminate saltiness.

Russian thistle is a much-branched annual weed, the branches mostly from the base, growing outward at first, then curving upward and inward to form a ball-shaped or globular mass. The main stem and its branches are sharply ridged. The lower leaves and some of the leaves on the primary branches are long and narrow, to nearly three inches long. The leaves on the smaller twigs are very similar but shorter and end in sharp spines. This is a notorious member of the "tumbleweeds" and a pernicious pest. Even so, the younger plants (before the thorns form) are very good when boiled as greens, and such plants will develop from earliest spring to late fall, springing up after every rain. The plant is salt-tolerant but will grow in other soils, and it is far too common and widespread in the drier areas of the West to moderate altitudes.

The several species of blite (*Suaeda*) are succulent weeds that are sprawling or only weakly erect, with fleshy leaves that are often nearly round in cross section, these ending in sharp but not hardened points. They grow only in salty or alkaline soils of the western states, but reach fairly high altitudes. The leaves are edible when boiled in two waters, and can be eaten raw when mixed with other and less salty foods.

Glasswort or chicken claws is an erect or sprawling plant with round, lead-colored internode sections shaped like baseball bats and with the vestigial leaves forming complete disks at the nodes. A reddish species occurs. It is found in salt marshes along the coast but occasionally grows in salty or alkaline marshes inland. Wherever found, the entire plant is edible either raw or cooked. It is extremely salty and may be used to add salt to other foods.

Five-hook bassia is a much-branched annual weed to three feet or more tall. The stems are finely hairy throughout, and this hair becomes white and woolly near the stem and branch tips. The leaves are largest at the tip, pointed-oval, to nearly an inch long, smooth edged, and covered with fine, silky hair. The single flowers grow in the axils, and each of the five sepals is equipped with a long and sharply hooked spine. This is a widespread plant in the drier areas of the West and is a valuable forage plant, especially after the nutritious seeds develop. The whole plant is both edible and good. Boil the foliage as greens and grind the seeds to use as flour or cook them as mush.

Patata is one of several species of *Monolepis* that are edible. Its much-branched stems are sprawling or weakly erect, succulent, smooth and hairless, with lance-shaped leaves that have a pair of wide-spreading lobes at the base. The inconspicuous flowers are in dense clusters in the axils (leaf-stem junctions). These plants grow in damp salty or alkaline soils throughout the drier parts of the western states. The entire above-ground plant is edible when boiled for greens. The other species are very similar to patata and are just as edible.

The purslane family produces a rather large number of edible species. These are succulent and fleshy herbs of various habit and are widely distributed.

Purslane or pussley is a sprawling plant, much-branched from the root crown, with reddish, smooth, and very fleshy stems. It has almost or quite stemless green leaves to three quarters of an inch long, long-oval but widest at the tip, and thick and fleshy. The flowers are tiny and bright yellow, in clusters at the stem tips. The seeds form in urn-shaped capsules with hinged lids. It is common and very widespread in the Southwest, and occasional in the Northwest, mostly in disturbed soils. This is a weed of worldwide distribution, originally from Europe, where it has been used for food since ancient times. Cook as greens, using no water other than the drops that cling after washing, fry in fat, or eat raw as in salads or out of hand. You will find it both nourishing and very tasty.

Spring beauties are widely admired for their flowers, but they are also appreciated for the flavor of their edible roots. The several species are perennial herbs with fleshy bulbs or almost carrot-form roots, with many long-stemmed basal leaves and usually only one pair of leaves on the erect flower stem. The leaves vary from diamond, to spoon, to lance-shaped. The flowers are shaped like saucers or like shallow bells, with whitish to pure pink petals veined with darker pink to rose-red, in an elongate cluster at the stem tip. The plants are common and extremely abundant in the sagebrush areas, usually in the wake of melting snow, but are also available in wooded areas and in wet scree or talus to very high altitudes. The roots can be eaten either raw or cooked, but

Figure 44: Fairy spuds

are at their best when cooked as with potatoes. Indeed, they are often known as "fairy spuds." The foliage is also good either cooked or raw. (See Figure 44.)

Miner's lettuce is the name normally given to one species of *Montia.* This plant is very distinctive, with numerous slender but succulent stems rising from a basal cluster of leaves that vary from diamond- to spoon-shaped, with each of these itself having a slender stem almost as long as the flower stems. An interesting feature of the flower stems is a separable threadlike core. Each flower stem grows through the middle of a bowl or cone-shaped leaf (actually two fused leaves) just below the flowers, which are white or pinkish. The other species of this genus are very similar, but have a pair of leaves instead of the fused, bowl-shaped leaf on the flower stem. They occur from the

Figure 45: Miners' lettuce

sagebrush areas of the western deserts (in moist spots only) to the forests of the Pacific slope. They tend to be small and often reddish in areas of little moisture and low fertility, but grow very lushly and are a rich, vivid green in moist and fertile soils. In many forested parts of the Pacific Northwest, these plants form extensive ground covers. They are delightful in salads, good as boiled greens, and rather tasty when eaten out of hand. (See Figure 45.)

Bitterroot is one of the plants that formed dietary staples for some western Indians. This plant has short, fleshy, almost cylindrical leaves that wither before blooming time. The flower stems are so short that the spectacular, cactus-like, white or pink flowers appear to be lying on the sand or rocks, like a dropped bouquet. These flowers close tightly at night, to reopen only when the day has warmed, and barren hillsides will suddenly be transformed into a flower garden when the blooms open. This is an arid-country plant, occurring from the high sagebrush country to sterile mountain slopes and ridges over much of the West. The fleshy, branched roots are edible, nourishing, and even almost tasty when peeled and boiled, but the skin is intensely bitter. Common and usually abundant where found, this is both a very beautiful wildflower and a useful source of emergency food.

The mustard family produces a tremendous number of edible plants in a large number of different genera, but only a few of the more valuable food plants will be mentioned here. All of the plants are characterized by, and they are named for, the cruciform (cross-shaped), four-petaled flowers. The seeds form in podlike capsules, these of wildly varied shape. All the members of this family are edible in the sense that none are toxic in small amounts, but most should not be eaten in large quantities because of the irritant mustard oils that give the family its distinctive taste.

Spoonwort is a sprawling or weakly erect, many-branched plant with kidney-shaped or spoon-shaped dark green leaves that are very coarsely or not at all toothed, often with both types on the same plant. They are long-stemmed near the main stem base, but become short-stemmed or completely stemless near the tips. The plants occur only along the immediate coastline from northern Oregon to the Aleutian Islands. You can eat the leaves raw, but they really shine as cooked greens.

Mustard is a broad common name that covers several genera. Most of the plants are tall, weedy, annual herbs with distinctively shaped divided or deeply cut leaves and bright-yellow flowers in terminal clusters. Whole fields are often painted by the profusion of mustard plants. The seeds are borne in slender, usually curved, pods. Common and very widespread, occurring almost throughout the continent, these are a valuable food resource. The plants make delightful greens when young and tender, and the roots are pungent but good either raw or cooked. Radishes, turnips, and rutabagas, as well as the many forms of cabbage, are members of this clan. The flower buds or the flowers themselves are very similar to broccoli when boiled until just tender, and the seeds can be ground to make the familiar condiment or used to season other foods. The hot or pungent taste of mustard plants is produced by highly irritant mustard oil, and either the seeds or the older foliage can cause intestinal irritation if eaten in too large an amount.

Watercress is one member of the mustard family that was deliberately imported from Europe, where it has been used for food throughout history. Indeed, some of the ancient Greek and Roman writers wrote effusively of its virtue both as food and curative herb. The plant grows in shallow water, has typically mustard-shaped leaves, and the floating or submersed stems are festooned with white threadlike roots. The flowers are white. The typical mustard taste is present but subdued, and the raw plants are very pleasant tasting when eaten out of hand or in sandwiches or salads. *Do not use them raw if the area is or may be polluted!* They are also a splendid additive to blander greens and are good when cooked alone.

The toothworts or crinkleroots are low-growing herbs with lobed or compound leaves from the base, these sometimes springing up at a distance from the main stem, and usually with much smaller parted or lobed leaves on the stem. The roots of these plants vary from fleshy rootstocks to actual tubers, and these are very tasty when eaten raw. Many people regularly seek these plants to use the roots as a very mild substitute for horseradish. The plants are very common and widespread, mostly in woods or thin timber. The flowers are sometimes locally known as spring beauties.

Shepherd's purse is a common weed known primarily for its persistence in lawns. It has a basal rosette of oblong leaves that are wavy edged and thinly hairy, and a few smaller leaves on the slender, branching flower stem. The flowers are tiny, inconspicuous, on rather long pedicels in an elongate terminal raceme. The single most interesting feature, and the most positive means of identifying the plant, is the unique shape of the seed pods. These look exactly like little green valentines that are attached by their small ends to the threadlike pedicels. These pods are easily stripped by the handful and have a pleasantly tangy "zip" when eaten raw. The leaves are excellent as greens, and it is said that Boy Scouts prefer this plant to all others for their camp cooking.

Knotweed is a very large family of plants that furnishes edible species in several genera. One or another of these species can be found in almost any area of North America not covered in snow or ice.

Wild buckwheat is a large genus with plants generally found in areas of low rainfall, and is especially well represented in sagebrush communities. The various species are annual or perennial, generally with clusters of thinly to densely woolly leaves of various shapes in basal clumps, and with many naked flower stems, these forking again and again into two or three equal branches. The flowers are various shades of yellow, orange, red, or white, heavily scented, generally in ball-shaped compound heads cupped in brightly-colored saucers (involucres) of modified leaves or bracts, but sometimes in branching, terminal clusters. The flowers of several species dry to a paperlike texture, and the dried heads then remain showy into early winter. All of the species are edible in all their parts, but only the basal leaves are available in sufficient quantity to be useful as emergency food. Boil these leaves in two or more changes of water to reduce the overly strong taste.

The docks are abundant and widespread weeds that are easily recognized by the dark green leaves and the panicles of dark brown, reddish-brown, or rose-colored three-winged seeds. There are a number of species, several of which densely cover dried creekbeds or pond bottoms in otherwise arid country. The leaves of all species are edible in small amount, and some taste good as well. *Don't eat in large quantity unless you change cooking water at least once!* The "lemony" taste of these plants is imparted by soluble oxalic acid, and this is toxic if substantial amounts are eaten without proper preparation. The seeds are edible either when ground as meal or when cooked as mush, and it is not necessary to change water unless to eliminate strong taste. Rub the three-winged seed hulls briskly between the palms to free the seeds, letting the wind blow the husk fragments away. If there is no wind, use a fan or your breath.

Sheep sorrel is a dainty form of dock, varying drastically in size with growth conditions. In lawns or other moist and fertile spots it is a cushion-shaped mound of halberd-shaped leaves of vivid green, eventually developing a cluster of slender stems decked out with enormous numbers of small reddish seeds. In areas of low fertility or dry soils, the plants show as small clumps of pale green leaves connected by long, underground runners. It has been said that no French chef could possibly cook without sheep sorrel. Whether or not this is so, the plant is indeed a delicious component of salads or a pot of mixed greens and adds a delightful flavor to gravies or sauces, soups or stews. It can also be eaten out of hand, but sparingly. The piquant taste is imparted by soluble oxalic acid, and this is toxic if ingested in considerable amounts. When cooked in two waters, the acid is largely dissolved and poured out with the first water; and the plant is then perfectly safe to eat in any normal amount. (See Figure 46.)

Figure 46:
Sheep sorrel

Mountain sorrel is a smallish alpine plant with heart- or kidney-shaped leaves that are deeply indented at the point of attachment to the long petioles (leaf stems). The seed hulls are flattened, round or nearly so, rose-red, each on a different threadlike stem. These plants are found at high altitudes nearly throughout the continent, and in such profusion that mountain slopes are colored by the seeds as if by red paint. This plant, too, contains rather high levels of soluble oxalic acid and can be dangerous if eaten raw in large amounts. It is very tasty, however, even after being boiled in two waters, and is a highly valuable food source both because of the ease of identification and its choice of habitat. You can safely eat a sprig or two raw, but don't overdo it!

Wood sorrel or wild shamrock is an annual herbaceous plant. Various species grow in damp, wooded, or forested areas nearly throughout the continent. The three-lobed leaves look exactly like those of the shamrock or like a monstrous three-leaf clover, with each leaf creased or folded in the middle. The leaves close at night and reopen with the return of day. They are tasty when eaten out of hand, in sandwiches, or in salads, but they contain too much soluble oxalic acid to be eaten in quantity unless boiled in two waters.

The soluble oxalic acid (salt of lemon) that makes these plants so tasty also makes them dangerous. The acid is dangerous because of its solubility and its affinity for calcium. The solubility permits the acid to enter the bloodstream, where it combines with calcium to form nonsoluble calcium oxalate. This precipitates out in the kidneys, where it both plugs the tubules and burns and kills all cells in contact with it. This causes renal failure and death. The acid readily dissolves in heated water and it will combine with calcium as readily in that water as in the bloodstream. Adding bone fragments, egg shells, or other sources of calcium to cooking water will transform the oxalic acid to nonsoluble calcium oxalate in the kettle, retaining the full flavor, but the acid is then no longer dangerous. If you have no such materials, simply pour out the first water after boiling for a time and replace with fresh water. These plants are excellent food when properly used, but they are potentially deadly if misused.

Amaranth is a genus that produces both edible and palatable products. Redroot pigweed grows from low to moderately high altitudes almost throughout North America. It grows to six feet or so tall in favorable locations or when started in spring; but it grows, matures, and even produces viable seed from a total height of three or four inches in unfavorable locations or when springing up from seed after late summer or early fall rains. It has erect, robust, slightly hairy stems that are often streaked with red, and the carrot-form root is distinctly reddish. The roughly triangular leaves are to eight inches long. The countless seeds are held in fuzzy to bristly spikes at stem and branch tips. The plants normally grow in dense colonies and can be obtained in good quantity where found. All parts of the plant can be eaten, but the seed husks should not be eaten raw because of their abrasive harshness. (See Figure 47.)

Figure 47: Amaranths

Tumbling amaranth is found in semidesert areas to moderate altitudes. The branches grow outward at first, then curve upward an inward to form a spherical shape, and the plant is one of the more common tumbleweeds. The leaves are pale green, more or less egg-shaped, not more than an inch and a half long. The younger plants are edible as cooked greens, and the seeds can be used as flour or mush. (See Figure 47.)

Sprawling or prostrate amaranth is similar in foliage and in food value. (See Figure 47.)

The grass family is one of the largest plant families, containing literally hundreds of genera and thousands of species, ranging from tiny annual plants to giant bamboo. All are characterized by jointed culms (stems), these usually but not always hollow, and by alternate, parallel-veined leaves, these long, narrow, and tapering more or less regularly to a point. These leaves normally sheath the stem at their bases, and most have a semitransparent membranous structure (a ligule) above the sheath-leaf junction. The flowers are inconspicuous (they are wind pollinated) in spikes, racemes, or panicles. The seeds or fruits are grains, differing mainly in size, color, shape, and flavor among the species.

The stems, leaves, and seeds are edible in all species, but one must be alert to the danger of mechanical injury from harsh, sharp bristles or saw-edged leaves in some species. Boiling will eliminate the hazard in the case of leaves or stems, and threshing and winnowing will get rid of bristly seed husks. One must also beware of either smut or ergot. Both appear as shapeless, moldlike masses on the seeds, black for smut and purplish for ergot.

The most efficient way of gathering grass seeds is to cut the grass and lay it on a blanket or other seed catcher, then beat it with a flail or a limby switch to knock the seeds off the spikelets. Another method is to weave a shallow, basket-shaped swatter out of limber switches of wood, then use this to knock the seeds off standing grasses into a waiting container. With many species, it is practical to bend the grass over until its seed-bearing tops are within or just over a container, then strike the tops a sharp blow with a stick to free the seeds. *These methods will work only if the seeds are ripe!* A more primitive method, and the only way with unripe seeds, is to strip the seeds by hand.

Once harvested, you must thresh and winnow the seeds to separate the edible grain from the inedible (or unwanted) chaff. Threshing is best accomplished by beating with a stick or flail, but it can be done by rubbing with a stone, or even by rolling between the palms. The chaff can then be removed by pouring the grain from a considerable height when a brisk breeze is blowing, by blowing the chaff out of a handful at a time with your breath, or by dumping both chaff and grain into a container of water. The lighter chaff will float high and dry, while the heavier grain will either sink or at least float less buoyantly. With those species having bristly husks that are difficult to separate, it is useful to thoroughly singe the husks before threshing.

Parch the threshed and winnowed grain to be eaten out of hand, grind it for use as flour by rubbing between stones, or cook it as mush. The seeds of many species are also very good when cooked with meat or in soup or stew. The boiled stems and leaves of grasses are also edible.

Various species of grass occur from ocean edge to well above timberline, and from semidesert to marshland. Indeed, these plants cover many thousands of square miles of the planet to the near exclusion of other plants. While man is not a grazing animal, there is no reason for anyone to starve while grasses are available in readily usable form.

Other edible plants abound, but a more comprehensive listing would serve no useful purpose. Those listed provide a sufficient selection of plant foods for any area and for any time of year. It is hoped that some readers will come to enjoy identifying and sampling or using some of them in the absence of need.

Chapter XX

Winter Problems

Winter presents many special problems whether or not one is lost or stranded. One of the worst hazards is the danger posed by snow-covered ice that often disguises shallow ponds or overflow areas as solid ground. Once the ice is blanketed with snow, it is insulated against the cold and will often remain much too thin to support a person's weight.

A heavy snowfall or drifting snow will often cover a stream, even when the stream is only thinly covered with ice. The stream will then erode the ice, chunks of snow will fall from the underside of the snow blanket, and the result will be a hidden snow tunnel. The roof of such a tunnel will not bear much weight and will cave in if you venture onto it, dropping you for an unknown distance and into water of unknown depth. A similar situation exists where the water level has subsided, leaving a sheet of ice suspended well above the water. Such spots are death traps for the unwary.

You can often hear the gurgling of a hidden stream, but you must not count on being able to do so; for snow is an efficient sound insulator. A pond or overflow makes no sound, of course; and your ears cannot help you detect its presence. Your eyes, too, are only partially effective in locating such dangers.

At the bottom of a canyon, you can safely assume that some sort of stream or at least a stream channel exists, and you can usually tell where the low point of the canyon floor is. In flat country, although a stream's channel may not be visible because of heavy or drifting snow, there are usually visible indicators of its presence. Streamside thickets will project above shallow snow, or will show up as parallel mounds even when completely buried. Streams in such country tend to meander, and those sections running in the direction of the prevailing wind will show up as depressions even when those sections at nearly right angles to the wind are drifted completely full. The channel will thus show up as an interrupted or disjointed series of depressions in the snow when seen from a distance.

Ponds and overflow areas usually appear as perfectly flat areas, but this is not always the case. Cattails, reeds, bulrushes, or other aquatic vegetation that projects above the ice catches and holds falling or drifting snow to create mounds or hummocks, and many overflow areas are choked with weeds and brush that grew before the flooding occurred. Drifting snow often creates shallow ripples even on level surfaces, too, and these will trap larger drifts once they have compacted.

Unless you are so thoroughly familiar with an area that you know beyond doubt that no ponds or overflows exist there, or know exactly where they are if they do, you should carry a pole and use it to probe suspicious spots before trusting your weight to them. The pole should be slender but fairly heavy, sharply pointed at the small end, and free of knots or other projections that would make it hard to jab through considerable thicknesses of snow.

Another hazard is crossing small streams when ice and snow obscure the dividing line between land and water, or when everything is slick with ice. If you must cross the stream, use extra caution in doing so. Do not attempt to cross by stepping from rock to rock unless these are so close together that you can easily step from one to another without stretching, jumping, or risking your balance, unless they are free of ice, and unless they are so solidly planted there is no danger of them moving under your feet. Use a staff of some kind as a prop or brace. Do not attempt to cross on a log unless it is large enough not to spring under your weight, solid enough to bear that weight without danger of breaking, and not slippery or covered with loose bark or rotted wood that could peel off under your foot. If the log is not large enough to offer secure footing but is otherwise suitable, straddle it and inch your way across.

It is possible to pole vault over a stream if it is not too wide. Ten to twelve feet would be the normal maximum. If at all possible, select a spot where you can vault from a higher to a lower bank. *The landing spot must be free of obstacles that could injure you!* The pole used in vaulting must be sturdy enough to avoid even the possibility of breaking, and it must be long enough to reach from the center of the stream to your bank plus your own height. To use it, plant the large end firmly in the center of the stream, working it about to make sure it is not resting on a loose or slippery rock or in soft sand or silt. Grasp the pole near its upper end and vault the stream. If you have not pole vaulted before, or if you are unsure of you ability to do so, practice on dry land before tackling the stream. This will increase both your proficiency and your confidence.

The less weight you carry, the easier it will be to vault. Use a long pole or two poles lashed together to transfer your extra gear (gun, pack, sleeping bag, snowshoes, etc.) to the far bank. It is even possible to build a fire there by transferring blazing material from a fire built on the takeoff bank. This is good insurance if weather conditions are such that an accidental wetting would be extremely dangerous, as it will eliminate the need to start a fire from scratch after you have been wetted. *Remember! Once you have transferred your gear, you cannot then change your mind about crossing!*

If none of these crossing systems is practical, you can wade the stream. Follow the stream until you find a shallow spot with a firm bottom and low banks. (A high, steep bank normally indicates deep water at its base.) Retreat to the closest narrow spot (regardless of depth there) and cut a pole long enough to reach across the stream with room to spare. Use it to transfer your gear and to build a fire on the far bank. Return to the shallow spot. Take off your boots and socks and roll up your pantlegs. If the water at your crossing spot is so deep that the trousers will surely become wet, take them off and throw them to the far bank. Put your boots on without socks to protect your feet. Wade the stream as quickly as possible without taking unnecessary risk, using the pole to probe for deep spots, to brace yourself against the current, to preserve your balance, and to break away thin ice in your pathway.

Once out of the water, go quickly to your pile of gear and prekindled fire. Towel yourself dry, even if you must use part of your clothing as a towel. Put on dry trousers and dry socks. If you are wearing rubber boots, simply wipe them dry inside and put them on again. You have then only to dry the material used as a towel and boot-wiping cloth and you are ready to proceed.

If you are wearing rubber boots with a fleece lining (and you should not be!) or leather boots or shoes, then you must either thoroughly dry them or use plastic or other thin, waterproof material to wrap your feet so you can wear them wet. *You must not attempt to dry leather boots or shoes by direct heat!* Too much heat will crack, deform, and harden wet leather to make the footgear unusable. Instead, wipe the boots free of excess water and stuff them full of heated absorbent material such as cloth, dry grasses, crumbled dead leaves, dry conifer needles, or well-dried moss. When this material has absorbed all the water it will hold, remove and replace it with fresh material or dry it for reuse. Repeat the process as often as necessary.

To use wet boots without drying them, wrap the bare feet with plastic film or a space blanket, put on one or more pairs of dry socks, then cover with another waterproof layer. If you lack material to make two layers, forgo the inner one. Moisture from the saturated boots cannot invade the socks to rob them of insulative capacity, and your feet will remain warm even if the boots freeze. If frozen boots begin to chafe and injure your feet, stop, make camp, and dry them. *Don't let them blister your feet!*

If much of your clothing has been soaked, there will probably be several different materials involved, and each of these presents unique drying problems of its own. Cotton fabrics may be dried rather quickly at fairly high temperatures. Anything made out of wool must be dried slowly and at low heat to prevent scorching and shrinking. (The "felt" liners used in some types of ski boots, in rubber overshoes, and in rubber-bottomed, leather-topped shoe pacs are made of wool.) Down is nearly impossible to dry under field conditions. Many of the synthetics will drip dry with no heat at all, and others will melt or evaporate if exposed to high temperatures!

Wind will dry clothing spread over a bush, even in low temperatures; and you can "freeze dry" clothing by allowing it to freeze when exposed to wind. The ice will evaporate (sublime) without thawing.

In many situations, small creeks will have frozen almost or quite to the bottom, and the ice will support your weight. You should test the ice by striking it a hard blow with the end of a heavy pole, just as if you were trying to jab a hole in it. Thick ice on streams or lakes often offers the easiest line of travel, but you must be absolutely sure that the ice is thick enough and solid enough to bear your weight safely.

Even then, you should carry a long pole, holding it by the middle and in a horizontal position. If you were then to break through the ice, the pole would span the hole and keep you from sinking down and under the ice. You can also use it to test any suspicious spot.

The best protection against the very real hazards of winter travel just described is good common sense. Ask yourself if it is really necessary to travel under such conditions or to cross that creek. *If you are lost, and if someone knows pretty much where you are, then the answer should be an emphatic no!* If you are not lost, then the answer would depend on a number of factors.

You should not undertake a really hazardous stream crossing (under conditions of severe cold or high wind all crossings of anything other than tiny streamlets could be so labeled) unless there is a compelling reason to do so. Compelling reasons could be a visible road, cabin, smoke, or even a more suitable shelter site on the opposite bank. Remember, unless you are actually traveling cross country from point A to point B, crossing a stream means you must recross it on your return.

Remember, too, when making such a decision as to how (or whether!) to proceed, that even a trivial accident or injury can be dangerous or life threatening under winter conditions. Remember also that you cannot afford to gamble, as the stakes are too high.

If a major part of your clothing has become wet during stream crossing or mishap, it is unlikely that you can fully dry them before dark, as winter days are short. Don't even try. Stop well before dark to make an overnight camp or shelter and to gather enough wood to last the night. You can turn and otherwise supervise the drying of your clothing as you stoke the fire during the night, and that will be often, believe me! Winter nights are long and cold, and a fire big enough to keep you warm without adequate bedding or shelter will burn an unbelievable amount of wood, so gather more than enough. If you travel until dark or near dark before stopping, you are sure to have a miserable night of it at best.

You must be alert to the danger of frostbite during winter weather. Ears, nose, cheeks, feet, and wrists are most likely to be affected. *Do not rub a frostbitten area with snow!* Even rubbing with the hands can seriously damage the tissue if done too vigorously. Rubbing with snow would tend to both extend the freezing and abrade and damage the frozen flesh.

Treat frostbite by applying mild heat to the frosted area. Cup an ear or nose in a warm palm, or cover them with a warm cloth. Frosted fingers can be thawed by holding them inside the clothes and clamped in an armpit. Another good method is to sponge the affected area with warmed water. The best way to thaw a frosted or frozen hand or foot is to immerse it in water warmed to body temperature or very slightly higher. (Test the water with your elbow, just as you would with a baby's bathwater.) If water is unavailable or you have no suitable container, use sand or dirt instead. It is also possible to heat rocks (never taken from a streambed or other wet area!) to a moderate temperature and use these as hotpacks around a well-wrapped foot or hand.

Do not attempt to thaw frozen hands or feet by immersing them in alcohol, gasoline, kerosene, antifreeze, or other such liquids! Unbelievable as it may seem, this has actually been attempted! These liquids remain liquid in severe cold because their freezing points are extremely low, and they are as cold as, or colder than, the temperature of the storage environment. To immerse a hand or foot in such liquids at low temperatures is to ensure that the limb will be frozen to the bone and that amputation or worse will result! Besides, petroleum-based products are toxic when absorbed through the skin!

If you must travel on foot to reach a known destination such as your camp or car, do not thaw frozen feet until you have reached that objective. Frostbitten or frozen flesh becomes very tender and is both painful and easily damaged when thawed; you could not walk any distance on freshly thawed feet without suffering extreme pain and incurring severe damage to your feet. Let the feet remain frozen until you have reached your destination, as long as this is within a few hours. You will not damage the frozen tissue by walking on it, and letting the feet remain frozen for a few hours will cause less damage than trying to walk any great distance on them freshly thawed.

If searchers are looking for you, make a camp and thaw your feet. But even if you choose to settle down and wait for rescue, you should make the camp and lay in a goodly store of wood before starting the thawing process.

When a frozen area begins to thaw, you will experience excruciating pain as feeling returns, and this is both unpleasant and disabling while it lasts. You can alleviate this effect somewhat by sponging the area with cold water or by holding a handful of snow against the flesh for a few seconds. Don't overdo this, as you do not want to retard the thawing process or risk refreezing.

Once thawed, the flesh becomes very sensitive to cold and is easily refrozen. You must be especially careful to prevent this, as refreezing will often lead to loss of the affected tissue or to gangrene.

Another real hazard in the winter is snow blindness. This is a painful irritation of the eyeballs and eyelids caused by sunlight reflected from snow. (Water can cause the same problem, but usually in milder form.) This can manifest itself as anything from a mildly painful irritation to total blindness. Blindness is temporary, but is no less disabling or incapacitating than permanent blindness while it lasts.

The sun need not be shining brightly to create this condition. Even on overcast days there is enough reflected light to be harmful. If you are forced to squint, your eyes need protection! Polarized sunglasses with close-fitting side shields are best, but regular snow goggles are nearly as good. Ordinary sunglasses will help, but you will either have to shield the sides or darken the skin in those areas, as with charcoal. You can make a domino mask from fabric, bark, leather, or even wood or bone that will furnish the needed protection. The mask must have narrow, horizontal slits to see through. You can also create a makeshift mask by plaiting cattail or other straplike leaves or by simply hanging a bushy evergreen bough or other screening material in front of the eyes. Even painting the sides of the nose and the skin around the eyes with dirt or charcoal will help to some degree. The objective in all cases is to keep light from being reflected from all angles into the eyes.

Treatment of snow blindness when no medicines are available consists of remaining in a darkened area or covering the eyes with a light-excluding bandage of some kind. The length of time required for recovery depends primarily upon the severity of the case, but normally the eyes should not be exposed to really bright light for at least a week. This could amount to a death sentence if alone in severe weather, as you could not do those things that had to be done in order to survive during that time. *If you are forced to squint, take steps to protect your eyes immediately!*

Another problem often overlooked by the uninitiated is the tremendous amount of energy required to wade through soft snow. With as little as eight or ten inches of soft snow, you would expend as much energy in traveling on level land as you would normally use in climbing a moderate hill, and each added inch imposes an additional burden. In snow sixteen or more inches deep, you could not hope to travel more than two or three miles before reaching a state of total or near total exhaustion. Crusted snow that will almost but not quite support your weight is even worse.

If you must travel in fresh snow or snow with a thin crust, you must improvise a set of snowshoes. These can be made from woven twigs, from strips of cloth or other fabric stretched across a hoop or frame, or even from an evergreen bough. One stranded hunter in southern Oregon walked out on two sections of corrugated roofing salvaged from a burned cabin! He had to tie a long stick to the front end of each "snowshoe" so he could alternately lift them by hand, and he was totally exhausted when he got out, but he did get out!

If you are forced to use evergreen boughs for snowshoes, point the main branch stub to the front and lay the bough with its convex side down. (Practically all conifer boughs grow with a pronounced curve.) Lash a cross stick across a main fork or crotch and weave a stick platform to support your foot. Tie a cord or a stick to the main stub to form a handle that will let you raise the front end as you step. Such makeshift snowshoes will be awkward and exhausting to use, but they will enable you to travel in soft snow that would otherwise prevent all travel. Making do with what's available—that is the name of the game!

Another hazard of winter travel is the danger of being caught in the path of an avalanche or snow slide. Fresh snow is especially subject to sliding when it is deposited in considerable depth upon an earlier and crusted deposit. Most low-level obstructions that would help anchor the snow in place are then buried under the lower layer, which has a smooth and slippery surface. Most avalanches are spontaneous, receiving their starting impetus from gravity alone, with the slide beginning when the pull of gravity overcomes the holding force of friction. Others, however, are triggered by an outside force. This can be lubrication of the lower surface by melt or rain water; the added weight of a person, an animal, or a falling or rolling rock; snow movement caused by wind; the shock and jar of another avalanche; an earth tremor; or even the sound of a shout, a shot, or a passing plane.

Do not cross open slopes of more than moderate incline or the areas below such slopes unless there is adequate tree cover, and be especially wary where steep side canyons or natural chutes are involved. Snow sliding in such areas is channeled and funneled by the contours to greatly increase both the amount of snow and the speed with which it travels. Such channeled avalanches actually become partially airborne and sweep everything in their path. No trees or other substantial growths are found in regular avalanche tracks, so such growth indicates that avalanches are infrequent or absent there.

If caught in an avalanche or snow slide, mountaineers try to "swim" in the snow, believing that such action tends to keep them at or near the surface. Anyone who has seen the tumbling, leap-frogging face of a snow slide has reason to doubt that this will help, and it seldom works in practice. You should avoid putting the theory to a test by carefully avoiding potential avalanche areas.

One final word on winter and its hazards: Water, whether for drinking, cooking, or other uses, is hard to come by. Ice and snow can be eaten or simply allowed to melt in the mouth, but this severely depletes body heat and is dangerous. Snow and ice can be melted to produce water, but this is a tedious and time-consuming process that requires a great deal of heat. It is usually far easier and simpler to obtain water in liquid form and to heat that water before drinking. In getting to the water, however, you may be faced with the fact that it lies at the bottom of a precipitous and very slippery bank, or is rimmed by thin ice. In such cases, you should carefully weigh the advantages and disadvantages of the various options and choose the one which promises the best result with the least danger or inconvenience. You must always remember, however, that no amount of simple inconvenience should justify taking a real risk.

Chapter XXI

Making Do

One of the prime essentials in many survival situations is cord, rope, or wire. You should have snare wire and some type of fishline in your emergency kit, but larger cords and ropes are often needed. Since you are not likely to have a rope with you unless you are traveling by car or boat or on horseback, you will have to improvise.

It is impossible to make wire, of course, but you can salvage useful quantities of insulated electrical wiring from a broken-down car or plane. You might blunder onto large steel wire in the form of an abandoned telephone line (when fire lookouts were abandoned or mines worked out, the lines were often left behind) or a disused barbwire fence. Abandoned and collapsed miners' huts and other buildings often have quantities of baling wire lying about (this is the "haywire" that caused a slipshod operation to be known as a "haywire outfit"), and some of this may still be in usable condition. It is too stiff to be used for snare nooses for any but large animals, but it is unexcelled for lashing things together or for suspending heavy objects such as counterweights or deadfalls.

You can make cord or rope from both vegetable- and animal-derived material. Some of the tree barks (inner barks in some cases, outer barks in others) that can be used in making ropes are: basswood, buckeye, cedar, cypress, elm, hawthorn, hickory, juniper, locust, mulberry, oak, Osage orange, and yew, and that from shrubs such as cliff rose, deer brush, hazel, wild lilac, and rabbitbrush. You can also use the twining, woody stems of vines such as clematis, grape, honeysuckle, and wisteria either as cords or as cord-making material.

Fibers from the stalks of burdock, wild flax, some grasses, Indian hemp, milkweed, nettles, sunflowers, and thistles make strong to very strong cord. The whole leaves of bear grass, some species of wild iris, and various species of grass and yucca make very strong cordage; the leaves of some sedges, rushes and tules make weak cordage.

The roots of many of the woody shrubs and those of such trees as aspen, cedar, cottonwood, fir, hemlock, juniper, larch, pine, spruce, tamarack, and yew have been used by the Indians to make thread for sewing and everything from binding twine to harpoon or climbing ropes. The long roots of reeds, some sedges, and sawgrass can also be used. The strength of these will vary with both the species and growth conditions, and these factors must be considered when deciding whether or not a material is suitable for the intended purpose.

This list is not meant to be exclusive! Test any and all vegetative material at hand that looks as if it might be suitable for making cordage. To test it, twist a thin strip of the material to see if it will break when tightly twisted. Use the whole stems of materials too small to be split. If it resists breakage, lay two or three such strips (or a group of fibers) parallel to each other and twist them together for a distance of several inches. Then, leaving them tightly twisted, grip one end of all but one strand and try to withdraw that strand by pulling on its other end. This measures resistance to end slippage. A final test is to tie a knot in the center of the potential cord material and pull hard on the ends to draw the knot tight. This will test to see whether or not the cord will cut itself when tightly tied.

If the material remains strong when twisted, offers considerable resistance to end slippage, and does not cut itself when knotted tightly, then it should make good cordage or rope. Those materials that will pass one or more of these tests but not all three (sagebrush bark is a prime example) will still make good baskets or other containers, sandals or outer soles for moccasins, or weak cordage suitable for binding things together. It is also possible to treat many such materials to make them pass all of the three tests.

Many barks, roots, and vines that will not pass these tests when gathered will easily pass when boiled, steamed, or merely soaked in hot water for a time. An easy way to steam them is in the Indian firepit. An easier alternative is to coil a length of material and tie it to hold it in a coil. Place the coil on the ground and cover it with several inches of ashes or dirt and build a fire atop this mound. If you think splitting the material would be easier after steaming, use a heap of it instead of the coil. Allow the material to steam in its own juices for at least an hour, then rinse to remove the lye. This is especially effective when preparing woody barks, roots, sprouts, and vines. After this treatment, most of these materials are nearly as flexible as twine, and you can then either use them whole or split them to make pieces of suitable size.

The size of cord you should make will be determined by the materials at hand and the purpose for which the cord is intended. When flexibility, small diameter, and considerable strength are required, as for fishing lines and snares for small animals, rely on the fibers from long-fibered herbaceous plants if you have a choice. For large cords or ropes where the only requirement is strength, you can use any suitable material, no matter how bulky.

Cord making is relatively simple. With fibers of considerable length (from flax, hemp, nettles, etc.), you can hold a bundle of them by one end and roll them between the palm of your other hand and your leg. When splicing more fibers to make the cord longer, be sure to feather or stagger the ends to make each fiber end at a different point. If there are two persons involved, you can actually make a crude spinning machine, but one person cannot operate such a contrivance. (See Figure 48.)

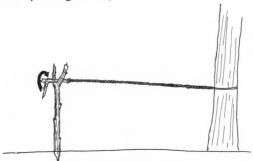

Figure 48: Hard finish crank

When the cord has been loosely twisted together in sufficient length, you can then use the pictured crank device to tighten the twist and to make a hard-finish cord. This cord will resemble a piece of commercial string or linen fishline in its surface texture. Again, however, you can make as good a cord by hand. It will just take more time and work.

To make a cord of considerably greater strength or size, or when it is necessary to use shorter materials, you must use the "Flemish twist" method. Hemp ropes, most steel cables, and a large proportion of ropes made from natural or synthetic fibers are so made. To make such a twist, divide the fibers into two or three bundles (two are easier to handle; three make stronger rope) or use two or three spun cords of the type just described. Lay these bundles or cords parallel to each other and tie them together at one end. Grasp the tied end firmly with the left hand (if right handed), with the bundles trailing across your lap. Grasp the bundle farthest from you, roll it away from you, then bring it up and over the other two bundles. This is called the "lay" of the rope. Repeat with each of the other bundles in turn and continue in this fashion until you run out of material or the rope reaches its intended length. *Remember: twist or roll to the right or clockwise, lay to the left or counterclockwise.* (See Figure 49.)

Figure 49: Flemish twist

You can cut leather thongs (variously known as babiche, shagnappie, or whangs) in any width and in one continuous piece that is limited in length only by the size of the stock. Find the exact center of the stock in its smallest dimension and punch a small hole there. Thread one end of a piece of string or cord through this hole and tie it to a small stick to hold it securely. Stretch the string to the nearest edge and tie it to a pencil, a piece of charred wood, or a sharpened stick. Use this "compass" to mark off the largest possible circle. Trim off all excess material. Cut a starting thong of the desired width at some point on the perimeter.

Make a jig by fastening a knife, a razor blade, a piece of sharp-edged glass or rock, or a hatchet at the proper distance from a smooth knot, peg, or other improvised guide, and cut by pulling on the thong and rotating the stock. For best results, the cutting edge should be very sharp and inclined toward the cut.

Use the same technique to cut even-width strips from any other suitable material, such as car floor mats or vinyl seat

Figure 50:
Whangs

covers. Any of these strips can then be plaited, braided, or twisted into ropes, but only those made of leather will be very strong. Whangs can be tied end to end with almost any kind of knot, but you can also make end-to-end splices without knotting. (See Figure 50.)

No other natural material you are likely to find can equal the strength of sinew. This is the fibrous material that transmits the force produced by animal muscles to the point of application. It is found in two basic forms: as massive, cordlike bundles known as tendons, which connect large muscles to joints of the skeleton, and as thin, sheathing layers attached to and covering large muscles. The most valuable of all sinews are those that cover the muscles surrounding the spine or backbone. These can be easily separated into individual, threadlike strands that are as long as the spine itself.

To retrieve the sinews in usable form, peel them from the underlying muscle, scrape them free of clinging flesh, then let them dry for an hour or two. You can then easily peel out the individual strands by pulling them apart. Let tendons dry more or less completely, then dampen them and gently pound them with a wooden club or hammer on a soft but firm surface such as a log or stump. This will separate the fibers, which can then be stripped out singly or in groups.

Individual strands can be used as sewing thread or to form cords, as already described. Strips containing several strands can be twisted for use as string or cord or can form one strand of a Flemish twist.

Once a sinew cord or rope has been twisted, it should be dampened and stretched between two points. You should then use a cloth or a piece of leather to rub the cord vigorously from end to end. This will heat the cord by friction, smooth it by eliminating or reducing the size of projections, and bind the separate fibers together with a gluelike substance drawn out of the sinew. Let the cord dry while stretched. If it then feels dry and stiff to the touch, rub it with tallow.

Use individual sinew strands or groups of strands for tying things together, as serving or seizing on cords or ropes, or for binding the handles on makeshift tools. When wrapped while wet, the sinew will dry almost bone hard and will shrink somewhat in drying.

The intestines of animals also make very strong cordage. Empty the contents, wash or rinse thoroughly, then scrape away both the outer and the inner membranous walls to leave only the fibrous main wall. It is often helpful to soak the split intestine in cold water for two or three days or in warm water for five or six hours before scraping, but you can get by without soaking if limited time or lack of water make this desirable. You will then have to substitute more muscle power, however.

Once you have removed the membranes, you should soak the now-fibrous intestine in a solution of wood ashes and water (hardwood ashes are much better for this purpose than those of the conifers) for four or five hours, then wash it thoroughly. You can then dry the material for later use or twist it while wet to make "catgut" cords or stings. You can either soak the dried material in water and use it the same way or separate it into individual fiber strands that can be used as with sinew. It is nearly as strong as sinew and is fully as useful.

To twist a wet section of intestine, lash one end firmly to a springy pole or stake and drive a short forked stake six inches or so beyond the other end. Cut a crank stick and lash its end to the free end of the intestine. Lay the crank in the forked stake and spin it to twist the gut. You must use a little care to see that the material is twisted smoothly and evenly throughout its length and does not knot up or stack in some spots while remaining untwisted in others. *Do not release the crank without tying it!* The crank handle will spin like a propeller if released and is capable of inflicting injury. Allow the twisted gut to dry while fully stretched, then coat it with fat or tallow and rub it briskly with a piece of leather or cloth to soften it and make it more flexible.

The intestines of large animals can also be used as canteens, as rainproof clothing, and as containers for storing food or other material. For clothing, simply split the gut after cutting it in suitable lengths, clean as described above, and sew the strips together to make a raincoat, poncho, rainhat, etc. For other uses, you'll have to clean and prepare the intestine without splitting it, but the technique for doing so is simple and easy.

To clean an unsplit piece of intestine, dump the contents, wash thoroughly, then scrape off the outer membrane. You will then have to turn the section wrong side out to get at the inner membrane. Turn a deep cuff on one end, grip the edges of this cuff, then dip it full of water. The weight of the water will pull the longer end of the gut down through the cuff and the gut will invert itself. If water is limited, you can use sand, dirt, or small pebbles instead. Remove the inner (now the outer) membrane, and wash again, and the gut is then ready for use.

Tie one end of a section tightly, tamp it full of prepared food (rendered fat, pemmican, jerky, dried berries, etc.) and tie the other end tightly to exclude air. Hang the filled section where sunlight or heat from a fire will shrink and dry it. If you have filled it with precooked meat scraps mixed with seasoning agents such as wild onions, smoking it will make a very respectable primitive sausage.

The bladders and the paunches or stomachs of large animals make useful containers, and you can even use a stomach as a boiling kettle! Open one end and tie off the other opening. Stretch the open end over a frame and suspend this to hold the pot directly over a bed of coals. You can also line a dug hole with it and use heated stones to boil the contents. The suspended pot will not burn through if flames are not allowed to touch it above the waterline, and a layer of cold rocks placed on the bottom will keep heated stones from burning a hole in the pit liner.

If you wish to use a paunch or stomach as a container, simply empty the contents, wash it thoroughly, remove the inner membrane, and stuff it with loose, fluffy materials that will both let it dry and hold it in shape. Preserve a bladder by washing it thoroughly, blowing it full of air, and tying off the opening to let it dry in inflated shape. The bladder will be parchmentlike when dry and will break or crack easily if not rubbed gently with tallow or fat to soften it.

Use turkey roasting bags (from your emergency kit) as suspended pots or kettles, or as pit liners. A piece of green hide or a piece of foil will serve as a pit liner, too. Peel flexible, nontoxic barks such as those from aspen, birch, cottonwood, and willow in large enough sections to fold into kettles. Steam the bark by holding the inner surface next to a fire to make it more flexible. You can often find suitable hollows in large rocks, and you can also burn and scrape depressions in fallen logs or stumps that will allow you to boil water with heated stones.

Make boiling kettles out of clay, either by rolling ropes of clay and coiling these into a pot or by lining a dug pit or a woven basket with a thick layer of clay. Smooth the interior surface with wetted hands to make the pot waterproof.

Fire the clay by building a small, hot fire in the pot itself or by slowly filling it with hot coals. Build a fire around the outside of a coiled pot or basket. The clay should be heated slowly, kept hot for several hours, then slowly cooled. If the pit liner cracks during firing, no great harm is done; you can simply force more clay into the crack and refire. With the coiled pot or lined basket (the basket will have burned away during firing), cracking will make the pot completely unusable for boiling, but you can still use it for baking or roasting.

Once again, however, nothing you can improvise or fabricate will be as good as material you can salvage from a car or plane or from materials discarded by humans. The hubcaps from many cars make splendid shallow kettles, frying pans, and Dutch oven lids, and the common tin can is famous as a "hobo kettle." Where old campfire pits or meat-poles between trees indicate a seasonal hunting camp, there is usually a garbage dump or covered garbage pit nearby. These dumps usually contain tin or aluminum food or beverage cans and other material that can be useful. Such camps often provide other useful material in the form of wire, nails, etc., and one can occasionally discover a cache of food or other camp goods. *Don't hesitate to use what you find if in desperate need!* You can always make the owner's loss good if you survive.

A clay pot set in a pit and surrounded by heated rocks or hot coals is excellent for baking or roasting, but a clay oven is even better. Make such an oven above ground by building it out of preformed bricks, by plastering rocks together with clay, or by using large ropelike coils of clay to make an oven shaped like a conical beehive. You can also dig a hole in a bank, lining this with clay or simply wetting and smoothing the interior surface if the dirt of the bank is suitable, then building a fire inside to fire the lining.

No matter how built, an oven must have a chimney hole at the back end or at the peak to enable a fire to burn briskly inside. When the fire is raked out of the oven and all openings sealed, the residual heat of the clay walls will bake bread or other baked goods almost as well as a kitchen range. If you have foil to place your loaves on, you will not have to clean your oven very carefully before use. If you have no foil or suitable substitute, you must sweep the floor of the oven carefully and then place your loaves directly on it.

It is also perfectly feasible to bake bread by coiling dough spiral fashion around a preheated, nontoxic stick an inch or more in diameter and propping this beside a fire. Ramrods were once commonly used for this. A branch stub or two left on the stick will help to secure the dough in position. This is the famous "bannock" or "stick bread" of Alaska.

If your fuel is nontoxic hardwood, you can actually bake small loaves by burying them directly in the ashes at the edge of the fire. These ashes will not cling to the loaf in any significant amount, and they will not penetrate the loaf at all. It is interesting to note that a spoonful of white hardwood ash is equivalent to a spoonful of bicarbonate of soda and can be used in place of soda when baking, cooking, or parboiling.

The Indian firepit is an excellent choice for baking or roasting foods, especially those that require long cooking times. Dig a pit, line the bottom and sides with rocks (never take these from a permanently wet area!), and then build a fire in the pit to heat the rocks. When the rocks are thoroughly heated, remove the fire and the ashes as best you can, put down a layer of nontoxic and bland-tasting vegetation (grasses or aspen, birch, cottonwood, and maple leaves are excellent choices), place the food on this, add another layer of vegetation, and cover the whole with dirt.

An alternative is to dig a pit and preheat a number of rocks in a fire built nearby, and to use these heated rocks to line the pit and cover the second layer of vegetation before piling on the dirt.

If the food is very moist and not in need of long cooking, simply leave the covered pit alone for the time you think necessary. If the food tends to be dry, pour some water through a hole or wet the vegetation layers just before covering. Either approach will create large volumes of steam within the pit. If very long cooking is required, build and maintain a fire atop the covered pit.

This device is unparalleled for cooking roots and bulbs or for tough meats. It is also splendid for shellfish and is good for steaming greens.

Cook small animals and birds in individual clay ovens. Wrap the eviscerated carcass is a blanket of wet clay or dip it several times in a thin clay "batter." You do not need to pluck or skin the animal when this method is used, unless you want or need to save the feathers or fur. The clay will penetrate the feathers or hair and, when baked and than broken off, it will take the skin with it, leaving only the cooked flesh behind. The hair or feathers will not taint or impart a flavor to the food. To cook, simply bury the clay-covered animal or bird in the ashes of your fire. You can do much the same by wrapping with foil, but you must skin or pluck the carcass before cooking. This also works splendidly for roots, bulbs, and tubers.

You can broil steaks, fish, or birds or small animals by skewering them with spits made of nontoxic wood (hundreds of people have been killed by using poisonous wood for spits), by clamping them between forks or woven basketwork grilles, by threading them on a piece of wire, or by placing them on or between heated rocks. You can also "plank" them by securing them to preheated slabs of nonresinous and nontoxic wood and propping this next to a fire. Remember, though, that you cannot use pitchy or resinous wood for fuel when broiling or planking and that whatever fuel you do use will impart a flavor to the food, as will the type of wood used for the plank.

If you have any type of metal cooking pot with a bail (or that you can make a bail for), you can make all sorts of arrangements for holding this above a fire. Make a "dingle stick" by weighting one end of a pole, resting the pole in a forked stake, in a tripod or a bipod, or by resting it on a rock or chunk of some kind. Hang the kettle from the raised end. Support a bar in two forked stakes or in two tripods and use forked and notched dangle sticks to hold the kettle at any preferred height. You can even make a swinging crane that will let you swing the kettle on and off the fire at will.

You can make all sorts of supports for a frying pan, for a rock or metal grill, for a hubcap used for cooking or for a pot without a bail. Place two green logs parallel to each other and close enough together to support the utensil, building your fire between the logs. Place rocks in or around the fire to rest the utensil on. Best of all, in most instances, is a narrow fire trench, with the utensil resting either on the banks or in shallow niches or ledges carved into them. Place a clay pot on the ground and build a fire around it.

You can actually make a stove of flat rocks if these are available, and you can then use the top as a grill to cook foods on. This will not produce food of the quality you are accustomed to, as the food will both tend to stick and to pick up a certain amount of sand or grit. It will work, however, and is well worth trying.

Make a set of fire tongs to handle heated rocks or hot pieces of metal used as cooking gear, or simply to move burning chunks from one place to another. The crudest form is simply a three-foot length of green stick an inch or so in diameter that is broken at the midpoint. The strands that hold the two halves together will act as a hinge, and you can pinch the hot object between the two ends. A somewhat better arrangement is to thin four inches or so at the center of a similar stick, removing the material from one side only. This will allow you to bend the stick in a **U** shape, but you must tie it in position to keep the two sides parallel to each other. You can also use a narrow forked stick, using the two branches to pinch the object. Best of all for handling heavy objects and for absolute security of grip is a set of tongs made of two forked sticks. This is a two-handed tool, but you can securely grasp anything from small rocks to large chunks of burning wood with it. (See Figure 51.)

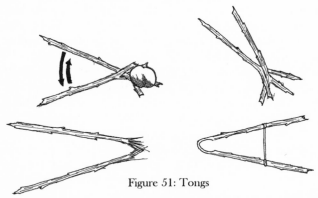

Figure 51: Tongs

Repeated reference has been made throughout this book to the use of hot rocks to heat or boil water, in cooking, to provide heat in a shelter, or as substitute heating pads or bed warmers. Most such references have been accompanied by the warning that rocks from wet areas should not be used. Rocks from saturated areas always contain some water, and the steam generated by heating sometimes causes these rocks to explode like hand grenades. Such explosions have blinded, maimed, and even killed people who have used such rocks for fire circles, to set kettles on, or for any other use where they were subjected to intense heat. Use only rocks from areas that are free of standing or running water throughout the year.

For use as hot water bottles or bed warmers, heated rocks must be wrapped in cloth or other material, and it is often best to substitute bags of sand or dirt for these purposes. A shirt or coat sleeve or a pants leg works admirably. A bag of loose material more closely conforms to a surface and is far more comfortable than an unyielding rock.

Repeated reference has been made, too, to the use of furs or skins. For anything but immediate use, these should be dressed or tanned. This entails both time and hard work, but the results are well worth the effort. The skins are made as flexible as cloth, are protected against decay, and objectionable odors are largely eliminated.

When an animal is taken, you should skin it immediately if possible, while it is still warm. If the animal has died in a snare or deadfall and has been dead or even frozen for a time, the skinning process will be more difficult and it will be much harder to keep from cutting the skin. There is no need to "case skin" the animals, even in the case of small fur-bearers, when skinning for use rather than for sale. Instead, skin all animals by slitting the skin from chin to base of tail, slitting the inside of all four legs from the foot or ankle to the main cut, then peeling the skin off. With fur animals you will want to skin the head and open up the tail. With animals such as deer, you will want to cut the skin off where the neck and head join. The skin must then be cut off at the knees or hocks, as it is nearly impossible to skin the lower legs and that skin would be of little value.

To peel the skin from a carcass, use your knife sparingly. Use your fist to force the skin away from the flesh in larger animals, stiffened fingers with smaller ones. If you are reluctant to use your hand for these operations or if the skin is reluctant to fall away, whittle a wood "spud" with a blunt, chisel-shaped end to use instead. In some cases, you can simply pull off the skin, as with rabbits and squirrels.

Whenever possible, the animal should be suspended for the skinning operation. This permits free access to all parts of the animal, keeps both the carcass and skin free of dirt and debris, and automatically keeps the freed skin out of the way. With large animals, hang by a "gambrel" thrust through slits made at the hocks. Hang smaller animals by the hind feet or the head.

Hoist with a rope thrown across a horizontal bar or simply place the gambrel or the leg or head ties over a limb stub. You can use a set of sheer poles or a single pole to help hang a deer-sized animal from a bent sapling. (See Figure 52.)

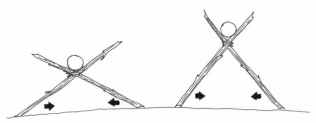

Figure 52: Sheer poles

Once the skin is off, the process of tanning or dressing should be started at once with any skin intended for use with the hair on. The first operation is to make sure that all foreign objects, such as hard mud balls, sticks, etc. are removed and that no felt-like hair balls or other lumps remain in the hair. Wash the hair or fur and rid it of clotted blood or other matter. Any lump or bump remaining in the hair will cause a puncture of the skin during defleshing or other operations.

The second operation is defleshing of the skin. This is best accomplished while the skin is soft and pliable. Drape the skin over a peeled pole or other smooth surface. Knots or bumps on the pole will cause punctures. Scrape adhering fat and scraps of flesh away, working from tail to head end. Any dull-edged implement such as the back of a fixed-blade knife, a rib bone or shoulder blade, a hardwood spud, or even the milled edge of a coin will work for smaller skins; and the wooden and bone tools can be improved by carving blunt and shallow teeth into the scraping edge. Use these tools with a hacking, scraping motion.

For larger skins that are thicker and more durable, you should use narrow, chisel-shaped fleshing tools not more than an inch or so wide. Make one from the legbone of a deer, a hardwood limb, an antler, or from a thin rock or a fifty cent piece set into a handle. Again, the tool is much improved by whittling or grinding small, blunt teeth into the striking edge. Hang the skin tail up on the side of a smooth-barked tree or drape it over a smooth log. Once again, any bump or projection, either in the hair or on the supporting surface, will produce punctures in the hide. Hold the fleshing tool at a shallow angle to the skin and strike with a stabbing, scraping motion.

When such a skin is intended for use with the hair on, stretch it tightly immediately after fleshing and allow it to dry. In winter or in humid weather, this normally means taking it into your shelter. *Do not do so in bear country, as a fresh skin is equivalent to an engraved invitation!* In sunny weather or drier areas, the skin will dry more quickly outside. *Do not expose it to direct sunlight or high heat at this stage.*

When the skin is completely dry, you will notice a sort of glazed membrane over the inner surface. Remove this by careful use of the fleshing tool. Every trace of this membrane must be removed, as it would keep tanning fluid from entering the skin.

You must now "stake" or work the skin to open the pores and to break up the cross-linkage between fibers. You can do this in several ways. Old-time professional tanners used either a stake (a dull-edged blade with rounded corners set into the top of a post) or a crutch knife (a blunt-edged circular blade set into the tip of a crutchlike handle).

You can use a coin or several coins set into the top of a post or even a stake with a smoothly rounded tip like a broom handle to work the skin. Hang the hide over the post with the flesh side down, then drag it back and forth as vigorously as you can without tearing the skin. Work it in every direction and make sure the entire hide is worked.

With a larger skin to be tanned for leather, you must both deflesh it and dehair it. The easiest method of dehairing is to submerge the whole hide in water for several days, testing it each day by pulling on the hair. When a clump of hair pulls free with little resistance, take the hide from the water, drape it over a smooth log and scrape the hair off. An outer layer of skin (the grain) will scrape off with it. Then stretch the hide tightly and let it dry.

The hide after drying will be very stiff and harsh. This is rawhide, untanned but usable where toughness but no flexibility is required. There are several methods of softening it and opening the pores to allow the tanning solution to enter the skin. First dampen the skin, then stake it as described for furs, peg it down over a yielding pad of dry vegetation and strike it repeated, glancing blows with a club or a smooth stone hammer, or wring or twist it.

The wringing and twisting is the easiest, fastest, and most effective method. Soak the skin in water, then drape it over a crossbar lashed head-high between trees or other supports. Lap the ends and tie them securely. Thrust a crossbar through the loop thus created, then twist this bar to wring and stretch the skin. Twist first in one direction, then in the other, moving the skin loop each time to have different sections on the bars.

Once all parts of the skin have been thoroughly twisted and all excess water has been wrung from it, lash the movable crossbar in position or jam it between the rigid crossbar and upright to keep the skin tightly twisted. *It is dangerous to release the crossbar lever without securing it!* Let the skin dry until just slightly damp, then release and untwist it and treat with the tanning solution.

The tanning fluid may be rubbed into the damp skin with the hands or the skin can be soaked with the solution for several hours, perhaps overnight. Allow the treated skin to dry thoroughly, then wash with clear water and stretch it in a frame or between trees until nearly dry. Work the nearly dry skin by staking it or twisting as before. Every inch of it must be twisted or worked if it is to be soft and supple. If you run out of time and energy before the skin is completely worked, however, you can dampen the unworked areas later and work them until dry. If you think this is a lot of work, you can chew the skins as Innuit women did!

You will then have soft white leather that is suitable for any use where it will not be saturated. Wetted while in this stage, the leather will be stiff and harsh when dried and must again be worked to soften it and restore pliability. To make it remain soft after a soaking, you must smoke it.

Dig a shallow trench several feet long and roof it with sods, rocks, or dirt-covered bark. Build a firepit at one end (preferably downhill) and set up a tripod of small poles over the other end. Build a small, hot fire in the firepit, let it burn down to a bed of coals, then smother the coals with slightly damp, well-rotted nonresinous wood. You want to produce lots of smoke, very little heat, and almost no soot.

The best woods for smoking are alder, aspen, birch, cottonwood, poplar, willow, or similar soft, deciduous hardwoods; but any nonresinous wood that has rotted to a spongy state will do. You must make sure, however, that no large knots or unrotted sections remain in the wood, as these would produce too much heat and could damage the skin. Keep a close watch on the fire and control it by opening or closing off the draft or by dampening the wood as necessary.

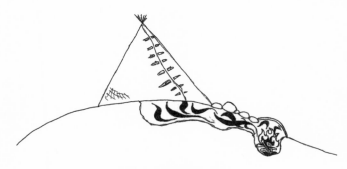

Figure 53: Smoking skins

When the fire is producing the proper smoke, drape the skin around the tripod, pinning or sewing the edges together to form a smoke-tight tepee. Weight or peg the bottom to retain the smoke. Allow to smoke for one to several hours, depending on the color wanted. Lay your palm on the outside of the skin frequently to make sure it is no more than reasonably warm. You can check for color by turning a flap at the bottom or by lifting the whole cone off the tripod. When satisfied, turn the skin wrong side out and smoke the other side.

Remove the skin from the tripod when checking on or refueling the fire, as increased draft may cause the fire to produce too much heat. (See Figure 53.)

You now have true "Indian tanned buckskin" that is suitable for clothing, moccasins, or any other use requiring soft and pliable leather. It will stretch somewhat when wetted, but will remain soft as ever when redried. No insect or wasp can sting through it, it is perfectly comfortable when worn against the skin (when it's dry, that is!), it is completely windproof, and it provides more insulation than cloth. It feels clammy when wet, but it has almost no wicking action, and it thus continues to provide considerable insulation even when saturated. Best of all its qualities, however, is the fact that it is available where little else is and that it comes wrapped around a considerable quantity of nutritious and palatable food.

The tanning fluid or solution so often mentioned in the preceding instructions is simply a mixture of the animal's brain and water. Some Indians added liver and fat, while others used equal parts of brain and fat, but this is not necessary with deer skins. With heavier skins such as those of elk or moose, where treatment must be repeated, fat should be used to supplement the brain.

To prepare the solution, remove the brain from the skull and immerse it in a quart or so of very warm water. Work the brain with the fingers, reducing it to a pulp that mixes readily with the water to form a slurry. Remove any bone fragments during this process. When the brain and water are of uniform consistency, simmer the solution gently for an hour or so, then allow it to cool to approximate body temperature. A small deer should produce about one quart of solution, a large deer about one and a half quarts. Rub the warm solution into the prepared skin.

If you must store the solution for later use, as when tanning a skin without the hair, the best method is to freeze it if the weather permits. If the weather is too warm for this, simmer it to a jellylike state and store this in a section of intestine. An Indian method was to blot the solution up in bunches of tree moss or dried grass, dry these, and store them in a cool place until needed. The moss or grass was then heated in water and the liquid poured off. You can also slice the whole brain thinly and dry it for later use. Do not neglect such preservation, as decomposing brain tissue has to be smelled to be believed!

Remember, both skin and brain are edible, both to you and to animals, birds, and insects. You must therefore take all possible steps to protect both skin and brain from predation while processing.

Boil a piece of hide with the hair removed to the point of disintegration in a small quantity of water to produce glue. Boil the hooves and the foot and ankle bones of ungulates for one or two hours in a small amount of water to produce neat's-foot oil, which is unexcelled for softening or restoring leather. Render fat or tallow for use as cooking lard or for making pemmican.

Hair removed from skins is valuable as insulation or padding, and you can use bones and antlers to make tools or weapons. Even the soup left after neat's-foot oil has been skimmed off and the cracklings left after fat is rendered are useful, either as food in the one case or as bait in the other. Be like the commercial butcher who "uses every part of a pig but the squeal," or like the Indians, who used almost every part of the buffalo for something. The uses of animal parts are limited only by your imagination and your willingness to experiment.

Weaving was one of the earliest and most valuable crafts practiced by man, and a knowledge of the basic techniques involved is of real value to anyone who must take advantage of every available resource to survive under primitive conditions. When weaving is practiced for the making of useful rather than decorative articles, the technique involved is relatively simple and easy to learn.

The simplest form of weaving is designed to produce flat mats suitable for walls, floors, or other structural parts of a shelter, or for making clothing, blankets, hammocks, etc. This weaving requires a number of "warp" strands laid parallel to each other at more or less regular intervals, and a number of "woof" strands laid at right angles to the warps. The first woof is laid over the first warp, under the second, over the third, and so on. The second woof then lies under the first warp, over the second, and under the third.

Tie the warp pieces between two horizontal or vertical bars and weave the woofs into them. This can be done by hand with thick, wide material, or with a shuttle in the case of thinner and more flexible material. You can also make a mechanical loom and eliminate much of the tedious work involved. (See Figure 54.)

Tie all of the warp strands to a fixed horizontal bar tied at waist level between two trees. Tie the other end of every

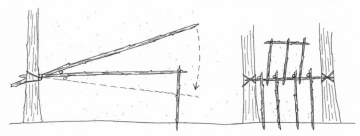

Figure 54: Loom

other one of these at the same height to vertical stakes set at the opposite end of the loom. The alternate and slightly longer strands are tied to a movable horizontal bar just past these stakes. This bar can be raised and lowered at will, with the attached warps moving up and down between the stakes.

In operation, this bar is lowered and the first woof piece is simply passed between the lowered and the fixed warps. The bar is then raised and the next woof is placed between the raised and the fixed warps. It then only remains to force the two woofs together and to continue this process until the mat is completed.

Anything even reasonably flexible is grist for the weaver's mill under survival conditions. Use evergreen boughs, deciduous branches, cattails, fern fronds, tules, reeds, grasses or sedges, strips of bark, or almost any other such material for the woofs, and you can use these or even stiff, rigid sticks for the warps, lashing them at each end with other material.

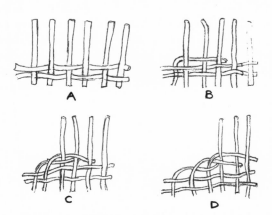

Figure 55: Basket rims. Cut each splint with the
stub outside. Seize or wrap with finer material if desired.

Basket-making involves the same basic technique, but the warp is usually formed of more or less rigid pieces with more flexible woofs woven into them. The usual method is to have warps long enough to reach clear down both sides and across the bottom, with an excess projecting above the rims; but it is perfectly feasible to splice the warps by overlapping two pieces for several inches, allowing the woofs to hold them in position. The woofs, too, can be spliced by overlapping. The basket rims can be formed by several different methods. (See Figure 55.)

This concludes the informative part of this book. I have tried to pass on to you, the reader, those bits of knowledge of survival and outdoor lore that I have acquired over a considerable span of life. If some of this seems to have been carried to the point of tedium, I make no apology.

No single person could possibly have need of all this information, but some particular item might be absolutely vital to someone at some time, and no one can foretell which item it might be. It is certainly better to have the knowledge and never need it than to need it and not have it. Many readers will also discover that each tidbit of knowledge gained and each outdoor skill learned will enhance their enjoyment of their outdoor pursuits. This has certainly been true for me.

It may become automatic for you to catalogue the resources available in any area you find yourself in and to plan the course of action you would take if you were forced to depend upon those resources for survival. It may also become your habit to collect and use those wild plants and plant products that interest you, and you may find real satisfaction in using the parts of the animals you take to make jerky, leather, pemmican, sausage, tools, etc. Practice in such skills will improve your chances of surviving in a real emergency and will afford you considerable pleasure as well.

In the final analysis, however, survival does not depend solely upon knowledge, practice, or acquired skills, although each will make survival easier. Survival, instead, depends primarily upon attitude and applied ingenuity.

One person will perish with every resource needed for survival and even comfort readily available, even in marginally severe conditions. He panics, fails to recognize the emergency until too late, or simply fails to correctly evaluate the situation and take the necessary steps to cope with it.

Another person, lacking even the minimal equipment normally required for survival, will come out of the most extreme situations without any ill effects. He will have diagnosed the emergency quickly and correctly, will have evaluated the risks and the benefits of the options open to him, and will have chosen those offering the most benefit with the least risk and effort. He will have used the best survival equipment of all: common sense.

Whether or not you will survive an emergency situation at all, and whether you will do so in relative comfort or abject misery, is thus largely dependent upon your attitude and common sense. I trust that you will survive if faced with such an emergency, and I hope that this book will help you do so in comfort. In any case, you will decide the outcome. Good luck!